T0408876

All God's Creatures

DEVOTIONS
for ANIMAL LOVERS

2026

G Guideposts

A Gift from Guideposts

Thank you for your purchase! We want to express our gratitude for your support with a special gift just for you.

Dive into *Spirit Lifters*, a complimentary e-book that will fortify your faith, offering solace during challenging moments. Its 31 carefully selected scripture verses will soothe and uplift your soul.

Please use the QR code or go to **guideposts.org/ spiritlifters** to download.

All God's Creatures 2026

Published by Guideposts
100 Reserve Road, Suite E200
Danbury, CT 06810
Guideposts.org

Copyright © 2026 by Guideposts. All rights reserved. This book, or parts thereof, may not be reproduced, stored in a retrieval system, or transmitted in any form or by any means, electronic, mechanical, photocopying, recording or otherwise, without the written permission of the publisher.

Cover and interior design by Mullerhaus
Cover photos: Horses: georgeclerk, Getty Images; corgi: Nataba, Getty Images; guinea pig: undefined, Getty Images; butterfly: Sonika Agarwal, Unsplash; hummingbird: Alexander Rotker, Unsplash; sea turtle: Marcoriveroph, Getty Images; deer: Andyworks, Getty Images; squirrel: suefeldberg, Getty Images.
Monthly page photos: January: Sjo/Getty Images; February: GuannanJANG/Getty Images; March: Kanujan Singarajah/Getty Images; April: PPAMPicture/Getty Images; May: Alex v ujcmPPxhxT8/Unsplash; June: martin-oslic/Unsplash; July: dnberty/Getty Images; August: Leoba/Getty Images; September: GettyTim82/Getty Images; October: Ksuksa/Getty Images; November: Cameris, Getty Images; December: Byrdyak/Getty Images.
Typeset by Aptara, Inc.

ISBN (hardcover): 978-1-961442-21-4
ISBN (softcover): 978-1-961442-22-1
ISBN (epub): 978-1-961442-23-8

Printed and bound in the United States of America
10 9 8 7 6 5 4 3 2 1

Introduction

A few months back, overwhelmed with troubles, I poured them all into a prayer list. Before bed, I turned them over to the Great Healer. As I drifted off to sleep, the one worry I kept in my heart was about Reggie, our charmingly defiant, big-eyed, chocolate-colored 15-year-old Chihuahua, who adopted us 5 years ago.

As Reggie has aged, he's become less tolerant of visits to the vet. We discontinued his nail trimmings because he got so aggravated by his paws being touched that he would attack the vet tech. No harm was ever done (he's toothless and weighs only 5 pounds), but I worried that he would hurt himself in his fits of rage. I bought a sandpaper nail trimmer, and we eased into a routine (including so many treats that he gained an extra pound).

This was effective except for one nail—his right paw dewclaw. I simply could not reach it from any angle without his trying to twist out of my grasp and becoming hostile. For 18 months I tried, and it had grown to the point of curling around and touching the pad. It had to be cut, or it would start growing into his skin.

It weighed on me. Should I take him in to be sedated for a nail trim? It would be potentially dangerous, considering his age and health, as well as an expensive measure for a simple nail clipping, but I had exhausted all other ideas.

The alarm clock went off at 5 a.m. I reached over to turn it off and heard a voice. The voice was not so much in my ears as it was in my heart.

It said, *Why don't you ask Me for help with Reggie?*

I was startled. I was groggy. I tried to get my bearings, reaching down to pat Reggie, who was snuggled by my hip.

"What?" I whispered. (Since I don't often hear ambient voices, I strongly suspected where this message was coming from.)

Don't you think I can help you with Reggie?

My heart pounded. Of course, I knew with complete confidence that God could help me with Reggie. My thoughts swirled. I hadn't included Reggie in my prayers because there were more important things for God to focus on, right? I had the list, and I had it prioritized. I should be able to take care of Reggie. He is such a small responsibility (literally). Why should I bother God with Reggie's nail care?

That was as far as I got before I realized the silliness of my thinking. I paused and listened for the voice. Nothing. My heart was calm.

I sighed at my foolishness. First Peter 5:7 tells us to cast all our anxiety on Him because He cares for us. All our anxiety—not just some.

Before I got out of bed, I prayed over Reggie and asked that God give me the strength, ingenuity, and patience to trim that dewclaw.

I was talking to a friend about it later that day, and she mentioned a video she saw of someone dealing with an irritable cat who did not want his nails trimmed. She described how the person successfully managed the feline, and I thought the technique might work for Reggie. What a blessing . . . there was hope!

It would take precise timing and assistance, so I enlisted my husband's help. He stood in front of Reggie while I held him in my lap with the traditional nail clippers. As I twisted myself around to address the dewclaw, my husband focused only on feeding Reggie peanut butter smeared on a big spoon. As Reggie slobbered his way through it, I gently maneuvered his nail into place, and CLIP! It was done—with only a minor growl. Hallelujah!

The authors of this year's special collection of devotions have found hope, inspiration, and delight in all the ways God shows Himself to us through His magnificent creations we call animals. I pray these stories are an encouragement. May they open our eyes to not only the grand ways but also the small and subtle ways our good Lord watches over us, our pets, and all those dear to our hearts.

Many blessings,
Jean Alfieri, author, speaker, dog fan,
and *All God's Creatures 2025* contributor

ALL GOD'S CREATURES

JANUARY 1

Wings of Comfort

The LORD said, "Go out and stand on the mountain in the presence of the
LORD, for the LORD is about to pass by." . . . After the earthquake came a fire,
but the LORD was not in the fire. And after the fire came a gentle whisper.

—1 KINGS 19:11–12 (NIV)

EMERGENCY HEART SURGERY and a weeklong hospital stay not long after Christmas didn't start the new year off very well. Already feeling tired and discouraged, we arrived home to empty bird feeders, a bad thing in cold January weather when other food sources for our feathered friends were scarce. The empty feeders were an apt picture of our empty emotional and physical reserves, and we prayed that God would show us He cared.

When we refilled the feeders, we had visitors that we had not seen before. A group of six common ground doves arrived. One or two mourning doves had visited before, but these were different, and they exhibited unusual behavior. They stayed close together underneath the feeder, as if they were a flock rather than individuals. One day we found them sitting in two rows facing the house, like people attending a lecture. They remained seated when we opened our back door to go outside, an encroachment into their territory that usually startled the birds away. At other times they wandered onto our patio and seemed unafraid when we joined them.

This visitation perplexed me until one day I remembered the words of an old country song, "Wings of a Dove," written by Bob Ferguson and recorded by Ferlin Husky—"He sends down His love on the wings of a dove."

I asked my wife, "Could the doves be messengers from God telling us that everything will be OK?" When I asked our preacher the same question, his simple response was, "That's how He does." After we had that realization, the doves left and did not return.

The doves' visitation was a wonderful reminder that God was with us through all our troubles. It just took us a short time to recognize His constant presence. —Harold Nichols

A song fluttered down in the form of a dove,
And it bore me a message, the one word—Love!
—Paul Laurence Dunbar

JANUARY 2

Stopping by Woods with Snowy

"Be still, and know that I am God!"

—PSALM 46:10 (NKJV)

SNOWY, MY 2-YEAR-OLD golden retriever, overwhelms me with her joy. Her paw gently nudges me if I try to sleep beyond her breakfast hour. Her giant smile and wagging tail instantly respond to my every word. She greets me excitedly each time I return home from the shortest errand.

One thing that doesn't excite Snowy is riding in the car. The modern automobile perplexes and intimidates my furry sidekick. Perhaps the motion upsets her stomach. Maybe she just feels out of control riding along at 60 miles per hour. Whatever the reason, she dreads getting into the car.

On a cold winter day, Snowy and I headed for the veterinarian's office for a routine exam and vaccinations. Since my white hairy beast loves people, she doesn't mind at all once we arrive. Snowy warmly greets the schnauzer and beagle in the waiting room. She tries to climb over the front desk to love on the receptionist. She gives a welcome bark to the vet. Once in an exam room, she happily tolerates shots in exchange for a generous portion of treats.

After the visit, we head to the car, and I boost her heavy behind into my Nissan once more. A gentle snow has blanketed the car and lent a magical, clean scent to the air. Heading home, I can't resist turning into the parking lot of a wooded preserve. With my window down, Snowy sits up in the back seat and leans her head on my shoulder. Gone is the perpetual motion that defines our daily lives together. The peace and breathless quiet overwhelm me with God's presence.

Why can't I summon this stillness more often? It is often available. As they do for Snowy, certain parts of my life come with difficulty, but when I stop—be still—God reminds me that He has it all under control. He blankets me with His peace. —David L. Winters

Walk of Faith: *Stop periodically today to witness and recognize the glory of God.*

ALL GOD'S CREATURES

JANUARY 3

The Joy of the Jump

When I was a child, I spoke and thought and reasoned as a child. But when I grew up, I put away childish things.

—1 CORINTHIANS 13:11 (NLT)

MY HUSBAND AND I chose the timing of our trip to Maui so that we could see a particular endangered species—humpback whales. From January to March, females give birth to their calves in the largely protected waters of Maui's southern and western shores. Every year these beautiful whales are visible even from the shoreline as they breach, blow, and slap their tail fins.

Taking a whale-watching tour is vital to get closer. We were thrilled to see a whale pod right away from our catamaran. An underwater microphone attached to the boat allowed us to hear the beautiful whale song being communicated beneath the surface.

As I walked to the side of the boat to search for more humpbacks, I saw three—a massive male principal escort, a female, and her calf. There was a splash as the calf leaped out of the water—our first breach! Over and over the calf jumped around the catamaran's bow while we cheered. The calf would disappear and begin again from her starting point. She repeated this pattern, breaching dozens of times to the joy of all. Even our crew was shocked at how many times the calf leaped out of the water. The calf was like a kid learning to ride a bike, yelling, "Look, Mom! I can do it!"

I laughed, thinking how little kids want their parents to be proud of them while doing something big kids can do. As I slowly mature in my walk with Christ, sometimes I want to shout, "Look, God, I didn't get angry that time!" or "Look, Father! I ignored that behavior and didn't engage." I wonder if God smiles at me and cheers me on, saying, "I am proud of you, My daughter." —Twila Bennett

Father, I long to please You in all I do, more and more each day.
May my thoughts, words, and actions make You proud of me.

JANUARY 4

Togo Makes the Front of the Pack

"His master replied, 'Well done, good and faithful servant! You have been faithful with a few things; I will put you in charge of many things. Come and share your master's happiness!'"

—MATTHEW 25:21 (NIV)

ONE WEEKEND I took my granddaughters to the library to meet some sled dogs and hear the story of Togo, a young husky who, in 1925, led a team of dogs to deliver lifesaving serum in Alaska. We patted the gray-and-white dogs, who were compact, energetic, and agile. One dog represented Togo. An actor dressed in heavy furs played the part of Leonhard Seppala, the musher. "Togo was a young mischief-maker when I first got him," the actor said. "He wouldn't listen to me or do as I said, so I put him in the back of the pack, where I could keep an eye on him."

I thought of my relationship with God. *When He asks something of me, do I hesitate or balk? When I sometimes forget to listen, does He have to keep an eye on me?*

"Then Togo began to demonstrate his capabilities. He was fast and determined, so I put him in the middle of the pack," the man continued, scratching the dog's head.

It seemed like this is where I was on my journey—the middle of the pack, wondering which way to go, yet trying to be obedient to God.

"Finally, when it came time for the important journey, Togo became my lead dog. He had proven that he was strong and made good decisions." The actor demonstrated by hitching the dog to a rope at the front of the pack. The dog wagged his tail happily.

This was where I strive to be in life's journey—in a position of reliability, making good decisions, cheerfully following God's directives, without doubt or question.

It turned out that Togo had traveled 260 miles in treacherous conditions, valiantly leading the sled dog team. Could it be because the musher trusted him and he trusted the musher? —Peggy Frezon

Lord and Master, Almighty God, I long to be obedient and show You that I am dependable and strong. I trust You. Help me to be worthy of a place in Your pack.

ALL GOD'S CREATURES

JANUARY 5

A Fur-Mom's Love

Where can I go from your Spirit? Where can I flee from your presence? If I go up to the heavens, you are there; if I make my bed in the depths, you are there.

—PSALM 139:7–8 (NIV)

BRRR! DAY FOUR with no electricity, no heat, and subzero temperatures. Winter storms had hit hard, leaving 20,000 people in the same predicament. My husband could leave every day and go to work in warm customers' offices, drinking coffee. But not me, not our dog.

And there lay the problem. No family could allow me to bring the dog if I came. Oh, they loved him, but one's landlord didn't allow pets. Two others had dogs of their own. Another's community allowed registered pets only.

Today's twenty-nine degrees had me layered up—three shirts, two pairs of pants, hooded sweatshirt, hat, gloves, and several fleece blankets. I wasn't toasty, but I stopped shivering occasionally. Bundled in my rocking chair, I couldn't write because the computer's battery had run down, and I couldn't hold a pen with my shaking, glove-covered hands.

And Kenai! Poor baby! He had his heavy winter coat, but it didn't afford much help in this frigid house. Plus, his bones had always minded the cold, and he often groaned when he moved. I'd put his thickest blanket on the couch and used extra ones to cover him.

The problem? Kenai is not a dog to stay put. He likes to move around—couch, Daddy's chair, his memory-foam bed. Whenever he got up and changed places, I disentangled myself from my cocoon to move his blankets with him. EVERY TIME! At one point, I laughed aloud at the seeming senselessness of this activity. Get swaddled in blankets . . . see Kenai move . . . get out and cover him to keep him toasty . . . get settled in . . . and do it again.

Yet isn't that just like our God? Every time we move away, He stops what He's doing and draws closer to us, keeping us near to His warming love. I'm guessing Kenai knows I love him, just as I know God loves me. —Cathy Mayfield

I could feel the warmth of His presence as if a soft blanket had been wrapped around my soul, around my heart.
—Colleen Houck

JANUARY 6

The Squirrel's Treasure

"But store up for yourselves treasures in heaven, where moths and vermin do not destroy, and where thieves do not break in and steal. For where your treasure is, there your heart will be also."

—MATTHEW 6:20–21 (NIV)

I LOVE WATCHING the squirrels in my yard chase one another and seeing their ingenuity as they try to break into my bird feeder. Just between you and me, I always leave a little extra birdseed on the ground just for them. But my favorite thing about my backyard squirrels is the way they use their small paws to quickly dig little holes and bury acorns. They scamper around, carrying these acorns, then stash them away like buried treasure. And somehow, when winter comes, they always seem to remember just where they hid these acorns in my yard.

As I watched one of my squirrels hide its acorn this afternoon, I began to think about my own treasure. Firstl, what *is* my treasure? Jesus said, in essence, that our heart resides where our treasure is held. Am I putting my efforts and time and heart into temporal returns that won't last by the time winter comes? Or am I seeking a heavenly treasure, carefully guarding and investing in God's gifts in my life? Do I see those heavenly treasures as valuable?

I find it so interesting that the Bible describes our treasure and our heart as intertwined. The location of my treasure shows the location of my heart, and the opposite also applies. Just as the squirrel remembers where it buries its precious acorns, my heart will lead me toward that which I consider valuable. May I find my treasure in the heart of God, so my paths will lead me home. —Ashley Clark

Father, sometimes I catch myself storing up treasures in this world, but You have given me the chance to make a heavenly investment with my life. Show me how to do just that. Amen.

ALL GOD'S CREATURES   7

JANUARY 7

All the Days of My Life

*Surely your goodness and love will follow me all the days of
my life, and I will dwell in the house of the Lord forever.*

—PSALM 23:6 (NIV)

ONE WINTER EVENING my husband, Kyle, suggested that we watch the Minnesota Department of Natural Resources eagle camera live stream. Earlier that day, he had read in the news that the mama eagle was preparing to lay her eggs. We don't watch much TV with our kids, so they were excited. The kids watched the live stream in awe and amazement, and what started that evening became a daily interest for several weeks.

Kyle kept reading updates about the mama eagle and sharing them with us. As soon as she started laying her eggs, our family watched and learned more about the eagle's journey to life. After the eggs hatched, our kids looked on in awe as the mama eagle fed the eaglets several times a day, until, eventually, the eaglets grew, matured, and left the nest.

The following year, we decided to make the eagle camera a family tradition, and once more we watched the mama eagle and her preparation for her family. Seeing nature unfold before our eyes again allowed my husband and me to talk more with our children about God and His loving care, like the mama eagle's care for her eggs and her hatchlings as they grew. We watched as the eagle parents cared for them, from the moment she laid her eggs until they grew up and left her nest.

As our family watched together and Kyle and I talked about these things with them, I was reminded anew that God has cared for me since He "knit me together in my mother's womb" (Psalm 139:14, NIV), and He will care for me "*all* the days of my life" (Psalm 23:6, NIV; italics added)—not just until the time comes for me to leave the nest of this earth, but in heaven for all eternity. —Stacey Thureen

*Like a bird protecting its young, God will cover you with His feathers,
will protect you under His great wings; His faithfulness will form
a shield around you, a rock-solid wall to protect you.*
—Psalm 91:4 (VOICE)

JANUARY 8

Always by My Side

Nevertheless I am continually with You; You hold me by my right hand.

—PSALM 73:23 (NKJV)

MY HUSBAND, TIM, was the first to notice the opossum by our house. After he mentioned it, I saw the opossum a couple of times but only from a distance. Each time our Yorkie was with me, and I wanted to keep her safe, since the animal was almost twice her size. Minnie didn't know what to do with the visitor, so I picked my dog up and got her to safety, afraid that the wild creature would hurt her.

I decided to learn more about this shy marsupial, and I was excited to discover that opossums were one of the animals featured at the Wildlife Animal Show at the nearby Sarasota Jungle Gardens in Florida.

The presenter shared opossum facts. Often misunderstood and seen as dangerous, they're quite harmless. They carry no diseases, such as rabies, because of their low body temperature, which causes them to seek a warm place—a shed or garage, for example—to survive the cold winter nights.

The opossum diet consists of slugs, bugs, small rodents, and sometimes avocados. That last one is my guess. My proof is the licked-clean avocado seeds I've seen at the bottom of our neighbor's tree with the skin some distance away. This was after Tim saw an opossum sleeping in our neighbor's avocado tree.

The presenter brought a live opossum for the audience to interact with, so at the end of the show, I went to get a closer look. The presenter invited me to pet her coarse fur, which felt soft to me. She looked cute with her tan face, pink nose, and almost crossed eyes.

I fear what I don't know, and I remind myself often that God is always with me to soothe my anxious heart. Thanks to that presentation, I know that if I hear an opossum hiss, it's only for show. And if scared, it'll play dead. I'll still give the opossum her space, but I might get close enough to see her cute face. Because the One who made me made the opossum too. —Crystal Storms

With the power of God within us, we need never fear the powers around us.
—Woodrow Kroll

ALL GOD'S CREATURES

JANUARY 9

Perilous Paths

And you were dead in the trespasses and sins in which you once walked,
following the course of this world, following the prince of the power of
the air, the spirit that is now at work in the sons of disobedience.

—EPHESIANS 2:1–2 (ESV)

ITHREW THE toy as far as I could, and it fell into the snow. Galen loped toward it but didn't take a direct route as he usually would. Instead, the giant Leonberger ran along the easier paths he had already worn into the foot of snow. It took him longer to reach the toy by the indirect route, and when he reached the limits of the "easy path," he stopped. He stared at the toy, which was lying only 4 feet from him. Then he turned and walked away, sticking to his path and leaving the toy behind.

For the rest of that winter, Galen continued his path-following behavior. When fresh snow first fell, he'd leap through the drifts with joyful abandon, forging new paths. But as soon as paths were created, he stayed on them, never wanting to venture away to enjoy other parts of the yard or play with toys.

I had noticed Galen was staying on paths rather than venturing into untouched snow, but I didn't realize how extreme he'd gotten. An adolescent Leonberger passing up the chance to play? Odd, to say the least. I couldn't make sense of his behavior, but I laughed, because I saw myself in Galen. Sometimes I'm reluctant to leave certain paths too—not in snow, but in life. It's scary to deviate from the popular, well-worn path of our culture. Society, friends, and family may expect us to fit in and follow the common path. But what happens when that path follows the world instead of Christ?

I no longer belong to the world. I belong to a Savior who leads me on His own paths. They may not be popular, but they will lead me in righteousness all the way home. —Jerusha Agen

Make me to know your ways, O LORD; teach me your paths.
—Psalm 25:4 (ESV)

10   ALL GOD'S CREATURES

JANUARY 10

Unexpected Blessing

Nehemiah said, "Go and enjoy choice food and sweet drinks, and send some to those who have nothing prepared. This day is holy to our LORD. Do not grieve, for the joy of the LORD is your strength."

—NEHEMIAH 8:10 (NIV)

WHEN MY HUSBAND traveled to Hawaii on business, I happily tagged along. We stayed in a hotel near the famous Waikiki beach in Honolulu. While Bill spent his days in meetings, I strolled along the beach, read a book under a shady palm, and enjoyed shopping at the Royal Hawaiian Center. But what thrilled me the most during our stay was something I'd not expected: I discovered a pair of white fairy terns nesting in the park nearby.

These snow-white birds with large black eyes took my breath away. Common in urban Honolulu, they appear to be buoyant and graceful in flight and curious about humans. When I realized the pair had a nestling, I was even more delighted. Fairy terns don't build nests but rather incubate their single egg directly on a ledge or tree branch. The parents fed their little puffball with small fish they carried from the ocean in their bills. Several times a day, I meandered to the park to check on what I'd dubbed "my fairies."

The unexpected gift of seeing the nesting *manu-o-Kū*, the Hawaiian name for this bird, was the highlight of my trip. Our Lord has often blessed people in unexpected ways. The anonymous cash gift that arrives just in time to avoid eviction. The encouraging call from an old friend that helps us keep going in difficult times. The scary checkup that ends with a clean bill of health. Who can explain such things? Not me. I'm simply grateful for the many unexpected joys He has blessed me with throughout my lifetime—including the lovely fairy terns "nesting" in the Honolulu park. —Shirley Raye Redmond

Walk of Faith: *In Jesus's name, bless someone in an unexpected way today: donate to a worthy ministry or charity. Invite someone to lunch. Send a thinking-of-you card to someone you've not seen for a while.*

ALL GOD'S CREATURES

JANUARY 11

Chin-Gnawing Love

*"Therefore do not worry, saying, 'What will we eat?' or 'What will we drink?'
or 'What will we wear?' For it is the gentiles who seek all these things,
and indeed your heavenly Father knows that you need all these things."*

—MATTHEW 6:31–32 (NRSVUE)

OUR DOG SIMONE was a rescue that came to us out of an abusive situation. For the first year, we had to be very gentle with her and not move too quickly, or she would cower. But she began to trust us and finally grew totally comfortable in our home. Yet she still lacked confidence.

After she'd been a part of our family for nearly 2 years, though, that began to change. Whenever it got to be nearly time for dinner, she would climb in my lap and get in my face as if trying to get my attention. Once I looked up, she'd start to gnaw on my chin. I always laughed hysterically as I tried to push her away because it tickled! But at 60 pounds, she was strong and persistent. When she started this behavior, I couldn't figure out what she was trying to do, so I looked it up. I discovered that chewing on the mother dog's chin is a way for puppies to let her know they're hungry. I was so touched by this, I nearly cried. Simone now feels bonded enough with me to treat me as if I were her mother, and she is communicating her needs to me.

Simone has come a long way from that cowering addition to our family. I'm thankful that, just as Simone has confidence in me, I can have confidence in God's love. With His unconditional love, I feel accepted, cherished, and protected. Like Simone gnawing on my chin when she's hungry, I can take my needs to God in prayer and trust Him for provision.
—Missy Tippens

*And since He bids me seek His face, believe His Word, and trust His grace,
I'll cast on Him my every care, and wait for thee, sweet hour of prayer!*
—W. W. Walford

JANUARY 12

Flamingo Moments

*He said, "Come." So Peter got out of the boat and
walked on the water and came to Jesus.*

—MATTHEW 14:29 (ESV)

MY DAUGHTER AND I were driving across the southern portion of
Spain when a flock of birds flew over our heads. As I craned my neck
to see them better, I blurted, "What in the world is that?" I looked again.
"Are those *flamingos*?"

"Yep," she said with a shrug. She'd been living in Spain, and apparently
flying flamingos were an everyday occurrence. "They nest in Andalusia
every winter. Doñana National Park has a huge colony of them."

The closest I'd ever come to a flamingo was our local zoo. I loved to
watch them gracefully lift their long spindly legs as they waded through
the shallow water in their habitat.

But flying? With three feet of legs trailing out behind them?

Decidedly *not* graceful. And yet, there they were, soaring above our
heads, making a salmon-colored canopy against the sapphire sky.

I've had a few flying flamingo moments recently. In response to a
last-minute SOS, I helped in children's church. Not my area of giftedness,
for sure. I knew none of the songs and only half the memory verses. I felt
awkward, out of my element, slightly terrified—decidedly *not* graceful.
But they had a need, and I felt the Lord nudge me to volunteer.

And then there was the time my dental patient burst into tears. When
I laid a sympathetic hand on her arm, she shared how her marriage was
shaky and her grandmother had just passed away. My dental hygiene
training hadn't prepared me for that, but I listened compassionately and
asked if I could pray with her. My words were disjointed and decidedly
not graceful, but when she rose to leave, she hugged and thanked me.

The memory of those Andalusian flamingos reminds me that not
everything I do will be graceful. But if I seek God and respond to the
opportunities He brings my way, I'll fly for His glory, and it will be a
beautiful thing. —Lori Hatcher

The will of God will never take us where the grace of God cannot sustain us.
—Billy Graham

JANUARY 13

The View Finder

Then Elisha prayed and said, "O LORD, please open his eyes that he may see." So the LORD opened the eyes of the young man, and he saw, and behold, the mountain was full of horses and chariots of fire all around Elisha.

—2 KINGS 6:17 (ESV)

THE LAST WILD flock of endangered whooping cranes winters at the Aransas National Wildlife Refuge in Austwell, Texas. People travel from around the world to see these enormous cranes. When my friend invited me to see them before they migrated back to Canada, I was excited.

Sunlight danced on the water as our boat cruised the bays looking for the whoopers. Anticipation was high. Finally, someone called out, "There they are!"

Eight cranes picked their way through the scrubby brush, three snowy pairs of adults with two rusty-feathered adolescents. My friend's camera clicked and whirred. Eventually, the cranes wandered away, and we motored on to find more. Over the course of the afternoon, we saw many more cranes, some making their whooping calls and others in flight.

I knew what I was seeing was rare. I wanted to have a transcendent moment. But I didn't. Intellectually, I appreciated these birds, but emotionally I wasn't feeling it.

When we got back to the house and my friend showed me her pictures, everything changed. Each click had captured a nuance of the birds: the energy of their enormous wings, the personalities of the families, the bold color of their heads. Looking through her eyes and recalling all I had learned on the boat, I was filled with awe.

I needed to be taught how to see the cranes, to have my eyes opened to their wonders. Having a friend who understood them elevated my entire experience.

The world overflows with miracles. Some I can recognize right away, and some I need explained to me. But each time another is revealed to me, no matter how much help I may need to understand, I am more able to feel the wonder and trust more deeply in the God who created it all.
—Lucy Chambers

Faith is to believe what you do not see;
the reward of this faith is to see what you believe.
—Saint Augustine

JANUARY 14

From Rough Mornings to Good Days

This is the day the Lord has made. We will rejoice and be glad in it.

—PSALM 118:24 (NLT)

MY DAY HADN'T started off very well. First thing in the morning, the school nurse called. My son Nathan had been hit by a ball in gym class, leaving him with a bloody nose and broken glasses. The nurse said he was pretty upset and wanted to come home. As I hurried to pick him up, I fretted over everything I'd planned to do that day. Work projects, housework, and a church obligation, and now I needed to squeeze in a visit to the eye doctor too. I was also concerned about the unexpected expense. "Lord, nothing today is going as planned. Please help me," I prayed as I headed into the school.

When I saw Nathan, he was surprisingly cheerful. "Can we get my glasses fixed and then get some ice cream?"

As we drove to the eye doctor, Nathan recounted what he'd learned in science class the day before. "Did you know that mother giraffes give birth standing up, so when the baby giraffe is born, he falls 6 or 7 feet to the ground? Falling 7 feet is the first thing that ever happens to him. But he doesn't let that stop him. Baby giraffes learn to walk when they're only an hour old."

I smiled, enjoying his enthusiastic storytelling. But he wasn't done. "After I got hurt, I thought about the baby giraffe. I decided to be like him. I had to get back up and keep going."

My smile grew bigger. "That's pretty wise, Bud." I remembered my prayer that morning and decided that I, too, would emulate that baby giraffe. I could choose to not let a rough start make my whole day bad. Each day is a gift from God, and we honor Him when we treat it that way.

The bill at the eye doctor was smaller than I feared, and the other tasks got done eventually too. Even Nathan's ice-cream cone. It was a good day after all. —Diane Stark

Give every day the chance to become the most beautiful day of your life.
—Mark Twain

ALL GOD'S CREATURES 15

JANUARY 15

A Higher Porpoise

I press toward the goal for the prize of the upward call of God in Christ Jesus.
—PHILIPPIANS 3:14 (NKJV)

OUR FAMILY VACATION was winding down, and so was my endurance. Tired from endless walking and long car rides, I sat on a bench, enjoying an ice-cream cone and staring across the San Francisco Bay. The rest of my family stood in line at a nearby fast-food restaurant while I rested.

As my brain tried to wrap itself around the differences between San Francisco and my small town in Ohio, a pair of harbor porpoises swam up to the water's edge to get a look at me. The top side of their bodies shone dark gray in the sun while their underbody appeared almost white. One of the pair rose up just a little above the waterline and beeped an unintelligible greeting.

"I'm tired," I responded. "We've been traveling for a week, and I'm ready to go home."

My new porpoise friends seemed intrigued by my comments. As one opened his or her mouth, I spotted a single row of teeth, which hinted at a smile. They chirped loudly at me.

As quickly as they had appeared, both porpoises dropped their faces downward and raised their triangular-shaped dorsal fins above the waterline. With a brief kick, they were on their way, leaving my pants leg noticeably damp from the splash.

I pondered the purpose of these gorgeous mammals. How carefree porpoises seemed, just doing laps in the bay, eating fish here and there. These mammals always seem to be in a good mood. Perhaps God instilled in them a simple understanding of their purpose that gave them peace to just live life without worry.

Suddenly, my weariness subsided. I realized it wasn't the long trip that created the heaviness I felt. Worry had drained me of energy. In that moment, I made the decision to release my worry to God, and immediately I felt life infusing my heart.

God sent the porpoises along at the perfect time. An ice-cream cone and a bench with a view slowed me down enough to hear these good-natured teachers. —David L. Winters

"Which of you by worrying can add one cubit to his stature?"
—Matthew 6:27 (NKJV)

JANUARY 16

The Snow Monkey's Secret

Carry each other's burdens, and in this way you will fulfill the law of Christ.

—GALATIANS 6:2 (NIV)

I STUDIED THE Japanese macaque, trying not to look like I was staring. Was the female snow monkey walking with a limp? She sat down before I could tell for sure.

Lowering my clipboard, I adopted a casual stance as visitors approached the monkeys' enclosure. My job as a zoo volunteer was to watch the animals and record observations about their behavior and health. When I had chatted with a zookeeper that morning, she'd shared they were concerned about the older female, Paddy. But as was typical for most animals, she was hiding her problem from the zookeepers.

I watched as Paddy stood again. This time I was certain—she was favoring one leg. I documented her injury on my clipboard. I would make sure to also tell a zookeeper about her limp before I left for the day.

As I observed Paddy and the other monkeys, checking them all to make certain they appeared healthy, I wondered at their secrecy. Why were they more comfortable letting strangers see their vulnerabilities than the zookeepers, the people who could help them most? Such behavior seemed the ultimate in folly, since it could prevent them from getting the care they needed to survive and thrive.

I swallowed as a realization crept into my mind. Don't I often commit the same folly? I often try to hide or ignore my struggles. Sometimes I might admit an issue in a joke to a friendly stranger. But I don't like to confess to someone close to me that I have a struggle and need help.

I want to believe I can win my struggles alone, healing my own wounds and inner sickness. But that is indeed the ultimate folly. God gives us brothers and sisters in the church to carry each other's burdens. When I allow my church family and loved ones to help, they can be God's means of bringing me the healing I need. —Jerusha Agen

Walk of Faith: *Are you struggling with an issue you're trying to keep hidden? Share your burden with a trusted friend or loved one today. You'll find their support lightens your load.*

JANUARY 17

Night Heron

"My prayer is not that you take them out of the world but that you protect them from the evil one. They are not of the world, even as I am not of it."

—JOHN 17:15–16 (NIV)

ISAW THE black-crowned night heron standing still and quiet on a rock in the middle of the creek. It stood on one leg, head tucked down close to its body, motionless. I would hardly have noticed it except I was actively looking for animals to photograph. It blended into its surroundings beautifully, not drawing attention to itself but also not hidden. At that moment, I was reminded of the saying that Christians are to be "in the world, not of the world."

The heron was in its natural habitat attending to its practical concerns—it was either resting or waiting to catch food. The creek is its home; and the heron was an integral and useful part of the overall ecosystem. It belonged there. And this is where the heron and I differ greatly.

I also live in the world, and I must attend to my own practical concerns—work, sleep, family, and worship, to name a few. I can also be useful in my community. But though it may be my "natural habitat," the world is not my home. My true forever home is in heaven with God. And my daily concerns are not simply to provide for myself or my family, but to let others know about their own forever home in heaven with the God who loves them.

I was privileged to spot the night heron in the creek. It's a beautiful bird, and seeing it brightened my day. Can I be a "beautiful bird" in a hurting world, sharing the love of Christ with those around me? Can I brighten someone's day by telling them about God's love for them? Yes! —Marianne Campbell

Dear Lord, I know I'm not "of" the world, but please give me opportunities to tell others about You so they may also know there is something beyond this world. There is eternity with You and Your love. Amen.

18　ALL GOD'S CREATURES

JANUARY 18

More Than a Begging Spot

Rejoice always, pray continually, give thanks in all circumstances;
for this is God's will for you in Christ Jesus.

—1 THESSALONIANS 5:16–18 (NIV)

I SAT DOWN in my favorite chair, a cup of coffee in my hand. My two dogs, Piper and Peyton, hopped up and nestled in on each side of me. Every morning, the three of us sat in that chair while I read my Bible and prayed. It was usually one of the best parts of my day, but today, I was just going through the motions. I was struggling with a relationship problem, and honestly, I didn't even feel like talking to God about it. Instead, I rubbed a hand over each dog's back and poured out my troubles to them. Piper and Peyton are good listeners, but I knew I should be talking to God.

Hours later, I went downstairs to fix lunch and nearly tripped over Piper. She was sitting on the rug in front of the kitchen sink, just as she always did when I cooked. We called it her "begging spot" because when she sat there, she was definitely hoping I'd share a few scraps with her.

I smiled as she watched me with hope in her eyes. I sneaked her a few bites of cooked chicken. Even after the casserole was in the oven, Piper remained on her begging spot, still hopeful.

I realized that, in a way, I have my own begging spot. It was my favorite chair, where I usually sat when I read my Bible and prayed. But it was more than a spot to ask God for things. It was also a place to praise God and thank Him for the things He'd already done. It was where I worked on the most important relationship in my life. But today, I'd held back from God, and that needed to change. The dogs and I settled back in my chair, and I shared my heart with my heavenly Father, who was always ready to listen. —Diane Stark

Make your relationship with God your number-one focus.
If you take care of that, God will take care of everything else.
—Anonymous

JANUARY 19

A Furry Example

There is neither Jew nor Gentile, neither slave nor free, nor is there male and female, for you are all one in Christ Jesus.

—GALATIANS 3:28 (NIV)

MY HUSBAND, NEIL, and I enjoy feeding the birds in winter. We relax by sitting in our recliners and watching them out our picture window. A bonus is that the sunflower seeds we set out for the birds draw other critters too. Squirrels and chipmunks come most often. They scrounge around the base of the feeder pole and gobble up the seeds that get swept to the ground by the birds' heads and feet.

The first four-legged creature to show up this winter was an adorable-looking red squirrel. We could identify him by his small size. However, except for his head and a thin red streak on his back and the top of his tail, his fur was all gray. *He must be a hybrid*, I thought. But when I looked it up, I learned that red and gray squirrels are different species. They don't interbreed.

The second squirrel was twice Red's size, with a big, fluffy tail. A gray squirrel, for sure. Only he wasn't the right color either. His body was gray, but his head and ears were red!

Lastly, a jet-black squirrel appeared. My research said he was a variant gray squirrel, called melanic, and that this variant was becoming more common in New York State.

We had three squirrels, none of whom conformed to their official descriptions. And sometimes all three came at once. Equally surprising, they all got along. It was fun to watch these odd-looking creatures sharing a meal without a cross word between them.

They made me think of us humans, who can be quick to judge others based on superficial appearances. The squirrels' unquestioned acceptance of each other reinforced my conviction that God means for us to get along. And with His help, I'll do my part. —Aline Newman

Never judge someone by the way he looks or a book by the way it's covered; for inside those tattered pages, there's a lot to be discovered.
—Stephen Cosgrove

ALL GOD'S CREATURES

JANUARY 20

Temptation behind the Door

Do not despise the LORD's instruction, my son, and do not loathe his discipline; for the LORD disciplines the one he loves, just as a father disciplines the son in whom he delights.

—PROVERBS 3:11–12 (CSB)

NO, YOU DON'T!" I said to our son's visiting cat. Isla was trying to sneak into the back basement of our home. Whenever she heard someone's footsteps on the stairs, she would race downstairs, hoping that the person would enter the "great unknown."

The back portion of our basement, which contained the furnace, storage shelving, and workbench, was unfinished. While it didn't have drywall, it did have access to the finished walls in the other parts of the basement. If one was skinny enough—say, the size of an exploring cat—one could enter through the working part of the basement and walk behind the walls in the finished area. Some of the areas were quite tight, and we were worried that Isla would get stuck.

There are many things in this world that can tempt us. Left to our own devices, we find ourselves in places where we shouldn't be and where we most likely will get stuck. God knows that. God gave us protection through His commandments so that we would be safe. It is not that He wants to deny us access to anything He created but that He knows we wouldn't be able to handle some situations and could get hurt.

While Isla has sometimes gotten into the back basement, we were quick to remove her for her safety. In the same way, God watches over me, especially in the times when I have gotten into a situation that requires some help. If only I ask, He will show me the way out. —Virginia Ruth

Guardian of all, thank You that You care for us so much that You give us instruction to keep us safe. Amen.

ALL GOD'S CREATURES

JANUARY 21

Lean into Me

The LORD is good, a refuge in times of trouble.
He cares for those who trust in him.

—NAHUM 1:7 (NIV)

SINCE SHE WAS a puppy, my dog, Honey, has been a *leaner*. She leans against the kitchen island, typically underfoot, while I make dinner for the family. She bounds to the top of the stairs only to lean against the wall there, observing our comings and goings. And most especially, Honey greets me in the morning, leaning into me, pressing heavily against my knees. Occasionally I fear I'll be knocked over as she mashes against me with her whole body.

When I observed Honey leaning against the wall as a puppy, I declared, "What a lazy little puppy!" I would chuckle over her casual posture. As time passed, however, and I became a solid presence that Honey leaned upon, I realized there was much more to it than lethargic passivity.

I now see and know there is a deep, abiding sense of trust demonstrated in Honey's leaning. Even as a tiny puppy, she was certain the wall would not give way and the kitchen island would support her. As she has grown and put her full trust in me as a caregiver, she knows not only that I can and will support her but that I will also pet, comfort, soothe, and speak sweetness to her. I am a solace to Honey. She leans in because she knows in her heart of hearts that I care for her.

As I have gone through stormy seasons in life and trouble has piled high around me, I have been certain of one thing, and that is the fact that God, the Lord, is my strong refuge. I can lean into God with my full weight and all the heaviness of my heart, and He will care for me. I have learned over a lifetime that I can trust God to be a strong and present help to me at all times. I can lean into Him, my unmoving refuge, and He will soothe and speak sweet words to me. —Katy W. Sundararajan

O God, be my strength and my salvation today and every day. Amen.

JANUARY 22

Raccoons in the Pool

"Do not fear, for I am with you; do not be dismayed, for I am your God. I will strengthen you and help you; I will uphold you with my righteous right hand."

—ISAIAH 41:10 (NIV)

LOUD SCREECHING FROM outside my bedroom woke me up at midnight. Splashing—and lots of it—followed. What in the world was that? And what was it doing in my pool?

I got out of bed, my heart racing, and opened the window shutters to see our backyard. Four large raccoons were swimming across the water. Was I dreaming? As they each pulled themselves out, shook off the water, and waddled out of our side yard and over the fence, I knew what I'd seen was real.

Four raccoons had just taken a swim in my pool with a half moon as a night-light. That was a first. My husband and I and two boys had just moved into our house a week ago. Everything around me was brand-new, and I was still getting used to living there.

What had chased the nursery (which I learned is the name for a group of raccoons) of raccoons into our yard? We had coyotes and mountain lions where we lived. Something terrified them enough to jump our fence and rush into the water.

I was scared that this was going to be a common occurrence. I love wildlife, but raccoons in the pool wasn't what I'd signed up for in this new neighborhood!

As I went back to bed, I chided myself. This unrealized fear was only the fear of the unknown. There was nothing to be afraid of—having raccoons in the pool was odd, for sure, but they weren't here to hurt us. My home was safe, we were safe, and I was just going to have to adjust to the antics of my new "neighbors" from time to time.

God reminded me that He is right there with me even in new circumstances. I had nothing to fear. And in the 11 years we've been at this house, the raccoons have never returned for a midnight swim. —Heather Spiva

Lord, thank You for watching over me! Help me to remember that I don't need to be afraid, even when it feels rational to be fearful. Amen.

JANUARY 23

Restored, Not Tamed

God made the wild animals according to their kinds, the livestock according to their kinds, and all the creatures that move along the ground according to their kinds. And God saw that it was good.

—GENESIS 1:25 (NIV)

I WAS SO close I could see the individual tan spots on the female barn owl's chest feathers. When I glanced up, I was staring into her heart-shaped face and wide dark eyes. Perhaps not the wisest action I have ever taken, but the handler had secured the raptor on her arm. This was a rare opportunity to meet Fern, the ambassador of Raptors Rise Rehabilitation. At this facility the staff rehabilitates injured birds of prey and returns them to the wild. Only a few of the recovered birds, like Fern, live permanently at the southern Indiana refuge.

I wanted to know all about the barn owls, which are endangered in Indiana due to loss of habitat. They don't hoot like I thought all owls did. Fern hisses, which would sound very eerie at night. This type of owl weighs less than two pounds. As far as hunting skills, the barn owl has excellent night vision and acute hearing for locating elusive prey.

When the director, Lola, told me that all the raptors have distinct personalities, I asked her if the staff tamed Fern and the other permanent residents.

Lola said, "No, we keep them wild, just as they were meant to be. We heal the injury, not their nature."

While I was driving home, I reflected on Lola's words. When I am bruised and broken, God offers me refuge and restores me, but He doesn't ask that I change my personality traits. In fact, He never requires a transformation into perfection. He requires only that I be me. I am slowly learning to appreciate my quirks and not become so frustrated when I stumble. God made me with a unique personality, just as God made each kind of wild animal with its own distinctive nature. —Glenda Ferguson

Rescue the perishing, care for the dying;
Jesus is merciful, Jesus will save.
—Fanny J. Crosby

JANUARY 24

Never Alone

*Do not be afraid; do not be discouraged, for the LORD
your God will be with you wherever you go.*

—JOSHUA 1:9 (NIV)

I WAS COMPLETELY alone—which was precisely why I came to the woods. Each winter, my husband gifts me three nights alone in a cabin in the Rocky Mountains. The first year, the silence felt awkward. Away from our four young children, I didn't know what to do with myself. Solitude can be uncomfortable. But this was my third solo trip, and these retreats have become a time of refreshment, worship, and creative energy. I walk in the woods between focused times of working on writing projects. On this particular afternoon, the forest was silenced. Any noise was absorbed by fresh snowfall. The day before, it had snowed from before sunup to after sundown. No one had yet walked this trail, and it was pristine, without a track in sight besides those of the deer.

I stopped to enjoy the rare silence and admire a ponderosa pine tree dressed in fresh snow. Only when I looked up did I realize I was not alone. Thirty feet away, a large animal ran full speed down the path toward me. I stood, stunned, as frozen as the snowy landscape. It took a moment to register what animal this was: a coyote. As I was standing beside the tree, he did not notice me. He was about 10 feet away when he finally veered to my right and ran around rather than into me. A moment later, a second coyote followed and ran past me on the opposite side. My heart rate began to calm as I watched the wild canids run silently into the forest.

I walked back to the cabin, suddenly conscious of the birds flitting above in branches. Walking through the wintry woods with an awakened awareness, I was reminded I am never truly alone. It's not just the animals of the forest—God is always with me, and I wouldn't want it any other way. —Eryn Lynum

Walk of Faith: *Enjoy a walk in a nature area while engaging all
your senses. Pay close attention to God's creatures around you.*

JANUARY 25

I Missed You So Much!

*I long to see you so that I may impart to you some spiritual
gift to make you strong—that is, that you and I may
be mutually encouraged by each other's faith.*

—ROMANS 1:11–12 (NIV)

LEADING A trip to Ireland with my friend Susy would not be complete without a visit to The Donkey Sanctuary in Liscarroll. We were eager to catch up with her friend Patrick (Susy wrote the book *Sanctuary* with him) and get a glimpse of Jacksie, the donkey Patrick had bottle-raised while recovering from addiction and PTSD.

I didn't know until we arrived that Patrick hadn't seen Jacksie in over 2 weeks. An emergency eye surgery required him to avoid dirt, which meant no contact with the donkeys. As soon as Jacksie heard Patrick calling him, he broke into loud brays. The image of him literally running into Patrick's outstretched arms moved me to tears. I could almost hear Jacksie crying, "I missed you so, so much. Don't ever leave me again." I felt the depth of their bond—the abandoned donkey and the once-wounded man who'd spent long nights nursing him to health—as they reunited, oblivious to our phone cameras capturing the reunion.

I thought of the friend I reconnected with at a conference after a long season when both of us had endured separate trials and could only pray for each other from afar. I remembered a sister in Christ who saw me through a hard transition and then moved away. One morning, after a difficult week, she made a surprise appearance as my ride to Bible study. In both cases, my friend and I hugged and cried like Jacksie and Patrick.

That moment at The Donkey Sanctuary reminded me that there is something special about friendships formed in hard times, especially when the bond includes mutual faith. We ache to be together, and when we finally can be, the reunion is sweet. —Jeanette Hanscome

Shared joy is a double joy; shared sorrow is half a sorrow.
—Swedish proverb

JANUARY 26

Hidden Things

"Now then, stand still and see this great thing the
Lord is about to do before your eyes!"

—1 Samuel 12:16 (NIV)

DURING A RECENT family trip to Costa Rica, one of our favorite things to do was walk along the beach and collect colorful shells. We'd stand in the surf, waiting for the waters to recede, then my girls and I would scan the newly revealed sand in search of treasures. When our plastic bags were full, we returned to our rental, set all the shells on a back porch table, and went inside.

Later, when we headed out to the porch, the positions of the shells had changed. In fact, some had disappeared altogether. At that point, we realized the shells were not as lifeless as we'd first assumed. They had tiny hermit crabs living in them. Tucked up inside the folds of their shell homes, the crabs became invisible. After that realization, upon returning to the rental, we'd place all our shells on the back porch table. Throughout the evening, crabs living in any of the shells would poke their legs out to start their return journey to the ocean.

In my life, I often find this kind of "shell" collecting as it relates to Scripture. Trinkets of God's Word that I memorized throughout my life sit on the table of my heart for days, weeks, or years. Then, on the perfect day that I need to hear a word from God, I find that scripture has legs. It comes to life and walks around, burrowing into my heart even more because of my present experience.

When my daughter had a panic attack, I was able to pray with her, declaring that God did not give her "a spirit of fear, but one of power, love, and sound judgment" (2 Timothy 1:7, CSB). It calmed her down and helped me to stay calm as well. I was very thankful to have that hidden treasure in my heart so that when we needed comfort, God's Word came alive, just like our "shells" in Costa Rica. —Kristen G. Johnson

Don't wait until the moment of crisis.
Plan ahead, hide God's Word in your heart.
—David Jeremiah

ALL GOD'S CREATURES   27

JANUARY 27

Spudnik, the Mustang

A person's wisdom yields patience; it is to one's glory to overlook an offense.

—PROVERBS 19:11 (NIV)

WORKING WITH THE Nashville based Mustang Heritage Foundation, I was blessed with the opportunity to go to a wild mustang "pickup," where horse trainers from all over the country pick up wild horses that were brought in from areas stewarded by the US Forest Service in order to control population and keep the environment sound for all wildlife.

I felt the powerful energy of these wild horses. Fear, uncertainty, dominance, and anger—all the emotions you would expect from a wild animal taken from the familiar and dropped into a strange situation. We as humans know that these animals will now get proper food, medical care, and love in a new home, but the recipients of all that good cannot fathom any benefit to them from our efforts.

I watched one frightened little gelding loaded into a trailer with his trainer, Jessica. She helped him recover from injuries sustained in the wild—foot abscesses, broken teeth, and so much more. She patiently worked with the little "potato" she named Spudnik, and love began to take root. This beat-up wild boy didn't even know how to handle such a soft landing. But his trainer moved slowly, giving him the chance to react until reaction turned to response. It wasn't overnight and it wasn't easy. Patience is always the key to any journey back from trauma.

As I follow Spudnik's journey, I can see the wild mustang in all of us. We carry scars from our families of origin. We carry fear, anger, and resentment for all the things perpetrated upon us, and we get transplanted into situations with no idea how we got there or where we are going. When this happens, I remind myself to stop. Breathe. And look for people willing to be patient with my progress. When I let the healing happen at the speed of life, the results will be a miracle, because that's how God works. —Devon O'Day

*God, please send me patient people who will understand where
I have come from. Give me patience with those You send me.
Let me remember that that's when miracles happen.*

28   ALL GOD'S CREATURES

JANUARY 28

Keiko

Praise the LORD from the earth, you great sea creatures and all ocean depths.
—**PSALM 148:7–8** (NIV)

WHEN KEIKO, THE famous orca, was transported in a special tank aboard a UPS plane to the Oregon Coast in 1996, I knew I had to take my family to see this unique marine mammal.

Also called killer whales, orcas are the largest member of the dolphin family, which includes porpoises, dolphins, and some whales. Orcas are the top predators of the ocean and often hunt in coordinated packs.

Captured in Iceland waters at the age of two or three, Keiko was sold to perform in marine circuses. He then became the star in the movie *Free Willy*, about a boy who teaches the orca to jump high enough to go over a breakwater structure to freedom in the sea. But in real life, Keiko lived in inhumane conditions in a small tank in a warehouse in Mexico City with his health failing.

Donors provided funds for Keiko's transfer to the Oregon Coast Aquarium in Newport, which built a $7.3-million rehabilitation tank to prepare him for a return to the ocean. The indoor pool was filled with 850,000 gallons of fresh seawater pumped in from Yaquina Bay at high tide.

I walked with my family through the tunnel in the exhibit, "Passages of the Deep," and I will never forget the black-and-white marvel in front of me. Keiko came up to the window as if to say hello to his fans, then swam in a sea dance, displaying his talents for all to see. His size and distinctive coloring touched my soul with appreciation for our Creator. This magnificent creature deserved to be free—to be home—where he was meant to be.

This experience prompted me to ask if I am abiding where I am meant to be. I was born to know God, to love Him, to fulfill His plan for me, and to display His glory. Jesus is my Living Water. As I jump into the depths of His love, I will be forever in His presence—my true home.
—Kathleen R. Ruckman

"Therefore if the Son makes you free, you shall be free indeed."
—John 8:36 (NKJV)

JANUARY 29

A New Heart and Mind

"I will give you a new heart and put a new spirit in you; I will remove from you your heart of stone and give you a heart of flesh."

—EZEKIEL 36:26 (NIV)

I HAD ASSUMED the creature with a frilly headdress that my children kept talking about was mythical. But one day during our homeschool studies, they convinced me that the axolotl (AX-uh-laht-uhl) is a real animal. All my planned curriculum for that day went out the window as we dove deep into axolotl research. By the end of the day, we had set up an aquarium, contacted a local breeder, and brought home our very own axolotl, Spud. We have since added two baby axolotls, Hash and Tater Tot, to our family.

It wasn't only their existence that surprised me; this animal, close to extinct in the wild, has incredible regenerative qualities. An axolotl can create new cells, tissues, and body parts, much like a starfish or lizard. We witnessed this after one of ours damaged its fin, and it repaired itself over the following weeks. However, axolotls win first place for regeneration, as they can regrow parts of their vital organs, including their hearts and brains.

I've enjoyed taking Spud into classrooms and teaching kids about these fascinating creatures and the amazing abilities God has granted them.

As I watch Spud, Hash, and Tater Tot playfully swim around their tanks, I am reminded of God's design and how, just as they can regrow parts of their hearts and brains, God can make our hearts and minds new. He replaces my old, stubborn heart with a soft heart ready to obey Him. He renews my mind, helping me take every thought captive and think upon everything lovely and true. —Eryn Lynum

Do not conform to the pattern of this world, but be transformed by the renewing of your mind. Then you will be able to test and approve what God's will is—his good, pleasing and perfect will.
—Romans 12:2 (NIV)

JANUARY 30

Learning by Imitating

Be imitators of me, as I am of Christ.

—1 CORINTHIANS 11:1 (ESV)

MY FIRST DOG, Jack, a Lhasa apso mix, was proud, confident, intelligent, and independent. He understood and learned things quickly. Friendly and charming, he garnered a few fans in our neighborhood.

My second dog was nothing like Jack. Rescued from a factory that illegally used dogs for testing, Ginger had never lived in a house before. She did not know how to walk down or up a flight of stairs. Housebreaking her was difficult. She was afraid of loud noises and men and would rather hide than socialize with people. At first, my family wondered if Ginger would ever behave like a normal dog because our efforts to train and help her were not yielding results as expected. But after a few days, we realized that Ginger was learning more from Jack than from us. By imitating him, she learned how to take the stairs, walk on a leash, how to sit on command, and when to go potty, among other things. Within a few months, she became more confident and overcame her fear of strangers.

When I think about how Ginger copied Jack, I'm reminded that as a disciple of Jesus, my goal is to become like Him. I can get to know Jesus and His character by spending time with Him through prayer and Bible study, and I can pattern my life after His by loving, forgiving, and serving others like He did when He lived on earth. Jesus set an example for how to obey God, endure suffering, and overcome temptation. By imitating Him through the power of the Holy Spirit, I can learn how to live a godly life in this world, growing in Christlikeness in the process and pointing others to Him. —Mabel Ninan

> Walk of Faith: *Make a list of qualities you admire in two or three godly men and women in your life. Think of a few practical steps you can take to follow their example.*

JANUARY 31

Too Much of a Good Thing

"I have the right to do anything," you say—but not everything is beneficial. "I have the right to do anything"—but I will not be mastered by anything.

—1 CORINTHIANS 6:12 (NIV)

THE CREEK NEAR my home is a magnet for waterfowl. I see ducks on every morning walk, of course, and Canada geese in season. But my favorite is the great blue heron. I love to spot one of these gangly waders standing stock-still in the babbling stream, fishing with the patience of Hemingway's long-suffering character in *The Old Man and the Sea*.

I've seldom seen a great blue heron in flight and never, that I recall, on the shore. These solitary birds love the water and depend on it for life. Of course, they must nest somewhere, but they always seem most at home in the water.

Heavy rain brought the creek to flood stage, and I was curious about what I'd find on my walk through the park. There are always ripples in this rocky creek, but days of rain had created white water worthy of the Colorado River. Ducks huddled on the shore. Canada geese too. And there on the creek bank, just above the bridge, sat a lone blue heron. He was motionless, as usual, trying his best to look dignified under the circumstances, but he looked more miserable than a wet cat.

Water is a good thing. Aquatic birds love it. They need it. They would die without it. But even they know that too much of a good thing can be dangerous.

Many things are like that—fine in and of themselves, perhaps good and necessary. But in excess, they become dangerous, even deadly. Alcohol can be a useful substance or a deadly poison. Food is required for life, but excessive consumption can undermine health. Work, money, leisure, exercise, and knowledge all have great value, but they are best treated as servants, not masters. They are a means to an end, not an end in themselves. —Lawrence W. Wilson

O God, help me to use things but love only You.

FEBRUARY 1

Open Your Wings!

"In the same way, let your light shine before others, that they may see your good deeds and glorify your Father in heaven."

—MATTHEW 5:16 (NIV)

THE THICK, WARM air transported us to another world. Just minutes before, we'd been shivering in the winter chill. Now, inside the glass dome, we were surrounded by tropical plants, waterfalls, and thousands of butterflies!

We were visiting the Niagara Parks Butterfly Conservatory in Niagara Falls, Canada. Signs encouraged us to identify as many of the flying wonders as possible. Feeding stations stocked with wedges of fruit attracted clusters of shimmering beauties—the perfect place to snap a few photos.

But the most peaceful part was wandering the curving pathways and feeling the gentle flights all around us. Butterflies of all sizes and colors drifted through the air. As I stood there, taking in the beauty, a blue morpho landed on my arm.

Blue morphos are striking! Their wingspan extends up to 8 inches across, making them one of the largest butterflies in the world. But the most enchanting part is their coloring. When opened, their wings are an iridescent sky blue. They're unashamed in their brightness and beauty. They just radiate light! But when closed, they disappear. Brown and gold markings on their closed wings allow them to camouflage perfectly with their natural surroundings.

The seemingly weightless butterfly had wandered down my arm and was now perched on the tips of my fingers. He lazily opened and closed his wings, revealing flashes of blue, then hiding them with walls of brown.

In that moment, I was reminded of being a Christian. Sometimes, we want to close ourselves up and disappear. We hide our light so we can camouflage into the crowd. But Jesus asked us to let our light shine! God wants us to open our wings, show our colors, and bring His light into the world, just like the glorious, joy-giving blue morpho. —Allison Lynn Flemming

Butterflies are God's confetti, thrown upon the Earth in celebration of His love.
—Kristen Dangelo

FEBRUARY 2

A Prickly Encounter

*Yea, though I walk through the valley of the shadow of
death, I will fear no evil: for thou art with me.*

—PSALM 23:4 (KJV)

BELIEVE ME, MY young friend, there is *nothing*—absolutely nothing—half so much worth doing as simply messing about in boats," says Water Rat to Mole in *The Wind in the Willows*. I am messing about in my boat just now, gliding along, silent and slow, going nowhere in particular, when up ahead I see motion on the shoreline.

Two coyotes, lean and bristly-haired, are snarling at their prey, which at first I identify as a woodchuck. But gliding closer I see that the object of the coyotes' attention is a spiky little fuzzball, short and stout, with a small black face—a porcupine. The coyotes take turns lunging at the prickly rodent, then stepping back, always keeping a respectful distance. The porcupine, meanwhile, plods along, slow and cumbersome, exhibiting not the slightest sign of fear or anxiety. She ignores the coyotes; it's as though they don't even exist. She knows, and the coyotes know, that anyone who tangles with her will pay a painful price. And so she lumbers along, oblivious to her attackers, and even stops to gnaw on a fresh aspen branch blown down by the wind. There she sits, gnawing on her branch, utterly unafraid. Finally the coyotes retreat, trotting away in search of easier pickings.

On a recent episode of *Jeopardy!* the clue was: This Bible book gives us the line, *Yea, though I walk through the valley of the shadow of death, I will fear no evil: for thou art with me.* None of the three contestants knew the answer. But I do. I committed that verse from the twenty-third psalm to memory when I was a child, and I have savored it ever since. When I remind myself that God is with me, then I am not afraid. That doesn't mean bad things will never happen to me. It means that whatever happens to me, God is with me. And when I know that, I know enough. —Louis Lotz

I sought the LORD, and he heard me, and delivered me from all my fears.
—Psalm 34:4 (KJV)

FEBRUARY 3

Entangled!

God is our refuge and strength, a very present help in trouble.

—PSALM 46:1 (NKJV)

WE FREQUENTLY HAVE deer in the backyard of our New Mexico home in the foothills of the Rockies. But one winter afternoon a large eight-point buck wandered in to lick the seeds from my bird feeder. A long, frayed rope appeared to be tangled in his antlers on one side of his head. The rope was so long that it dangled between the buck's front legs. While not frantic, the buck was obviously hampered by the trailing rope. When he moved forward, he would sometimes step on the rope, which would then jerk his head sharply to one side. Seemingly exhausted from his ordeal, the buck finally settled underneath my apricot tree to rest.

I felt a surge of pity for the poor creature, but there was no way for me to get close enough to help. Occasionally, I have felt that my life was a messy tangle too—the sort of tangle that leaves one feeling both physically and emotionally drained—the kind of mess I cannot extricate myself from on my own no matter how hard I try. Perhaps we've all experienced situations like that. Over the years, I've learned to turn to God for help. He understands how helpless we can be. That's why He sent His Son, Jesus, to free us from the coils and tangles of sin.

Eventually, the buck moved on, but not before a neighbor snapped a photo with his phone and called the local US Fish and Wildlife office. Later I learned that the animal had been tranquilized and the rope removed from his antlers. I said a silent prayer of thanksgiving for the deer's rescue—and for my own. —Shirley Raye Redmond

Cast all your anxiety on him because he cares for you.
—1 Peter 5:7 (NIV)

FEBRUARY 4

A (Not) Chance Meeting

"Your Father knows what you need before you ask him."
—MATTHEW 6:8 (NIV)

I'D BEEN IN a funk all morning, spinning my wheels and getting nowhere fast. The kaleidoscope of tracked changes on my computer pounded the writer's block deeper into my psyche. Filled with self-pity, I closed the blinds and decided to hibernate the day away. But Lucy, our spirited papillon, wasn't having it. She stirred beside me, her curly tail thumping in time with her expressive black button eyes, as if to say, *Mailbox! Mailbox! Mailbox!*

Indifferent to my gloom, she raced past me and retrieved her leash. Despite my mood, I surrendered to the pint-size dictator and headed up the driveway. While I lowered my hat and shielded my face with oversize sunglasses, Lucy strutted like a rock star. We'd just passed the long, curvy part of the driveway when I spotted a woman strolling leisurely along the road.

"Busted," I muttered, contemplating a hasty retreat back to the house or deliberately slowing my steps to avoid chatting. When I tugged on the leash, Lucy picked up her pace, ensuring our path intersected with the walker's. Once we reached the mailbox, the little traitor planted herself squarely in front of the smiling lady.

"Well, aren't you a cutie? What's your name?" she asked Lucy.

In response, Lucy pranced and trilled a greeting, her hallmark papillon ears spreading like the butterfly wings that gave her breed its name. Since she couldn't talk, I had no choice but to speak for her.

Soon a few pleasantries turned into a lovely conversation, and before long, I couldn't recall why I'd been so grumpy. As Lucy and I walked back to the house, I noted the undeniable joy in her gait, realizing it perfectly matched my own!

How merciful and loving our God is! Despite my resistance, God saw beyond my "funk" and provided what I *needed* the most, if not what I *wanted*. Because He knows me better than anyone, He understands my tendency toward defeatism, and on this day, like Lucy, He wasn't having it. Even if that meant using a sprightly papillon to encourage my path. —Hallie Lee

The God who knows you best knows the best for you.
—Woodrow Kroll

FEBRUARY 5

Small but Not Insignificant

And don't forget to do good and to share with those in need. These are the sacrifices that please God.

—HEBREWS 13:16 (NLT)

IT'S NOT UNUSUAL to see gray squirrels racing about, zigzagging and chasing one another over the nearly 2,000 acres at our favorite arboretum. Today, I saw something new. A squirrel was carrying another adult squirrel sprawled across its back. As I watched, transfixed, the carrying squirrel moved slowly across the visitor center's roof, half carrying, half dragging its burden.

The mystery of its behavior sent me on a Google search. I found that squirrels, being the social animals that they are, have been observed carrying a squirrel because it is injured or ill and—this surprised me—the carrying squirrel may even take care of the other until it gets well. This was my first experience encountering a squirrel as rescuer and caregiver, and I was impressed by the difference it made in another's life, even though it was small.

Here I had thought that squirrels were all about creating caches of nuts, running across my attic at daybreak, and chewing a trapdoor along my roofline. Apparently, they can have their moments of nobility, just like you and me.

Stories in the Bible often capture ordinary people in their noblest of moments. Some of them have BIG moments, such as Queen Esther saving her people from genocide. Yet we'll also find relational actions that did not play out on the grand stage of history—small acts that have touched hearts and set an example for us today, such as King David's loyalty to rescue and care for Jonathan's disabled son and Ruth's loyalty and care for Naomi.

I may never carry someone on my back across rooftops. I may never save a people from genocide. But I will daily encounter opportunities to serve selflessly and help others. And I am sure that my actions, whether great or small, are never insignificant to my Father in heaven. They are noted and not forgotten by the One who matters most. —Darlene Kerr

I long to accomplish a great and noble task, but it is my chief duty to accomplish small tasks as if they were great and noble.
—Helen Keller

FEBRUARY 6

Joyful Work

I saw that there is nothing better for a person than to enjoy their work, because that is their lot.

—ECCLESIASTES 3:22 (NIV)

THERE IS A coffeehouse nearby, a friendly neighborhood place where everyone feels welcome. And yesterday "everyone" included a small rat who scurried back and forth between the shop and the dumpster. Back and forth, back and forth.

Suddenly the little rat's efforts were interrupted by a two-man crew of garbage collectors who wheeled the dumpster out to a waiting truck and returned the dumpster empty. I felt a bit disappointed for the industrious rat whose livelihood had seemingly been withdrawn, but once the crew had retreated, the rat returned to running his route, undeterred.

I was outside the café at a picnic table, facing my open laptop for a remote work meeting. It was a serious meeting. We were doing serious work things and doing them seriously. But something about that little rat feverishly racing across my line of sight made me giggle and then chuckle.

I explained to my colleagues why I was snickering, and as I described the frenetic rat, our conversation shifted topic, and we began to see ourselves as frenetic too. Soon we were no longer laughing at the rat but laughing at ourselves.

Laughing at ourselves together transformed our serious work into shared joy. We did get our work done, but we did it together with lighter hearts and more love for one another. —Susie Colby

Joy, not grit, is the hallmark of holy obedience. We need to be lighthearted in what we do to avoid taking ourselves too seriously. It is a cheerful revolt against self and pride.
—Richard J. Foster

FEBRUARY 7

A Little Moo for Stevie

*Julius, in kindness to Paul, allowed him to go to his
friends so they might provide for his needs.*

—ACTS 27:3 (NIV)

FOR 2 YEARS Stevie, my blind steer, had been all alone in the pasture. He was the only bovine on the farm, and the horses wanted nothing to do with him. They weren't mean, but they left Stevie alone, and isolation was its own type of pain. Cows are quite affectionate, and Stevie's loneliness was apparent.

Can you imagine being alone, with no one who spoke your language? A dear friend called about a dairy steer who'd been taken from his mama at two days old and bottle-fed by a sweet lady and was now too large for her to handle. I agreed to take him in, against all my plans to begin winding down on the farm.

When Little Moo, as he was called, was released into the pasture, the horses chased him, and he ran in fear. As I stood next to Little Moo, I heard a deep bellow from Stevie, who'd blindly made his way into the front pasture. Little Moo answered that bellow with a high-pitched moo that stopped them both in their tracks. Neither had ever been in the presence of other cows, and suddenly, someone else in their world spoke "cow"! Little Moo ran to Stevie, and they have been inseparable ever since.

Maybe you, like Stevie and Little Moo, are alone in your world right now, just waiting for someone to walk into your chaos speaking your language. God hears us in whatever language we use and answers in ways we can't always see coming, and often He uses friends to provide comfort when all we have been able to do is wander and wait. Inspired by Stevie and Moo, I want to be one of those friends to others. —Devon O'Day

A real friend is one who walks in when the rest of the world walks out.
—Walter Winchell

FEBRUARY 8

Time for the Puppy Bowl

*It is God who works in you to will and to act
in order to fulfill his good purpose.*

—PHILIPPIANS 2:13 (NIV)

ON SUPER BOWL Sunday, when my husband and son, along with sports fanatics all across the country, are watching football, I sneak away to the den, turn on *Animal Planet*, and settle in with my favorite sporting competition—the Puppy Bowl.

Played inside a scaled-down stadium, the Puppy Bowl consists of two squads of pups rollicking across the Astroturf, carrying toys—some of them footballs—across the end zone to score goals for their team. I enjoy the program because it brings awareness to a good cause—dog rescue.

Last year my 8-year-old granddaughter joined me in the den. The dogs tumbled onto the field. "I'm rooting for that little white one," Grace said, referring to a terrier mix from Team Ruff.

I noticed a lanky Lab mix on Team Fluff. He moved with excited bounds. The announcer explained that the dog was both hearing and sight impaired. I watched as he joyfully joined in with the others and even scored a touchdown!

The Puppy Bowl participants are all adoptable dogs, several with special needs. Some of the dogs are tri-pawed—dogs with only three legs. Others are deaf or sight-impaired or have neurological disorders. Putting these dogs on television highlights their amazing spirit and helps them get adopted. And their can-do attitude gives me pause. I have friends who maintain a positive attitude despite physical or emotional challenges. They inspire me by demonstrating what God can do through them. Although I don't face similar challenges, sometimes I feel the challenge of being shorter, older, or less agile than another. But that doesn't mean I'm not capable. God has given me wisdom, compassion, and perseverance. He has prepared me to show what He can do through me too!

Teamwork, pet adoption, and celebrating different abilities—all lessons to be thankful for—and lessons that I, via the Puppy Bowl, am grateful to share with my granddaughter. —Peggy Frezon

Thank You, God, for working in me to make me willing and able to obey You. Through Your power and grace, I am capable of great things.

ALL GOD'S CREATURES   41

FEBRUARY 9

One-Cat SWAT Team

*Those who guard their mouths and their tongues
keep themselves from calamity.*

—PROVERBS 21:23 (NIV)

FOR THE PAST 13 years, our rescue cat Speckles has been a one-member SWAT team. This tactical tortoiseshell patrols our property and home all by herself. No matter the hour, day or night, she is vigilant in defending our acre from wildlife and the occasional stray cat. Even when there seems to be no threat, Speckles is engaging in rigorous training by sharpening her claws and scaling trees. I must say she excels at her duties.

Then, one midnight, a small tabby kitten infiltrated our garage. We named her Scrappy. The adorable stray has not been able to crack Speckles's tough exterior. There is the hissing, the growling, the swatting. Yes, Speckles gave a whole new meaning to SWAT—Swipes With Attitude and Temper. Because Scrappy attempts contact over and over and we want to keep the kitten safe (and maintain our sanity), my husband erected a screen barrier by the back door that allowed Speckles to travel inside and outdoors. The two partitions separate eating and catnapping areas.

Their precarious relationship reminds me of a time when my sister-in-law came to live with us for a short time. Barbara had suffered a house fire that wiped out all her belongings. We invited her to sleep on our couch in our tiny house. I went from having a sanctuary with plenty of alone time for writing and reading to sharing my living room, my kitchen, my closet. I wasn't adjusting well and frequently spoke without thinking. There were many days when I shut my bedroom door, closing off any interactions with her. I tried managing on my own, but I failed miserably. I prayed for guidance, and all of us began cooperatively planning schedules, spaces, and solitude.

I pray that our two cats will develop some degree of cooperation. Perhaps that won't happen with whisker-to-whisker meetings, but maybe on either side of the barrier. —Glenda Ferguson

*Dear loving Father, I pray that in developing harmony in my
relationships, You will provide me the love and discernment to know
when to speak and when to remain silent. Amen.*

FEBRUARY 10

Bring a Friend

The first thing Andrew did was to find his brother Simon and tell him, "We have found the Messiah" (that is, the Christ). And he brought him to Jesus.

—JOHN 1:41-42 (NIV)

DON'T FEED THE BIRDS. The sign admonishing me to avoid the temptation to share a tidbit of my lunch with my feathered friends was prominently displayed in the outdoor café where I enjoyed a leisurely meal. Although somewhat disappointed, as I love watching birds—especially when they seek me out to get a free crumb of food—I understood the need for the sign. Whenever a person feeds one bird, all its friends seem to get the message and flock to the scene. Are they all tweeting about it?

Birds are some of the most intelligent animals on earth. They tell each other about food sources through visual cues, vocalizations, and body language. Just like humans, birds share information about the best places to eat. But a group of birds descending on patrons in an outdoor restaurant can be a nuisance.

I think about how we, as Christians, should not only flock to Jesus but bring our friends, as well. Jesus will not view a group of people eager to meet Him as a nuisance. But how faithful am I about telling people about Jesus? Do I want to keep the crumbs of the Gospel all for myself, or do I want all my friends to know that spiritual food is available to anyone who's hungry?

The first thing Andrew did when he met Jesus was bring his brother, Simon (Peter), to Him. How difficult is it to invite someone to church? As an introvert, I find it easy to make up excuses for why I don't invite people more often. I have to force myself outside my comfort zone. Yet, I know God has put people in my path and my life who need to hear the Gospel. I need to be more like the birds in pointing people to spiritual nourishment. —Ellen Fannon

I love to tell the story of unseen things above,
of Jesus and his glory, of Jesus and his love.
I love to tell the story because I know it's true;
it satisfies my longings as nothing else can do.
—Katherine Hankey

FEBRUARY 11

The Clinging Cockroach

Abhor what is evil; hold fast to what is good.

—ROMANS 12:9 (ESV)

WANT TO HOLD him?"
My heart raced as I stared at the Madagascar hissing cockroach in the zookeeper's hand. "Sure." I managed to push out the word, trying to be as brave as the zookeeper who fearlessly cared for all animals, including the giant bug I was about to . . . touch. As a zoo volunteer, I'd already held snakes without a problem. But handling insects was at the top of my list of the most disgusting and frightening things I could do.

I braced myself as the zookeeper placed the 3-inch-long cockroach in my palm. The horror I'd expected didn't come. The cockroach held still, and it didn't feel repulsive. I stroked its deep-red shell—dry and smooth except for the slight ridges.

The touch of its small feet on my skin was light and gentle. I reached with my other hand to pick it up.

"Careful." The zookeeper's warning stopped me. "These critters don't like to let go." She reached for the cockroach instead and gently lifted it a microinch. Its feet stayed connected to my skin with a slight tug. She pointed out tiny hooks on the cockroach's feet and legs that enabled it to hold fast to any surface. "If you pull it away before it lets go, you could break its legs."

Concern for the cockroach prevented any squeamishness I might've felt from its painless grip. *It shouldn't hold on so tightly when doing so could cause harm*, I thought.

But didn't I do the same thing? The thought struck me hard. I often hold on to things I shouldn't. Whether I'm clinging to a loved one, something I'm afraid to lose, or bitterness and anger, I'm risking more than a broken leg. I'm putting my heart and soul in danger. I need to let go and cling only to Jesus, the One who holds me fast. —Jerusha Agen

Lord, help me to let go of anything I'm holding too tightly to, those things that keep my heart and mind from belonging only to You. Amen.

44   ALL GOD'S CREATURES

FEBRUARY 12

Being Hospitable

Do not forget to show hospitality to strangers, for by so doing some people have shown hospitality to angels without knowing it.

—HEBREWS 13:2 (NIV)

OUR PET PUP, Snowy, greets everyone who comes to our home with a wag and a lick. His attention makes our guests feel welcome, and they appreciate his eagerness to bond, even those who are not "dog people."

One spring, a couple from out of town came to stay with us for a week. When we learned that the wife was scared of dogs, we did our best to keep Snowy away from her. Though our friend ignored Snowy, he found ways to gain her favor. He would sit near her and look up at her with longing eyes. Sometimes, he would place his toy at her feet, inviting her to play with him. When she finally found the courage to pet him, he responded by snuggling close to her. By the end of the week, Snowy's gentleness and persistence had won over my friend. To our surprise, she became comfortable around him, even happy to have him on her lap.

Sometimes when we host a party, our pooch goes about greeting everyone but attaches himself to one or two people and makes them feel special. Children, too, enjoy coming to our house, partly because they feel wanted and welcomed by our Maltese.

I believe God sent Snowy to our family to teach me valuable lessons in hospitality. Being hospitable has less to do with a tidy home and immaculate table settings and more to do with creating an atmosphere where people feel loved and accepted as they are. I can show interest in getting to know my guests, and like Snowy, I can give them my full attention by listening to them and being thoughtful about their needs and preferences. I pray that, through my hospitality (and Snowy's), my guests can get a glimpse of God's love for them. —Mabel Ninan

The heart of hospitality is about creating space for someone to feel seen and heard and loved. It's about declaring your table a safe zone, a place of warmth and nourishment.
—Shauna Niequist

FEBRUARY 13

Who's Holding Your Hand?

"For I am the LORD your God who takes hold of your right hand."

—ISAIAH 41:13 (NIV)

IF YOU STAND near the otter habitat at Riverbanks Zoo in Columbia, South Carolina, you'll probably see two sleek-bodied animals racing around the habitat like children playing tag. When they tire of land tag, one will launch itself into the water, and the other will follow close behind. Almost effortlessly, they circle the plexiglass pond with increasing speed until they burst from the water and the chase continues.

It's rare to see the otters when they're not running helter-skelter around the exhibit, but one gray day, shortly after the zoo opened, I caught them sleeping. Floating on their backs with their eyes closed, the pair dozed peacefully on the surface of the water holding hands!

"Otters do that a lot in the wild," a nearby keeper said in response to my gasp of delight. "It keeps them from getting separated, especially if the current is strong."

As the otters snoozed, I thought of the times I've held someone's hand. As a little girl, I loved tucking my tiny hand into Dad's big warm one. I felt safe and loved. My fiancé and I held hands so often that friends teased us about it. I held my children's hands as they learned to walk, cross a busy street, or navigate a crowded area. Most recently I've experienced the pleasure of my grandson or granddaughter slipping their hand in mine as we walk together.

Sweeter than otters, fiancées, or grandchildren, however, is the knowledge that God my heavenly Father always holds my hand. He told the prophet Isaiah, "For I am the LORD your God who takes hold of your right hand and says to you, Do not fear; I will help you" (41:13, NIV). Whether I'm learning to walk in faith, crossing a confusing intersection, or navigating a season crowded with choices, He is always with me. His right hand guides, comforts, and protects me.

Like the otters, when I lie down to sleep, I can close my eyes in peace, knowing He will hold me secure. —Lori Hatcher

> Walk of Faith: *When you need comfort today or through your week, picture yourself slipping your hand into God's strong one. Rest in the peace this brings.*

FEBRUARY 14

Always with Us

"Do not fear, for I am with you; do not be dismayed, for I am your God. I will strengthen you and help you; I will uphold you with my righteous right hand."

—ISAIAH 41:10 (NIV)

WHEN MY HUSBAND, Eric, and I married, it was a second marriage for both of us. We each had two children from our previous marriage. My kids, Jordan and Julia, were eight and five when we packed up everything we owned to move into Eric's house. While the kids were happy to be getting a bonus dad and two more siblings, they were worried about moving to a new town and starting at a new school. I tried to comfort them, but they still felt nervous.

While we were packing the car, one of the tubes on our hamster cage broke. "What are we going to do now?" I asked. With the tube detached, Pumpkin the teddy bear hamster could escape his cage, get loose in the car, and get hurt or cause an accident.

"Can you hold him in your hands?" Eric asked.

"It's a 3-hour drive," I said. "But I have an idea." I slipped Pumpkin into my hoodie pocket, hoping he'd sleep on the drive home. But of course, he didn't. He kept poking his head out to see where we were going. The kids loved it. "He looks so safe and cozy in there," Julia said.

"Pumpkin is getting a new house too, but he doesn't seem scared. So I'm not scared either," Jordan said.

"I'm not scared because I love everyone at the new house," Julia added. She said the name of everyone in our new family, plus Pumpkin's name. "And Jesus will be there too. So I'm not scared."

Eric squeezed my hand. "Yes, Jesus goes everywhere with us, so we never need to be afraid."

I reached into my hoodie pocket to pet Pumpkin. He'd helped the kids feel at peace with the move just by being curious, instead of scared. "Thank you, Buddy," I whispered. Then I closed my eyes and thanked God for being with us every day, no matter where we lived. —Diane Stark

God, thank You for Your constant presence in my life. Amen.

ALL GOD'S CREATURES   47

FEBRUARY 15

One of His Flock

Know that the LORD, He is God; it is He who has made us, and not we ourselves; we are His people and the sheep of His pasture.

—PSALM 100:3 (NKJV)

MY BROTHER MARRIED a wonderful lady who came from a farming family. Her brother was a cattle rancher and family farmer. From their earliest years in 4-H, my brother's son and daughter were encouraged by their uncle to raise cattle, not sheep. This advice held sway for a while, but eventually, my brother's knee received an untimely kick from a calf, ending his love affair with cows. From then on, my brother's children raised only sheep.

The whole extended family enjoyed watching his children show lambs and sheep. Sheep have rectangular pupils, allowing them to see from 270 to 320 degrees on the horizon. In the wild, this protects them from predators. Sheep have great memories and can recognize the faces of up to fifty other sheep. So they know their friends and enemies—not to mention those that feed them.

Sheep are emotionally complex—self-evident if you study their facial expressions and responses to their various handlers. So are my niece and nephew. The reactions in their faces and demeanor delighted us as we watched them win blue ribbons (and occasionally not come in first) at the county fair. How wonderful to know the many references to sheep in Scripture and watch them play out in front of us with my brother's children.

As I watched the sheep hang out after their time in the show ring, I felt the tug of God's Spirit. The sheep would slurp a drink of water and then move over to a sheep in the adjoining pen for a quick snuggle. Sheep and people are social animals. They know the safety in numbers and revel in the affection of their friends—just as Scripture teaches that we all should. —David L. Winters

Lord, may we look after each other as the Shepherd looks after us. Amen.

FEBRUARY 16

Joy Shared

Light in a messenger's eyes brings joy to the heart.

—PROVERBS 15:30 (NIV)

WE NAMED HIM Bubba. This little Holland Lop rabbit was born a "peanut." When two bunnies with the dwarf gene have babies, there is a chance the little kits will get two dwarf genes and become peanuts. They usually do not survive past two weeks, and more often die within a few days of birth, because their pituitary gland doesn't function properly. When we saw Bubba, and how tiny he was compared to his siblings, we understood this reality, but we wanted to give him a fighting chance. We helped feed him and made sure he kept warm in his nesting box.

With our help and his mother's sweet patience, he grew! We couldn't believe he'd lived as long as he had and grown to be a 5-inch-long fluffy fireball. I loved Bubba's bubbly personality. Any time I went out to the rabbit hutches, he would jump out of the nesting box and race toward me. If I put my hand down next to him, he would climb up my arm and sit on my shoulder. When we put him on the back of the couch, he would race along the top one way, freak out the cat, then turn around and race back the other way. I thought maybe, just maybe, this spunky, energetic baby would beat the odds.

Unfortunately, as we feared, Bubba lived only about 6 weeks. But his short life made a huge impact on me. He taught me that even when we deal with obstacles and issues and life is hard, we can still choose joy and spread that joy to others. His excitement when I greeted him each morning filled me with a sense of value and importance. Thanks to Bubba, I remember that I can offer that same feeling to others when I share with them the joy God has given me. —Kristen G. Johnson

Keep the joy of loving God in your heart and share this joy with all you meet, especially your family.
—Mother Teresa

FEBRUARY 17

Guard Your Home

*Keep me as the apple of your eye; hide me in the shadow
of your wings from the wicked who are out to destroy
me, from my mortal enemies who surround me.*

—PSALM 17:8–9 (NIV)

BACK DURING THE uncertainty of Covid-19, my husband and I placed a wooden cross in our front yard, like many other people we knew. Near our mailbox and streetlamp, it serves as a reminder of God's provision and care during a scary and challenging time for our entire globe.

Recently, I noticed a bluebird sitting on the edge of the cross. For several years now bluebirds have nested in a house we tacked to the light pole. We enjoy watching them fledge new babies into the world. He seemed out of place sitting on the cross when we typically see him on the powerline, watching for insects to devour or feed chirping mouths. The female bluebird stood on top of the birdhouse, twitching her head back and forth. Both seemed to be guarding their home anxiously. Closer inspection revealed twigs, bits of straw, and snakeskin sheds spilling from the opening, with more of the same inside the box in an unkempt nest. We knew that wasn't usual for bluebirds, so we kept a close eye. Over the next several days, two great crested flycatchers and the bluebird pair tussled over ownership of the box. We silently rooted for the bluebirds, just because they felt like part of the family. The male bluebird stood guard on the horizontal beam of the cross most days.

When David and I checked the box several days later, we beamed with joy to see five bluebird eggs nestled in a neatly prepared bluebird nest. No sign of snakeskins or extra debris. We certainly hope the flycatchers found their own place to nest, but we're glad the bluebirds' persistence and watchfulness won out.

With God's help, I want to guard my home from evil and debris. And if any sneaks in, then I hope I'll be diligent to remove it immediately.
—Julie Lavender

*He will cover you with his feathers, and under his wings you will
find refuge; his faithfulness will be your shield and rampart.*
—Psalm 91:4 (NIV)

FEBRUARY 18

Giraffe Out the Window

And God said, "Let the land produce living creatures according to their kinds: the livestock, the creatures that move along the ground, and the wild animals, each according to its kind." And it was so.

—GENESIS 1:24 (NIV)

ONE OF OUR favorite resorts is Disney's Animal Kingdom Lodge in Lake Buena Vista, Florida, where we can watch African animals wander freely on a savannah outside our window. On the second day of a recent visit, I received an early morning text from our son in the adjoining room: "Giraffe out our window." My wife and I hurried to look, and there it was, a tall, stately giraffe moving from tree to tree, grabbing leaves and branches for its breakfast. It was an amazing moment. As Jane Goodall said, "However much you know giraffes, to see one in the wild for the first time feels prehistoric." And that's exactly how I felt when I saw this majestic beast. It looked up at a branch that was far above its head. Our daughter-in-law whispered, "It will never reach it." And we looked in awe as the giraffe stuck out its long tongue and pulled down the branch it wanted.

A giraffe's tongue is a creation marvel. A quick bit of internet research after watching this scene revealed that the tongue of an adult is usually 18 to 20 inches in length, and it is prehensile, meaning that the giraffe can use the tongue to grasp and pull things. This moment made me think of how amazing God's creation is. He has given every animal the equipment that it needs to deal with its environment. If we take the time to look for them, the details in God's creation are astounding. —Harold Nichols

Walk of Faith: *As you encounter God's creation today, be aware of the little details that make our world and the creatures in it so unique and amazing.*

ALL GOD'S CREATURES

FEBRUARY 19

Watching Like a Hawk

The LORD watches over you—the Lord is your shade at your right hand.

—PSALM 121:5 (NIV)

IN THE MORNING, as soon as I wake up, I head to the large picture window in my bedroom and open the wooden blinds. From there, I survey my backyard: yep, the pool's still there; my orange tree is blooming and beautiful. Oh, look, a squirrel is running across the fence.

But one morning, I opened the blinds to see a hawk sitting on our pergola just a few yards from me. His back was turned toward me, and he was surveying the yard much like I was. He strained his neck to see to his right and his left, and his head bobbed and weaved, slowly checking out everything within his view.

Both of us were looking out from our perch, making sure things were in order. I opened the blinds a little further, hoping he wouldn't hear or see me. I even grabbed my phone and snapped a photo.

Getting to see this magnificent bird up close was a treat. I also felt strangely protected, as if he were a security guard watching the place for me. It was both a relief and a comfort at the same time. The hawk flew away after glancing at me for the shortest of moments. Of course, he had seen me. He was watching like a hawk.

Seeing the majesty of this bird, and feeling his protection, reminded me that I already have all the protection I need. I have God, my Lord and Savior, taking care and noting every move I make. He watches over me constantly. There is nothing in my life He doesn't know, doesn't see, or doesn't care about.

Knowing I have a God who watches me "like a hawk" comforts my soul like nothing else. I am free to go about my life knowing He's in control and loving me. —Heather Spiva

Dear Lord, I thank You for watching over me like a hawk,
every day, without fail. Your eyes miss nothing, and
I can rest and hope, protected by Your vigilance.

ALL GOD'S CREATURES

FEBRUARY 20

What's Up, Doc?

The Lord opens the eyes of the blind; the Lord raises those who are bowed down; the Lord loves the righteous.

—PSALM 146:8 (NKJV)

I LOVE VISITING my sister's animal sanctuary. She has a special heart to care for animals that, for any number of reasons, cannot be adopted. She gives refuge to everything from horses to dogs, cats, ducks, chickens, and pigs. Sometimes other sanctuaries will call her when they come across an unadoptable animal. Other times people literally drop off their animals at the end of her driveway. She once found a potbellied pig on her driveway, complete with everything needed to care for him. Clearly this was from someone who'd bought the piglet, not realizing potbellied pigs get big. Like—*big*!

As for myself, I've been a horse person from the time I've been old enough to say the word. My favorite thing to do at the sanctuary is simply to stand in the middle of the herd of horses and breathe. There's just something special about horses. I've seen simply amazing ways horses can reach people, especially kids and those with trauma. On my sister's farm, there is one horse in particular who is absolutely amazing with children.

The catch is, Doc is blind.

But not being able to see doesn't slow him down. He loves to eat and frolics in the field, kicking up his heels and playing with the other horses. Best of all, he loves kids. He's patient and gentle. He is so kind and tender in all his interactions with people, and his special personality brings a smile to everyone he meets.

Sometimes I grumble about things I don't have, or trials, illnesses, or other challenges that make life difficult. I can learn a lot from Doc, who doesn't let his disability define him. —Deb Kastner

There is much we can learn from a friend who happens to be a horse.
—Aleksandra Layland

ALL GOD'S CREATURES   53

FEBRUARY 21

Winged Escorts

May the God of hope fill you with all joy and peace as you trust in him,
so that you may overflow with hope by the power of the Holy Spirit.

—ROMANS 15:13 (NIV)

THE SKIES HAD been overcast for weeks, and everyone was grumpy, especially me. I had a bad case of the February blues, and the usual antidotes—doing something nice for someone else, drinking herbal tea, reading a good book under a blanket—weren't helping. I prayed for something to knock me out of my rut and make me feel appropriately thankful for all the blessings I could still clearly recognize that I enjoyed.

I brought up this malaise to my husband. He listened patiently, and then he asked, "Is there anything you're looking forward to?" When I couldn't think of anything, he said, "Let's go for a ride in the car."

"Why?" I asked.

"Well, it makes the dogs happy," he replied. I couldn't even muster a laugh.

Still, I bundled up and got in the car. We drove around aimlessly, not talking much. As we turned into the drive through the park, red flashes began appearing along the road on my side of the car. More cardinals than I could count were flying next to me. Their feathers lit up the gray skies and the dark woods, and they seemed to be beckoning me forward.

"Look at the cardinals!" I cried. "They're messengers, you know!"

"What are they telling you to do?" asked my husband.

I thought for a minute. What were they telling me? Nothing had changed. It was still deep February, and I still had nothing to look forward to. But I felt good again. These bright little messengers reminded me to just have faith. The seasons would change, spring would come, new opportunities would arise. In the meantime, I was once again clear that I had much to be thankful for, including an extraordinary winged escort right out of my rut. —Lucy Chambers

Beams of heaven as I go through this wilderness below.
Guide my feet in peaceful ways, turn my midnights into days.
—Charles Albert Tindley

FEBRUARY 22

The Three Musketeers

God places the lonely in families; he sets the prisoners free and gives them joy.
—PSALM 68:6 (NLT)

ROSE PETAL WAS a tiny, sweet, sociable bichon who was loved by her humans. Circumstances arose in their lives that made it necessary to find her a different home. Once adopted by her new family, she quickly became part of a menagerie that also included a rabbit and a parakeet. Before long the three of them had become fast friends.

Rose was very maternal in nature yet wasn't able to have her own litter. She insisted on feeding her food to the rabbit, not eating anything until he was satisfied. An outside mama cat on the property took some offense at Rose's interference with her kittens. It stressed Rose when the babies climbed up to every precarious perch they could find. She tried rescuing them by the scruff of their necks before their true mama convinced Rose to stand down. In time she learned that their behavior was natural for felines.

But the three inside pets were inseparable. When the two-legged residents left home for any length of time, the adventures began. Rose had figured out how to free both of her friends from their cages. The release mechanism for the rabbit's cage was pretty easy, while the parakeet's took a bit of practice. Soon she was a pro at bumping the bottom of the birdcage with her head. This motion shifted the lid on the cage so that the bird could escape. Once that happened, the three of them explored the house together with the parakeet perched securely on Rose's back. Their favorite spot to visit was the kitchen pantry.

Just as for these three, when it comes to family, God knew what I needed. I ended up with three moms, two dads, four brothers, and two sisters. We, too, were a menagerie of whole, half, and step-siblings. None of that mattered, because God had assembled us. We weren't perfect, but He made us one. —Liz Kimmel

> *You don't choose your family. They are God's gift to you,*
> *as you are to them.*
> —Desmond Tutu

FEBRUARY 23

A Mouse's Treasures

*"Do not store up for yourselves treasures on earth, where moths
and vermin destroy, and where thieves break in and steal. But store
up for yourselves treasures in heaven, where moths and vermin do
not destroy, and where thieves do not break in and steal."*

—MATTHEW 6:19–20 (NIV)

I ADJUSTED THE laundry basket in my arms and headed toward the cellar stairs. "Oh no," my husband, Mike, said, inspecting a khaki jacket he'd retrieved from the hall closet. "There's a hole in my old coat." I paused to inspect the damage. Sure enough, there was a good-sized, frayed opening at the bottom of the left front pocket. Mike poked his hand inside. "Look!" he said, laughing, and pulled out the remnants of a forgotten fun-size bag of peanut M&Ms.

"I guess a little mouse found himself a treasure!" I said.

As I continued downstairs and set the laundry basket on the basement floor, I found a nibbled piece of blue sugar-coated chocolate by the washing machine. And a green one in the corner behind the dryer. Apparently our little friend was stockpiling his treasures, hiding them for future use. I wondered where else I might find bits of colorful candy.

Looking around me, however, it appeared that Mr. Mouse wasn't the only culprit guilty of stockpiling possessions. The basement was full of boxes of mementos we had no place to display, collectibles too good to throw away, furniture and appliances we no longer had use for. Material things we just couldn't seem to get rid of. Could it be I was storing up treasures, of a sort, here in the basement, when I should be spending more time investing in others, being generous with my schedule and my resources? It would be a big job to sort through all the boxes. But in doing so, I could help others, while at the same time putting my focus on my most valuable treasure—God in heaven. He is my wealth that will never become inadequate or obsolete. —Peggy Frezon

> Walk of Faith: *Are you stockpiling too many material things?
> Start with one small area—one room, a closet, a drawer—and
> clean out and organize. Donate or upcycle what you can't use.*

ALL GOD'S CREATURES

FEBRUARY 24

Toe Beans

"But ask the beasts, and they will teach you; the birds of the heavens, and they will tell you; or the bushes of the earth, and they will teach you; and the fish of the sea will declare to you. Who among all these does not know that the hand of the LORD has done this?"

—JOB 12:7–9 (ESV)

"HEY, MOM, CHECK out these toe beans!" my daughter yelled from across the room.

"What in the world are toe beans?" I replied.

My daughter brought her phone over to show me the screen, which was filled with pictures of cat feet. Turns out that the term *toe beans* has developed online as a nickname for the soft bean-shaped cushions on the underside of the cat's paw.

Of course, now I was curious. With just a little internet searching, I found photo upon photo of "toe beans." In fact, there are innumerable online videos, websites, and Pinterest boards dedicated to cats and their feet. The scrolling possibilities are endless.

Toe beans was a term I had never even thought of. In fact, I hadn't thought very much about cat feet at all. But they clearly point to a created design, a God who planned our world a certain way. Padded feet aid in cushioning jumps and the silent walk of the predator. They also house those dangerous claws until they are needed. Cute but deadly, that is the cat.

Thinking about toe beans reminded me to take in all the wonder and joy of God's creation. And it made me think about what parts of creation I might be missing. I didn't know about toe beans, so what else might I not notice in my world?

From the jeweled back of a beetle to the beautiful web of a spider, from the wonder of a duck floating on a pond to a vulture riding an air current, the whole world inspires wonder. And it all points to a God who creates not only with purpose but also with whimsy. What a reason to celebrate!

—Heather Jepsen

Dear God, thank You for the joy and wonder of Your creation. Help me to notice wonderful things and offer You thanks and praise today. Amen.

ALL GOD'S CREATURES

FEBRUARY 25

Speaking the Truth in Love

Speaking the truth in love, we are to grow up in every way into him who is the head, into Christ.

—EPHESIANS 4:15 (ESV)

MY FRIEND MARTY often brings Gus, her sweetheart of a golden retriever, to the nursing home where her mom lives. Gus makes the rounds, loving on the residents and offering sloppy kisses to every outstretched hand.

A hospital in my town took pet therapy to a whole new level when they added Grant, an 80-pound, laid-back Bouvier des Flandres, and Pip, a 50-pound, energetic Australian shepherd, to their staff of therapists. Unlike sessions where dogs like Gus dole out kisses and give residents an opportunity to pet and hug, animal-assisted therapy helps trauma victims emotionally heal from their experiences.

As I learned more about this program, I discovered that because many victims of abuse struggle with low self-esteem and negative thoughts toward themselves, therapists work with them to help them identify and change their thinking. They'll sometimes ask a patient to think of a negative statement they'd say to themselves, like, "You're not deserving of love," or "You'll never amount to anything." Then they ask them to say it to Grant or Pip.

Most patients struggle to speak these thoughts aloud to their furry friends. Instead, they rethink their words and say things like, "Oh goodness, you deserve the best things in life," or "You're amazing."

When their therapist asks them to repeat those same words to themselves, they are profoundly affected.

I've never participated in official pet therapy, but the next time I'm tempted to speak discouraging or negative words to myself, I'm going to picture Grant or Pip's soulful eyes and think again.

If I wouldn't say those words to a dog, why would I say them to myself?
—Lori Hatcher

Father, help me speak kind and true words—not only to others but also to myself. Amen.

58 ALL GOD'S CREATURES

FEBRUARY 26

Living with Purpose

"I know that you can do all things; no purpose of yours can be thwarted."

—JOB 42:2 (NIV)

I HEARD AN interesting science story on the news about toothed whales (a category that also includes dolphins and porpoises) and menopause. Killer whales, a type of toothed whale, are among the few mammals whose females outlive their reproductive years. Even though they may not be contributing to the propagation of the species, they are helping in protecting and rearing the young whales in the pods.

At the time I heard that news story, I was feeling a little blue. I am at the age where I wonder, *What's my purpose?* My children are grown, my original career is over, and I sometimes find myself feeling that I don't have anything left to contribute. Yet the story reminded me that until God calls me home, I have a purpose. Even if we are not experiencing dramatic signs of aging, all of us at times can feel "old." Sadly, in many cultures it is not to the aged that we look for help and wisdom, but rather to the young. In the whale pods, it is the experience of the older females that contributes to the overall pod well-being.

As I listened to how the older generation of whales helps rear the next, I realized that God also designed us with purpose and plans, whether that is helping the next generation or caring for our present one. We are designed to live in community, and as such, all of us have something to contribute to the well-being of that community. —Virginia Ruth

Creator of All Things, thank You that You designed every creature with a purpose and plan. May those who feel discouraged as we age take heart in knowing that You aren't finished with us yet. Amen.

ALL GOD'S CREATURES

FEBRUARY 27

Deer Feet

He makes my feet like the feet of deer and sets me on my high places.

—PSALM 18:33 (NKJV)

HERE IN COLORADO we are blessed to see Rocky Mountain bighorn sheep, both at the zoo and when we're driving mountain roads. Rams in particular are magnificent and serve as many schools' mascot, including Colorado State University and my own alma mater, Green Mountain High School. Go Rams!

Encountering these sheep, especially in the wild, is gripping. They traverse cliffsides that most experienced rock climbers couldn't handle, and they make it look easy. I especially love watching the little lambs. It's kind of scary seeing these little guys hopping around high cliffs without a care in the world. It's innate in them. And it's amazing to see.

My husband, a diabetic, recently had an episode of hypoglycemia (low blood sugar) and had a bad fall. The paramedics recommended he visit the emergency room, so off he went in an ambulance. In the ER, he started vomiting, which led the doctor to find follicular lymphoma—the big C word, with an enlarged liver and spleen. He was immediately admitted to the hospital and started on chemo.

It happened so fast and furious I could barely take it all in. I already felt over my head in my daily life, and now this? My dear husband. I'd made a vow. In sickness and in health. But hadn't we already had enough with the double stroke 8 years ago that left him walking with a cane?

I'll admit I felt a little sorry for myself, sleeping without my partner and trying to go about all my daily duties as well as embracing this new journey. I was down and didn't know how I could climb up this enormous cliff so I could be there for my husband, kids, and grandchildren. But God reminded me He is with me. He truly does grant me the ability to climb this enormous cliffside with the same ability to navigate the crags as the bighorn sheep. I simply need to listen for the Shepherd's voice. —Deb Kastner

"And when he brings out his own sheep, he goes before them; and the sheep follow him, for they know his voice."
—John 10:4 (NKJV)

FEBRUARY 28

Spread Too Thin

Again Jesus spoke to them, saying, "I am the light of the world. Whoever follows me will not walk in darkness, but will have the light of life."

—JOHN 8:12 (ESV)

ONE WARM FEBRUARY day, my husband and I visited north Florida's Gulfarium Marine Adventure Park. We had toured most of the animal exhibits, seen the dolphin and sea lion shows, and listened to various keeper chats. After passing the alligator and crocodile enclosures, we happened upon a lizard of some type sunning itself on the white sand. A keeper stood nearby and identified the stunning fellow as a bearded dragon.

Despite the imposing name of his species, the dragon's body was only 6 inches long with a tail about the same length. He was a beauty with his orange eyes, dusky beige hide, and rows of soft spikes lining a triangular head. But it was the little lizard's stance that caught my attention.

"Why is his body all flattened out like that?" I asked. "Is he trying to make himself look bigger and more intimidating?"

"No, he's a pretty docile creature," his keeper said. "With the cold temperatures we've had, he's just coming out of brumation, which is kind of like hibernation. He's loving this sunshine and spreading out to expose as much of his body to the sun as he can."

I laughed. Though I like to catch a few rays myself, I don't usually try to flatten myself into a pancake to do it.

Unfortunately, I do tend to spread myself a bit thin in other ways. Writing, editing, speaking, and traveling can leave me little time to spend with my Jesus. Sometimes I have to pull back to catch the "Son." Jesus's light warms me through time spent with Him and rejuvenates me, like a cold-blooded animal coming out of hibernation. With renewed energy, I can then spread the good news about my Savior to others. —Tracy Crump

Walk of Faith: *Study or think through your schedule and see where you can pull back from something to spend a few more minutes with Jesus, reading His Word and listening to His heart. You might be surprised how much His light energizes you.*

MARCH 1

Sing

But let all who take refuge in you be glad; let them ever sing for joy.

—Psalm 5:11 (NIV)

IT WAS A blustery winter day, the kind we get toward the end of the season—sunny but not quite warm enough to feel like spring. As I passed through an industrial area, I noticed a small bird sitting in the middle of the concrete sidewalk, singing its heart out. I wondered why it was there, as there were no noticeable trees or shrubs nearby. Was it blown off the course of its migratory pattern? Was it trying to find its family? Or was the bird just singing because it felt like it? Regardless of the reason, or perhaps despite it, the little bird was just singing.

Seeing and hearing this chipper bird made me think. Do I sing when I am afraid? Or heading in a wrong direction? Or when I feel lonely? Or just because?

I used to spontaneously sing a lot as a child, whether I was happy or upset, but in my adult years, I have forgotten. Sadly, singing is not my go-to expression anymore when things are difficult. My default seems to be more yelling than singing.

Though music can convey all human emotions, spontaneous singing most often flows from joy, and since joy is a gift from God, singing is also a gift from God—whether we realize it or not.

Seeing that little bird reminded me that I feel better when I sing. I have songs that will change my mood. When I feel a little blue, I listen to songs that inspire me, and before I know it, I'm singing along and my spirits lift. Any chore becomes much easier if I sing while I do it.

I like to think that little bird was taking a rest before continuing its journey, and singing a little song was its way to find motivation to continue on. And the next time I need a little oomph in my step, I will remember to sing like that little bird. —Virginia Ruth

I sing because I'm happy; I sing because I'm free.
His eye is on the sparrow, and I know He watches me.
—Civilla Martin

MARCH 2

Haystack Home

My people will abide in a peaceful habitation, in
secure dwellings, and in quiet resting places.

—ISAIAH 32:18 (ESV)

ON OUR RANCH in the Sierra Valley, a pair of geese have made their nesting home for several years on top of one of the eight-tier haystacks. They arrive at winter's end and seek out sites with an unobstructed view so they can see their surroundings and potential predators. It's fun to watch the female select the spot for the nest and build up a bowl-shaped structure using hay and then line the nest with feathers. When the eggs come, she sits on the nest while the male watches for predators, such as coyotes, foxes, or even eagles. The spot on the haystack is handy, since the geese have a convenient buffet of good alfalfa hay all around them.

It's their seasonal home, and the two geese are territorial about it—even making a fuss when my rancher husband approaches a nearby stack. So he gives them their peace until the goslings are ready to fly away.

One day a neighborhood cat headed toward the stacks—where field mice also can find a safe, cozy haven. Ever on the alert, the papa goose started honking and dive-bombing the cat, which quickly took off for home.

Just like that protective papa goose, our heavenly Father watches over us. He certainly wants us to live in a safe, peaceful place, but even more, He wants us to find our spiritual home in Him. Our Father guards us against all harm when we are safely nestled in His arms.
—Janet Holm McHenry

Dear God, thank You for Your loving, protective care for me.
Keep my home safe, and guard me from any advance
from the enemy on my heart, mind, and soul.

MARCH 3

Discomfort Zone

"Have I not commanded you? Be strong and courageous. Do not be afraid; do not be discouraged, for the LORD your God will be with you wherever you go."

—JOSHUA 1:9 (NIV)

WHEN MY NEIGHBOR asked if I'd feed her cat, Grae, while she and her husband were on vacation, I was thrilled. A cute little purring machine, Grae had frosty gray fur and dusty paws.

Because she was an outside cat, I wanted to make sure I was clear on the instructions before my neighbor left for her trip. I jotted notes as she pointed out the heated cat house, the water dispenser, and the food container. When I noticed that there were two bowls, my neighbor explained that Sheba, Grae's sidekick, popped in occasionally.

"She's not as trusting as Grae," she explained. "She hunts along the tree line and mostly fends for herself, but I leave food for her just in case." I was curious why one would be so trusting and the other so skittish.

Sure enough, a winter storm blew in the day my neighbors left for vacation. I trekked over at feeding time, and while Grae purred and threw herself in front of me dramatically, I was surprised to find Sheba huddling in the warm cat house. As soon as she saw me, she darted into the woods. I called out to her, but she was long gone. Why would she linger just beyond a safe haven?

On the heels of that thought, I was convicted. Didn't I do that as well? I certainly tarried on the perimeter when it came to my church community. While I didn't fear for my safety like Sheba, I didn't feel as "well-churched" as everyone else. What if I misquoted Scripture? Or couldn't verbalize my prayers or what was in my heart?

Just then, Grae stirred at my feet, and when I bent to pet her, I caught a flash of movement in my peripheral vision. Sheba cautiously crept from the tree line, stealthily making her way toward food, warmth—and me.

"Don't be afraid," I cooed. "I'll take good care of you. I promise."
—Hallie Lee

> *Lord, please give me courage and confidence that*
> *You're with me wherever I go!*

MARCH 4

He Loves Them Too

"I have other sheep that are not of this sheep pen. I must bring them also."
—JOHN 10:16 (NIV)

MOTHER ROBIN AND I have had an uneasy truce for the past 3 years. During the first year, she built her nest under the eaves of my front porch, opposite where I like to sit. I was a bit annoyed with the mess, but we otherwise got along fine. I decided to let her stay through the season, at least until her chicks had flown. I cleared out the nest that fall.

The next year she nested just above the place where I enjoy morning coffee and write in my journal. That spring was a tug-of-war between the two of us. Each time I sat on the porch, she flew out of the nest, then swooped back in every minute or two to see if I was still there. Meanwhile, the chicks howled for their breakfast. Most of the time, I gave up and went indoors. "Who's the actual landlord here?" I asked myself in disgust.

This year we reached a detente. I moved my writing table a few feet further from the nest. Mother was wary at first, but I sat facing away from the brood and kept still when she cautiously ventured in and out. Within a few days, she acclimated to my presence, and I to hers. She's at peace. The chicks are growing. And I'm enjoying my porch nearly every day.

Much of life, and much of life as a follower of Jesus, is learning to accept people who are different from us. We encounter them everywhere, and our needs and desires often seem to conflict. The simplest solution is to either push them away or move somewhere else. That's a mistake. Jesus has many, many children. And most of them are quite different from me. —Lawrence W. Wilson

Lord, give me a deep love for all Your children
and boundless patience to accept them.

MARCH 5

Stay, Little Buddy

"Come to me, all who labor and are heavy laden, and I will give you rest."
—MATTHEW 11:28 (NIV)

WHEN MY FAMILY and I embarked on our annual weeklong summer trip to the cabin, I wasn't expecting that my youngest child, Joy, would grow fond of slithery, slimy things. I'm not talking about fish. I'm talking about earthworms sitting around in the mud.

At first, when Joy met these itty-bitty creatures, she was apprehensive about them. Typically, she is not fazed by playing around in the dirt or even getting it on her face. So, when Joy saw her two older siblings being calm, cool, and collected around these creatures, she did the same. Joy would scoop the worms up into the palm of her hand and talk to them. It was so precious I took a couple of videos of her conversations to remember. Joy petted them and even named them. She told me how much she loved them. As if they had become her own special pets, Joy said to them, "Stay, little buddy," as they slithered around the palms of her hands. I think if Joy had it her way, she would have wanted to sleep with the worms like she did with one of her favorite stuffies.

Joy's care for them inspired me to think of creative ways to care for all of God's creatures. I admit, I'm not as fond of worms as she is. But every now and then, when we get a good downpour of rain and the worms come out of the ground, Joy spots them. Their habit of coming to the surface of the earth after it rains reminds me that when heavy circumstances in life pour down on me and become too much to bear, I, too, need to let His living water help me come to the surface to experience His friendship and gentle care. —Stacey Thureen

Walk of Faith: *Take a few minutes to thank God for how He loves you. Praise Him for holding you close, delicately, in the palm of His hand.*

ALL GOD'S CREATURES   67

MARCH 6

By-the-Wind Sailor

*Charm is deceptive, and beauty is fleeting; but a
woman who fears the LORD is to be praised.*

—PROVERBS 31:30 (NIV)

DURING SPRING MY local coastline can sometimes be awash in "by-the-wind sailors," scientifically known as *Velella velella*. They are tiny sea creatures similar to a Portuguese man-o'-war with a tiny sail and transparent body. Their most striking feature, in my humble opinion, is their color, a beautiful, iridescent cerulean blue. Without a means of self-propulsion, they are completely at the mercy of the elements. Blown in one direction by wind or carried in another direction by waves, they will finally be deposited upon the sand, their little sails standing upright, resembling a minuscule ocean wave about to break. But this structure and beauty last only a little while. Eventually being on land dries them out, and they end up looking like a piece of clear plastic. This is all part of their natural cycle.

Admiring these pretty but delicate creatures, I was reminded of what the Bible says about fleeting beauty. When I find myself overly concerned about my own fleeting youth or perhaps fretting about what material things I'll leave behind for my family, especially in a culture that too often values such things over fine character, I need to remember that every part of our reality this side of heaven is like the by-the-wind sailor—it won't last. But unlike those lovely little creatures, which, when washed ashore, turn into something that looks like discarded trash, I know something much better is in store for me at the end of my life.

In my life as a Christian, I am not a by-the-wind sailor. They don't last, and they aren't meant to. But I am. God created me to be with Him for eternity through faith in His Son, Jesus Christ. Each time I see a by-the-wind sailor, I'll remember that. —Marianne Campbell

*He has made everything beautiful in its time. He has also set
eternity in the human heart; yet no one can fathom what
God has done from beginning to end.*
—Ecclesiastes 3:11 (NIV)

MARCH 7

Butterflies, Stop Here!

Do not merely listen to the word, and so deceive yourselves. Do what it says.

—JAMES 1:22 (NIV)

I HAVE ALWAYS been enamored of butterflies. As a child, I would watch their whimsical flight and admire the intricate patterns on their wings—a beautiful display of God's handiwork. As an adult, I have provided food for many caterpillars and given them safe refuge as they go through their transformation.

Last year, my family planted some parsley in our garden, and the swallowtail butterflies made good use of it as a host plant, nibbling it all the way down to the ground. When the parsley sprang back up this year, I assumed the same thing would happen. So far, I've been wrong. In the meantime, our parsley has grown into a sprawling plant that is several feet tall. Imagine my excitement when a swallowtail finally fluttered through our yard a couple of weeks ago. Finally, a butterfly to eat this jungle of parsley! But to my surprise, the swallowtail kept flying.

As I watched it go, I considered that the problem may be the lack of flowers in that area of my yard. See, butterflies need two kinds of plants: flowers for nectar, and a host plant for their caterpillar eggs. To give them one without the other is not enough to maintain their life cycle.

As a follower of Christ, I need to be grounded in His Word, but that "host plant" is not enough. I also need the nectar that comes from following Him in prayer and obedience wherever He leads me. A daily surrender to Him in this way allows Scripture to take action in my heart. The butterfly and I need two kinds of food, and I must take care that I don't spiritually starve myself of the nourishment God graciously offers. —Ashley Clark

> Walk of Faith: *As you go through your day, take notice of the flowers (and any butterflies) you see. Let them be a reminder to you to devote yourself to Scripture, then ask God to help you do what it says.*

ALL GOD'S CREATURES   69

MARCH 8

Tunnel Vision

But the Lord answered and said unto her, Martha, Martha,
thou art anxious and troubled about many things.

—LUKE 10:41 (ASV)

I WAS RACING through my day. My self-imposed to-do list, burdened by my tendency to say yes to every need, had once again brought stress. My shoulders tensed as my thoughts raced and frustration mounted. Behind the wheel, I was eager to get the last of the errands completed while it was midday and traffic was light.

I exited our housing development and pulled out on a well-traveled road. I was barely underway when I saw movement to my right in the tree line. A doe materialized and ran across the road within a few yards of my car. I slammed on my brakes as she crossed the road. I remained motionless, recovering from the fright and remembering my husband's admonition that when you see one deer, you should assume there are more nearby. I started creeping forward with a wary eye on the dense brush. Suddenly, a young buck raced into the road and briefly froze in front of my car before resuming the chase after the doe. On his heels, another young buck crossed the road at high speed.

Yep, it was rutting season, a heedless time of year for bucks on the hunt for a mate. In the white-tailed mating dance, it's the doe who picks her partner. One theory holds that the courting chase facilitates this selection. By leading a male on a run through the woods, a female tests his fitness for breeding. Another theory contends that a noisy chase gets the attention of other, more dominant bucks.

I shook my head at the tunnel vision. They were unmindful of the big picture that included cars and dangerous roads. Yet, who am I to admonish them? How about my own tunnel vision that only sees tasks to complete? My flurry of activity often leaves little or no room in my day for true life-giving treasures. I'm the Martha desiring to be like her sister Mary—she who didn't focus on "what needs to be done" over precious moments with Jesus. —Darlene Kerr

Far too often we miss life by doing something that we call "life."
—Craig D. Lounsbrough

MARCH 9

Birds in the Bush

*Two are better than one, because they have a good return for their labor.
If either of them falls down, one can help the other up. But pity
anyone who falls and has no one to help them up.*

—ECCLESIASTES 4:9–10 (NIV)

I WAS DOING laundry when my husband, Neil, called to me. "Come. Come and see," he said. I dropped the pile of clean clothes I had in my arms on the dining room table and hurried into the family room. Neil was sitting in his recliner and watching the birds at the feeder outside our picture window.

Much to his surprise, a flock of ten blue jays suddenly flew into the lilac bush next to our feeder. Perched on various branches, they bobbed their bodies up and down, some so forcefully that their feet left the branches. And like feathered rock stars, they sang at the same time. Except that their song sounded less like music and more like a squeaky gate.

Just as intriguing, one bird would periodically fly away, with all the others in hot pursuit. When they all returned two minutes later, the bobbing and singing would start again. Neil and I couldn't stop watching. We were so fascinated that I did some research afterward.

It turns out that the bobbing up and down sometimes serves a territorial purpose but is usually a courtship display. A group of males will surround a female and all display at once, showing off for her. The watching female can tell by the speed and power of each bird's performance which one would make the fittest mate.

Eventually, everyone settled down, I think because the female had made her selection. And that's when I learned that once two jays pair off, they stay together for life, which can be up to 16 years!

Such committed companionship made me think about all the places in my life where I benefit from having someone else in my corner—my husband, family, close friends, people in my church and community. Alone, I can do only so much, but when I work with someone else, my burden is halved, and the fruit of our shared labor increases exponentially. —Aline Newman

Alone we can do so little; together we can do so much.
—Helen Keller

ALL GOD'S CREATURES

MARCH 10

Duncan's Doggie Door

When they came to the border of Mysia, they tried to enter Bithynia, but the Spirit of Jesus would not allow them to.

—ACTS 16:7 (NIV)

WATCHING DUNCAN, OUR independent-minded Scottish terrier, approach his doggie door one evening taught me a valuable lesson about trusting God. I'd slipped the panel in so he couldn't go outside. It was dark. There was a skunk either in our yard or moseying along the back fence. I could smell the unmistakable odor through an open window. Instead of banging his head against the closed door, Duncan simply turned around and went back to napping in his favorite corner of the den. Duncan always did that. He never flung himself against the door trying to get out. Occasionally, he might whimper, eager to chase whatever had intruded upon our property. But if I told him to go lie down, he did. It was as though he trusted me to let him out when the time was right. And I eventually did—when the coast was clear.

One evening I realized I should be more trusting when God closes a door in my life. I've pushed and shoved and insisted on having my way—getting through that closed door at all costs. But the task of an obedient Christian is to go through the doors the Lord opens for us—not force ourselves through the closed ones. I need to move on to the next step that God has for me, not insist on having my own way. The Apostle Paul wanted to preach in Asia, but twice the Holy Spirit closed that door to him and his companions. Paul obeyed and went elsewhere. He didn't waste time and energy banging on a closed door.

I had my reasons for shutting Duncan's doggie door that night. God has His reasons, too, when He closes a door in my life. I just need to trust Him. —Shirley Raye Redmond

Trust and obey, for there's no other way to be happy in Jesus,
but to trust and obey.
—John H. Sammis

MARCH 11

Basking in Love

Don't look out only for your own interests, but take an interest in others, too.

—**PHILIPPIANS 2:4** (NLT)

I HAVE A young friend who's afraid she'll never find love. She reads books, takes classes, consults with experts, and does everything imaginable to make herself attractive so that the love of her life will recognize her and she'll find the connection she longs for.

Recently, one of her experts advised her to get a turtle. "Why a turtle?" I asked my friend.

"Turtles are supposed to be good teachers," she explained. My friend brought home a handsome box turtle named Alden, a name she told me meant "wise old friend."

Alden wasn't as easy to care for as she had imagined. His habitat needs to be temperature and humidity controlled, he needed a burrow, and he needed a basking area with a heat lamp and ultraviolet light to provide vitamin D. Her refrigerator was filled with greens and berries that she shared with him, as well as boxes of worms and wet dog food that only Alden enjoyed.

Caring for the turtle had forced her to create a schedule that wasn't just focused on what she thought she lacked but instead was centered on caring for Alden. He didn't talk or wag his tail or cuddle with her like other pets might, but he was fascinating. He marched around her apartment, exploring and hiding and even coming out to greet her when she called. She had found him a vet, and she had already started making new friends at the pet store where she got the worms. She hadn't found love yet, but she was meeting new people and finding new meaning in caring for Alden.

Like my friend, I often try too hard when I am looking for validation. I get stacks of books and try to improve myself. But as her experience with Alden reminded me, the only way to find love is to get out of our shell and care for another creature. —Lucy Chambers

Let your teacher be love itself.
—Rumi

ALL GOD'S CREATURES 73

MARCH 12

Surprise from the Sand

*"They will feast on the abundance of the seas,
on the treasures hidden in the sand."*

—DEUTERONOMY 33:19 (NIV)

MY GAZE WAS glued to the sand beneath me as my husband and I strolled along. "I'd sure love to find a shark's tooth on this trip."

"Yeah, I've heard early morning's the best time, before all the others have beachcombed."

Since it was almost noon, I knew that finding such a treasure was unlikely, given the crowds gathered under umbrellas, sprawled out on towels, and playing along the shoreline. Still, God knew the desire of my heart. Small though this one was—both figuratively and literally—with Him, I believed all things were possible.

"Hey, look at that." I stopped walking and knelt down. "What's making all those bubbles and tiny balls?"

Bill knelt beside me. "I think it's a sand bubbler crab. He's somewhere, down in his burrow, and the balls are . . ." He paused and cleared his throat. "I think they're his poop."

"Ew." I giggled. "Well, I guess crabs have to go to the bathroom too."

We continued to watch as the little creature, though out of sight, pushed wet sand and petite pellets out of his abode.

"How cute is that? A housecleaning crab." I nudged my husband. "Isn't God creative?"

Before Bill could answer and right before our eyes, out of the sand bubbler's burrow popped—"You've got to be kidding me!" I could hardly believe it. Carefully, I picked up a small, shiny object. "Do you see this?"

I held it in my open palm, and Bill inspected it. "A shark's tooth. How in the world?"

And it's true. I have it with other gifts from the sea, kept safe in my treasure box. The shark's tooth serves as a reminder. God knows the desires of my heart, and with Him, all things—large and small—are possible. Amen! —Maureen Miller

Take delight in the LORD, and he will give you the desires of your heart.
—Psalm 37:4 (NIV)

MARCH 13

Too Close for Comfort

"I have seen God face to face, and yet my life has been delivered."
—GENESIS 32:30 (ESV)

AS A CHILD, I spent a lot of time at my grandparents' dairy farm. My grandparents would get up at 3 a.m. to go milk the cows each morning. I was only five or six at the time—too young to be left in the house alone. So they fashioned a bed for me in the barn: a large lounge chair, a pillow, and some blankets. They'd get me set up in the middle of the floor so they could keep an eye on me while they milked the cows, and I slept.

One morning, I woke to find myself face to face with a cow that had gotten loose. I'd always thought cows were cute and cuddly, but this was a bit too close for comfort.

She looked down on me curiously, breathing hot air in my face. I panicked, jumped up, and ran to find my grandparents. Up close and personal, the cow no longer seemed cute and cuddly. She was huge and scary! And while she didn't threaten me, I was alarmed at the realization that she could easily crush me if she wanted to. Poppa quickly rounded her up while Gram held me close.

As an adult looking back, I realize how this encounter reminded me of God. Up close, I saw the cow in a different light. I was overwhelmed by her power, no longer just seeing her cute and cuddly facade. I can only imagine how I would feel in such an encounter with God. In my mind sometimes, God can seem cuddly, but while I know He is gentle and loving, I don't want to forget that He is also infinitely large and powerful too.

Life can throw curveballs—or a cow!—my way. In those times, I can call out to Him, remembering that He is the Lord, strong and mighty, as well as my tender Shepherd, and knowing He not only *wants* to keep me safe but also has the power to do so. —Leslie L. McKee

Who is this King of glory? The LORD, strong and mighty,
the LORD, mighty in battle!
—Psalm 24:8 (ESV)

MARCH 14

A Snake Under the Car

This God—his way is perfect; the word of the LORD proves true; he is a shield for all those who take refuge in him.

—PSALM 18:30 (NIV)

THERE'S A SNAKE under my car," our son said when he called one morning. "I thought it was a branch until it moved and slithered into a pan under the engine."

He was on his way to meet his wife and five-year-old son, Jack, at a doctor's appointment, and he had two concerns. First, he lives across the road from a heavily wooded area with a variety of snakes, so he did not know if it was venomous. Second, he wondered how he would know if or when the snake had left the car, because once he returned home, the car would be parked near where our grandson played.

When he arrived at the doctor's office, our son got out of the car quickly and headed toward a swing set where his wife and Jack were waiting until it was time to go inside for the appointment. As he turned around, he saw the snake leave the car. It was big, but it was a harmless rat snake. It was probably more traumatized than they were after its bumpy car ride, and it quickly slithered away from the car.

The snake's life took an unexpected detour when he sought refuge in the wrong place. He easily could have been harmed or worse from seeking sanctuary in the undercarriage of the car.

Thinking about my son's snake saga later, I wondered if I, too, sometimes seek refuge in the wrong place. The world clamors for our attention, promising solace or comfort in places and ways that could lead to hurt or destruction. But God promises me refuge in Him, and His promises always prove to be true. I can trust His Word that when I seek refuge in Him, He will shelter me in His arms. —Harold Nichols

The Lord is my Refuge, my Strength, and Shield, and this of a truth I know;
His tender protection is o'er me still, my comfort where'er I go.
—Fanny Crosby

MARCH 15

Angels Unaware

Don't mistreat any foreigners who live in your land. Instead, treat them as well as you treat your own people and love them as much as you love yourself.

LEVITICUS 19:33–34 (CEV)

EARLY IN THE spring as I walked by the cove near our home, I watched the many birds swimming near shore or walking along the low-tide sands. Some were familiar to me because they were there most of the year, while others seemed to be passing through in their migratory travels.

What I found interesting was that they were all congregating without any squabbles. Not that they were completely mixed, but groupings of like birds were paddling beside groupings of different birds. If one from one group swam or waddled into another group, there wasn't much squawking. It was as if the "local" birds were welcoming the travelers.

Watching the birds, I wondered how welcoming and hospitable I may or may not be to people who travel through my life. Those transient people who pass through: college students in town, military families, temporary workers. Many are not "like me" in their stages of life, yet we are all similar in our humanness. Just as I may feel lonely and in need of a friend, so too may they.

The birds reminded me of the Hebrew writers and the admonition to welcome the sojourner and stranger. The birds weren't squabbling over resources. There appeared to be plenty to share. God has blessed me with many things that I could share with those who are passing through. Wherever we are in life, we can and should welcome those who are passing through. For we never know if we are entertaining angels unaware. —Virginia Ruth

Walk of Faith: *Today, make a point to welcome a new neighbor with a plant or baked good; pray for a family in need; tell someone who provides a service for you how much you appreciate their work; or just reach out to someone who is passing through your life.*

ALL GOD'S CREATURES

MARCH 16

Sweet Decorated Fawns

"Do you watch when the doe bears her fawn?"

—JOB 39:1 (NIV)

IAM GRATEFUL for the natural habitat around me, where springtime and early summer bring newborn fawns to the high desert of central Oregon. White speckles on their brown backs look like winter's snowflakes that stayed behind and left their design on the coats of these infant deer.

This past spring, a mother and her fawns walked across my backyard. The twins followed their mother with a prance that tugged at my heart. On another occasion, when visiting Wallowa Lake in northeast Oregon, I watched a doe and her baby come up to the lodge porch where I sat. They were so close, I could have petted them but would never dare. It was evident they were accustomed to humans, but my role was to appreciate them as wild and to know my boundaries. The fawn, out of the forest and in the open, stood out to me like a delicate work of art.

Our Creator put these adorable markings on fawns, and they hold a purpose. The spots mimic the dappled sunrays on the forest floor, as the sun filters through the leaves and branches. This makes the vulnerable fawns harder for predators to see. What strikes me most is that the spots are not arbitrary. They are as unique as human fingerprints and snowflakes. This identification helps a doe recognize her own offspring among the others, even from a distance, and this creates a special and loving bond between mother and baby.

As springtime approaches again, I will watch for the mother does and their fawns. I sense a "call" to peace when I see them—a call to be still and know that He is God and I am His child. The serenity of deer, especially with their babies, inspires me to declare the wonders of God and how He decorates His world and creation—such marvels to comprehend!
—Kathleen R. Ruckman

"Be still, and know that I am God."
—Psalm 46:10 (NKJV)

MARCH 17

Beware of Dog?

They were all terrified when they saw him. But Jesus spoke to them at once. "Don't be afraid," he said. "Take courage! I am here!"

—MARK 6:50 (NLT)

DURING ONE OF our last days visiting Ireland, my friends Susy and Teresa and I ventured down a stone alleyway that almost made us forget we were living in the twenty-first century. A Beware of Dog sign broke the illusion. We waited for an angry dog to start snarling at us. Just when we'd resorted to tiptoeing past the house, we spotted a Jack Russell terrier mix staring at us through her owner's gate.

I laughed. "Hi, there, scary little dog."

Susy carefully reached out her hand for the dog to sniff.

We took turns petting the black-and-white tyke and telling her how terrified we felt in her presence.

A young woman came outside in her slippers and robe, her hair damp. She chatted with us and introduced her dog. "Her name is Saoirse," she told us, the name sounding like SEER-shuh.

I admitted we'd been laughing at her Beware of Dog sign.

The woman laughed along with us. "I put that up because sometimes she just barks and barks. It's so embarrassing. I feel I need to warn people."

We visited a little longer, gave Saoirse a final pet each through the gate, then continued to dinner, uplifted by the encounter with a friendly Irish local.

It hit me how often life's Beware of Dog signs have turned out to have Jack Russells like Saoirse behind them—in other words, nothing to fear. Like when the disciples mistook the figure walking on the water for a ghost when it was actually Jesus. If we had let fear rule that day in Ireland, we would've missed out on meeting Saoirse and her owner. The memory continues to motivate me to pause before allowing fear to paralyze me. —Jeanette Hanscome

The peculiarity of sunrise is to make us laugh at all our terrors of the night, and our laugh is always proportioned to the fear we have had.
—Victor Hugo

ALL GOD'S CREATURES

MARCH 18

It's Their World Too

O Lord, You preserve man and beast.
—Psalm 36:6 (NKJV)

I MADE A contribution to a certain charity. A week later I received in the mail a thank-you gift—a spiral-bound desk calendar. Every calendar page bore a photo of poverty-stricken people the charity was striving to help: malnourished children scrounging for food in a garbage dump, stick-skinny tribespeople wandering in a windswept desert, hollow-eyed mothers cradling their babies. Photo after photo of human beings so poor they couldn't get much poorer without dying. Superimposed over the photos are the words, "It's Their World Too." Amen to that. The poor have just as much right to be alive and to have a meaningful and satisfying existence as I do. It's their world too.

It occurs to me that this saying could also be applied to animals. Billions of people now inhabit this small planet, and it is easy for humankind to keep pushing outward, to keep gobbling up natural habitat that once belonged to the animals. But it's their world too. In a nearby wooded acreage, there is a vernal pool, a shallow, quarter-acre depression that fills with water in springtime, then dries out come summer. I visit the pool every spring to look for frogs and salamanders. On today's visit I find a blue-spotted salamander, a slender amphibian about 4 inches long, with bluish-black skin freckled with white spots. He is a shy little guy who spends most of his life hiding under leaves and logs. Sadly, this will be my last visit to the vernal pool. A housing development is planned for this land, and bulldozers will start moving dirt next month.

I wonder what will become of the salamanders who live here. Birds and most mammals can easily relocate, but amphibians can't move fast or far. The landowner had every right to sell his property to the developer, and people need houses to live in. I get it. But I feel sad for the blue-spotted salamanders. It's their world too. —Louis Lotz

The greatness of a nation and its moral progress can be
judged by the way its animals are treated.
—Mahatma Gandhi

MARCH 19

Return of the Travelers

The LORD is good, a refuge in times of trouble.
He cares for those who trust in him

—NAHUM 1:7 (NIV)

EACH YEAR, I look forward to the return of a family of swallows I affectionately named The Travelers. In their honor, last spring I added a birdhouse shaped like a camper to the existing row of quirky wooden bird dwellings. With the exception of one season when The Travelers chose our roof as their summer home, dive-bombed anyone who tried to use the porch, and got "asked to leave" via a barrier, they always nest in an area outside my bedroom window, which has access to a shady place under the upstairs deck.

This year, the first Traveler started scouting out my row of birdhouses during the same week we were having a deck inspection and repairs done on the ceiling. The deck crew removed a row of bamboo lattice that the swallows liked to sit on.

I prepared for a year without The Travelers. Surely they would never tolerate having their campsite disrupted and workers coming and going with power tools.

But the swallows kept showing up. They seemed to enjoy the freedom of flying under the deck without lattice in the way. They sat on the birdhouses more than in the past, swung on the hanger chains, and perched on a ladder. The workers didn't frighten them a bit.

I realized my family had created a space where The Travelers knew they were welcome. That space under the deck lined with swinging birdhouses had become their yearly refuge—like the places of safety God provides for me when I need a break, a quiet place to write, time with friends who get me, or solitude with Him. Their presence prompts me to thank my heavenly Father for every refuge He makes available when I need it. —Jeanette Hanscome

Walk of Faith: How has God been a refuge to you lately? What forms of refuge has He provided? Take time today to thank Him for knowing how to make you feel welcome and safe.

ALL GOD'S CREATURES

MARCH 20

Misha's Car Naps

[Love] keeps no record of wrongs.
—1 CORINTHIANS 13:5 (NIV)

MISHA IS A Siamese cat who is very particular about her interactions with others. She likes to be patted only on her head and only for the length of time she deems long enough, and when she is ready to be done with her cuddle time, she lets you know in no uncertain terms that she is done. If you miss your cue and overstay your welcome, she will bat your hand with her claws or even administer a swift bite. But the ultimate way that she demands I show her love is her "car naps." When I pull into the driveway, she waits for the car door to open and then hops in to find a comfortable place to nap, making me wait for at least a half hour until she's ready to go back in the house.

Before you ask why I would love a cat so, one who bites and is so persnickety about her needs, I must tell you that to be loved by Misha is a joy. She has the loudest purr you have ever heard, and she loves being loved beyond all things. She has a look when she is happy that will melt your heart. That love look in those big blue Siamese eyes is how she convinced me to take her home when I found her in the rain outside my bank while making a night deposit. Misha has learned that the only road to love is to pursue it. She demands love. And by pursuing love, she gets it, even if her personality brings challenge.

Love doesn't ask for perfection. Love doesn't require all our days to be good. Love only requires our desire for it. When we pursue love, we find it. Love comes in many forms—platonic, spiritual, romantic, and the comfortable love that allows you to nap in inconvenient places without apology.

Misha has taught me that when I pursue love as God has pursued me with love, my life will be filled with a force stronger than anything that comes against me. —Devon O'Day

Pursue love, and earnestly desire the spiritual gifts.
—1 Corinthians 14:1 (ESV)

MARCH 21

A Wild Ride

*Therefore we will not fear, though the earth give way
and the mountains fall into the heart of the sea.*

—PSALM 46:2 (NIV)

FOR SEVERAL YEARS I've been trying to grow a fig tree in a pot. It came through the mail as a tender 4-inch shoot, and now, at nearly 3 feet tall and bushy, it had lived through the winter in a hefty, unwieldy pot. When it came time to move the fig outside in the spring, my husband helped me lug it through the patio doors; he watched the steps, and I watched the leaves as we inched our way outside.

That's when I saw a most amazing thing. Suddenly, a gigantic earthworm shot out of the dirt—a good 6 inches—straight into the air. I've never seen anything like it, but it seems that having its home and haven disturbed, the worm came to the surface to determine whether a crisis was at hand. All winter long, I had not a clue that an earthworm as big as a fresh no. 2 pencil was living with my fig tree, hidden safely in the dark depths of dirt.

Moments after the worm shot from the soil, it curled and twisted its way across the surface and immediately back down into the loamy depths of the pot. Though its earth had rocked and trembled, the worm must have determined it was still safe. Nothing to fear.

When my life shakes, when my world is wobbly, and when my shoulders stiffen with anxiety and worry, I want to be like the worm. I really do. I want to look around and know immediately that all is well. My life and my worries are all in God's hands; God holds me safe and secure; and I simply need to allow myself to settle into that safety. I need not fear. —Katy W. Sundararajan

If you look at the world, you'll be distressed. If you look within, you'll be depressed. If you look at God, you'll be at rest.
—Corrie Ten Boom

ALL GOD'S CREATURES   83

MARCH 22

Ducks Can Fly

I said, "Oh, that I had the wings of a dove! I would fly away and be at rest."

—PSALM 55:6 (NIV)

SPRING RAINS HAD brought the creek in our town park to flood level. White water cascaded over the small waterfall, creating a swift current in the pond below. The ducks, seemingly oblivious to the roaring falls and rushing stream, floated placidly—and very swiftly—toward the dam in the outlet of the pond. The water level there was at least 2 feet higher than normal, sending a torrent crashing several feet onto the rocks below.

The ducks had traveled nearly the length of the pond and were seconds away from cascading over the dam. Twenty feet. Ten feet. Why didn't they alter course? Five feet. *They'll certainly be injured in the fall.* I was about to cry out, but it was too late. The first of the ducks had reached the spillway. There was no turning back.

But the duck didn't drown. She didn't fall. Instead, she opened her wings and took off from the dam as if launched from an aircraft carrier. The others followed a moment later, looking for all the world like a contingent of Blue Angels, the famed US Navy precision flight team. They rose into the air, circled to the right, and soon landed safely on the grassy creek bank.

Oh, yeah, I thought. *Ducks can fly.* I suppose the urgency of the moment had made me forget.

Stress can do that. Hectic days, wayward children, conflict at work, a painful marriage—these and other circumstances can cause us to get lost in the moment, forgetting the tremendous gift and great power that Jesus has given us. We have knowledge of eternity. We are never limited by the situation before us. We have the power to rise above it and persevere.

Ducks can fly, and we can too. —Lawrence W. Wilson

Lord Jesus, give me the strength to live, a free person saved by grace and able to do all things in Your strength. And help me to remember that when life gets tough, I will find my rest in You. Amen.

MARCH 23

There Through It All

Everything is meaningless . . . everything beautiful in its time.
—ECCLESIASTES 1:2; 3:11 (NIV)

ANIMAL CRACKERS IN my soup . . ." The ditty from Shirley Temple's movie *Curly Top* sang through my mind, then belted out my mouth. Laughter bubbled up, helping to shove aside the sadness and anxiety filling my soul that morning. The mirth came from an early spring sighting of a white-tailed deer on my drive down our road. I thought I saw curls swirling between its ears, possibly the start of a young buck's antlers. The sight lifted the low spirits I'd left home with.

During my quiet time earlier, thoughts of a recent family upheaval had intruded. Instead of enjoying some peaceful moments with God, my soul felt burdened. Tears stung my eyes. I gave up and put my devotions away, trudged back down the hall, and got dressed. Shoulders slumped and head down, I got in the car to run errands. And then the deer sighting happened, shoving the sadness aside. Joy had returned!

As I continued on my journey, I thought about the two parts of my morning, one bringing despair to my spirit, the other causing immediate laughter and a fun song to brighten my mood. I considered how often God uses animals to bring me joy out of sorrow.

Yes, the anxiety would return. But so will happiness and joy. God's boundless grace is always with me, in both tears and laughter, and He makes all of it beautiful in its time.

The writer of Ecclesiastes talked of the "meaningless" parts of life. He considered the back and forth of "everything," including laughing and crying. Yet he described everything God has made as "beautiful." Everything—from scalding tears to a curly-topped deer. —Cathy Mayfield

I know that everything God does will endure forever.
—Ecclesiastes 3:14 (NIV)

MARCH 24

The Nest

"The Lord does not look at the things people look at. People look at the outward appearance, but the Lord looks at the heart."

—1 SAMUEL 16:7 (NIV)

ONE SPRING MORNING as I was peacefully working in my front flower patch, I heard a bloodcurdling scream. I looked up to see my daughter running away from the flowers. "What is it?" I frantically called. "What happened?"

"Snakes!" she screamed over her shoulder as she ran away.

My daughter had been helping me clean up the duff from winter and get the patch ready for spring. I looked where she was working, and sure enough, curled together in a lump right next to my irises was a whole nest of baby snakes. "It's OK," I said. "I know they're scary, but they won't hurt you."

Carefully we worked to put some dead leaves and mulch back on the baby snakes. "They are just trying to keep warm," I explained. "It's not time for them to come out yet."

Later that night my daughter brought up the nest again. "I hate snakes," she said. "Maybe we should try to get rid of them."

"No," I replied, "we want to have them in our garden." I patiently explained that snakes are part of a healthy ecosystem. They work to eat insects and other things that will eat our flowers. Without snakes, we couldn't have flowers. And we all love flowers.

I wondered how many times I had judged someone based on their outward appearance. Just as I can't judge an animal simply by how it looks, I also can't judge people that way. God looks to the heart of all things. All of creation, from people to snakes, has value in the eyes of our Creator. —Heather Jepsen

Loving God, help me look beyond the outward appearance and see others as You see them, with the eyes of grace and love. Amen.

MARCH 25

Woodpecker Wrecking Crew

When the trumpets sounded, the army shouted, and at the sound of the trumpet, when the men gave a loud shout, the wall collapsed; so everyone charged straight in, and they took the city.

—JOSHUA 6:20 (NIV)

THE TREE STUMP on our Indiana property was only 3 feet high, but it would not budge. My husband, Tim, oiled his handsaw. The blade bounced right off the wood. He powered up his chain saw. Nary a scratch. The stump was not moving. Tim admitted defeat, and we used the stump as a corn-feeding station for the wildlife.

This spring as I placed feed on the stump, I noticed bark and wood chips scattered around the bottom. Apparently a creature had succeeded where we could not. Tim and I decided to let the chips fall where they may.

Over the next two weeks, I heard the *cuk-cuk-cuk-cuk-cuk* of a pileated woodpecker, the largest of that species, swooping from one dead tree to another; the dead trees are perfect for nesting areas. Then I caught a glimpse of the woodpecker whacking away at the base of the stump. The black-and-white jackhammer encircled the stump to find the most vulnerable sections, searching for insects in the exposed areas. I read up on the bird's chisel-like beak and its excavations in dead wood. Not only is the beak like a stiff hammer, but its neck muscles provide the striking power.

That stump's demise reminded me of the city of Jericho with its impenetrable wall and how God directed Joshua in all he was to do in taking the city. Was it the trumpets, the shouting, or the army encircling the wall that caused the collapse? Taking the city certainly began with the faith of the leader, Joshua, in obeying God's commands.

Could I attack seemingly insurmountable problems like Joshua and the woodpecker did? Only if I pray, obey God's commands, and look for the weak spots. —Glenda Ferguson

When a problem comes along, study it until you are completely knowledgeable. Then find that weak spot, break the problem apart, and the rest will be easy.
—Norman Vincent Peale

ALL GOD'S CREATURES

MARCH 26

Building a Kingdom

[Jesus] answered them, "The kingdom of God is not coming in ways that can be observed, nor will they say, 'Look, here it is!' or 'There!' for behold, the kingdom of God is in the midst of you."

—LUKE 17:20–21 (ESV)

WHEN MY HUSBAND and I take our daily walks, we often see little hills of dirt that seem to pop up overnight along the levee around our neighborhood lakes. The mounds grow especially large during spring when the earth is soft. Though we know they hide somewhere inside, we rarely see the individual ants that build them. But wait until a nest is disturbed! Ants pour from their home, ready to defend it. Then they begin the job of repairing the damaged section and go back to gathering food for the seasons ahead.

I love to watch our industrious ants, whether they build mounds beside the road or in the cracks of my sidewalk. Scientists have classified more than 12,000 species of ants throughout the world. I don't know what kinds we have, but from the smallest to the largest, they work with their colonies to build their homes, one grain of dirt at a time.

God uses even the tiniest of creatures to teach me the qualities He wants me to develop. Just staying busy is not the lesson I learn. It's what I'm busy doing. Where ants dedicate themselves to building an earthly home, I can work with my fellow Christians to build God's kingdom, one person at a time.

Jesus stayed busy from morning to night gathering believers and teaching them about His Father's will for them. Though my work may not be noticed, the ants remind me the kingdom of God is in our midst. I don't have to wait until I'm disturbed about the state of our world. I can tell others of God's love and salvation and the heavenly home—one that can never be shaken—waiting just for them. —Tracy Crump

Walk of Faith: *Think of someone you know who might not have heard the Good News of Jesus. Pray for the person, and seek opportunities to tell them about the home in heaven He promised to build for all who place their faith in Him.*

MARCH 27

Niblet's Second Chance

"Forget the former things; do not dwell on the past. See, I am doing a new thing! Now it springs up; do you not perceive it? I am making a way in the wilderness and streams in the wasteland."

—ISAIAH 43:18–19 (NIV)

NIBLET WAS THE only chick that survived from one of her mother's hatchings. Niblet and Mavis, her mother, kept to themselves in the backyard. They nested together in a small pet igloo set high above ground. Once she grew old enough, Niblet hatched out her first six chicks. She was young and didn't know how to be a mother. She didn't fare very well at teaching and protecting them.

The next year, Niblet stayed on her nest in the little igloo and refused to leave the eggs she was nesting on. When they hatched, there were sixteen little baby chicks, and she was the perfect mama hen. She taught them how to find food as they free-ranged, covered them with her wings, and protected them with all she had. Her little flock has flourished, and Niblet gets a gold star for her second time around.

I am encouraged and inspired by Niblet's story of second chances after a first-time failure. How many times have I tried something the first time and been a total failure in my execution of it? We learn by making mistakes. We learn by falling down. We learn by watching others make mistakes and watching others do things well. The bottom line is, if I am living, I have a chance to learn.

When I have failed at something, I will eventually learn from that experience. I can try again with what I have learned and with God's help. One of the best things I have learned is that people forget my failures with every success I achieve. God is a God of new things and second chances. With His help, I want to follow Niblet's example and try, try again. —Devon O'Day

God, let me learn from every mistake and never hesitate to take You up on Your gift of a second chance.

MARCH 28

That Special Something

*The wolf will live with the lamb. . . . The infant
will play near the cobra's den.*

—ISAIAH 11:6, 8 (NIV)

WHEN WAS THE last time you witnessed that special something that passes between humans and animals? Small children and puppies, riders with horses, and the disabled with their service animals often feel a deep sense of connection.

I witnessed a magical exchange like this at our local zoo in Columbia, South Carolina. Only glass separates visitors from the family of gorillas who call Riverbanks home. Often we have to squint to see them foraging in the hilly terrain above the viewing area, but not that day.

Close enough to touch if it weren't for the glass, a female, two youngsters, and an imposing silverback lounged nearby. They watched children giggle from the other side of the glass as the young gorillas rolled and tumbled with each other in play that looked a lot like the young visitors' own playground tussles.

The silverback, however, sat, dignified and aloof, with his back to the viewing area. When Sammy, a curly haired boy of about four, approached the glass, he turned.

Sammy drew closer until he and the gorilla stood face to face, studying each other. Sammy raised his hand, pressed his palm against the glass, and grinned. The giant gorilla did the same, placing his palm on the other side of the glass to match Sammy's. He didn't grin, but I swear I saw a twinkle in his wise old eyes.

DNA, habitats, and mental ability separate humans from animals, but sometimes, like that day in the zoo, the threads of our common Creator link our hearts. It makes me long for the day when the wolf will live with the lamb, a child can play near a cobra's den without fear, and a boy can high-five a gorilla with no glass between them. —Lori Hatcher

Walk of Faith: *What aspect of Isaiah's prophecy about humanity's interaction with animals do you look forward to most? Ponder it today and be on the lookout for moments when animals and humans demonstrate their close connection here on earth.*

ALL GOD'S CREATURES

MARCH 29

Home Sweet Nest

*He who dwells in the secret place of the Most High
shall abide under the shadow of the Almighty.*

—PSALM 91:1 (NKJV)

SPRINGTIME IS WHEN I spruce up our Indiana home, yard, and front porch with Easter decorations, which are stored in plastic containers on our garage shelves. I abruptly stopped sorting through the items when I happened upon a ball-shaped nest fitted inside a rounded corner of the container. The little brown mama mouse and family were long gone. Apparently, the lid had not been snapped in place last spring, which left the safe, secret location available for occupancy during the freezing winter temperatures. The resourceful creature transformed long pink ribbon, white fuzzy string, brittle brown twigs, and a turquoise fabric into a perfect little snug home. I recognized the ribbon from my bunny display, the string from my garden gnome's beard, and the twigs from a wreath that decorates my door. I puzzled over the source of the fabric.

I recalled when my husband and I were newlyweds and moved onto this one wooded acre. We needed to acquire every household furnishing to transform our house into a home. My grandparents donated an antique bed. Our parents passed along a used table with mismatched chairs. I bought dishes and kitchen items from a flea market. Over time, as finances allowed, we replaced the hodgepodge of furniture with brand-new pieces. For four decades, we have prayed for peace and safety in our home sweet home, as well as God's blessings over our marriage during every season of our lives. As we welcome God into our presence, we abide under His care. I guess I shouldn't mind if one of His wild creatures desires a nook of our snug dwelling.

After removing all the damaged items from the container, I uncovered a forgotten turquoise garden flag tucked underneath the mouse nest. The fabric now had quite a number of holes in it, but I laughed at the message on the flag: "Bless This Nest!" —Glenda Ferguson

*Almighty God, I ask for Your blessing on this home for all who seek
peace and safety here, no matter the season. Amen.*

ALL GOD'S CREATURES   91

MARCH 30

The Ninja Fish

*And my God will meet all your needs according to
the riches of his glory in Christ Jesus.*

—PHILIPPIANS 4:19 (NIV)

OUR FAMILY VACATION plans fell through, and I was so disappointed. Because of some unexpected medical bills, we decided to forgo the trip. Lately, it seemed as though nothing was going right, and it was affecting my faith. "Where are You, God?" I wondered. "Don't You care that our family is struggling right now?"

In lieu of our vacation, the kids and I went to our county fair. They were excited about it. Honestly, their attitude was better than mine. After riding some rides, my son, Jordan, wanted to play a game and try to win a goldfish. I tried to talk him out of it, but he was insistent. He won and was thrilled when the man handed him a goldfish in a plastic bag.

"Can we buy a fish tank on the way home?" Jordan asked.

I sighed. "I think we'll put him in a bowl we already have." I wanted to avoid explaining that it was a waste of money because the fish wasn't going to live more than a few days.

But a month later, the fish was still with us. "Can we get a fish tank now?" Jordan asked. I broke down and bought one.

Six months later, Goldie was still going strong. By then, I'd told Jordan that I hadn't expected him to live long. "He's amazing," Jordan said. "He's like a ninja." That became Goldie's new name.

Every summer, Ninja Fish celebrated another birthday, and each time, Jordan reminded me that he'd never given up on his little goldfish. Every year, I reflected on that canceled vacation, the overwhelming medical bills, and the challenging time we'd gone through. I'd been proven wrong about the fish, and I realized that, even during that time, God had proven me wrong about His presence and care in my life. He'd always taken care of my family and me, and I could trust Him to provide for our needs. —Diane Stark

Walk of Faith: *Reflect on God's faithfulness during a difficult time
in your life, and thank Him for being there for you.*

MARCH 31

The Distracted Robin

Whoever works his land will have plenty of bread, but
he who follows worthless pursuits lacks sense.

—PROVERBS 12:11 (ESV)

A ROBIN LANDED atop the drainpipe at the back of my house, strands of straw clutched in its beak. I smiled as the bird added the straw to a nest it was building there. Soon, there might be darling baby robins.

Later, when I looked out the front window of my house, I saw a robin building a nest at the corner of our garage. Then another nest appeared on top of a fence post. Strangely, they stayed empty. As I continued to watch, I realized the same robin had apparently built all three nests.

Wondering if building more than one nest was common in robins, I researched the topic and found that robins are occasionally tempted to build more than one nest if they find ideal conditions. In such cases, the robin gets carried away and builds many nests when all she needs is one.

I chuckled at the distracted robin. Until a thought struck me. Wasn't I behaving the same way? I'd been fluttering from one activity to another too. I would sit down to tackle an important project only to recall I had laundry to wash or pets to feed. Sometimes I was led astray by the grass that needed to be cut or delivered packages I had to bring inside.

I was more distracted than the nest-building robin. The tasks themselves weren't bad, and some needed to be done. But when I allowed them to derail my focus, I neglected more important things. Like the robin, I became so distracted building my nests—partially doing many tasks—that I didn't complete any of the work God had for me.

Eventually the robin stopped building nests and committed to one, and I did the same. And I discovered that finishing God's work is the most rewarding task of all. —Jerusha Agen

Discipline without direction is drudgery.
—Donald Whitney

APRIL 1

The Cat's Pajamas

Where shall I go from your Spirit? Or where shall I flee from your presence? If I ascend to heaven, you are there! If I make my bed in Sheol, you are there!

—PSALM 139:7–8 (ESV)

I'D BEEN DOING laundry the day Benny the all-black house panther went missing. A skittish cat, he was known to hide, but I couldn't find him in any of his favorite hidey spots. As I hung clothes on an outside clothesline, I'd foolishly left the door open. My new neighborhood was perched on the edge of a canyon, where coyotes and other wild critters might consider Benny a light snack. I searched outside frantically, but he was nowhere to be found. I was devastated.

Later that day, I visited my elderly grandmother. I told her about Benny, about how he'd been found before, hiding between the bed sheets. Once on a trip to the vet, he'd wedged himself under the dash of my car, and it had taken two veterinarians to get him out. I teared up, saying, "But now my little Benny is gone."

Grandmother smiled. "I'm so sorry. Benny was the cat's pajamas." I remembered the saying *cat's pajamas* from the early twentieth century—it meant Benny was wonderful.

And then it hit me. The only place I hadn't looked was in a basket of laundry sitting next to the door. I kissed Grandma and raced home, heart pounding. Sure enough, the laundry basket still sat by the back door. I called, "Benny!" No response. I dug through the basket, still calling his name.

Like Benny, I sometimes wander and try to hide from the God who calls my name. My search for Benny reminded me of Jesus's parable of the lost sheep. God never stops searching for me until I'm safe and sound.

As I lifted out a pair of pj's, a pair of golden eyes looked up at me. At the bottom of the basket, Benny lay curled up. He sweetly mewed, as if to say, "Hey, you're disturbing my nap!" I buried my face in his soft black fur and whispered, "You really are the cat's pajamas." —Linda S. Clare

Lord, thank You for never giving up on me.

ALL GOD'S CREATURES

APRIL 2

Ten Horses

It is good that one should wait quietly for the salvation of the Lord.

—LAMENTATIONS 3:26 (ESV)

AFTER A FUN afternoon watching Houston's Art Car Parade downtown, I got stuck in traffic trying to get home. I sat in my car on a bridge and wondered how the gridlock of floats, cars, and overheated people lugging folding chairs would ever move. Frustrated and anxious, I was about to get out of the car and try to redirect the people who kept crowding onto the bridge. As I reached for the door handle, a little voice suggested that I would just make things worse.

I put my head on the wheel and prayed—for the self-control to not jump into the fray, for everyone to stop honking, for someone to come help. When I raised my head, a beautiful bay horse walked inches from my car.

Stepping carefully through the stopped traffic, the horse carried a police officer deep into the clustered area ahead. Soon after, a palomino brushed past. Horses of every color went by, until I counted ten horses, the last one a paint with its striking white-and-brown pattern. Despite the crowd, the cars, the blaring horns, and the exhaust all around them, the horses calmly carried the officers into the gridlock. The large group of powerful horses captured the attention of everyone they passed, and the honking suddenly stopped.

Within minutes, the traffic knots began to loosen, and I was on my way home. Passing the ten horses, now peacefully nibbling grass by the colorful art cars parked on the side of the road, I waved my thanks. In my frustration, I thought I had to fix the situation all by myself. But, as usual, taking a moment to pray was the better choice. I wasn't expecting that God would answer my prayer with ten horses, but guided by their riders, these magnificent creatures had the skills, strength, and presence to solve the problem. —Lucy Chambers

Horses are angels with hooves, sent to Earth to teach us about love, trust, and patience.
—Pam Brown

APRIL 3

Squirrel!

Look unto Jesus, the author and finisher of our faith, who for the joy that was set before Him endured the cross, despising the shame, and has sat down at the right hand of the throne of God.

—HEBREWS 12:2 (NKJV)

LAST YEAR I had the very great pleasure of driving cross-country through Canada on the Trans-Canada Highway on my way to the Stratford Festival in Ontario to see my favorite actor play King Lear. I could have flown, but I chose instead to drive, enjoying all the varying landscapes across the provinces, from farmland to forests and everything in between. One thing I could always count on was seeing wildlife and livestock along the way. There were deer crossings, moose crossings, and countless horses and cattle frolicking in the fields. I half expected Canada's national animal, the beaver, to have its own crossing as well.

What they didn't have, and perhaps should have had, was a sign for a squirrel crossing. Several times during my trip, a squirrel would dart directly in front of my car, causing me to swerve or stomp on my brakes to keep them safe. I remember one squirrel in particular who stood on his hind legs in the middle of the road, staring at me as if I were the problem, which I probably was. After all, this was *his* territory, and I was the interloper. He paused for a moment, then scurried back and forth, appearing not to know which direction he wanted to go. I had already stopped the car until I was sure the little guy was OK, but he certainly took a long time deciding which side of the road to choose.

I am so much like that squirrel. I get into one project only to be distracted by another. I half finish my sentence and then say something else completely unrelated. Like the squirrel, I can't decide which side of the road I want to be on. That's when I remind myself to look at the cross of Christ to guide me. —Deb Kastner

Most high, glorious God, enlighten the darkness of my heart and give me, Lord, a correct faith, certain hope, perfect charity, sense, and knowledge, so that I may carry out Your holy and true command.
—Saint Francis of Assisi

APRIL 4

An Epic Battle

*"They will make war on the Lamb, and the Lamb will
conquer them, for he is Lord of lords and King of kings, and
those with him are called and chosen and faithful."*

—REVELATION 17:14 (ESV)

I'D RETURNED TO our condo early, leaving the rest of my family to enjoy the beach a little while longer, when my husband called.

"Go out on the patio and look past the crowd gathered on the sand," he said. "There's a 10-foot hammerhead shark just offshore."

Grabbing the binoculars, I shook as I trained them on the shoreline. A dark, unmistakable shape swam back and forth through the water. Before long, my family returned to the room, all talking at once. As soon as they came through the door, our three-year-old grandson shouted, "We saw a shark!" The details of the battle they described made me weak with relief that no one was injured.

My husband, son, and granddaughter were playing in the waves when, not 20 feet away, the hammerhead attacked a huge stingray and flipped it into the air. A battle ensued. My husband didn't understand what was happening at first, but our daughter-in-law had a better view from the beach and yelled, "Get out of the water, you ding-dongs!" Another young woman later paddled out to the area on a surfboard. Her video showed the remains of the vanquished stingray with the hammerhead still circling its prey.

Neither the shark nor the stingray was evil. They were just doing what animals do to survive in the wild. But one day, a great battle between good and evil will ensue. Jesus will fight for me and for all who have trusted Him through faith.

Fortunately, Jesus has already won the ultimate victory for me through His sacrifice on the cross, and because of that, I will live with Him in heaven with nothing to fear. Not even sharks. —Tracy Crump

*Then I saw heaven opened, and behold, a white horse! The one sitting on it is
called Faithful and True, and in righteousness he judges and makes war.*
—Revelation 19:11 (ESV)

APRIL 5

Easter-Easter-Easter!

Let everything that has breath praise the LORD.

—PSALM 150:6 (NIV)

WE HADN'T ATTENDED a church with a true sunrise service—you know, the kind where you rise before dawn, gather on the lawn, and sing "He Lives!" as the sun comes up—for years. But there we were, dressed in our Easter clothes and seated under a group of oak trees with other Resurrection Day celebrants.

In the predawn hush, I heard a rustle overhead. I squinted, curious to see which feathered friend had joined our gathering. The canopy of leaves hid the bird from my sight, but when it hopped onto a low-hanging branch, I recognized its gray plumage and jaunty crest. A tufted titmouse. I often see them in my yard and smile at their cheery *"peter-peter-peter."*

This day, though, as the bird joined the believers from our fellowship and blended its voice with our praise, it seemed to sing a new song. Instead of *"peter-peter-peter,"* its little voice seemed to declare, *"Easter-Easter-Easter!"*

As Jesus made his way to Jerusalem long ago, Jewish leaders scolded Christ for allowing His disciples to cheer Him on with shouts of praise. "I tell you," Jesus replied, "if they keep quiet, the stones will cry out" (Luke 19:40, NIV).

Every Easter since then, Jesus's followers have heralded Him as Messiah and King, declaring His victory over sin, death, and the grave. I wasn't surprised, therefore, that a bird, the subject of so many of Jesus's parables, took up the stones' chorus and added its voice to our Easter celebration.

In the days following our sunrise service, I've often seen a tufted titmouse on the church grounds. The tiny bird still wears its spring plumage and chirps happily, but all I hear now is *"peter-peter-peter."* I guess our little soprano has closed its Easter hymnal until next year.

I, however, will continue to celebrate. Every time I think of the darkness of sin, death, and the grave, I'll remember the sunlit triumph of *"Easter, Easter, Easter!"* —Lori Hatcher

Praise be to the God and Father of our Lord Jesus Christ! In his great mercy he has given us new birth into a living hope through the resurrection of Jesus Christ from the dead.
—1 Peter 1:3 (NIV)

APRIL 6

My Own Special Serenade

The birds of the sky nest by the waters; they sing among the branches.

—PSALM 104:12 (NIV)

WHEN EASTER SUNDAY arrived at the end of March in 2024, we still had some snow on the ground where we live in Minnesota. Before I headed to church to volunteer in the preschool room, I noticed that the air temperature was just right to go outside for a morning walk.

As I made my way through the neighborhood, reflecting on the Easter message I'd heard the evening before, I saw a robin sitting in the tree singing its own sweet melody. The AllAboutBirds website I'd found described the robin's song as *"cheerily, cheer up, cheer up, cheerily, cheer up,"* and as I listened that morning, it seemed an apt description. The bird's song was indeed cheery, and I found it sweet and beautiful.

During the Covid pandemic, I often went for walks outside to seek refuge and solace from a busy and noisy household of five as we observed our state's shelter-in-place orders. The robins' song cheered me up and gave me a cozy feeling then—a sense that in all the upheaval the pandemic caused, nature's song continued, and God was still in control.

When the lockdown was lifted and life returned to its busy normal, my walks with the birds fell by the wayside. Hearing the robin's cheery song again that snowy Resurrection Sunday renewed my spirit. I was reminded that God has a song for me to sing, too, in all seasons of life, whether stressful or not, because He is still in control now just as He was in those uncertain times of Covid.

My songs of praise, like the robins' songs, can continue in good times and bad. And like the robin's springtime serenade, my song is my own unique way of praising Him. —Stacey Thureen

The LORD is my strength and my shield; my heart trusts in Him, and I am helped; therefore my heart triumphs, and with my song I shall thank Him.
—Psalm 28:7 (NASB)

APRIL 7

Cleo and the Egg

The LORD appeared to us in the past, saying: "I have loved you with an everlasting love; I have drawn you with unfailing kindness."

—JEREMIAH 31:3 (NIV)

ONE LAST LINDT chocolate egg remained in the bowl. The gold-wrapped eggs are white chocolate, and apparently my adult children and the friends who congregate in my kitchen don't care much for white chocolate. The gold-foil Easter eggs were the last to go.

Somehow Cleo, the kitten, maneuvered the one egg out of the bowl, tossed it to the ground, leaped down after it, pounced, and then dribbled it across the kitchen, shifting it between two front paws. This gleeful and raucous game went on for 20 minutes. Cleo caught it in her mouth and proudly carried the egg into the next room only to roll over on her back, toss the egg to herself, and begin dribbling like a four-legged soccer player once again.

The older cat, Tango, looked on like a sports fan following the action, occasionally glancing my way as if to wonder, "What's with Cleo?" Finally, the kitten shot the egg under the heater cover on which we store shoes. Uh-oh, toy lost.

But Cleo is persistent and quite clever. Twisting her body, she reached one paw as far under the cover as she could and pulled out a stick. Then with the stick, she levered out a pen. Unsatisfied with this new toy, Cleo switched paws, twisted, and using the stick, levered out the chocolate egg. Taking no chances, she carried it to her kitty tent in the next room where she resumed the game of catch with herself. I was tired just watching, impressed with her cleverness and persistence, and curious about her devotion to the egg.

Many times have I been assured God pursues us relentlessly with love, but watching my kitten chase the egg, it occurred to me for the first time that God's relentless pursuit could include playfulness and joy. What if God lovingly pursues us playfully, energetically, even joyfully? Can I sense God hidden and eager to pounce into my day? —Susie Colby

Joy is the infallible sign of the presence of God.
—Pierre Teilhard de Chardin

APRIL 8

What a Hippo Hides

"A good man out of the good treasure of his heart brings forth good things, and an evil man out of the evil treasure brings forth evil things."

—MATTHEW 12:35 (NKJV)

HIPPOPOTAMUSES ARE FASCINATING. Like nature's jack-in-the-box, their relatively small head and eyes rise from the water, revealing a mammoth body. Traveling through life, I've learned people can be a lot like hippos. What we see on the surface may or may not accurately reflect the enormity of their life experiences, character traits, and wisdom.

When we first meet, most people show us their best side: smiles, gracious words, and sometimes even warm gestures. Just like the small head and eyes of the hippo, this picture doesn't begin to reveal the whole person who lies beneath the waterline of their polite facade.

Many folks earn our respect with years of kind acts, honest dealings, and wise counsel. Over time, I've discovered the truth of Matthew 12:35, that whatever is in the heart eventually comes out. A hippopotamus-size storehouse of good things can delight us and add so much good to our lives.

Still, people—even those who profess to be Christians—don't always treat us kindly or do the right thing. When we face betrayal, dishonesty, or just insensitivity, it can feel like the hippo revealing what's beneath the surface. This leaves us with a question: How will I respond?

Jesus left us valuable instructions about understanding others and responding with love. He made us aware that not everyone will share our moral code or treat us with civility. Whether people do or do not have a relationship with Christ, our job is to speak honestly, love unconditionally, and respond graciously in every circumstance. Don't be surprised by what lurks beneath the surface, but celebrate those people who demonstrate goodness and mercy to us.

May God make us a light to all, including those who need God's cleansing power. Just planting a seed for a relationship with Jesus will bring forth a bumper crop of good in the future. —David L. Winters

Lord, may my actions always reflect Your saving grace to everyone I meet. Amen.

APRIL 9

Glowing Millipedes

*When Jesus spoke again to the people, he said, "I am the
light of the world. Whoever follows me will never walk
in darkness, but will have the light of life."*

—JOHN 8:12 (NIV)

I RECENTLY JOINED A group of people on a night walk through
California's Armstrong Redwoods State Natural Reserve, home to a few
old-growth redwoods and a thriving second-growth redwood grove. It
was dusk when we gathered. We'd been instructed to bring UV flashlights
so we could "see" certain creatures and mushrooms once the sun went
down. As the light of day faded away, the grove became profoundly dark
and silent. Our guides had glow sticks tied to their hats so we could see
them as we carefully picked our way along the trail.

Soon our UV lights showed us a few millipedes. There weren't many of
them at the edge of the trail. The insects had learned not to crawl near
the tramping feet of human visitors. I was beginning to think the grove
might be devoid of life on this particular night until our guide shone his
light up on a hillside. And there, like dozens of glittering gems scattered
on the dark hill, twinkled tiny lights as many millipedes lit up in the
night. We were surrounded by life!

Those millipedes shining on the hillside reminded me that I may feel
alone sometimes, but shining the light of Jesus everywhere, and especially
into what may seem like a dark space, will reveal that I'm not alone at
all. Jesus is there with me—often in surprising ways *and* surprising places.

Just as the millipedes couldn't be seen without the aid of a special light,
I must use my spiritual understanding to see Jesus all around me. The UV
light lit up the millipedes in the dark, and the Holy Spirit will guide my
vision as I look around my world. I pray it will enable me to shine for
others so they may see Him too. —Marianne Campbell

Don't shine so that others can see you.
Shine so that through you, others can see Him.
—C. S. Lewis

ALL GOD'S CREATURES

APRIL 10

Unexpected Visitors

*May the grace of the Lord Jesus Christ, and the love of God,
and the fellowship of the Holy Spirit be with you all.*

—2 CORINTHIANS 13:14 (NIV)

ONE EARLY APRIL afternoon, I was in the mudroom moving laundry from the washing machine to the dryer. My youngest child, Joy, was coloring in the family room. Suddenly, I noticed something moving outside on our front lawn. In my peripheral vision, it looked like a neighbor's dog. As I turned away from the laundry and focused my gaze outside, I realized it was a wild turkey! I had never seen a wild turkey in our neighborhood; we don't live in a rural area, and I'd assumed they wouldn't venture this close.

I made my way to the kitchen, where I peered out at our backyard to see not one but five wild turkeys—a male and four females. I called Joy to the windows and showed her our unexpected visitors. She was amazed by the large, regal, but awkward-looking birds in our yard.

As Joy smooshed her little face up against the windows, I searched on my phone to figure out why the male was fluffing his feathers so much. Turns out that where we live, in Minnesota, wild turkeys mate from April to May.

I watched my preschooler pull up a chair and sit on it for several minutes, looking at our backyard. Joy asked lots of questions, curious to know why they were there and what they were doing. I tried to answer her in a way she would understand. While her older two siblings were away at school, this became a special moment that only she and I got to share.

As a mom of three, I don't always get to have spontaneous one-on-one time with each of my kids. Usually, I have to plan for special time with them. Being surprised and inspired by one of God's creatures—the gift from Him of a rare sighting—became the catalyst for the connection I was looking for with one of them. —Stacey Thureen

Lord, thank You for the unexpected, surprising moments in life that You use to get my attention and draw me closer to You and others. Amen.

APRIL 11

The Wren House

*Are not two sparrows sold for a penny? Yet not one of them
will fall to the ground outside your Father's care.*

—MATTHEW 10:29 (NIV)

WHAT A WINDSTORM. From inside the house it sounded like a runaway freight train, a low, wailing howl, a chorus of banshees. I stepped out onto the porch, and immediately I had to lean into the wind to keep my balance. The sky was the color of a bad bruise, and the tall grass on the fields was blown flat. My old-fashioned metal lawn chair, gone from its customary place on the porch, was now cartwheeling merrily down the road. I saw shingles—not mine, hopefully—zipping through the sky.

And then there was the wren house. I'd hung it from a branch on the alder tree by the porch, suspended by a metal wire. The nest was swinging wildly in the wind. Inside were the mother and several recently hatched fledglings. I tried to imagine what was happening inside the birdhouse—the fledglings tumbling around in their little home, falling on top of one another, the mother squawking.

Mine is a genteel life, one of a retired clergyman living out in the country. But now and then the wind comes up, and my safe, stable existence gets rocked—a frightening medical diagnosis, the sudden death of a lifelong friend, a financial crisis. Suddenly, my safe little nest gets turned upside down. In times like that my soul reaches out for Him who rebuked the wind and the waves and stilled the storm. I remind myself that all windstorms eventually cease, and that when they do, God will still be God, and I will still be His beloved child.

I set the birdhouse in the garage. When the windstorm passed, I brought it back out and hung it again from the branch. I heard little peeps coming from inside the birdhouse, and a minute later Mama emerged, looked around, and flew off in search of food. —Louis Lotz

*Remind me yet again, O God, that whether I come or go, pass or fail,
win or lose, live or die, You are with me, always and forever. Amen.*

APRIL 12

Perfectly Hidden

For he will hide me in his shelter in the day of trouble.

—PSALM 27:5 (ESV)

EVERY DAY, I walk my dog. We nearly always follow the same route, and I know the terrain well. During the spring, I thrill to see the colors pop as the earth comes alive again—trees so full of blossoms they are cartoon-pink! The new grass so thick it will take two good mows for a nice crew cut. Breezes laced with the watery, pond-like scent of mud blow against my face.

Yesterday, I was enjoying the bright clumps of daffodils and the carpet of violets beneath them when my mouth widened into an O to see two brown rabbits lying in the wood chips surrounding the daffodils. The rabbits could not have been more than 5 feet from me and my sniffing dog. They were very still, not even twitching in their small sanctuary. Even more beautifully, they were not afraid. The master Creator, our brilliant God, had perfectly painted the rabbits into the picture, and they knew it. In His genius, they were safe.

Just like me, the rabbits were out enjoying the sun, the color, the glory. They were both glad and safe in creation. I am certain that God knows my needs just as He knows those of the rabbits. God knows how my very being yearns for color and rich breezes after a long, deadened winter. God also knows any pain and trouble that lurks around my life. God gives me beauty. God gives me safety.

In my life with God, I am not unlike the vulnerable rabbits, quite possibly 5 feet from a threat at any given moment. Yet I am alive and well in Christ, and I am beautifully sheltered by God's nearness and care. —Katy W. Sundararajan

Dear Lord, I pray that You would hide me in Your heart and by grace, grant me beauty and rest today. Amen.

APRIL 13

They Ate What?

We take captive every thought to make it obedient to Christ.

—2 CORINTHIANS 10:5 (NIV)

SINCE 2006, *The Veterinary Practice News*, a professional magazine, has featured an annual contest called "They Ate *What?*" Veterinarians submit radiographs of the strangest objects they have encountered in their patients' digestive tracts, hoping to win prizes and a brief moment of fame in the spotlighted article. From steak knives to rubber duckies, this contest features the odd and humorous items our furry friends have ingested.

Most veterinarians, myself included, have removed some bizarre nonedible materials from the digestive tracts of our patients. It's difficult to narrow down the list of the weirdest things I've taken out of my patients, beyond the mundane rocks, bones, towels, socks, underwear, string, sewing needles, coins, and toys that all veterinarians have likely seen. Perhaps the duck who swallowed a whole rubber glove tops the list. Or maybe the dog whose stomach looked like he was trying to build a bird's nest with twigs and leaves. Why do animals eat unusual things? God only knows. But nothing good can come of ingesting items that weren't meant to be eaten.

Thinking about these unusual dietary choices, I'm reminded that nothing good can come from allowing impurities into our minds. The expression "Garbage in, garbage out," a computer concept that the quality of the input determines the quality of the output, can be equally applied to our brains. Once unclean images or words have entered the mind, it is difficult to eradicate them.

I must guard against what I watch, read, or listen to. At times, I have turned off a promising movie or quit watching a television series I enjoyed because of foul language or the introduction of immoral plotlines. I've stopped reading books in the first chapter. When unwholesome thoughts cross my mind, I must consciously force myself to redirect my thinking to something God-honoring. Taking every thought captive is a practice I've learned to incorporate into my life, one that gets easier the more I do it.

Just as ingested garbage harms the bodies of our pets, garbage entering my mind harms my soul. —Ellen Fannon

Oh, be careful, little eyes, what you see.
—Anonymous

ALL GOD'S CREATURES   107

APRIL 14

Well, Well, Well

*Christ has truly set us free. Now make sure that you stay
free, and don't get tied up again in slavery to the law.*

—GALATIANS 5:1 (NLT)

MY FRIEND MANDIE'S basement bedroom includes an egress window as required by the city inspectors. It opens into a fairly deep window well. One morning Mandie and her sister heard a frenzied commotion emanating from the other side of their window. When they opened the curtain, they were surprised to see an angry, frightened muskrat desperately clawing at whatever surface he could find in an effort to free himself from this bondage. The screen was shredded to bits, but fortunately he hadn't managed to break the glass.

The sisters quickly dressed and went outside to see how they could help. A nearby shovel seemed a good possibility, but the muskrat wouldn't cooperate. They scouted the yard for another option and found a long-handled push broom. They extended it into the well and tried to maneuver it underneath him. Fortunately, his claws were able to grip the wooden pole, and he scampered up and out.

Muskrats are much more mobile in the water, so it was hard to gauge his anxiety level by his movements. He did a half walk/half hop past the garage, around the house, between the cars parked in the driveway, and back to his starting place. At that point he fell ignominiously back into the window well and had to be rescued again.

This critter's unwitting repeat fall paints a vivid picture for me of just how easy it is to sin, get rescued, be forgiven, and then stumble once again over the same issue. Jesus never said my life would be easy. I will encounter pitfalls. I will sometimes triumph over temptation, but I could just as easily succumb to whatever it is that entices me. I need the freedom that He supplies, and I need His strength to continue living in that place no matter what comes my way. —Liz Kimmel

*Whether we get to avoid pain and suffering or we must persevere
in the midst of it, our deliverance comes when we're dragged from
the enemy of our souls to the heart of God.*
—Beth Moore

APRIL 15

Exceptional Communication

Do not be anxious for anything, but in everything by prayer and supplication with thanksgiving let your requests be made known to God.

—PHILIPPIANS 4:6 (ESV)

MANAGING BEES TAKES a lot of work. The longer I spend with honeybees, the more I realize I have a lot more to learn. I never stop learning.

As I study the bees, I'm impressed by how well they communicate with one another. I've learned to understand them if I take the time to "listen," And I've discovered five ways honeybees communicate to better function as one colony.

- Sound: The level of intensity of buzzing relays their mood.
- Taste: The scout shares the taste of the nectar she has found with her sisters.
- Smell: The queen produces her own pheromone that is unique to her colony.
- Dance: The waggle dance tells workers the direction, distance, and quantity of nectar.
- Sign Language: A lost bee will perform motions to seek asylum within another colony.

Honeybees communicate exceptionally well. Me, not so much. My sharp responses can send unhealthy messages that weaken my relationships. I have been learning from my bees to improve my communication skills. As I discovered with my bees, I realize there is much more to learn in God's Word. God gives me five ways to communicate with Him.

- Prayer: This is simply talking with God as I would a friend.
- Supplication: This is more intense because the issue or concern is deeper.
- Thanksgiving: Here, I get to offer praise to Him, even during tough times.
- Meditation: Now I am dwelling on His Word more to understand how to apply it to my life (Joshua 1:8).
- Groanings: God hears me even when I can't find the words to say (Romans 8:26).

What a wonderful discovery finding that God gives me so many exceptional ways to communicate with Him. I can see how effective it is in my bees, and I am confident it works even better between God and me. —Ben Cooper

Walk of Faith: *Over the next few days, make a point of using each of the five ways of praying described above.*

ALL GOD'S CREATURES 109

APRIL 16

The Ikebana Ducks

For everything that was written in the past was written to teach us, so that through the endurance taught in the Scriptures and the encouragement they provide we might have hope.

—ROMANS 15:4 (NIV)

THE DAY HAD been sparkling and unseasonably cool for the Gulf Coast spring. As long golden rays stretched between the trees, I realized I had walked too far along the bayou and needed to head home for dinner. Despite my hurry, I noticed a large flock of mallards gliding on the water.

On the shoreline, a group of the ducks seemed to be putting on a striking tableau for some turtles soaking up the last of the sun. The contrast between the colorful, feathery actors with their flashy blue-and-green markings and their mellow brown audience captivated me. Three mottled brown-and-black ducks nestled on the ground, bills tucked into wings. Three more stood over them, with gleaming, deep green heads highlighted by bright yellow bills. A very large duck stood behind all the others, facing away, wings spread wide and high. The iridescent blue patches of its large wings looked like lively eyes, watching over all of us.

Their coloring and positions reminded me of ikebana, an ancient Japanese flower-arranging practice—emphasizing form and balance—I had learned about from my grandmother. She loved nature. She reverently named every animal, every flower, and every tree we saw together. She explained to me that each arrangement always contains three elements: earth, human, and heaven. This idea of people grounded in nature and reaching up to God seemed so beautiful to me. Now these ducks had positioned themselves in a living ikebana arrangement, each element adding color, texture, and pattern to the visual story.

The sky got rosier, the sun began to set, and the turtles slipped back into the bayou. As I continued home, I thought of the many beautiful ways God shows me how connected we all are—to each other, to God's beloved creatures, and to Him, who watches over us with loving eyes as we move through the patterns of our days. —Lucy Chambers

Where heaven meets earth, where God is near,
His tender mercies often appear.
—John Connolly

110 ALL GOD'S CREATURES

APRIL 17

Wrong Spot for a Nest

Whoever dwells in the shelter of the Most High
will rest in the shadow of the Almighty.

—PSALM 91:1 (NIV)

IT WAS A beautiful spring day. After my husband and I set up our RV, we went for a hike. We watched birds flit about, gathering nesting material. When we returned to our site, I rested in a chair next to the RV, enjoying the breeze. A small sparrow flew past. I didn't pay it much attention at first.

After it flew past several more times, I noticed it was carrying small twigs and dried leaves in its beak. Intrigued as to where this sparrow was building its nest, I watched the next time it flew past me. Unfortunately, the sparrow had chosen the wrong spot for its nest—the covered area above the section of our RV that slides out when we camp. Although the protected spot made perfect sense, it was not safe. When it was time to leave the campground and we pulled the slide in, the nest and any eggs that might be there would be crushed.

My husband climbed onto the RV's roof and cleared out the nest. We felt bad about destroying the beginnings of the nest but knew it was the right thing to do. Still, the sparrow was undeterred. The next day there was another nest. This time, further back in the slide-out area, making it harder to reach. One more time after that, we found nesting material. Again, it was built deeper inside the area.

That bird thought it had chosen the perfect spot for its nest. However, it didn't know what we knew. The spot it had chosen might have looked safe, but it wasn't.

When things don't work out the way I plan, I need to remember a sparrow whose nest didn't work out like it planned. I need to remember that, just as we protected the bird, God protects me from dangers that I don't see. I trust Him with the details. —Sandy Kirby Quandt

> *"For as the heavens are higher than the earth, so are My ways*
> *higher than your ways, and My thoughts than your thoughts."*
> —Isaiah 55:9 (NKJV)

APRIL 18

Holy Roly-Poly

Then God blessed the seventh day and made it holy, because on
it he rested from all the work of creating that he had done.

—GENESIS 2:3 (NIV)

THAT BUG'S A basketball." My daughter pointed at the pill bug on the
porch. "Aw, looks like he's sleepin'."

I chuckled. "I think it's how he protects himself, dear, but let's read
about him."

And we did, discovering this small land-dwelling crustacean has a great
big name—Armadillidiidae. Best known as roly-polies in the United States
and Canada, in other places, they're called many different names, among
them pill bugs, woodlice, Parsons pigs, and (ahem!) in the Netherlands
a name I won't repeat. Much like armadillos, they roll into a ball as a
protective measure—a process called conglobation—but they also do this
to conserve water.

Smart little creatures! Seems they know what's best. By His creative
design, God instilled in them the instinct to ward off predators and to
stay hydrated—both by rolling up. And although roly-polies aren't resting
when they roll into a ball, this action reminds us we need rest too.

The Lord asked that we honor the Sabbath and keep it holy—something
He demonstrated when He rested on the seventh day. He knew what
we would need—for our health and safety, not to mention our sanity.
Sabbath is necessary for humankind too, much like the reminder offered
by those little Chuckie pigs, as they're known in some parts of the South!

How fun it must have been to name them. Maybe Eve said to Adam,
"Hey, dear—how 'bout doodlebug?"

After a moment, perhaps one of them declared, "Sure looks like it's
taking a Sabbath rest, so how 'bout we call it a holy roly-poly. Has a nice
ring, don't you think?"

And I'm guessing, as God yawned and stretched, He smiled!
—Maureen Miller

Kind and creative Father, You set the example, so why do we try
to live differently? You've called us to rest as You rested.
Following Your ways always leads to blessing.
Help us to be obedient to Your Word. Amen.

APRIL 19

Life Upside Down

But I tell you, love your enemies and pray for those who persecute you.
—**MATTHEW 5:44** (NIV)

OUR FAMILY TAKES a beach vacation each year. In truth, it's more of a reading retreat. We spend just enough time on the beach to take a few selfies and get a mild sunburn. Most of the week is passed on the second-story deck of our rented cottage. There, nestled among the treetops, we drink copious amounts of coffee and read to our hearts' content.

The Florida Panhandle teems with wildlife, and we are often surrounded by more birds than books. Looking up from a novel one afternoon, I noticed a downy woodpecker among the branches of a live oak. She moved effortlessly from limb to limb, barely fluttering her wings and often simply hopping from one place to the next.

In her foraging, this delicate little bird seemed to move in every direction. She hopped from side to side, turned around, circled a branch, flew to another, and started the process again. At last, she arrived at the underside of a rather steeply rising branch, head pointed toward the earth, and sat there, suspended upside down like a bat in a cave. I've never seen a bird fly upside down, but this little woodpecker was more than happy to sit, walk, hunt, and eat in an almost completely inverted position. What an advantage that must be.

In truth, that's the natural attitude for a Christian as well. In Christ's kingdom, values and priorities are inverted from those of the world. Humility is rewarded over ambition, generosity is valued more than greed, service is preferable to leadership, and weakness is more useful than strength. True, we continue to live within the world. But we are not defined by it. That means spending a lot of time upside down.
—Lawrence W. Wilson

But God chose the foolish things of the world to shame the wise;
God chose the weak things of the world to shame the strong.
—1 Corinthians 1:27 (NIV)

ALL GOD'S CREATURES   113

APRIL 20

Flies in the Buttermilk, Shoo Fly Shoo!

To everything there is a season, a time for every purpose under heaven.

—ECCLESIASTES 3:1 (NKJV)

SKIP TO MY Lou" is a fun children's song I enjoy singing to my young grandchildren. We "swat" the air and laugh and sing, "Flies in the buttermilk, shoo fly shoo, skip to my Lou, my darling." (Of course, skipping goes along with the song too.) Flies have always been shooed or swatted. The Amish named their extra-sweet dessert "shoofly pie," because they shooed flies from their pies cooling in the window.

When my grandson (the bug collector in our family) showed me his insect book, he said, "Grandma, why don't you write about flies?" At first, I resisted the thought, but then I said, "God must have a purpose for creating them. Let's find out."

We learned together that flies are second only to bees in importance as pollinators, and they live in nearly every environment on earth. Some types are attracted to specific flowers, and some are generalists. We learned that flies pollinate more than one hundred types of crops. We laughed when we learned we should thank flies for chocolate, because a particular species of small flies is the prime pollinator of cacao trees. Unlike honeybees, flies don't have to carry pollen and nectar back to a hive; they simply sip on the nectar and carry the pollen from one flower or plant to the next. *Smithsonian* magazine defined flies as "the unsung heroes of pollination."

The next time I'm tempted to swat an annoying and buzzing fly, I think I'll just open my window or door and say, "Shoo, fly, shoo!" and watch it fly away to do its work in this world. —Kathleen R. Ruckman

Dear God, help me to take a closer look at
Your creation—for all things have a purpose.

APRIL 21

Imagine What You Will Become

Your eyes saw my unformed body; all the days ordained for me
were written in your book before one of them came to be.

—PSALM 139:16 (NIV)

IT'S STARTING!" MY son exclaimed. His attention, mine, and that of his three siblings snapped up from our homeschool studies as we fixed our eyes on the large glass container at the center of our table. Over the past several days, we'd watched as the chrysalis holding our monarch caterpillar changed from bright lime green to translucent, revealing a butterfly's vivid orange-and-black wings. Now, we watched attentively as the chrysalis cracked open and the butterfly pushed itself out into the world. We remembered with wonder how a very different creature had wrapped itself up into the chrysalis just over a week before. We thought about the mystery of what took place inside.

In our studies, we had learned how a caterpillar liquifies nearly its entire body and how a special group of cells called *imaginal discs* forms the new parts of a butterfly.

"Think about God tucking those imaginal disc cells into the caterpillar," I told my children. "It's as if He designed the caterpillar with the imaginal discs and said, 'Imagine what you'll become!'"

A similar statement runs through my mind as I watch my children while we release the new butterfly into our backyard. *Imagine what you'll become*, I think, as we move through our days of learning, growing, and maturing. In many ways, I hear God speaking the same words over me. Even now, with a family and career, He is forming me into the person He planned in my mother's womb. I am fearfully and wonderfully made, and just as He did for a caterpillar with imaginal discs, God has tucked potential within me that will flourish in time. —Eryn Lynum

Therefore, if anyone is in Christ, the new creation has come:
The old has gone, the new is here!
—2 Corinthians 5:17 (NIV)

ALL GOD'S CREATURES

APRIL 22

All the Burning Bushes

"Do not come any closer," God said. "Take off your sandals, for the place where you are standing is holy ground."

—EXODUS 3:5 (NIV)

WHILE I LONG for a steady faith, too often I find myself drifting, feeling distant from God. At a point when my usual devotional practices weren't creating connection, I entered a redfish tournament with some friends. I put my spiritual seeking aside for the weekend and focused on fishing.

We left the pier at 5 a.m. A thick mist lay over the water, and we couldn't see further than the short reach of the boat's headlamps. Baitfish jumped on either side of us, and insects cut iridescent paths through the light. The sun emerged as a rosy disc too shrouded by mist to reveal its power.

We weren't catching any fish, but we encountered a glittering array of sea creatures: turquoise and indigo crabs with bright orange pinchers, tawny stingrays with whiplike tails, silver-speckled trout with razor teeth, and pulsing jellyfish of all shapes and sizes. The mist had burned off, and each one gleamed in the sun, scales glittering, colors blazing.

Just before we headed in, my rod bent nearly double. In the distance, the biggest redfish I've ever seen leaped up into the air. The afternoon sun caught its scales, and it glowed like red neon as it splashed back into the sparkling green water. I reeled hard, but the big fish pulled harder. Suddenly, the line went slack. My legendary fish had gotten away. But I realized something more important had happened.

When I'm seeking God, I'm always looking for a voice from a burning bush. That day on the bay, God's light blazed in every creature. I had been surrounded by His presence all day, and once I realized that, I was filled with thanks, reminded that God connects with us in limitless ways.
—Lucy H. Chambers

It is an incalculable added pleasure to any one's sum of happiness if he or she grows to know, even slightly and imperfectly, how to read and enjoy the wonder-book of nature.
—Theodore Roosevelt

APRIL 23

The Changing Lizard

Do not conform to the pattern of this world, but be transformed by the renewing of your mind. Then you will be able to test and approve what God's will is—his good, pleasing and perfect will.

—ROMANS 12:2 (NIV)

AS IT PEEKS out from between two pots of bright-red geraniums, I spot the anole lizard that has made itself at home on my doorstep. Every time I leave the house or get my mail, I say a quick hello to my new garden friend, who then tilts its head to the side and studies me as though wondering why I am interrupting its day.

One thing I have always loved about these lizards is the way they change colors according to their surroundings. The same lizard may be bright green or dark brown depending on its environment. A range of factors from heat to stress level can have an effect, as well. The lizard on my doorstep is no exception. I have found his shades of color vary widely from day to day.

To me, the lizard's changing color pattern is a striking picture of the way our own environments affect us. On days I am weary, discouraged, or anxious, it's easy to feel overwhelmed—as though I don't have much control over my circumstances. When I remember and follow the important principle in Romans 12:2—when I allow my mind to be renewed by the Spirit of God—I can be transformed by His truth rather than by the trials or struggles that tear me down.

If, like the anole, I am bound to be affected by my surroundings, I want to choose them well. I want to become more like God—full of His love, His hope, His truth—instead of taking on the stress of this world.
—Ashley Clark

May these words of my mouth and this meditation of my heart be pleasing in your sight, LORD, my Rock and my Redeemer.
—Psalm 19:14 (NIV)

APRIL 24

Chasing Chickens

How beautiful on the mountains are the feet of those who bring good news, who proclaim peace, who bring good tidings, who proclaim salvation, who say to Zion, "Your God reigns!"

—ISAIAH 52:7 (NIV)

MY HUSBAND, TIM, and I had been cooped up all winter in southern Indiana. Spring weather meant the outdoor ice-cream shop was open. We were more than ready to sit at the picnic table and enjoy satisfying sundaes. From past experience, we knew the owner often let her colorful chickens out as entertainment. In the rural area where I grew up, I knew about yellow chicks and white hens, but these Hoosier free-ranging fowl went by the names such as Golden Laced Wyandotte, Brown Leghorn, and Black Barred Plymouth Rock.

As we ate our treats, we observed two children wanting to pet the chickens. No matter how sweetly the youngsters tried calling, the speedsters maneuvered just beyond the reach of their outstretched arms. Chicken feet pivoted quicker than little kid feet could turn.

Tim told them, "That's no way to catch a chicken. Watch this." He placed his almost empty bowl of ice cream down on the ground. First one, then two more hens flocked to us while we sat quietly. Soon the children calmed down and joined us at the table for close-up views of the peeps.

As we drove away, the children chasing the chickens reminded me of the first time I wanted to spread the good news of God's love and grace. As a new Christian, my method was reminding my closest friends of the consequences of their poor choices. I pelted them with scriptures about examples of living daily in a godly way. Of course, they were not enticed to know more about my new way of life. I only chased them away with my squawking. Finally, I shared in small portions about what God was doing in my life and attempted to demonstrate what that meant in my daily walk with Him. Soon all of us were flocking toward the sweetness of God's love and grace. —Glenda Ferguson

The way we live is often more convincing than the words we say.
—Billy Graham

APRIL 25

Messy Devotion

The Word became flesh and made his dwelling among us.
—JOHN 1:14 (NIV)

PART OF MY own devotional practice is to read, reflect, and sometimes write in my journal in the morning. My older cat, Tango, has long been a faithful companion in devotion, nestling beside me on the couch, occasionally interfering by sitting on my writing hand or open journal. The addition of our new kitten, Cleo, has disrupted our routine. Cleo zooms around the house, putting both Tango and me on alert in a manner not at all conducive to contemplation. Or, as she has just done, Cleo nudges Tango off the couch and takes up residence in Tango's spot. Cleo is trying to burrow under my sweater. It's endearing, until—ouch!—she bites my bare skin.

I've been reflecting that the devotional pieces I write are so much neater and tidier than the devotional life I live. Cats frolicking and nibbling are but a few of the distractions that threaten my focus and devotion. Real life—work deadlines, household chores, social engagements, broken appliances (and don't get me started on plumbing!)—all seem to conspire against my attentiveness to God's presence in my life.

But the promise is that the Word became flesh and made His dwelling among us, among the *real* us, not our idealized selves. That must mean that God is here in the mess, the upended plans and unexpected challenges. What if I were to burrow into His side like the kitten burrows into me? Would I find refuge amid chaos?

Just as I close my eyes to contemplate burrowing, I hear the unmistakable sound of Tango vomiting at the top of the stairs. Sigh . . . Today will not be the day of "neat and tidy" devotion. But devotion it is, nonetheless. I will scrub the floor and pet the cat, welcome the real cat, not the idealized version of memes and on Instagram. Sometimes devotion invites us to our knees in prayer; other times devotion invites us to our knees with water and paper towels. —Susie Colby

Until one has loved an animal, a part of one's soul remains unawakened.
—Anatole France

ALL GOD'S CREATURES

APRIL 26

Basking in the Bird Feeder

"Look at the birds of the air; they do not sow or reap or store away in barns, and yet your heavenly Father feeds them."

—MATTHEW 6:26 (NIV)

THE WORRIES OF my life were swirling around my head. The afternoon sun was beginning to set on California's Central Valley as I sat outside on my shaded patio, contemplating things.

Life has its bright moments and blessings, but that day, I was worried. I was worried about our finances, worried about getting our debts paid, and worried about inconsequential things. Once I began down that rabbit hole of worry, it was hard to climb back out. How was this all going to work out?

I heard a flutter of wings and the high-pitched chirps frequently emitted by hummingbirds. There was one at my hummingbird feeder! He swooped in, perched comfortably on the feeder, and took a few sips. He even glanced my way for a moment, then finished his afternoon drink and went his way with chirps and a flutter of wings.

I smiled. He seemed to be at complete ease. His provision was right in front of him. But that thought jarred something in me. Was I not important to God, just like these little birds were to me? I provided food for them, and they didn't worry one bit about where their next meal was coming from. Why was I worrying?

That bird feeder was symbolic of God's provision to me as well. I had so much: my home, my family, and food on the table. He would provide what I needed as He always did. My bird feeder was God Himself, and I could bask in His provision as I trusted Him. —Heather Spiva

Walk of Faith: *What areas of your life are causing you the most stress right now? Jot down a list on your phone or a slip of paper today, and ask God to help you trust Him for them, crossing them off one by one as you pray.*

APRIL 27

New Skin

*. . . and have put on the new self, which is being renewed
in knowledge after the image of its creator.*

—COLOSSIANS 3:10 (ESV)

EACH YEAR LIKE clockwork, I go into my barn and find an intact
shed black snakeskin next to the narrow ladder leading upward to the
small hayloft. I carefully unravel it and store it with the others in a plastic
bucket. I can measure the growth and any anomalies by examining the
previous shed cycles. A few years ago, this black snake was injured and
received a nasty cut. The process of healing to repair and restore the skin
took a couple of shedding cycles. I hold the evidence of the improvement
in my plastic bucket.

That collection of sheds records the growth and major impacts of the
snake's life. The skins that remain are now fragile reminders of everything
this snake has gone through. The past cut has been healed, and it now
has a new skin. It took a gradual change during the regeneration cycle
to allow the scar to fade away. Looking at the new skin, I can't tell the
snake was ever cut.

My physical, emotional, and even spiritual skin has taken a few cuts
over the years. If I had to continue living in my old skin, my appearance
would show the evidence of those scars. Thankfully, I put on my new self
when I trusted in the Lord for my salvation. I am being renewed every
day into the image of my Creator.

My past scars are fading away, and the evidence is seen in my new skin,
just like it is with the friendly black snake that lives in my barn. I am
looking forward to the day when I will shed my current skin and get one
that will last throughout all eternity. While I wait for that day to come,
my desire is to be found faithfully serving Him. —Ben Cooper

*Therefore, beloved, since you are waiting for these, be diligent to be
found by him without spot or blemish, and at peace.*
—2 Peter 3:14 (ESV)

ALL GOD'S CREATURES

APRIL 28

God's Familiar Face

You made [Jesus] for a little while lower than the angels.

—**HEBREWS 2:7** (ESV)

A WILDLIFE CENTER IN Virginia is raising a wild fox baby (called a kit). The kit was so young when found that its eyes weren't yet open. The individuals tending to it are very careful to ensure that the kit has no human interaction, since they want to release this abandoned little one back into the wild once it is grown. In order to do this, the caregivers wear fox masks so that as the little fox grows, it identifies with its "own" kind.

It makes me think of what Jesus had to do to make it possible for us to see God as our "own" kind. Jesus took on our form so that we would know that God's teaching was for us. The God of the universe emptied Himself and took on a form lower than the angels so that Jesus could speak to us directly, save us from death, and offer us the opportunity to be with Him forever.

The wildlife center based its approach on what Chinese researchers had done in raising orphaned panda cubs, which was to smear themselves with panda feces and other panda scents so the cubs would recognize their own. When Jesus took on our form, He became well aware of our human "messiness"—physically, emotionally, and spiritually. He experienced it all. Hebrews 4:15 says Jesus can empathize with us because He "faced all of the same testings we do" (NLT).

Because He became one of us, we can trust Him with all our experiences. Just like the little fox can trust the caregivers to do all they can to tend to its needs and help him develop into a grown fox, we can trust the God of the universe to tend to our needs so that we can spiritually grow and have a relationship with Him forever. —Virginia Ruth

Thank You, Jesus, that You came to earth as one of us with all our messiness and troubles. Your sacrifice allows us to live forever with You. Amen.

APRIL 29

Following Him

Then Jesus told his disciples, "If anyone would come after me,
let him deny himself and take up his cross and follow me."

—MATTHEW 16:24 (ESV)

AFTER MY DAD retired, he started a part-time job with an auto dealer's exchange that auctioned used vehicles to dealerships. He occasionally made out-of-town trips to pick up cars. One night, Dad returned to the auction lot later than usual and was on his way home at midnight when his car broke down. Since he was within a mile of his house, he decided to walk rather than wake my mom to come get him.

Trudging along the dark country road, Dad suddenly got the eerie feeling he wasn't alone. He passed nothing but open fields surrounded by fences, yet he couldn't shake the feeling. As he walked alongside a hedgerow that stretched for at least a half mile, the moon came out from behind a cloud. He could barely make out several massive creatures behind the trees, silently following him.

Then a cowbell jangled.

Dad laughed when he told the story of his midnight stalkers. We never knew the cows' objective, but they were intent on their mission, at least until they got to the end of the fence.

As a Christ follower, I want to be just as intent on my mission. But when I stop and think—really think—of what the cross signifies, I can become overwhelmed. To take up my cross and follow Jesus means letting go of my objectives, my desires, myself. Yet that's what He calls me to do. To follow Him, no matter the cost.

Following Jesus is no easy proposition. It requires making a daily decision to let Christ lead me along whatever dark paths I may face without knowing the outcome, but I wouldn't have it any other way. And unlike the cows, I won't let anything stop me. —Tracy Crump

Jesus says, "I want you to follow me so fully, so intensely, so enduringly
that all other attachments in your life look weak by comparison."
—Timothy Keller

APRIL 30

Bella Blues

The lowly he sets on high, and those who mourn are lifted to safety.
—JOB 5:11 (NIV)

WHEN MY DAUGHTER first adopted her new puppy, I was afraid the pup might break. Bella the teacup Chihuahua, who weighed only three pounds, seemed fragile, especially when I considered her doggie brother—a full-grown pit bull named Blue. For the first few days, we carefully watched the two dogs, fearing Blue might accidentally seriously injure the tiny Bella.

I didn't say so, but I also worried Blue might intentionally harm Bella. Blue's head was as big as a basketball, and although he seemed docile, his breed's reputation was fierce. He outweighed Bella by at least 60 pounds. I prayed God would keep everyone safe.

Then I had to dog-sit while my daughter was away. I'd met Blue before, but this was the first time I'd spent an extended amount of time with him by myself. I told myself not to act scared—I'd heard dogs could smell fear. As I unlocked the front door, the barking started. I cracked open the door, expecting to see Blue's snarling teeth. Instead, Bella's frantic yipping met me, while over in the corner, Blue, the ferocious guard dog, lounged on his bed.

I made my way inside, careful not to step on Bella. She ran circles around my legs, still growling and barking up a storm. Blue lifted his massive head and, seeing that it was only me, went back to lounging.

Bella kept looking back at Blue as if to ask if all was well. She reminded me of the many times I've been afraid or in sorrow, growling and barking at the world. But when I finally remember to look to God for protection, I can climb into His lap and feel safe.

Bella glanced at Blue once more and quieted, even allowing me to pet her ears. She clambered onto Blue, sprawling out on top of his head. They both napped in a blade of sunshine like the best of friends. —Linda S. Clare

A friend is one soul abiding in two bodies.
—Aristotle

MAY 1

Night Ninja

*For you know very well that the day of the Lord
will come like a thief in the night.*

—1 THESSALONIANS 5:2 (NIV)

MY HUSBAND, TIM, and I love living in southern Indiana on one acre of wooded land where the wild things are. But when we first moved here with our cat, Speckles, we didn't realize how close those wild things could come. We installed pet doors, providing access to the outdoors and indoors for Speckles's wanderings, with food and water bowls in the kitchen. One morning, muddy footprints covered the kitchen floor and the bar. The cat food had disappeared, and the water in the bowl was filthy. We blamed Speckles.

That evening, after we went to bed, we heard a commotion in the kitchen. We got up to find out what shenanigans Speckles had gotten into. My husband flipped on the light. The eyes that stared back at us weren't cat eyes. This animal had two wet front paws and a black mask—a raccoon. He was just as startled as we were and leaped to the top of our kitchen cabinets near the ceiling. After scrutinizing his options, the night ninja bounded to the bar and vaulted to the floor, sticking his landing. He darted through the pet doors just as if he had been training for this escape. We should have realized from the kitchen clues that Speckles was not to blame for the mess, and we did apologize to her. From then on, we adjusted the pet doors so they restricted any other unexpected nocturnal visitors.

The incident with the raccoon and the pet doors reminds me to be on guard in my walk with God, especially against any negative thoughts wanting to steal my peace of mind. In the mornings, instead of opening social media first, I begin my day by reading His Word and reflecting on its meaning. During my working hours, I am particular regarding what enters my thoughts (what I watch, hear, and read). At night, I count my blessings and shut out worries about tomorrow. —Glenda Ferguson

> *Lord, help me reflect the light of Jesus's love so that I can
> remain confident, even if the unexpected occurs.*

MAY 2

A Bumblebee's Search for Beauty

Finally, brothers and sisters, whatever is true, whatever is noble, whatever is right, whatever is pure, whatever is lovely, whatever is admirable— if anything is excellent or praiseworthy—think about such things.

—PHILIPPIANS 4:8 (NIV)

AS THE SPRING flowers fell from my garden, I began waiting rather impatiently for my agapanthus to bloom. I have always loved the whimsical purple-blue flowers of this plant, and this year, they took so long to blossom that I was particularly grateful to see them when they finally did. As it turns out, I was not the only one! A fuzzy bumblebee buzzed from flower to flower, enjoying the nectar. To the bumblebee, the cluster of tall agapanthus blooms must have looked like a buffet.

I marveled as I watched this bumblebee and considered the value and complexity of pollination. Bumblebees spend much of their days searching out flowers, drinking nectar, and collecting pollen on their bodies. When they land on other plants and spread this pollen, they essentially feed the other plants nearby—and this process of pollination is a key component in plants producing food for humans and animals, not to mention the beauty of the blooms.

Watching that bumblebee reminded me that what I may deem small or insignificant during my day may actually hold great importance—a whispered prayer, a pause to change my attitude, choosing gratitude. If bees and pollination were to disappear, the effects on the human food chain would be profound. But what strikes me most is the reality that the entire process begins with bees seeking beauty, searching for lovely, fragrant flowers in the world around them. In the same way, I must actively seek out the beauty God has placed in my life and consume the sweet nectar of these metaphorical blossoms. Only then can I share the good news of faith in a way that produces fruit. —Ashley Clark

Father, I am guilty of taking the "blooms" in my life for granted. Open my eyes to the beauty and blessings all around me, and help me to think on these things. Amen.

MAY 3

Follow the King

Then Pilate said to him, "So you are a king?" Jesus answered, "You say that I am a king. For this purpose I was born and for this purpose I have come into the world—to bear witness to the truth. Everyone who is of the truth listens to my voice."

—JOHN 18:37 (ESV)

NORMALLY, I ENJOY seeing posts of my family on social media. This video made me cringe.

My son, Jeremy, stood on a ladder balanced against a pole, scooping handfuls of writhing honeybees from a birdhouse and putting them in a box. Granted, he wore a full beekeeping suit, complete with gloves and veiled cap, but the sight still sent shivers up my spine.

The homeowners had called Jeremy to remove the swarm that had taken up residence in the penthouse of their six-room birdhouse. As our son worked to relocate the docile insects, he later told me, he suddenly noticed five or six worker bees standing around the rim of the box with their back ends in the air, fanning madly. Knowing it meant he had the queen in the box, Jeremy stepped back. All he had to do now was wait while the workers spread pheromones to call the rest of the swarm to their queen. The remaining bees would enter the container on their own. An hour or so later, he closed the lid and headed home, where he set them up in their own beehive.

Honeybees and several other insect species follow their queen to ensure the survival of the hive. They are lost without her. In the same way, I am lost without my King. Jesus ensured my spiritual survival through His sacrifice on the cross. He holds the truth and the key to eternal life. But unlike Jeremy, I can't step back and wait for others to follow Him. Jesus commissioned me to tell the lost world that He is the way to salvation. —Tracy Crump

He's King of kings, oh, hallelujah! He's Lord of lords, oh, praise His name! The Lamb of God, who brought salvation, endured the cross with all its shame.
—Thomas Kelly

128   ALL GOD'S CREATURES

MAY 4

Squirrel Smart

. . . to reach all the riches of full assurance of understanding and the knowledge of God's mystery, which is Christ, in whom are hidden all the treasures of wisdom and knowledge. I say this in order that no one may delude you with plausible arguments.

—COLOSSIANS 2:2–4 (ESV)

MY MIDDLE-SCHOOL-AGE SON has been trying in vain to make a squirrel trap. This isn't something malicious; it's motivated by curiosity and a desire to outsmart the wily squirrels. He sees them scampering up tree trunks, leaping brazenly from branch to branch at high altitude, and sneaking snacks from Mom's garden. From Reuben's perspective, squirrels have superpowers, and he wants to challenge them.

To date, all of Reuben's "traps" have involved utility buckets, cardboard, duct tape, and birdseed. Always birdseed. The traps never work, and I would never allow him to make a trap that would actually harm a squirrel. If anything, I've seen this as a test of his intelligence, not the squirrels'.

Squirrels are pretty smart. They have shown themselves smarter than me with every vegetable garden I've ever planted and with nearly every bird feeder I've hung. Squirrels have an uncanny knack for knowing where food is and how to get to it. They know how to get what they want, and most of the time, I must admit, that's pretty awesome.

I wish I could be so certain, so focused, so persistent. There is so much information blasted at me in life day by day, hour by hour, and via social media, even minute by minute. It is overwhelming attempting to find the truth in all of it.

I want to be as cunning and as driven as a squirrel as I go after what I want—the wisdom and knowledge of Christ. I don't want to be deceived by flimsy traps or deluded by the glut of words, arguments, and philosophies out there in the world, attempting to lead me astray. I want to fix my eyes on Jesus and find my way toward His truth. —Katy W. Sundararajan

Let us run with perseverance the race marked out for us, fixing our eyes on Jesus, the pioneer and perfecter of faith.
—Hebrews 12:1–2 (NIV)

MAY 5

The Peace You Seek

Once, on being asked by the Pharisees when the kingdom of God would come, Jesus replied, "The coming of the kingdom of God is not something that can be observed, nor will people say, 'Here it is,' or 'There it is,' because the kingdom of God is in your midst."

—LUKE 17:20–21 (NIV)

THERE IS SOMETHING about the month of May that seems to make everyone crazy. Perhaps, no matter what our age or stage in life, it's the transition from the school year to summer, the feeling that everything must be wrapped up before people begin taking off to cooler climes. This May seemed to be even more crowded with events and deadlines, and I found myself racing to finish projects. My husband kindly offered to take care of our rabbit hutch, something that I usually enjoy doing.

Even with the extra help, I felt overwhelmed. One to-do list seemed to bleed into the next, and no matter how much I got done, I couldn't relax. I kept fantasizing about summer vacations in the past—trips to the mountains when life was easy and time seemed to stop. *Happiness is right around the corner*, I promised myself. *Once I get through all this, I'll feel good.*

Then my husband had to go out of town for work. At first, I panicked and thought I would never get everything done, but I headed out to the hutch. I started to speed through the checklist of chores—food, water, litter box, hay, greens, herbal forage, and a few little treats. As I worked, Lemon and Nimbus hopped around me, darting in and out of their tunnels. They stopped, sat up on their haunches, and groomed themselves, pulling first one ear down and then the other, extending their long legs and carefully cleaning them. Then they groomed each other behind the ears where they couldn't reach themselves. When they were done, they flopped down and curled up next to each other.

I stopped cleaning and just sat and watched them. Their hay smelled like summer, and the herbal forage like an amazing salad. They exuded peace. I realized they were the very thing that I had been lacking. Giving up the responsibility of their care had not lightened my load; it had denied me the opportunity to observe these wonderful creatures. I didn't need to go to the mountains to relax in nature. I just needed to take a deep breath and give my full attention to the bunnies. The peace of God is all around me, all the time. Sometimes I just need to stop chasing it to be able to feel it. —Lucy H. Chambers

One of the persistent follies of human nature is to imagine true happiness is just out of reach.
—Gretchen Rubin

MAY 6

Mayflies

*Our light and momentary troubles are achieving for us
an eternal glory that far outweighs them all.*

—2 CORINTHIANS 4:17 (NIV)

I WAS RUNNING late to my dental appointment that warm May morning, so when mayflies swarmed me at my Jeep, I groaned a bit and brushed them away. While they're pleasant creatures that just have one or two days of life, I didn't really like them and didn't want them flying into my car. Each year they congregate around the large snowball bush that sits at the driveway corner of our house in the Sierra Valley.

But partway through my half-hour drive across the valley, a single mayfly that had made its way into the Jeep parked himself on me. Although I knew mayflies do not bite because they do not eat—hence, their short lifespan—I waved the guy aside a few times. Finally, I decided to pull over to the shoulder of the road, opened my door, and escorted him out. My temporary annoyance brushed away now, I faced the larger one ahead: dental work.

But as I thought about those mayflies and the one that had taken up short-term residence with me, I realized that just as their season is short, so would my time be in the dental chair. And actually, that momentary discomfort could provide the opportunity for me to learn patience and develop a grace-filled perspective, as well as spread kindness, sympathy, and even a bit of laughter to those in the dental office.

Later, as I returned home, I parked farther away from the snowball bush with its mayfly reunion. Perhaps, I thought, even mayflies needed a bit of sympathy and understanding. —Janet Holm McHenry

*Consider it pure joy, my brothers and sisters,
whenever you face trials of many kinds,
because you know that the testing of your
faith produces perseverance.*
—James 1:2–3 (NIV)

MAY 7

Ever-Present Help

God is our refuge and strength, an ever-present help in trouble.

—PSALM 46:1 (NIV)

IT WAS EARLY May, and our yard was a bustle of activity with flowers blooming and birds returning. A red-winged blackbird trilled from the top of our poplar tree, demanding attention, but mine was on the house sparrows who had recently taken up residence in our sparrow condominium. The condominium, a large birdhouse fixed to the top of an 8-foot vertical tree trunk, has fourteen openings and room for several house sparrow families. One door was particularly busy that afternoon as a mom and dad house sparrow took turns hunting and returning with insects for their chicks inside.

I watched through binoculars as the mom perched outside the door with a fly in her beak. She sat patiently, every few moments turning an ear toward the door or poking her head inside as if waiting for her chicks to be ready to eat. After a few minutes, she disappeared through the hole as the father sparrow arrived to take over the perch and stand guard over their home. Even without binoculars, I could see the sizable winged insect in his beak, the chicks' next meal delivery. The mama emerged, her beak empty, and took off into our bushes for her turn to hunt.

As I sit on our back porch watching the condominium throughout spring, I am struck by the parents' attentiveness and devotion. The perch outside their door is nearly always occupied by dad or mom, and they always have an insect waiting for their chicks. I'm reminded of God's careful attention to creatures as small as a sparrow and that, like the sparrow parents, He is always at hand and ever present, protecting and providing for me. —Eryn Lynum

> *"Look at the birds of the air; they do not sow or reap or store away in barns, and yet your heavenly Father feeds them. Are you not much more valuable than they?"*
> —Matthew 6:26 (NIV)

132   ALL GOD'S CREATURES

MAY 8

The Ants and the Peonies

*But in fact God has placed the parts in the body, every
one of them, just as he wanted them to be.*

—1 CORINTHIANS 12:18 (NIV)

WHEREVER YOU SEE peonies, you'll see ants."
Decades later, I can still hear my grandmother's voice. Every spring she'd gather a huge bouquet of peonies from her flower garden, fill a vase with fresh water, and set it in the center of her dining-room table. For the next two days, my sisters and I would be on the lookout for the tiny black ants that scurried among the fragrant blossoms onto the table.

My grandmother believed the folk wisdom that without ants the peonies wouldn't bloom. As legend has it, ants, attracted by the sticky sap that coats the buds, lick off the droplets, thus freeing the blossoms to burst open.

Years later, I learned that ants and peonies do enjoy a special relationship, called *mutualism,* in which both parties derive benefit from a relationship. The peonies provide a food source of sugars, amino acids, and other compounds the ants need. In return, the ants protect the plant from other pests that may cause damage.

Ants and peonies aren't the only members of God's creation that enjoy mutualism. Brothers and sisters in the body of Christ do too. God gave us differing gifts, and we need one another to live full and fruitful lives.

My friend Jean helps me with sticky theological questions. I help her with time management. My friend Mandy prays with me when I have a concern. I do the same for her. Maryann challenges me to share my faith. I challenge her to love and serve her difficult family members.

Science tells us peonies will open with or without their ant friends, but I won't become all I can be in Christ without faithful members of the body of Christ to help me along. I'm glad God places us in a family when He calls us to Him. Just as my grandmother's bouquet of ants and peonies benefits from mutualism, my life wouldn't be as sweet or as beautiful without my brothers and sisters in Christ. —Lori Hatcher

Now to each one the manifestation of the Spirit is given for the common good.
—1 Corinthians 12:7 (NIV)

ALL GOD'S CREATURES   133

MAY 9

Ladybug, Ladybug

But God chose the foolish things of the world, that he might put to shame them that are wise; and God chose the weak things of the world, that he might put to shame the things that are strong.

—1 CORINTHIANS 1:27 (ASV)

MY LITTLE GRANDDAUGHTER Edelweiss skipped toward me with her chubby hand thrust forward. "Look," she declared. "It's a ladybug." The small red beetle covered with black spots walked across her palm. I recalled catching ladybugs myself as a child and remembered how adults told me the insect was a sign of good luck.

Perhaps that's because they are so beneficial to farmers. Although small, ladybugs can eat as many as seventy-five aphids in a single day! Aphids cause millions of dollars of damage to crops every year. Thankfully, the small and humble ladybug helps keep the population down by consuming five thousand aphids during its short lifetime.

I don't think it's a coincidence that such a tiny insect makes a vast difference in our world. The Lord often uses what others consider small and insignificant to manifest His glory.

Consider the beautiful Hebrew orphan named Esther who saved her people from mass annihilation. God chose another Hebrew girl of humble origins to give birth to His one and only Son, Jesus. Consider a young widow named Elisabeth Elliot. She bravely took her baby daughter to live among a violent tribe in Ecuador, the same people who had murdered her missionary husband. Over time, she won many of these villagers to Christ. And what about Fanny Crosby? Blind from infancy, Fanny grew up to write hundreds of hymns that are still being sung by believers today.

There are no insignificant roles in the Lord's kingdom. The ladybug performs an important task in God's creation, as do all of us. You, me, and the ladybug—we are working together for the glory of God.
—Shirley Raye Redmond

There are no ordinary people.
—C. S. Lewis

MAY 10

A Mama's Heart

The LORD will work out his plans for my life.
—PSALM 138:8 (NLT)

MY PASTORS RAISE chickens, and we are the delighted recipients of an occasional carton of beautiful brown and beige eggs. They have a number of laying hens but no roosters. That reality did not deter one of the hens from entering into a broody state. She really wanted to hatch some eggs. She really wanted to be a mama. But without a boy chicken in the roost, that was not going to happen.

My friends recognized the strength of this desire in their hen and sought ways to help her. First they bought four fertilized eggs and exchanged them for the eggs Buffy was sitting on. After a prolonged period of waiting, it was evident that this wouldn't work.

Then they attempted to purchase day-old chicks in hopes that Buffy would bond with them. But chicks that young were not to be found. The youngest were over a week old, which is technically too old to be introduced to a new hen. They purchased some of the week-olds anyway and carefully snuck them underneath the would-be mama.

She was delighted to feel movement in the nest. And the babies, even though they had already interacted with tons of potential maternal figures, bonded and fell in love with this wonderful hen who so obviously loved them. It was a win-win situation all around. They were inseparable and happy to be a family. Buffy was thrilled to be a mama to her adopted babies.

There have been many roles I've wanted over the course of my life—graduate, teacher, wife, mother, grandma, writer, friend. Some of those roles came easier than others, but God always made a way. My perseverance wasn't necessarily the answer. There were times when I just needed to wait and trust and know that if it was meant to be, it would be. God knew who He made me to be, and He would help me to follow His plan when the time was right. —Liz Kimmel

Thank You, Father, for Your plan for my life. Thank You for bringing me through hard times when life just doesn't look like I think it should. Teach me to trust that from Your heart was birthed my beautiful life, designed to bring You glory

ALL GOD'S CREATURES

MAY 11

Perfect in Every Way

I will give thanks to You, because I am awesomely and wonderfully made; wonderful are Your works, and my soul knows it very well.

—PSALM 139:14 (NASB)

OUT ON THE back porch one afternoon, I happened upon a tiny snail. He was quietly sliding along the railing, minding his own business, so I stopped awhile to watch him.

I couldn't help but marvel at his shell. Such a perfect spiral. So well balanced and pleasing to the eye. The snail shell is such a wonder of creation. It provides the necessary protection for the vulnerable creature inside, yet it also looks so perfect. What a marvel created by a loving God!

Marveling at the beauty of the snail shell got me to thinking. *Am I not also the beautiful and wondrous creation of a loving God?* When I imagine the intricate map of blood vessels or the tree of bronchial tubes in my lungs, I know I am as marvelous and beautiful as the shell of the snail. How often do we succumb to the voices around us telling us what beauty standards are, while we neglect the inner truth of our own creation?

The psalmist said, "I am awesomely and wonderfully made." All of creation is beautiful. All of creation is declared to be "good" by a loving creator God (Genesis 1:31), and that includes you and me. I need to spend less time considering such things as my wrinkles or my weight and more time remembering that God made me as perfectly as the snail's spiral shell. And beyond that, I am made in the image of God. What a wonderful gift to enjoy each and every day! Thanks be to God! —Heather Jepsen

Dear Lord, I praise You that I was awesomely and wonderfully made by You. Please help me keep that in mind, especially in those times when I worry about my outward appearance.

MAY 12

Have a Max-imum Morning!

*Because of the L*ORD*'s great love we are not consumed, for his compassions never fail. They are new every morning; great is your faithfulness.*

—LAMENTATIONS 3:22–23 (NIV)

MAX CAME TO us as a 2-pound bundle of furry love. He was a round, soft Pomeranian puppy, with silky ears and a penchant for nibbling on fingers. It had been many years since we'd owned a puppy, and my husband, Gerald, and I were excited for these early days.

But a week after Max came to live with us, our lives entered a downward spiral. We both contracted Covid, and it hit us hard. A month after our recovery, Gerald's dad became ill and passed away. And just as we were getting through the immediate rush of grief, funeral arrangements, and estate laws, we were knocked out by Covid again!

And through all this, we were trying to raise and train an active little puppy.

There were days when we dreaded getting up in the morning, overwhelmed before we even lifted our heads off the pillow. But there would be Max, smiling at us from his crate. *Good morning!* he seemed to say. *This is an amazing day! Let's go see what's happening!*

He'd bound into each day full of enthusiastic joy. Every meal and trip into the backyard made him spin with excitement. He danced for his squeaky toys and his little fleece blanket. Gerald and I couldn't stop laughing the day Max discovered reusable cloth shopping bags. He'd grab one by the handle and run, letting it billow behind him like a kite.

Lamentations reminds us that God's compassions are new every morning, but it is easy to let the weight of yesterday and worries of what lies ahead cloud that sunrise view.

In a challenging year, Max's enthusiasm reminded us of that daily newness. This morning belongs to God, and because of that, we can approach it filled with hope, trusting in God's faithful love. —Allison Lynn Flemming

*This is the day the L*ORD *has made; we will rejoice and be glad in it.*
—Psalm 118:24 (NKJV)

ALL GOD'S CREATURES 137

MAY 13

Simian Safe Space

*Love is patient, love is kind. It does not envy, it does not boast,
it is not proud. It does not dishonor others, it is not self-seeking,
it is not easily angered, it keeps no record of wrongs.*

—1 CORINTHIANS 13:4–5 (NIV)

MY HUSBAND, SIMON, took our son to the Oakland Zoo during the summer. They were disappointed at first because they could only spot a few animals in their habitats. The rest took shelter from the sweltering heat in covered enclosures or under shady trees.

Some animals, like the primates, did not seem to mind the sun. It was just another lazy afternoon for the zoo's hamadryas baboons. Some ate fruit while others groomed each other's silver manes. Then there was Jasiri, the newest member of the family. Only an infant, he was a ball of energy, swinging from tree to tree. Ryan, our son, noticed that the adult baboons tolerated the infant baboon's antics. Sometimes, the energetic Jasiri got in their way or interrupted them when they were foraging, but the baboons did not chastise him. This troop of baboons provided a safe environment for the inquisitive infant to fail, to learn, and to grow.

When Ryan shared Jasiri's story with me, it occurred to me that the baboons served as a great example of godly community. There are people with varying degrees of faith and levels of spiritual maturity in a spiritual community. The Bible encourages us to be patient with one another, especially with those who are new to God's household.

I was reminded of my Bible study group, which is multigenerational and diverse. Sometimes, I get frustrated when a member spiritually drifts away or misunderstands biblical truths. But I'm called to encourage and support new believers or young ones, being patient with their faults or weaknesses and extending grace to them. A spiritual community should be a safe space where new and younger members can express their doubts and make mistakes. Adults like me who are more experienced in matters of faith can gently correct and counsel them, modeling Christlike love in community. —Mabel Ninan

*Be completely humble and gentle;
be patient, bearing with one another in love.*
—Ephesians 4:2 (NIV)

MAY 14

Magnificent Ostrich

"The beast of the field will honor Me, the jackals and the ostriches."

—ISAIAH 43:20 (NKJV)

WILDLIFE SAFARI IS a drive-through zoological park on the outskirts of Winston, a southwestern Oregon town. There are 615 acres of pastures and enclosed fields that allow for close-up encounters with wildlife from Africa, Asia, and the Americas.

During one of our visits to Wildlife Safari, a curious and bold South African ostrich strutted up to the driver's side of our parked car. I'm convinced that this social but territorial bird would have poked his entire head inside our car had we not shut our windows after seeing the warning signs. Stunning, with black feathers, white wings, and a white tail, this large male ostrich took us by surprise, pressing its beak against the glass.

The size of the ostrich amazed me. The world's largest, heaviest, and most powerful bird stands up to nine feet tall and weighs from 220 to 287 pounds. Too heavy to fly, it uses its wings for balance, as it did when it ran toward us—the fastest two-legged land animal on earth. I will never forget its huge eyes—the largest eyes of any land animal—its sweeping eyelashes, and curious intent. Separated by a mere window, I could almost have encountered this giant bird in the open grasslands of Africa face-to-face.

I learned that day to respect the wild and powerful creatures on earth. The window we shut tightly revealed that respect—that we could get close, but not *too* close. Isaiah 43:20 has intrigued me since my encounter with the ostrich because it says one of the most magnificent birds on earth, the ostrich, honors God, its creator. The verse reminds me that someday, all knees will bow to the One who spoke the breath of life into every living being and said, "It is good." —Kathleen R. Ruckman

Lord, may I always respect nature, as nature ultimately honors You.
And may I have wisdom to know when
a barrier is needed to keep me safe—in all of life.

MAY 15

Taking the Leap

Immediately they left the boat and their father and followed him.

—MATTHEW 4:22 (ESV)

COME ON UP, Vinter." I patted my lap and looked down at the white-and-gray Turkish Van cat. He stretched up to touch my leg with his paws as I sat in the chair. Lowering himself to the floor after his reconnaissance, he prepared to jump. Or so I thought. Instead, he met my eyes and meowed.

"You can do it, buddy." Vinter could easily make the jump to my lap; he had done so many times. But for unknown reasons, he sometimes hesitated. He would act uncertain, as if something wasn't right. He'd survey my lap, then tense as if about to jump but wouldn't follow through. It seemed he was waiting for everything to be perfect before he took the leap.

That morning, as Vinter finally prepared to jump up to me, a calico kitty landed in my lap from the opposite side. Videa, my female cat, had secured my lap instead.

"Sorry, Vinter." I shook my head. "You shouldn't have hesitated." I chuckled at the familiar scenario. Vinter's hesitation often resulted in him losing the coveted lap position to Videa. She never delayed when she wanted something or needed to act.

As I pondered the contrast between my two cats, I realized there was a lesson for me in their behavior. When God calls me to do something, my instinct is to hesitate, as Vinter does. I first make sure I have the time, resources, and desire to do what He wants me to. I want everything to align perfectly before I'll take a leap. But when Jesus called His disciples to follow Him, they *immediately* left everything to obey. What blessings am I missing because I hesitate? I want to be more like Videa and the disciples. If God says, "Leap," I want to jump into action, knowing He will catch me and the rewards will be great. —Jerusha Agen

The blessedness and the blessing of
God's Word is only to be known by doing it.
—Andrew Murray

MAY 16

An Army of Help

With your help I can advance against a troop; with my God I can scale a wall.
—**PSALM 18:29** (NIV)

GROWING UP IN the Arizona desert, I used to make my own ant farms from jars filled with soil. Ants have always fascinated me, but I'm glad that army ants weren't around then.

These little terrors are usually found in the tropical regions of Central and South America, although their smaller cousins inhabit the southern United States. Larger than most ant species, army ant soldiers possess bigger jaws than the workers. Army ants are known for swarming aggressively and devouring anything they meet. Some species dine on lizards, chickens, and even goats. I've watched nature documentaries where, like Roman legions, army ants march through forests, looking for spiders, bugs, and other ants to conquer and eat. Together, they overpower their prey and, when faced with obstacles, even become a live ant bridge that allows their brothers to cross a gulf safely.

I'm relieved that army ants never invaded my childhood, but I can't help but admire them from afar. They're fearless, and their secret seems to be attacking problems as one unit. As the horde of army ants advances, they work together to meet the needs of the whole. What would be insurmountable for one ant becomes possible as a colony works together.

Observing army ants reminds me of my human community. They say that many hands make light work, and when people come together, like army ants, in friendship and purpose, more is accomplished than whatever one person alone can give.

I don't ever want to become a target for these six-legged meanies, but I can learn from them. God shows me the steadfast ways of the army ant and holds up their teamwork as an example I can follow, lending a hand wherever it's needed. You never know when someone might need help to cross a bridge to a better day. —Linda S. Clare

Lord, show me the places where I can join other helping hands in love.

ALL GOD'S CREATURES

MAY 17

Inconceivable Beauty

*Oh, the depth of the riches both of the wisdom and knowledge of God!
How unsearchable are His judgments and His ways past finding out!*
—ROMANS 11:33 (NKJV)

I WOKE UP late after sleeping fitfully. The electricity remained off from a storm during the night. After a hurried shower, I left the house looking like a kindergartener had picked out my clothes. On the way to work, I remembered my overnight bag, which was sitting safely in the bedroom closet, empty and unready for the weekend retreat for which I should depart right after work. A lunch trip to the drugstore yielded enough essentials to make it through two nights away. After an unbelievably long, stressful day, I embarked on the 2-hour drive through rush-hour traffic to Sunset Vista campground. The evening service passed quickly. I was among the first to bed.

Surprisingly, I roused before my bunkmates and opted for a walk to occupy my stomach until breakfast. Not far down the mountain path, a dramatic vista unfolded below me, a fabulous green valley. In the clear, cool morning, a lone raptor rode the breeze overhead. I stared as the huge bird effortlessly circled.

Every one of my five senses sprang to life as I watched the sun rise behind the soaring bird. The smell of the evergreens, the feel of the flat rock beneath me, even the taste of the gum in my mouth shouted how wonderful it felt to be alive. How peaceful that eagle looked as it defied gravity and made loop after loop.

For a moment, I forgot about my troubles getting to the retreat. Scriptures from the night before flowed through my brain. Stress melted, and the Holy Spirit awakened within like a bird leaping from its aerie home.

Without a preacher near, I heard God's voice loud and clear. *Wake up to the wonderful world I've created for you. Fly like the eagle. Circle above life's petty drama, and take it all in.* —David L. Winters

Walk of Faith: *Make a conscious effort today to notice
and experience life in all its beauty.*

MAY 18

Watch for the Wonder

O LORD, what a variety of things you have made! In wisdom you have made them all. The earth is full of your creatures. Here is the ocean, vast and wide, teeming with life of every kind, both large and small.

—PSALM 104:24–25 (NLT)

MY HUSBAND, DAN, and I lowered ourselves into the ocean near "Turtle Town" for the second half of a snorkeling trip off Maui. We floated around, watching the underwater world through tiny masks, looking for the promised abundance of sea turtles. A single giant turtle with a gnarly shell floated by as gracefully as a ballerina despite his size, but any other turtles seemed nonexistent.

Dan dove down to get a closer view of the rocks and fish. He later told me that he had seen a small turtle fin sticking out from under a rock. He began to surface, and through the hazy water, a sea turtle quickly swim up near his head. Dan was surprised, to say the least, to have a turtle next to his face when he turned. It's tough to float in one place in the always-moving ocean, and Dan had to back-paddle from the turtle in order to keep our required distance.

I swam nearer to Dan. Our friendly turtle stayed next to us, as curious about us as we were about him, calmly looking right into our eyes with his sweet expression and half-smiling mouth. The detail on his skin and shell was amazing to view at such close proximity. What a joy and honor!

I am constantly amazed at the creatures God has been placing in my path since I began challenging myself to watch for His goodness in nature. This surprise visit by a sea turtle was a thrilling reminder of my Father and His incredible creativity. —Twila Bennett

Life can be great, but not when you can't see it. So, open your eyes to life: to see it in the vivid colors that God gave us as a precious gift to His children, to enjoy life to the fullest, and to make it count. Say yes to your life.
—Nancy Reagan

MAY 19

Nocturnal Nibbler

*Your words were found and I ate them, and Your words
became a joy to me and the delight of my heart.*

—JEREMIAH 15:16 (AMP)

THERE WERE SIGNS, though he clearly worked in the dark of night. Despite never seeing him, I believed he was there, evidence of his presence discovered in nooks and crannies, high on shelves, and behind books in my office.

It wasn't until my family took a vacation, leaving home for a week, that he overstepped his bounds. Upon our return, I ventured to my workspace, a small building situated yards from our primary dwelling. There I found it, the frayed edges of my women's study Bible—a Mother's Day gift from my daughter—clear indication that a mouse was sharing my tiny house.

I chuckled as I considered what to do, asking my husband how we might solve this problem. "Perhaps we could set a live trap, get the little guy out once and for all?"

We live on a farm, surrounded by acres abundant with rodents. Why this mouse chose to live in the confines of my office where there was rarely any food and no water—not to mention, no friends—was a mystery to me.

Finally, the trap worked, and our tiny guest was set free some distance from my tiny house. I imagined him scampering among the other field mice, telling them of the goodness of that one meal, unlike any sustenance he'd ever consumed: "I feasted on the Bread of Life, my thirst quenched by the Living Water," perhaps he proclaimed.

And though I'm happy he's able to share his good news, I'd prefer he not invite others to partake. Still, the signposts this nocturnal nibbler left on the edges of my Bible serve to remind me . . . I, too, should fill up on a portion of God's Word daily, then share with others the joy and delight reading the Bible brings. —Maureen Miller

Walk of Faith: *The psalmist described God's Word as "sweeter than
honey to my mouth!" (Psalm 119:103, NIV). Read chapter 119,
verses 97–104 in your favorite translation today, and memorize verse 103.*

MAY 20

Insistent Lizard

*And be kind to one another, tenderhearted, forgiving
one other, even as God in Christ forgave you.*

—EPHESIANS 4:32 (NKJV)

"SCOTT!" I HOLLERED to my husband. "Come get this lizard!"
I was never squeamish about picking up small critters, but for some reason I can't bring myself to do it anymore. I wasn't afraid of the lizard, but I was not about to pick up the squirmy reptile. My husband, Scott, on the other hand, has a tender heart for little animals like lizards, and he could do the job easily.

I'd opened the door to check the mailbox when a 6-inch-long western fence lizard darted into the house. What it *thought* it was doing is anyone's guess. I called for Scott, and it didn't take him long to capture the little intruder. But no sooner did he gently place it outside the door than the lizard launched itself back into the house! Scott and I were really laughing then. This lizard did *not* want to be outside. We checked around for predators—there were none we could see—and removed the lizard again, this time putting it farther into the yard among the flowers and being quicker to close the door before it could find its way back. I sincerely hoped it found its way to a more lizard-friendly environment.

How patient and gentle Scott had been with that lizard! It reminded me of how patient and kind God is with me. I can be pesky and insistent, stubborn and selfish, but God lovingly guides me through my life and protects me from harm. What a blessing it is to have a God like that! My prayer is to follow His example and not only be gentle with lizards but be a blessing to the people in my life, treating them with kindness, gentleness, and forgiveness. —Marianne Campbell

Oh, that gentleness! how far more potent is it than force!
—Charlotte Brontë

MAY 21

The Willet Walk

*I press on toward the goal to win the prize for which
God has called me heavenward in Christ Jesus.*

—PHILIPPIANS 3:14 (NIV)

AT THE END of a long road trip, we made an overnight stop at
Pensacola Beach in the Florida Panhandle. It was a place where we
had stopped before, but this time we noticed a bird we did not recognize
strolling the sand. It exhibited some of the behavior of a sandpiper in
searching for food in the sand, but it showed none of the sandpiper's
typical darting behavior, and this bird went a few feet further offshore and
deeper into the water. An internet search revealed that this was a willet,
a larger member of the sandpiper family.

The willet is noted for its deliberate walk, and this individual was clearly
exhibiting that behavior. When it encountered a person, it didn't run
away; it simply changed course to go around. Its long legs allowed it to
go deeper into the water than its smaller cousin could. This meant that
the willet exposed itself to small waves, a couple of which washed over
its head. It was not fazed in the slightest and continued its pursuit of
whatever it was trying to catch. It was a perfect example of ignoring life's
distractions and pursuing a fixed purpose.

What a great example the willet sets for me in my daily Christian walk!
Life is filled with a multitude of distractions: home repair emergencies,
minor health issues, phone calls, text messages, notifications, and on
and on. Carving out the time for prayer and Bible study is hard enough,
and once found, keeping that time free of distractions is also difficult. I
need to remember the example of the willet and keep my gaze straight
ahead. —Harold Nichols

*Dear Lord, please help me to remember the willet and be as
determined in following my Christian calling as the willet
is in pursuing its goal down the beach. Amen.*

MAY 22

The Hollow of His Hand

I know what it is to be in need, and I know what it is to have plenty.
I have learned the secret of being content in any and every situation,
whether well fed or hungry, whether living in plenty or in want.

—PHILIPPIANS 4:12 (NIV)

WE WERE ON vacation in the high desert. The mountain biking and hiking adventure I had planned turned out to be a challenging week in a heat wave with no air-conditioning. Every morning we set out with big plans; before lunchtime, the pulsing heat of the sun drove us home. We'd spend the rest of the day rocking slowly on the front porch, listlessly fanning ourselves and watching the aspen leaves quiver.

One afternoon, as we lamented missing the planned activities because of the heat, we saw a brown rabbit in the yard. We watched it slowly progress across the yard, passing patches of daisies, mounds of feather-grass, and wiry mesquite. When it got to a space under two big clumps of chamisa, it lay down. I was afraid it was dying. But then it stood up and dug rapidly with its front paws, making a hollow. The little rabbit spread out in it and rested there all afternoon.

That evening it hopped away energetically, and the next day it returned and did the same thing again. We realized that just underneath the hot top layer of dirt, there was enough coolness to sustain the rabbit until sundown. Under stress, it rested peacefully, wasting no energy. Watching it reminded me that even in challenging circumstances, I can rest in the Lord and find comfort. Our trip to the desert wasn't what I had planned, but I left refreshed and grateful, thanks to one wise brown rabbit. —Lucy Chambers

Seek the rest you need, and a little bit more. It is a sacred space.
—Kate Bowler

MAY 23

Finding Joy Each Day

This is the day that the LORD has made; let us rejoice and be glad in it.

—PSALM 118:24 (ESV)

THE DAY DAWNED bright and clear, perfect for a whale watch. My high-school classmates and I saw three whales jumping through the water. Imagine our excitement when another whale surfaced right beside our boat! Hearing the splash, we raced to look over the edge at this beautiful animal until it disappeared. We heard sounds on the other side of the boat and dashed across to see the whale popping out of the water, as if it was looking for us as much as we were looking for the whale. And then it disappeared again.

This game of peekaboo continued for at least 10 minutes, with the whale popping up and "waving" a flipper at us before disappearing, only to reappear again on the other side of the boat. Our tour guide explained that such playfulness indicated that this was a young whale.

I'd seen photos and movies that featured whales, but this was my first time seeing this magnificent creature in person. Being up close and personal really put into perspective just how big they are—and it reminded me that God is even bigger!

Though this senior trip to Boston happened many years ago, it's something I vividly recall to this day. I remember being elated yet nervous, not just about the trip but also about the fact that I would soon be leaving home to head to college. While the prospect was exciting, it was also a bit daunting. Watching that whale go back and forth under our boat—filled with sheer joy in being alive and in the moment—reminded me to live for the day. The whale didn't seem concerned about what it would find on the other side of the boat. Likewise, I did not need to worry about the future ahead of me, because God was in control. I could just enjoy the moment each day—because this truly is the day that the Lord has made. —Leslie L. McKee

Lord, help me to always delight in each day as I see the way
You are working in my life and the world around me. Amen.

MAY 24

A Baby Mockingbird and the Value of Caregiving

"The King will reply, 'Truly I tell you, whatever you did for one of the least of these brothers and sisters of mine, you did for me.'"

—MATTHEW 25:40 (NIV)

WHILE WALKING MY dog one beautiful evening, I noticed the birds vocalizing danger. I looked up and saw a hawk circling overhead. A short way further down the sidewalk, I noticed a baby bird standing in a neighbor's driveway—a mockingbird—and my mind flashed to the cover of P. D. Eastman's beloved children's classic *Are You My Mother?* The fledgling looked at me wide-eyed, its only apparent concern seemed to be for worms.

Remembering the hawk threat moments prior and having some experience with mockingbirds, I grew concerned. Where *was* this little bird's mother? If she were nearby, she would likely be swooping me and my dog since we were so close to her youngster. The fledgling hopped around in an adorable way but could not yet fly. I had no choice but to wait for the mama bird to return.

My dog stood patiently, unsure why I was standing outside the neighbor's driveway. A couple of other neighbors passed by. But I was determined to watch over the juvenile mockingbird as long as it might take—or to transport the bird to a wildlife sanctuary if necessary. To my relief, the mother bird showed up with a worm in her beak after just a couple of minutes. The baby bird hopped beneath the cover of bushes. And the hawk settled far away, having never spotted the vulnerable youngster.

As I walked off, the spiritual resonance of this event echoed in my heart. I have the ability to keep hawks away by simply standing nearby. I do not need fancy qualifications, expert knowledge, or practice. I just need to be there. In the same way, God has given me the privilege of caring for people in my life, simply as I am. I can protect the vulnerable around me whenever I remain near—just by seeing their value and remaining faithful. —Ashley Clark

Father, sometimes caregiving can be a difficult and wearisome endeavor. Help me remember my work is valuable, and remind me that Your presence is also there. Amen.

ALL GOD'S CREATURES

MAY 25

The Beginning and the Ending

I am Alpha and Omega, the beginning and the ending, saith the Lord, which is, and which was, and which is to come, the Almighty.

—REVELATION 1:8 (KJV)

OUR GRANDDAUGHTER'S DOG, Minnie, began her life with our family when Nellie was just four. Nellie was visiting with us that day when our son called and instructed us to have her sit on the hill in our backyard with her eyes closed. Jeremy and his wife arrived a moment later with a tiny puppy, which they placed in Nellie's arms, where she snuggled right in.

An adopted sister joined Minnie a few months later, and the two raced around our backyard during visits. They stayed with us while their family went on vacation, because they felt right at home here. Though they often got into mischief, Minnie was the best vacuum cleaner we ever had.

Several years passed. Jeremy and his family sold their house and moved into a camper until they could find property on which to build. Five days later, Minnie became very ill and passed away from liver cancer. Jeremy called from the vet's office. "We have no place to bury Minnie. Can we bury her in your backyard?"

Of course!

We found a shady spot under a fragrant cedar tree, and Jeremy plunged a shovel into the rock-hard ground while we all cried. I sprinkled pink impatiens petals into the grave and spread zinnia blooms on top. Minnie had come full circle, resting at home in our backyard where she first snuggled her way into our hearts.

I never look forward to losing a beloved pet and have shed tears over many, but they remind me that physical life has a beginning and an ending. The good news is that Jesus made a way for me to live forever with Him, and in heaven, there will be no more sickness or death or tears. I can snuggle in with Jesus because He *is* the beginning and the ending.

—Tracy Crump

No more sickness, No more tears.
For Your purchase spans the years.

—TC

ALL GOD'S CREATURES

MAY 26

Mudpuppy Wisdom

Search for wisdom as you would search for silver or hidden treasure.

—**PROVERBS 2:4** (CEV)

TRY THAT ROCK over there. The big flat one. But make sure you lift it slowly so the water doesn't get too cloudy from the silt."

Teaching our daughters how to search for mudpuppies, a brown salamander that frequented Pennsylvania's creeks, brought smiles as I remembered how my mom loved finding the slippery little critters. While my brothers sought the fat crayfish, squealing over their claws, my mom and I spent time in shaded areas of the streambed, gently turning over the flattest silt-covered rocks, hoping to see a tiny wiggling brown creature. Even if we did see them, catching them could be tricky. Their slimy bodies would dart under the creek bottom and blend in, while also stirring up the soft dirt, making the water too cloudy. A lesson in patience went along with slow motions and quick hands

At this writing, several of our grandchildren enjoy creek beds. I'm waiting to spend some time with them to teach them the art of capturing mudpuppies, though it's harder now because they are not as plentiful as they once were. Still, it's worth the try to finally hold one in the palm of your hand, feeling it slip across your skin.

In Proverbs, the Preacher, as the writer identified himself, urged his readers to search diligently for something too—wisdom. Though it's not slimy like mudpuppies, wisdom still takes time to find, and when I do find it, I know it's something special to be kept sacred and used for righteousness and truth. Seeking it won't get my hands covered in brown muck, but it may take me a few rounds of trial and error to hold on to it. Sometimes, I find it, grab it, use it, and then promptly forget about it. As a Christian, though, I have Someone who will remind me—the Holy Spirit implanted in me the moment I accepted our Savior's gift.

Like the mudpuppy, I want to spend time in the riverbed—the river of God's Word—seeking wisdom. I know it's worth the time. —Cathy Mayfield

Walk of Faith: *Spend time outside seeking hidden treasures—a flower petal, a unique rock, a spiderweb. Take a photo, and keep it to remind you to seek treasure in God's Word.*

ALL GOD'S CREATURES 151

MAY 27

God's Tiny Creatures

*Now faith is confidence in what we hope for and
assurance about what we do not see.*

—HEBREWS 11:1 (NIV)

WHEN MY HUSBAND'S professional status changed from wildlife biologist to retiree, we couldn't wait to spend more time gardening. We planted fennel, dill, and parsley for black swallowtail butterflies; salvia, red cardinal flower, and cypress vine for hummingbirds; and bee balm, verbena, and milkweed for other pollinators.

Imagine our joy when we spotted a black swallowtail butterfly flitting among the fennel. Sure enough, she deposited eggs on its slim branches. To the untrained eye, the eggs were mere minuscule dots on the green plant. Our hopeful hearts helped us find them with no problem.

On one of our daily egg checks, we found nothing. Discouraged, we discussed what might have gotten them, like a hungry ant or some other insect. About this time, two of our six adult children—four kids and two sons-in-love—were searching for jobs because of work-related challenges. Praying often for those two kids distracted me, though I was sad about the missing eggs.

David continued to baby his plants. "You've got to see this," he said after a morning fennel visit. "Come look really close." He pointed to the tiniest black line, just slightly bigger than an errant pencil mark, where an egg had been. We counted four more thin marks. Nothing had eaten or taken our eggs. The black swallowtail caterpillars started out so small, we hadn't noticed them previously.

I couldn't help but think about my kids' job situations. So many times, I can't see what God is doing, and I fret. To my untrained eyes and faltering heart, His plan seems insignificant or not in line with my ideas. I fail to recognize He's working on my behalf all the time. Who knows what God is doing right now to give both of our kids new jobs that might be the best thing that ever happened to them. I can't wait to see what unfolds in both our kids' and caterpillars' lives. —Julie Lavender

*Dear Father, who hast all things made, and carest for them all,
There's none too great for thy great love, nor anything too small.*
—G. W. Briggs

ALL GOD'S CREATURES

MAY 28

Storing Up What I Need

I have hidden your word in my heart that I might not sin against you.

—PSALM 119:11 (NIV)

BUZZING FILLED AND overwhelmed my ears as I opened our front window.

"Quick, come here!" I exclaimed to my children. Our cherry tree, just a couple of feet from the open window, had erupted in fragrant blossoms, and it was swarming with honeybees collecting pollen. I walked outside and stood beneath the tree, observing the busy workers. After a moment, I noticed bright yellow blobs on the back of the bees' legs. I texted a friend who is a beekeeper, and she confirmed these are their pollen baskets, where they store pollen to take back to the hive. Over the next few days, we watched as dozens of bees frequented our tree, collecting what they needed and storing it in their pollen baskets. I thought about what might happen if God had not designed bees with this unique ability to carry their sustenance. Indeed, they would not survive. But because God equipped them to store their food source and carry it with them, they thrive.

Watching the bees, I consider how God calls me to store His Word in my heart. He has given me what I need—a mind to memorize and a heart to absorb His truth, so I am never without my sustenance and what I need to thrive. Like the bees collecting pollen from our cherry tree, I can collect God's peace and promises as I spend time in Scripture and hide His Word in my heart. I can carry the comfort and blessings of His Word throughout my day and into whatever challenge might come. As eager as a bee gathering pollen, I want to store up and treasure God's Word, then bring it wherever I go. —Eryn Lynum

Jesus answered, "It is written: 'Man shall not live on bread alone, but on every word that comes from the mouth of God.'"
—Matthew 4:4 (NIV)

MAY 29

Chicken Church

*And let us consider how to stir up one another to love
and good works, not neglecting to meet together, as is
the habit of some, but encouraging one another.*

—HEBREWS 10:24–25 (ESV)

AN ABANDONED DOGHOUSE rests under an aging apple tree in our yard. It hasn't been used by a dog in years. However, our free-range chickens have claimed it and use it every morning. About half of our flock cram themselves into the box for roughly 20 minutes after their morning feeding. Then, one by one, they exit the structure and proceed on their way. Years ago, my youngest daughter dubbed this activity "chicken church."

I often wonder what this behavior represents. Are they holding daily planning meetings? Giving safety tips on how to avoid predators? Maybe, since they are very quiet, they simply share a peaceful moment of encouragement. Whatever the reason, they do it together.

Many other animals display this gathering tendency, as seen in groupings such as schools of fish, herds of elk, and flocks of geese. In nature, there is safety in numbers. I am sure there is a level of comfort and encouragement as well.

People also like to gather. I've seen it at sporting events, coffee shops, birthday parties, and during the holidays. We were created as social beings with a desire to go through life together. When the first-century church began, many of the Christians would meet daily to encourage each other. The scriptural text reminds me that sometime later some of the people neglected this practice long enough to forget to do it.

Maybe our chickens in the backyard have it right. They take the time to have a quiet morning break together to find encouragement for the day. I appreciate the ability to allow these simple examples in nature to teach me spiritual applications in my life. —Ben Cooper

*Father God, keep the desire in me to regularly gather with those
of like precious faith to be encouraged and strengthened wherever
my new day takes me. In Jesus's name. Amen.*

MAY 30

Annie

For every animal of the forest is mine, and the cattle on a thousand hills
—**PSALM 50:10** (NIV)

ANNIE IS A sweet girl, calm and docile—a Jersey heifer calf. She is fawn-colored, with large doe-like brown eyes, a dark brown face, and a whitish muzzle. She is curious and playful, always poking her big nose at you, sniffing. She has only three legs.

"She was born that way," says our friend Bob, "so she doesn't know anything different." Bob works this small farmstead with his wife and two daughters. "When she was born, I was going to put her down right away," he says. "I mean, a calf with only three legs?"

"What stopped you?" I ask.

Bob says that Annie's salvation was Clarabell, the mama cow. The moment Annie flopped to the ground, all gooey with birth, Clarabell started licking her and nuzzling her, oblivious to the fact that her offspring was deformed. After about a half hour, Annie was trying to stand up. She'd get upright for a few seconds, wobble, tip over. Clarabell would go back to licking, nuzzling, prodding her baby, pushing her. *Come on, you can do it!* Finally Annie got up and stayed up. On three legs. An hour later she was nursing. "I guess we figured that if Clarabell didn't care about imperfections, why should we?" says Bob. Why indeed?

It seems like everywhere I turn in life, I am judged for my imperfections. The world grants acceptance only if I am talented enough, smart enough, wealthy enough, popular enough. But my heavenly Father says *I* am enough, just me myself, and that I am loved despite my flaws and failings. It feels good to know that.

I give Annie a hug, running my hands over her withers, scratching her forehead. As I begin to walk away, she walks with me, toddling along on her three legs.

Thumbtacked to the wall in the farmhouse kitchen is a diagram titled *Conformation Standards, Jersey Cows.* It shows what a perfect Jersey looks like. Annie is glaringly imperfect, but that doesn't seem to bother her. I, too, am imperfect, and it doesn't bother me either. —Louis Lotz

Thank You, Father, for loving me despite my flaws and failings. Amen.

MAY 31

Tiny Messengers

We love because he first loved us.

—1 JOHN 4:19 (NIV)

IN THE FIRST trimester of my daughter-in-law Nicole's pregnancy, she was hit with extreme morning sickness. At one point before their first ob-gyn appointment, she also got sick with a cold. Because she had miscarried twice that year, she and my son began to struggle with fear of losing the baby.

After a particularly rough day, Nicole noticed a ladybug on the ceiling over the bed. The next morning, it was on the wall in their bathroom. Later that night, it was crawling on her bedside lamp. She began to feel as if it were nearby for a purpose. Since her grandfather's passing, she had always felt him close, and she wondered if he was trying to let her know all was well, and that God was taking care of her through the pregnancy. The thought of God sending that special message was a comfort.

Over the coming days, she saw ladybugs everywhere: on her car windshield, in the screened-in porch, on the living room curtain, and even more in the next couple of weeks. On a trip to the mountains with her parents, a ladybug was on the car door near her mom. Since her beloved grandfather was her mother's father, Nicole felt as if he was sending another message. While Nicole walked away from the car, the ladybug flew a little dance of circles over her and her mom's heads, and Nicole was overwhelmed by God's reassurance that He was with them.

Once they learned they were having twins, Nicole began to refer to them as her "ladybugs" and decided to decorate the nursery with a ladybug theme in honor of the comfort she'd received throughout her pregnancy.

I am always amazed how God can use the smallest things—including ladybugs—to bring peace in our difficult times and to help us learn to trust in His provision. —Missy Tippens

> *Be not dismayed whate'er betide, God will take care of you;*
> *Beneath his wings of love abide, God will take care of you.*
> —Civilla D. Martin

ALL GOD'S CREATURES 157

JUNE 1

Raise Up a Cub

Train up a child in the way he should go.

—PROVERBS 22:6 (ESV)

MANAGING MY BEEHIVES requires knowledge. The available information about honeybees is always changing. I need ongoing educational updates regarding new threats, diseases, and predators. There are known threats too. I happen to live in an area with a high black bear population. I have had bears attack my bee yard, but I realize they are part of the ecosystem. Managing multiple species increases my need to understand about more than just my bees.

Honeybees are well adapted for communication, and passing on information to the next generation is crucial since a bee lives for only 6 weeks during their peak active season. They have a short window to teach young sister bees.

In contrast, black bears take up to 16 months to teach their cubs. Mama bear teaches them what to eat and how to survive winter hibernation. Cubs are born during hibernation and stay with Mama over their second winter. The sow engages with her young to improve their foraging and behavior so they have a better chance of surviving the cold winter. Mama bear spends much of her time training her young cubs.

As parents of five now-adult children, my wife and I have done our best to nurture our children to adulthood. Bees, bears, and humans aren't all that different. We each teach our young how to survive a world of threats and predators. My wife and I want our children to thrive rather than just survive. Our family teaching methods include a spiritual component to prepare them for an eternal life in heaven. I am sure my lessons and examples are not sufficient. Thankfully, my children have a better teacher than me—the Holy Spirit, who is far more capable of instructing them in the way they should go. —Ben Cooper

Walk of Faith: *Think of someone you know in a younger generation—a child, grandchild, niece or nephew, or church youth-group member. Pray today for that person or those persons, asking God to help you model His wisdom to them and asking for the Holy Spirit to guide them.*

JUNE 2

Following the Leaf-Cutter

*Then Jesus said, "Come to me, all of you who are weary and carry heavy
burdens, and I will give you rest. Take my yoke upon you. Let me teach you,
because I am humble and gentle at heart, and you will find rest for your
souls. For my yoke is easy to bear, and the burden I give you is light."*

—MATTHEW 11:28–30 (NLT)

I TRUDGED ALONG, carrying my complaints: My day bag is heavy; it's
too hot; I can't breathe (an exaggeration, but not by much in the close,
steamy tropical air). Oh, and my back has been aching for the last 3 hours.
Another day in Costa Rica on a bird-watching tour.

I'm not alone traversing this trail. One doesn't walk far before seeing
numerous long lines of leaf-cutter ants—fellow travelers alongside or even
crisscrossing our trail. I'm careful where I step. *Just how many colonies of
leaf-cutter ants are there, anyway?* Yet their efforts and industry begin to
mesmerize me.

The ants follow a well-worn path, evidence of their many workers taking frequent trips to and from the underground nest. Those ants carrying
loads often stagger, seemingly unable to walk a straight line. But they
keep on, because there is no one else to take their burdens.

Personally, I wouldn't relish a life of endless trips with heavy burdens.
Yet, I stop to consider: Who among us doesn't carry heavy loads? I've got
mine and you've got yours. All of us experience carrying heavy burdens
during our time on earth.

When it comes to burdens, I rejoice in this: At one time, I carried the
heaviest burden—the one that separated me from God. On that day when
I believed in the Lord Jesus Christ, that burden was forever removed,
because He took it upon Himself. Better yet, my right standing with Him
is a free gift; I'm not required to work for my keep in His kingdom. In
Him, I found my rest and peace, and I'm forever grateful. —Darlene Kerr

*I hear the Savior say, "Thy strength indeed is small;
Child of weakness, watch and pray, find in Me thine all in all."*
—Elvina M. Hall

ALL GOD'S CREATURES

JUNE 3

Chasing After the Wind and a Tail

I have seen all the things that are done under the sun; all of them are meaningless, a chasing after the wind.

—ECCLESIASTES 1:14 (NIV)

MY SON'S DOG, Chio, loves to chase her tail. A mutt of indeterminate origin, Chio is a silly animal who never fails to amuse me. I have never seen another dog with such a fascination for her tail. Chio catches sight of the strange appendage sprouting from her hind end and starts to growl. Soon she turns in frenzied circles trying to latch onto the elusive tail. When that approach doesn't work, she sits with her tail between her legs and attacks it from that angle. Sometimes she gets tired and lies down to scoot around on her side, as if that approach might yield the desired results. Whenever Chio gets in "tail chasing mode," I have to stop whatever I'm doing and watch the entertaining show.

As funny as Chio's antics are, I have to wonder if I sometimes get in tail-chasing mode, with the same lack of success. Some days I get busy with unproductive activities that yield little result, often starting out without taking a few moments to read a devotion or pray. Sometimes I find it easy to fall into the trap of living selfishly, which leaves me feeling empty, as if my life has no meaning. Apart from God, all my accomplishments and possessions have no value. Like the writer of Ecclesiastes, I pursue meaningless things with no eternal consequence.

Doing anything in my own power and thinking I can control the outcome is like chasing my tail. Without godly wisdom, my pursuits are nothing but folly. As Jesus instructed in Matthew, "Seek first his kingdom and his righteousness, and all these things will be given to you as well" (6:33, NIV). I don't need to waste time chasing my tail to get the good things God has in store for me. I just need to put Him first. —Ellen Fannon

Take delight in the LORD, and he will give you the desires of your heart.
—Psalm 37:4 (NIV)

JUNE 4

Crafting a Home

By wisdom a house is built, and through understanding it is established.

—PROVERBS 24:3 (NIV)

"OH WOW, I have never seen this." I had seen Bullock's orioles many times but never in the act of nest weaving. My binoculars remained fixed on the olive-colored bird as she swayed on a branch over the river. My friend with whom I often bird-watch stood next to me, her binoculars also trained on the bird.

Years before, I'd learned to identify oriole nests, which look like balls of twine, hair, and straw hanging like grocery sacks from cottonwood branches. But I'd never been able to watch one of these skilled weavers at work.

A long strand of straw hung from the oriole's beak as she carefully maneuvered it around the branch, grabbing then releasing the straw with her beak and feet. With patience and finesse, these crafty birds begin by weaving long, sturdy fibers into the outer bowl of their abode, then they fill it with soft fibers and downy feathers to cushion their eggs.

After a few moments of trying to weave the straw to begin her nest, the oriole must have decided this spot was not ideal, as she flew off to find another option.

In 15 years of marriage, my husband and I have had 10 homes, including rental units, rundown houses we've purchased and restored together, and even a 20-foot travel trailer in which we lived and traveled with three-going-on-four kids and our dog. In all these spaces, we have learned what a home truly is and isn't.

Like the oriole, I have discovered that being choosy about where we set down roots—or weave our twine—matters. It took us many moves to find out what we wanted for our family and what matters to us, like a restful space with trees, wildlife, and a community nearby. Of course, we can't always choose our surroundings; at times, ours have been less than ideal. But we can determine what we fill our home with and the atmosphere we create. — Eryn Lynum

My people will live in peaceful dwelling places,
in secure homes, in undisturbed places of rest.
—Isaiah 32:18 (NIV)

JUNE 5

Luther Has No Pride

When pride comes, then comes disgrace, but with humility comes wisdom.

—Proverbs 11:2 (NIV)

A NEW CAT showed up one night when I was outside feeding the barn cats. One ear was almost gone, and his head was swollen from years of fighting. I was sure he had some sort of untreated injury going on because his walk was stiff and sore.

My name for him was Luther. I don't know why, but he seemed like a Luther. He had wisdom from years on the streets fighting off so many dangers we could never know the full extent of. He was hungry, and he must have shown up at my house because it seemed like a place where he could find safety and food.

Luther didn't demand attention. He didn't ask for much. He didn't jockey for position with the other cats, who were quite territorial. Luther simply waited. He was hungry. That was all. He didn't have to be king. He has shown up in the darkness and disappeared the same way for almost a year now. He seems content to spend his elder years in a place where he has nothing to prove.

Have you ever reached a point where you have nothing to prove anymore? Where what matters is not what rung of the ladder you are on but that you have a ladder? There is peace in falling into the trust of provision without the fight. When there is a race, it is often the real win of finishing that brings the most satisfaction.

Luther came to me at a time in my life and career when I felt I deserved more than I was getting. More recognition. More money. More. More. More. And in our nightly feedings, this old survivor taught me that just living to this point and finding a good place to be fed and safe—that was the real prize. —Devon O'Day

God, let me realize when to stop fighting and to start enjoying all the goodness You have given me.

JUNE 6

Love Multiplies

"A new command I give you: Love one another. As I have loved you, so you must love one another."

—JOHN 13:34 (NIV)

MY MOM HAS fallen for a younger man with face tattoos. She's never met him, but his tender care for a few stray cats has won her over. Our extended family follows a family of cats on what we refer to as "the KittenCam," a livestream broadcast from an animal rescue organization. It all started when, during a difficult season of my daughter's life, a stray cat adopted her. The cat showed up on my daughter's porch and returned to visit each morning and evening. Being beloved by the cat and loving the cat in return was solace.

Due to household allergies, the stray cat stayed outdoors, but the kitty was at home on the porch until it became evident she would soon give birth. Suddenly the porch seemed less hospitable, and my daughter struggled to find her a new home. The rescue organization took the pregnant cat and provided shelter and medical care for her and her newborn kittens.

We watched on screen as the tiny kittens nursed and ventured over their mother. When at 2 weeks their eyes began to open, we cheered with delight. As the kittens learned to play, their personalities emerged. But theirs were not the only personalities we came to know; a parade of caretakers appeared on camera, feeding, weighing, cleaning, and cuddling the kitties.

One of those caretakers was a rough-looking but especially attentive man. His gentle love for the cats was evident. My mom was enamored.

I get it. I first noticed the man who would become my husband when I saw him care for and enjoy children. Recently at a cat café, my other daughter and I watched a young couple on their first date. What a great way to discover someone's personality, by observing how they love cats or children. Even better, what a way to become lovable. Love begets love; affection begets affection, and tender care builds a foundation for the love we long to share in our families and communities. —Susie Colby

If you would be loved, love and be lovable.
—Ben Franklin

ALL GOD'S CREATURES 163

JUNE 7

The Flamingo Filter

I will study your commandments and reflect on your ways.

—PSALM 119:15 (NLT)

THE FLAMINGOS AT Disney's Animal Kingdom were great fun to watch. In addition to their beauty, their behavior was interesting. A flamingo would duck its head underwater to grab a bite to eat and then shake its head vigorously from side to side once it surfaced. It looked similar to a dog shaking to remove excess water after exiting its bath, but as I listened to an animal specialist talk to my five-year-old grandson, I learned that wasn't the purpose at all.

The flamingo, he explained, is one of the few land animals that is a filter feeder. It contains a specialized mechanism in its beak that allows the flamingo to shake out the water it has taken in and retain the small items that it wants to consume. There are other filter feeders, such as the baleen whale, but most of these live underwater.

When I was growing up, the sources of daily information seemed relatively limited: Walter Cronkite, Huntley and Brinkley, and a couple of daily newspapers. These days there are multiple news channels, lots of "commentators," blogs, podcasts, social media, and innumerable other ways of getting information and disparate views via the internet. Filtering in today's world seems overwhelming. How do I know what to believe and what to respond to? I found myself wishing I had a filter that allowed me to sift through the information that assaults me on a daily basis.

And then I realized that God has already given me a filter. It's called the Bible, and it contains God's revealed Word, against which I can measure the information I receive. With more Bible reading and Bible study, I will be better equipped to discern the way God wants me to live.
—Harold Nichols

Am I willing to trade my addiction to the world's
entertainment for more time with my Bible?
—Leslie Ludy

JUNE 8

Fly Away Home

Children are a gift from the LORD; they are a reward from him.

—PSALM 127:3 (NLT)

WHILE WE WERE visiting our grandson in Chattanooga, my son-in-law announced, "Wednesday is Insect Day for the letter *I* in Benaiah's pre-K classroom. I messaged his teacher that you guys could visit his class." My husband, David, had spent 20 years as a navy entomologist, so this idea thrilled us. Benaiah, David, and I caught six ladybugs at the park in preparation for the visit. We carefully tucked them into a plastic container we keep handy in the car for critter observations.

Just after lunch, eager four- and five-year-olds sat on carpet squares in rapt attention as David shared scientific facts about insects and elaborated on each of the critters brought in for show and tell. Next, I read insect books to the kids until recess, and then we all trekked outside, plastic containers in hand, to release our finds. Swings and slides took a back seat to crawling, flying, and creeping critters.

After a big squeezy hug, we said goodbye to Benaiah and reluctantly headed back to Georgia. It's hard to leave no matter how often we visit any of our adult kids and grandchildren, who are scattered across three states.

A few tears and a lot of miles later, we arrived home. David unpacked the car, and I started laundry in a too-quiet house. Hurrying inside, David handed me the empty ladybug container. Only it wasn't so empty after all. "Look close," he said. Tiny white dots clung to the inside of the jar.

"Ladybug eggs." Unbeknownst to us, we'd brought home little memories. Soon, itty-bitty ladybug larva emerged from the eggs. David placed the container in our flower bed so they could exit at will.

God used six ladybugs to remind me that I always carry a piece of my kids and grandkids back home in my heart, no matter how far apart we may be. We can't wait to take the critter jar on another family adventure.
—Julie Lavender

I'll love you forever, I'll like you for always,
as long as I'm living, my baby you'll be.
—Robert Munsch

ALL GOD'S CREATURES 165

JUNE 9

What a Spectacle!

*When Jesus reached the spot, he looked up and said to him,
"Zacchaeus, come down immediately. I must stay at your house
today." So he came down at once and welcomed him gladly.*

—LUKE 19:5–6 (NIV)

ONE MORNING IN early summer, my teenage son dashed in through kitchen door, urging me to follow him to the soccer field across the street. "You're never going to believe it! There are hundreds of birds eating something in the grass."

"What kind of birds?" I asked, dropping the dish towel on the counter and following him outside. He didn't know. They were gray with black wing bars. And noisy. Very noisy! There were indeed hundreds of them in the field. Where had they come from? Where were they going? Others witnessed the spectacle too. Some people driving by pulled their cars over to the curb. Pedestrians paused to stare at the unusual scene. Jordan and I leaned against the fence encircling the field to watch and listen.

Later, when I had time to consult my birder's guide, I learned we'd witnessed a flock of Clark's nutcrackers—the only bird that William Clark of Lewis and Clark Expedition fame had named for himself back in the early 1800s. I also learned that such a sudden appearance of unexpected birds is called an "irruption" (not *eruption*). Scientists suggest that such appearances are caused by food shortages in the birds' usual habitat.

We'd witnessed something exciting that day. I wonder if Zacchaeus felt like that when he heard about Jesus coming to Jericho. The Lord had been attracting curious crowds everywhere He went. Zacchaeus, wanting to see for himself, climbed a tree to get a good look. How thrilled he must have been when Jesus announced he was spending the day with him at his home. Even before Jesus asked him to, Zacchaeus offered to right all the wrongs he'd done. That must have been quite a spectacle to witness too— even more so than a flock of Clark's nutcrackers. —Shirley Raye Redmond

*Lord, help me to be like Zacchaeus, eager to be near You
and willing to do the right thing without being asked. Amen.*

JUNE 10

Lifted Up

He lifted me out of the pit of despair, out of the mud and the mire. He set my feet on solid ground and steadied me as I walked along.

—PSALM 40:2 (NLT)

ROUNDING THE CORNER to head across the levee on my daily walk, I startled a flock of twenty-five to thirty Canada geese that immediately took flight from the lake.

Wait a minute. Canada geese aren't that easy to frighten. In fact, they often stand their ground and hiss at me when I pass by, making *me* just a little afraid. Not until the flock settled again in the water a safe distance away did I realize they weren't floating on *top* of the water. Their bodies sank *under* the surface with only their necks and heads showing. The timid birds were cormorants, not geese.

These waterfowl are apparently so common in nearby lakes that one community is named Lake Cormorant, but we rarely see them in our subdivision. When we do, I love watching the goose-size birds dive under the water to catch their dinner. I later learned that unlike ducks and geese, the cormorants' feathers are not very waterproof, which they use to their advantage. Since they lack the oil that would allow them to float, they're better able to dive underwater. However, that means they must frequently perch in the sun and dry their feathers to avoid becoming waterlogged.

Like the cormorants, I often become overloaded with the cares of this world and start to sink. Unfortunately, I can't sit on a branch and shake my feathers to rid myself of the cares. Instead, I go to the Lord, who applies a healing balm to my spirit. It may involve confession and humbling myself, because I have a habit of taking on more than God intends me to handle. But with Bible study and prayer, I find God lifts me up and allows me to shed my burdens. Then I can move boldly forward to accomplish His purposes for my day. —Tracy Crump

Humble yourselves in the sight of the Lord, and he shall lift you up.
—James 4:10 (KJV)

ALL GOD'S CREATURES

JUNE 11

A Squirrelly Situation

*Jesus answered, "It is written: 'Man shall not live on bread alone,
but on every word that comes from the mouth of God.'"*

—MATTHEW 4:4 (NIV)

AS MY HUSBAND and I enjoyed a leisurely breakfast at the picnic table of our campsite, a sudden movement caught my eye. *What in the world?* When I looked closer, I saw a squirrel with an empty peanut butter jar. The squirrel held the jar with its front paws and poked its head inside, trying to lap up the little bit of peanut butter still clinging to the sides. After thoroughly cleaning out as much of the treat as it could reach, the squirrel dropped the jar and crawled inside to lick the bottom. Fascinated with the acrobatics of the industrious squirrel, I became so engrossed in the little creature's eagerness to polish off as much of the discarded treasure as possible that I forgot about my own uneaten breakfast. The squirrel didn't seem to be bothered in the least by how silly he looked with half his body inside the jar and his bushy tail poking out.

I began to compare the squirrel's determination to do whatever it took to obtain physical nourishment with my determination to obtain spiritual nourishment. Am I willing to do whatever it takes to be spiritually fed? I'm afraid some days I let my spiritual needs go hungry. Some mornings I am running late and skip my morning devotion. Some evenings I am just too tired to read my Bible. My prayer time doesn't always receive top priority either. There are even times when I feel silly trying to meet my spiritual needs in a secular world that doesn't understand those needs.

Yet, when I take the time to study and dig deep into God's Word, I am always energized and refreshed. I know that just like the squirrel, the deeper I dig, the more I will be rewarded—and my reward is something that will satisfy my soul in a way that physical food never could. —Ellen Fannon

*Father, please place in my heart the burning desire
to be spiritually fed with Your Word and Your presence.*

JUNE 12

Copycat

What the Father does, the Son does. The Father loves the Son and includes him in everything he is doing.

—JOHN 5:19–20 (MSG)

MY SISTER MARI was cat-sitting for our brother recently while he was out of town. David was never big on coming up with names for the family pets. He left that job to his daughters. When they were all grown and out on their own, it was just him, his dog, and his cat. The dog got a name, but the feline family member didn't. She answers to "Kitty."

Kitty never wants to be more than 2 inches away from her humans. This is not an issue if the human is seated. But whenever Mari moved about the room, she had to guard against tripping over the energetic and excitable fur in motion. Kitty even wanted in on the action when Mari bent at the bathroom sink to wash her face in the evening. From her perch on the counter Kitty focused intently on the stream of water coming out of the faucet. Mari cupped her hands to catch a bit and splash it on her face. At first, Kitty tentatively stretched her paw toward the water but quickly pulled it back when it got wet. The next time she kept her paw in place slightly longer. Soon she allowed water to soak her fur. Then, just as Mari had done, she used the moisture to rub her face and wash away the grime of the day's activities.

I want to be like Kitty in the way that she observed and then wholeheartedly copied the behavior of her trusted friend. I, too, have a trusted Friend whose character I want to copy. He has given me plenty of good examples to mimic as I walk out my Christian faith, both in my life and in His Word, and I pray that, as I do so, I will grow to be more like Him. —Liz Kimmel

> *Dear Father, Son, and Holy Spirit, there is no one I want to be more like than You. Please give me eyes to see and ears to hear what You are doing and saying.*

ALL GOD'S CREATURES   169

JUNE 13

Just Call Me Grace

But He gives more grace. Therefore He says: "God resists the proud, but gives grace to the humble."

—JAMES 4:6 (NKJV)

MY HUSBAND, JOE, and I live in landlocked Colorado, so it was a special treat for us to visit Belize on a cruise. We decided to tool around on a motorboat on the clear blue water as one of our excursions. The sea spray, the wind in my hair, and the speed of the boat were exhilarating, but perhaps the best part was when we saw signs indicating a manatee swimming area. The skipper of the boat turned the motor down to a trolling speed to keep the animals safe—and to allow us the opportunity to catch sight of the lovely creatures.

The skipper instructed us to watch for snouts sticking out of the water, as manatees are mammals and breathe air. I was so delighted that after our cruise, I went home and immersed myself in manatee discovery via online videos and nature shows to watch how incredibly graceful these huge, lumbering sea creatures are when in their natural habitat underneath the water. It blew my mind that 13 to 15 feet and 3,500 pounds of animal could look that good.

Compare this to me trying to walk up a flight of stairs. Sure, I've occasionally seen people slip and fall *down* stairs, but it takes real talent to trip up the stairs. My mother used to laugh when she did something like that and say, "Just call me Grace."

While I may not be as graceful as a manatee, I do know where to turn to ask for more grace in my life. Whether I'm wishing for more physical grace after tripping on the stairs or more emotional or spiritual grace during difficult times, Jesus is always there to uplift me. —Deb Kastner

Lord, thank You for the grace You anticipate on my behalf in every day and every way I need it.

170   ALL GOD'S CREATURES

JUNE 14

A Distinctive Mark

*By this all will know that you are My disciples,
if you have love for one another.*

—JOHN 13:35 (NKJV)

HE WAS ABSOLUTELY adorable, from his fluffy tuft of hair to his spotted legs. I'd encountered him at an 1800s farm-life historical site. He was reddish-brown and white. He had a white strip along his spine. His legs were brown and white. However, it was his distinctive forehead that set this bull apart. Between eyes circled in brown and below two stubby horns was a star. I'd never seen a bull like him before.

Over several years, every time I visited this site, I looked for the bull. He'd walk to the fence, let me scratch his forehead, then wander off to find some shade or eat some grass. One day, though, I couldn't find him in any of the pastures. When I asked a docent about him, I described his distinctive star. She smiled. "Oh. You mean Ajax. He's been sold." She must have noticed my distressed look. "Don't worry. He'll live out the rest of his days in luxury surrounded by a herd of cows."

When I described Ajax's distinctive star, the docent knew immediately which bull I meant. His star set him apart. I didn't need to say anything else. It was one attribute that stood out. It was obvious. There was no mistaking some other bull for Ajax. Even as he grew, each time I visited the farm, his star stood out.

I want to live in such a way that, like Ajax, if someone described what was different about me, others would know who they meant. Not because I have a distinctive star on my forehead, but because I have the love of God inside me. A love that shines from within and shows I belong to Him. —Sandy Kirby Quandt

*To be yourself in a world that is constantly trying to make you
something else is the greatest accomplishment.*
—Ralph Waldo Emerson

JUNE 15

Batter Up?

*"For the life of every living thing is in his hand,
and the breath of every human being."*

—JOB 12:10 (NLT)

DAVID AND I looked forward to our grandson's baseball tournament. Though we couldn't wait to watch our five-year-old's batting abilities, I'd admit that part of the attraction was that we'd get to see swarms of periodical cicadas making their debut after spending the last 13 years underground. It was the highlight of every recent FaceTime conversation with our grandson. "Maybe Benaiah will grow up to be an entomologist, just like you," I told my husband.

On tournament day, after driving 6 hours the night before, we set up chairs and a tent. Cicadas buzzed and flew, especially in the thick forest of trees behind the park. Some made their way to the baseball fields, landing on fences, picnic tables, soccer chairs, and spectators' pant legs. Big orange eyes contrasted with iridescent green bodies.

The synchronicity of their loud calls—males attempting to attract a mate—came in waves. The sound seemed deafening at first, but we tuned it out once the ballgame began.

Benaiah's teammate Olivia, however, couldn't take her eyes—or hands—off the insect visitors. Each time she came up to bat, the coach yelled over the din of the tournament, "Put the cicada down!" She was my kinda gal—one who enjoyed playing in the dirt more than stealing second and playing in the grass rather than fielding balls.

She eventually complied and set down her treasure. Regretting her decision, Olivia hopped after the freed cicada, bat trailing behind. Finally, the umpire intervened and guided the cicada away from the field. Olivia had no idea whether her team won the game because baseball just didn't seem that important to her. More interested in the beauty of God's creations, she didn't want to miss a minute of the bug-eyed critters that wouldn't emerge again for another 13 years.

I'm glad I enjoy God's creations as much as Olivia does. We're two of a kind! —Julie Lavender

*Dear God, thank You for magnificent creations, from the
mighty to the miniature. Help me stay in awe of Your creativity,
especially those parts that might be easy to miss. Amen.*

JUNE 16

Snoopy the Rabbit

How good and pleasant it is when God's people live together in unity!

—PSALM 133:1 (NIV)

AS OFTEN HAPPENS in our neighborhood, my husband and I noticed a group of rabbits hopping across the street just ahead of where we were walking our dog. We did a bit of a double take, however, as the last of the bunch crossed the road. You see, all of the rabbits in our neighborhood are a standard woody-brown color, but this one was white. Even better, it was white with black ears and a black nose. It looked a lot like Snoopy, actually.

We spent some time wondering if this was someone's pet bunny that had escaped or gotten lost somehow, but we ultimately decided that didn't matter at this point. It was obvious that the rabbit was among friends. It looked nothing at all like its compatriots, but you would never know from the way they interacted. Neither the standard brown rabbits nor the Snoopy-colored rabbit acted as though something unusual was taking place. They were together, united; they were friends.

More than once in my life I've had to make new friends. I've moved a few times, and I went off to college in a different state. I have traveled and lived abroad. I have joined a new church. Making new friends during these transitions has sometimes felt like a painful or awkward challenge, and sometimes I've been lonely. But when people have come along and allowed me into the fold no matter how I look or sound or act, I've been aware that God is at work. Time and again, God has given me the gift of friendship and community, safety and security, and true gladness of heart with others. I'm so very thankful that God gives me places and people to belong with, always allowing for my individual uniqueness.
—Katy W. Sundararajan

Friendship is born at that moment when one person says to another: "What! You, too? I thought I was the only one."
—C. S. Lewis

ALL GOD'S CREATURES

JUNE 17

Giving Back

Each of you should use whatever gift you have received to serve others, as faithful stewards of God's grace in its various forms.

—1 PETER 4:10 (NIV)

SEVERAL MONTHS AGO, my husband, Mike, fell ill in the middle of the night. "Mike, I'm calling the ambulance," I said, praying for his health as we waited. Our golden retriever, Sophie, appeared at Mike's side and stayed there, pressing in against him. Her comforting instincts came naturally. "Thank you, Sophie," Mike said, stroking her neck. We both felt a little calmer. In short time, the EMTs bustled in the door and transported Mike to the hospital, where he was treated and, in a few days, was as good as new.

Mike and I discussed many times how thankful we were for the EMTs' calm and comforting response. Things might not have gone so well if they hadn't helped. We wanted to do something to express our gratitude. But donuts or cookies didn't seem enough. Then I got an idea. Sophie was a certified therapy dog. She'd taken classes and passed a test to earn her certificate. Surely the EMTs with the stressful job could use the same comfort as Sophie had shown Mike that night.

We arranged to visit the Emergency Medical Services Corps. Sophie walked in the door as if she knew why she was there. Her tail wagged as the employees smiled and patted her. She led us up and down the halls to a large room with desks and monitors. There we saw the very EMTs who had assisted Mike. "You took me out in the ambulance a few weeks ago," Mike said. "Thank you for what you do."

God has equipped certain people to come to the aid of others. In the same way, He has equipped certain dogs. Sophie's calm presence and attentive manner comforted the rescue workers, much as their same virtues had comforted Mike and me on that scary night. —Peggy Frezon

Walk of Faith: *How has God equipped you to serve others? Make a list of your skills and experience. Is there a way any of these could line up with a need in your community?*

174   ALL GOD'S CREATURES

JUNE 18

Duck One, Duck Two

*But do not forget to do good and to share, for with
such sacrifices God is well pleased.*

—HEBREWS 13:16 (NKJV)

I WAS WATCHING A couple of ducks presumably trying to build a
nest in the meadow by the bank of the small stream that runs behind
our house.

In any case, Duck One was efficiently scraping dirt out of the hole and
making a nice space for her eggs. Duck Two, however, evidently wasn't
happy with Duck One's housing and wanted to overhaul the place. She
moved around the nest, using her webbed feet to brush the newly dug-
out dirt back into Duck One's carefully made hole. Duck One would scoop,
scoop, scoop, and then Duck Two would brush, brush, brush, essentially leaving them both back where they'd started. Talk about cross-communication.
And yet I still had the feeling both were fully committed to doing the
right thing for the baby ducklings.

Like those ducks, I all too often find myself miscommunicating with
my spouse or kids. I say something, and they hear it a whole different
way. Perhaps I need to step back and reconsider my words. There have
been times when I'm supposed to watch my granddaughter, and in all
the craziness of my life, I write the wrong date in my planner. Surprise!
It's always a good surprise when I get to spend time with her, but I do try
to plan my days. Other times I get into a tussle with my husband, when
really we are saying the exact same thing in different ways.

Duck One and Duck Two. Scoop, brush. Scoop, brush.

At times like this, rather than getting frustrated with Duck Two, I am
trying to make it a habit to turn to the Lord and ask for wisdom and
patience. I've learned to think before I speak or act and revisit my words
or actions if I seem to be causing a reaction that's the opposite of what I
expected. —Deb Kastner

*Do you see that faith was working together with his works,
and by works faith was made perfect?*
—James 2:22 (NKJV)

ALL GOD'S CREATURES   175

JUNE 19

My Joy Comes at the Dawn

Let the morning bring me word of your unfailing love, for I have put my trust in you. Show me the way I should go, for to you I entrust my life.

—PSALM 143:8 (NIV)

WE HAVE A very small backyard. When we moved into our house, there were trees and open space all around us. As the older houses got replaced by bigger ones, we found ourselves boxed in a tiny patch of green. We put in a postage-stamp-size pool, surrounded it with native plants, and painted our old iron lawn furniture a cheery green.

In the summer, just before dawn, I sit out there and look to the east. I can't see the horizon because of the house next door, but the glow in the sky and the singing of the birds tells me when the sun rises. Soon the bees will electrify the oak leaf hydrangea with their buzzing. Lizards come next, looking for the hot rays of the sun. My dogs, Red and Ruby, come out and sit quietly.

The faithful cardinals, displaced by new construction, have made a new nest in the holly trees behind the hydrangea. Their morning song is one of my favorites. High-flying hawks and herons shoot across the sky, dragonflies dance over the pool, and hummingbirds zoom from flower to flower.

I think about how much life this small patch of green supports. The world won't wait long before it starts honking and shouting and closing in on my peace of mind. But in this tiny haven, surrounded by the wide variety of creatures, I trust that the Lord has made this day. The Lord has made these amazing animals. And the Lord has given me the ability to carry the peace of this moment in my heart wherever I go. —Lucy Chambers

I can see the light of a clear blue morning.
Oh, everything's gonna be all right. It's gonna be okay.
—Dolly Parton

JUNE 20

Come-Along Cat

He guides me along the right paths for his name's sake.
—PSALM 23:3 (NIV)

EVERY MORNING, I take my dogs for a walk. Off we go, the three of us, around the neighborhood for a daily stroll. Sometimes even my cat Kiki comes along.

Kiki is a wild little thing. She prefers to come and go by her own schedule. She knows where she can find safety and food, but she also knows that she is free to wander as she likes.

Some mornings, she decides she wants to walk with me and the dogs. She won't walk right next to us; instead, she is about 15 paces behind. She will meow and call for me, and when I turn and look at her, she runs to catch up with us. The further we get from home, the more nervous she becomes. I can tell she is torn. She wants to stay with me, but she is afraid to leave behind the safety and security of familiar territory.

I can feel this struggle in my own faith life sometimes. God will be calling me to follow in new and daring ways, but I am hesitant. It can take a lot to make me step out of my comfort zone in faith. Like Kiki, I want to stick close to the familiar, but I also want to follow where God leads me out in the big world.

Kiki can trust that I won't let her get hurt. So, too, I can trust God to lead me on right paths. I just need to find the courage to get out the door.
—Heather Jepsen

He brings my wandering spirit back when I forsake His ways;
He leads me, for His mercy's sake, in paths of truth and grace.
—Isaac Watts

JUNE 21

Bullfrog Insomnia

Behold, He who keeps Israel shall neither slumber nor sleep.

—PSALM 121:4 (NKJV)

SLEEPING UNDER THE stars in a tent brings to mind wondrous night skies and the gentle chirping of crickets in the distance. Little did I anticipate the nearly deafening cacophony that would accompany our trip to a Christian music festival.

After our busy, eventful day, I figured sleep would come quickly and proceed uninterrupted through the night. I was wrong.

My air mattress inflated obediently, and my battery-operated fan whirred quietly from the edge of my tent. I snuggled into my sleeping bag and prepared to drift off. Suddenly, the sound of a bullfrog emanated from the pond nearby. Then another chimed in. And another.

Despite my aching body and tired mind, I was kept awake as bullfrogs large and small gave a ribbiting performance. The basses croaked low and loud. The soprano bullfrogs intoned much higher. The altos came in a bit off-pitch, and the tenors waxed loudest of all. A bullfrog chorus serenaded all who dared try to sleep in their neighborhood.

As I tossed and turned in my bed, God listened patiently to me. *I'm too old for this, Lord. It's one thing to get dragged out here for 3 days of music and roughing it. It's something else to go through sleep deprivation at the mercy of all these crazy bullfrogs.*

To pass the time and try to calm down, I used my phone to look up bullfrogs on the internet. Perhaps I could find out how soon they might knock off the racket for the night. To my chagrin, I learned of their sometimes weekslong insomnia.

This reminded me that our heavenly Father neither slumbers nor sleeps. He never takes a break while looking after us. He protects our world day and night. Perhaps He watches over us to the rhythm of the insomniac bullfrogs, ready to come to our aid at any hour. All we need to do is ask Him.

Thankfully, the prayer and thoughts of the Father's love calmed me, and I drifted off to sleep. —David L. Winters

Blessed be God, even the Father of our Lord Jesus Christ,
the Father of mercies, and the God of all comfort.
—2 Corinthians 1:3 (NKJV)

178 ALL GOD'S CREATURES

JUNE 22

The Escape Bandits

Whoever dwells in the shelter of the Most High will rest in the shadow of the Almighty. I will say of the LORD, "He is my refuge and my fortress, my God, in whom I trust."

—PSALM 91:1–2 (NIV)

THE PHONE RANG once, then stopped. A few dings followed, so I picked up the phone. A text message from an unknown number caught my eye. "I found your dogs on the road. Your phone went straight to voicemail, and I took them to the animal hospital. Call the hospital to find out how to pick them up." Attached was a picture of the fugitives, Tracy and Nikki, looking guilty as charged. Before I could reply, I received an urgent phone call from the dogsitter. Crying inconsolably, she told me the dogs had run away.

"Are they back with you?" I asked, wanting only to know if they were safely at home.

"Yes, they're here," she said. Kara proceeded to tell me the escape story. "I didn't know they could run away. They were so happy playing outside in the fenced yard, like they did all weekend. Nati was with me the whole time, and I didn't realize the other two were gone."

Tracy and Nikki were expert escape artists who consistently outwitted their humans and tormented their sitters. On the other hand, Nati, my formerly abused street dog, preferred the safety and love of her caregivers to wayward adventures.

I was on vacation trying to regroup after months of personal turmoil. I realized that, like Tracy and Nikki, I was escaping from my personal problems, when my safety and well-being lay in the presence of God. I had allowed my troubles to separate me from my Creator, who wants only the best for me and provides it in unlimited supply.

My return home brought the joy of reuniting with my always faithful Nati and my two prodigal dogs and the realization that everything I needed existed in the holy presence of God. It awaited me for the taking. At home or abroad. —Sonia Frontera

Lord, in times of trouble keep me close to You. Help me realize You are all I need. My safety and my strength lie in You alone.

ALL GOD'S CREATURES 179

JUNE 23

Friends Look Out for Each Other

A friend loves at all times.

—PROVERBS 17:17 (NIV)

AS I TUCKED my four-year-old grandson, Collin, into bed one night, I read him a story (that night we recounted the highlights of Joshua and the battle of Jericho) and prayed with him. His eyes, droopy with sleep, had almost closed when he sat up in bed with a gasp.

"Gigi," he said. "I forgot to release my salamander."

My grands have a small pond in their backyard where they spend hours catching frogs, lizards, and salamanders. They place them into carefully constructed outdoor habitats containing food and water and delight in learning their ways.

Their parents have two rules: First, they must treat every animal kindly. Second, they must release whatever they catch at the end of the day.

Collin remembered this second rule as he was drifting off to sleep.

To be honest, the last thing I wanted to do was go stumbling through the woods in the dark to release a salamander. But rules are rules, and this was a good one.

"I'm glad you remembered, Collin," I said. "We don't want the salamander to die. Let me grab a flashlight, and you can show me where you left it."

I didn't know if salamanders were nocturnal (it turns out they are) or if we woke it up, but when Collin led me to the side of the stream where he'd left the creature, there it sat, gazing up at us with shiny black eyes.

I knew you'd be back, it seemed to say.

Ten minutes later, as I tucked Collin into bed for the second time, he closed his eyes with a satisfied smile.

"Thanks, Gigi," he said. "We had to release him. He was my friend."

"And you were his," I said, hugging him tightly. "Friends look out for each other." —Lori Hatcher

> *It seems they had always been, and always would be,*
> *friends. Time could change, but not that.*
> —Often attributed to A. A. Milne

JUNE 24

Outsize Courage

"The least of you will become a thousand, the smallest a mighty nation."

—ISAIAH 60:22 (NIV)

WHILE A STUDENT, I worked as a security guard. Each evening, I walked through the deserted buildings and grounds of a small manufacturing plant. My job was to ensure there were no intruders, fires, or other disasters. In those duties, I was aided by an unusual deputy—a mockingbird.

Most evenings as I began my rounds, I could see the little fellow perched atop one of the tall lampposts that lined the parking lot. He stood there, all 5 inches of him, with an ego larger than his long tail. He surveyed the property as if every inch of it belonged to him. When a larger bird like a crow or a turkey vulture invaded his airspace, the plucky watchman swooped into action.

Smaller and more agile than his foes, the little mockingbird would dive on them repeatedly, literally flying circles around them. Though often outnumbered, he attacked relentlessly, like a fighter plane ripping into a squadron of bombers. The battle always ended the same. The bigger birds flew away, and Top Gun returned to his perch to await the next strike.

That little fellow taught me that courage is not a function of size or strength, but it is a force multiplier. One courageous person can rout many half-hearted opponents. The same is true in our spiritual battles. Temptations appear overwhelming and irresistible. They aren't. A confident word of faith will banish them. Those who oppose the Gospel and even your own efforts to live a righteous life often appear to have the upper hand. They may have the affirmation of the world and the backing of popular culture.

So what? The One who is in you is greater than he who is in the world.
—Lawrence W. Wilson

Guide me, O Thou great Jehovah,
Pilgrim thro' this barren land.
I am weak, but Thou art mighty,
Hold me with Thy pow'rful hand.
—Thomas Hastings

JUNE 25

The Forbidden Mulch

*No temptation has overtaken you that is not common to man.
God is faithful, and he will not let you be tempted beyond
your ability, but with the temptation he will also provide
the way of escape, that you may be able to endure it.*

—1 CORINTHIANS 10:13 (ESV)

GALEN, LEAVE IT." My giant Leonberger stuck his head through the short fence and leaned forward, reaching for the coveted chunk of mulch. I walked toward him, knowing that he wouldn't listen to my command, and that I would be too late to enforce it.

Galen pulled back, the wood chunk clutched in his mouth. The three-year-old didn't realize that chewing on that block of wood was much more dangerous than chewing a normal stick. It could break into splinters that would cut his mouth or, if swallowed, damage his throat and stomach.

So despite his happiness as he lay down and began to chew the wood, I had to tell him to drop it. This time he obeyed and released the wood, accepting the treat I offered as a reward.

When I returned the chunk of wood to the other side of the fence, I spotted an equally large wood block on the ground at my feet. It sat, easily reachable, on our side of the fence. Galen could've picked it up at any time, yet he went through all the effort of forcing his large head through the fence and stretching as far as he could for another piece of wood. The forbidden piece of wood.

I suddenly had a clearer understanding of Adam and Eve in the garden of Eden. God told them to eat the fruit from any tree in the garden except one. Given that they were in a perfect paradise, I'm sure all the fruit was amazing. But since God forbade Adam and Eve to eat from one particular tree, that became the fruit they most wanted.

Was I striving to have or achieve something God had forbidden? I hoped not. Because like me protecting Galen, God only forbids that which would cause me harm. —Jerusha Agen

*For because he himself has suffered when tempted,
he is able to help those who are being tempted.*
—Hebrews 2:18 (ESV)

JUNE 26

Fireflies, Strawberry Pies

I remember the days of long ago; I meditate on all your works and consider what your hands have done.

—PSALM 143:5 (NIV)

WHENEVER MY MOTHER saw fireflies, she would sing this little lyric, "Fireflies bring strawberry pies." As a small child I formed the mental image of a squadron of fireflies sailing low over the lawn on a summer evening, holding aloft a fresh-baked strawberry pie, steam still rising from the flaky crust. Only much later in life did I learn that fireflies break hibernation and begin flying at about the same time that wild strawberries ripen. What I'd always assumed to be a nonsensical ditty was actually a nugget of folk wisdom: when you see fireflies, it's time to go strawberry picking. Fireflies bring strawberry pies.

And now on this soft summer evening, watching fireflies drifting above the fields, like torches being carried by a distant search party, my memory clicks on, and I smile and remember my mom. What a dazzling, breathtaking gift of God is memory.

Sometimes I misuse the gift. I store up unpleasant memories. I hold on to hurts and humiliations, filing them away for future reference. In the morning I tear the scab off old wounds and feel their pain all over again. What a waste of God's precious gift. I need to let go of unhappy, unhealthy memories.

But this evening, all the memories are good. I am a child again, chasing fireflies on the lawn with a Mason jar with holes punched in the lid. Frolicking with the dog. Having water-pistol battles with my big sister. The smell of citronella candles. Falling asleep under a mulch pile of Superman comics. Life is full of memories good and bad, and we choose which we shall dwell on. This evening, by God's grace, I choose the good ones. I enjoy the ethereal lights bouncing above the gently undulating grass, like so many pixies flitting about holding their little lamps. There is a soft breeze blowing, my gardening chores are done for the day, and there is a strawberry pie in my future. —Louis Lotz

Nothing is ever really lost to us as long as we remember it.
—Lucy Maud Montgomery

JUNE 27

At the Top of the To-Do List

"The LORD your God in your midst, the Mighty One, will save;
He will rejoice over you with gladness, He will quiet you
with His love, He will rejoice over you with singing."

—ZEPHANIAH 3:17 (NKJV)

ONE PARTICULARLY BUSY day, I was bent over, petting my dog, Honey, in our entryway as she greeted me. I had just returned from the store and was distracted, thinking about the next task at hand, an online meeting I was running late for. Honey, as usual, had brought me a favorite toy and was wagging her tail with great exuberance. To further gain my attention, she was bouncing along in front of me as I headed toward my office.

"Hi, Honey-baby. How are you?" I said, planning to brush her off so I could get to my meeting, but then I heard myself say, "What's on your to-do list today?" And do you know what? Honey just bounced around some more, showing me her toy. In fact, at any given moment, my steadfast and loving dog's entire to-do list is to pay attention to me. She never fails to welcome me home, ever. She keeps an eye on me even while she is curled in a ball on her bed. If I leave the room, Honey follows me just to be sure she won't miss a single part of my day. Her to-do list, if she had one, would simply have my name on it, nothing more.

The way Honey shows up in my life is a lot like the way God is always present and available to me: mighty to save, rejoicing over me, quieting me with His love. I spend a good deal of my life rushing about, attending to my to-do list and the tyranny of much that is urgent. It can leave me feeling scattered, stressed out, unfocused. I know that none of this will change, however, unless I settle into God's saving presence and the quiet peace of His gladness and love for me. God's love can completely change my focus. —Katy W. Sundararajan

> Walk of Faith: *As you go through your to-do list today,*
> *envision God's to-do list with your name at the top.*

JUNE 28

Snake in the House

"Have I not commanded you? Be strong and courageous. Do not be afraid; do not be discouraged, for the LORD your God will be with you wherever you go."

—JOSHUA 1:9 (NIV)

BOYS, COME QUICKLY! There's a snake in the house."
Despite the panic in my voice, those words fell on deaf ears. My teenage boys said it was "rad" that there was a snake, but honestly, they didn't want to get close to it any more than I did.

I knew I had to get the snake out of the house. If I didn't, it would find a way to crawl into a hole, crack, or crevice, and I would be up all night wondering where it was and if it was coming to get me. (It was a garden snake, nothing dangerous. But that didn't matter.) My husband was at work, so that left me to do it. There was no way out of it. *Why did it have to be a snake?*

I said a short prayer, asking God to give me courage, then grabbed a plastic tub and a lid and corralled the thing into a corner. I maneuvered it into the bin, and in a short time had it contained.

I told one of my boys to open the door, and I ran out with the snake in the plastic container, putting it into the grass as far away from the house as possible. Whew! Mission accomplished: the snake was back outside where it belonged.

Adrenaline coursed through my veins, and my legs shook. Regardless, I had done it. God was right there beside me, giving me the courage to face my daunting task. While I never want to face removing another snake from the house, I now know I can if I have to.

Courage was doing what I didn't want to do and acting as if I could do it all along. And as I discovered that day, with God's help, there is never a reason not to feel courageous. —Heather Spiva

Walk of Faith: *Is there a situation in your life that you have been dreading? Ask for God's help and, if you can, take the first necessary step to address that situation. Proceed as if God is right next to you—because He is.*

JUNE 29

A Stroke of Luck

Do not be astonished at this; for the hour is coming when all who are in their graves will hear his voice.

—**JOHN 5:28** (NRSVUE)

ONE DAY BEFORE my wedding, our elderly black poodle looked up, met my eyes, and tipped over sideways on the porch. Mom scooped up Missy and took her to the vet while I entertained out-of-town guests. Mom returned home without our dog. The vet had determined Missy had suffered a catastrophic stroke, there was no chance of recovery, and the best thing would be to put her down. But Mom refused to add "our dog died" to the story of my wedding and convinced the vet to keep Missy until Monday.

Friends and family gathered, we rehearsed and dined, I slept (a little), got dressed, wedded, and attended the reception, and then my new husband and I left for our honeymoon. Tuesday, our coastal road trip brought us back through town. As we approached Mom's house, I spotted a curly-haired head in the front window. Missy? Mom told us that when she arrived at the vet's clinic Monday morning, she found a sheepish, smiling vet and a "miraculously" recovered Missy.

This isn't a story about resurrection, exactly, but it is a story about hope and expectation. At our wedding, the homily referenced the wedding at Cana, where Jesus turned water into very good wine. Our pastor claimed the story promises that Jesus will surprise us with good things, even when the outlook is bleak. "Be expectant," he charged us. Over 30 years of marriage, I came to expect good things. I was not disappointed, and even though my future sometimes feels bleak in the years following my husband's passing, I cling to the anticipation of the blessings God has yet to bestow.

We enjoyed one more delightful year with Missy. That plentiful good wine at Cana eventually ran out, but in the meantime, oh the party the wedding guests enjoyed! Our best celebrations are mere foretastes of the day when "all who are in their graves hear His voice and come out." That will be a party worth the wait! —Susie Colby

You might never have been, but you are because the party wouldn't have been complete without you.
—Frederick Buechner

JUNE 30

Down but Not Out

Oh, that I had the wings of a dove! I would fly away and be at rest.

—PSALM 55:6 (NIV)

*T*HWACK! I WAS washing our car. All the while I was cleaning it, I had heard the squawk of two orioles fighting over territory. It was during one of these aerial fights that one dived right into the car window.

"Oh no!" I cried. I looked at the ground, and the bird just lay there. *What should I do?* I remembered that there was a nearby bird sanctuary and called them. The volunteer rescuer was very calm and helpful over the phone.

"Just let the bird be. If the bird doesn't move in about an hour, then call me back. You might have to bring it in."

I went back outside, not wanting to disturb the bird, but it hadn't moved. I returned inside, tried to get involved in another project, and then returned to check on the bird. I continued this for a while, all the time praying that in one of my checks, the bird would be gone.

Sure enough, almost exactly an hour from the time the bird hurt itself, it was gone and had flown away.

The bird reminded me of the time our dear friends received devastating news that the husband had ALS (also known as Lou Gehrig's disease). They were shocked and stunned. The husband sent out an email to his friends and asked that we let them be for a while until they processed the situation. While we waited, we prayed and allowed our friends to go through their grieving process as they faced a changed future.

It took some time, but eventually, after processing the situation, they were able to discuss it with friends. Just like the oriole, they needed the time to regroup.

Anyone may be downed by life circumstances. Sometimes all we need is time to seek God and process with Him the plan He has for us.
—Virginia Ruth

Gracious God, thank You that You have plans for us. May
we turn to You when life circumstances knock us down.
May You lift us up with renewed hope. Amen.

ALL GOD'S CREATURES

JULY 1

God Wink

"For I know the plans I have for you," declares the LORD, "plans to prosper you and not to harm you, plans to give you hope and a future."

—JEREMIAH 29:11 (NIV)

LOSING OUR PAPILLON, Lucy, to cancer was hard, but when our 22-year-old cat died, it broke me. Inconsolable, I didn't want another pet, but my daughter, Bree, insisted that that was *exactly* what I needed.

She began texting pictures of adoptable kittens daily, and while hesitant, I found myself in PetSmart one day staring at empty cages. On the way out, I crossed paths with Linda, a woman who ran a local shelter. She explained that while she didn't have the kittens yet, she expected a litter soon and would send pictures.

Although a week passed without word from her, I remained steadfast, encouraged when I received my Guideposts *All God's Creatures* magazine in the mail. I opened the July/August 2023 issue to find an orange kitten on the cover! Seconds later my phone vibrated with a photo from Linda. An *orange* kitten with white freckles across her nose beamed back at me, along with Linda's promise to contact me once she received the litter.

In anticipation of meeting Piper (yes, I named her), I bought toys and treats and gazed endlessly at her precious photo. But a week later I got bad news. Linda apologized and explained that not only had the kittens not arrived to be vetted for adoption, but the owners weren't returning her calls. Devastated and heartbroken, I gave up.

Even though Bree continued to find adoptable kittens, I declined. I simply couldn't get the freckle-faced Piper out of my head. But on June 30, I got an emphatic text from Linda. "I've got her!" Piper and her littermates had miraculously arrived!

The next morning, after reading my *All God's Creatures* devotional—the one with the orange kitten on the cover—Bree and I picked up Piper.

I marvel at God's wondrous hand in bringing us together! Despite the incredible highs and lows along the way, He followed through on His plan to give me hope—and a future—with Piper! Definitely a God wink.
—Hallie Lee

Thank You, Lord, for Your grand plans!

JULY 2

When Fear Strikes

"Be strong and of good courage, do not fear nor be afraid of them; for the LORD your God, He is the One who goes with you. He will not leave you nor forsake you."

—DEUTERONOMY 31:6 (NKJV)

I'D HEARD THE expression "playing possum." But that summer I got to see this adage put into action. Or lack of action, as it were.

I was drying dishes in the kitchen when I heard our golden retrievers in the backyard, frantically barking. I went outside to investigate. There, I spotted a motionless gray animal beside the fence. Inching forward, I realized it was an opossum, its body curled up stiffly, its eyes closed, the mouth on its pointy white face open to reveal numerous sharp teeth. It didn't move at all, even when I approached cautiously.

"Oh, the poor thing is dead," I said. It didn't appear as if the dogs had hurt it. Perhaps the unfortunate creature had been ill and stumbled into our yard, where it took its last breath. I herded the dogs inside, opting to deal with the remains later.

Sometime that evening, before the unpleasant job was done, I looked out back, only to see the animal get up and scarper away into the woods. That's when it dawned on me that it had been "playing possum"! An involuntary response to fear, triggered by the dogs barking and a perceived predatory attack, the frightened possum had fallen to the ground, its body temporarily immobile.

Playing dead may be an effective way to handle fear when you're a possum, but it's not the most effective strategy for me. Playing dead indicates that one is alone and defenseless. Yet, I know that I am never alone in my circumstances. That doesn't mean that I will never experience fear in my life, but God has promised that He will never leave me alone, no matter what. He will calm me, comfort me, and guide me. Never do I have to be frozen in fear when I have my Protector beside me. —Peggy Frezon

Focus on Christ instead of your fears, and your fears will begin to fade.
—Billy Graham

190   ALL GOD'S CREATURES

JULY 3

Dragonfly Rescue

A generous person will prosper; whoever refreshes others will be refreshed.

—PROVERBS 11:25 (NIV)

OUR NEIGHBORHOOD IS blessed with dragonflies. These marvelous insects help keep the mosquito population under control, with each insect consuming about one hundred mosquitos a day. We were visiting a neighbor one morning when she said, "Let me show you something. I found it on my patio." What she showed us was a dragonfly. It was clearly alive; but it appeared frozen, unable to move, perhaps a victim of the Louisiana heat. Our neighbor brought out a plate of water and slipped it under the dragonfly. The insect did not fly away but rather perched itself on the edge. We all hoped that making some water available might help revive it.

For the next two days, we checked on the dragonfly. It remained still, but it clung to life. Then one morning our neighbor reported, "Today it just flew away." What our neighbor did was such a simple gesture. Anyone could have done it. It did not take special skill or knowledge. It took only a minute or two of her time—but to that dragonfly it was lifesaving.

As the playwright, poet, and religious writer Hannah More (1745–1833) put it, "One kernel is felt in a hogshead; one drop of water helps to swell the ocean; a spark of fire helps to give light to the world. None are too small, too feeble, too poor to be of service. Think of this and act."

The dragonfly and its fate made me question myself. How often do I pause and take the time to do the little things that might make a difference in someone's life, such as making a phone call, sending a message, mailing a card, stopping in my walk to greet a neighbor, or rescuing a dragonfly? I need to be more aware of the power of little things. —Harold Nichols

The King will reply, "Truly I tell you, whatever you did for one of the least of these brothers and sisters of mine, you did for me."
—Matthew 25:40 (NIV)

JULY 4

Gentle Giants

Let your gentleness be evident to all. The Lord is near.

—PHILIPPIANS 4:5 (NIV)

I LOVE PARADES. THE high school bands always put a pep in my step as I watch majorettes twirl their batons and hear the instruments, especially the drums. Last summer, my husband, Tom, and I went to the Fourth of July parade and got there extra early so we could sit up close.

Little ones waited on the sidelines to catch candy thrown from fire trucks, and rodeo queens smiled and waved from vintage convertibles. But when I saw the Clydesdale horses and heard the *clomp, clomp, clomp* of their feet, that was the highlight of the celebration for me.

Veterans followed the band, marching in step with patriotic songs. A man dressed as Uncle Sam stood in the center of a large open wagon with patriots waving flags—but what brought majesty to the celebration were the large Clydesdale horses that pulled the heavy wagon.

The horses' regal "feathered" feet feature long flowing hair around hooves that can reach the size of dinner plates. This unique feature gives these draft horses an exquisite beauty. Their gorgeous manes and a height of up to 8 feet almost took my breath away.

Clydesdale horses are called gentle giants. As big and strong as they are, they are easy to train, and they have a gentle demeanor. They remain peaceful under duress and were originally used as warhorses for their strength and because they stayed calm and in control through tough circumstances. Later, many became farm horses, always willing to learn and do the task at hand.

This characteristic reminds me of Moses, who was called a meek man (Numbers 12:3, ESV)—*meek* meaning "power under control." A strong leader, he allowed God to take the reins of his life and lead him.

I can't wait for the next parade when I sit on the sidelines and look *up* at the Clydesdales who teach us the importance of strength with gentleness. —Kathleen R. Ruckman

Nothing is so strong as gentleness, and nothing is so gentle as real strength.
—Saint Francis de Sales

JULY 5

Bring Others Joy

*Therefore encourage one another and build each
other up, just as in fact you are doing.*

—1 THESSALONIANS 5:11 (NIV)

THERE IS A clear demarcation of responsibilities in our household when it comes to our pooch. I feed and groom Snowy, our Maltese mix, and take care of his medical needs. My 12-year-old son picks up after the dog does his business in the backyard and accompanies me on walks, and my husband replenishes the dog food in the pantry every month. Some of our duties also happen to align with our personalities. Since my husband and son are more energetic than I am, they play fetch with Snowy and make up all kinds of silly games that make them roll with laughter. Our clever furry friend knows what to expect from each member of the family, so I was surprised when one afternoon he dropped his favorite toy at my feet, urging me with excited barks to play with him. Hesitantly, I threw the stuffed shark toy in the backyard and watched as Snowy dashed into the bushes to retrieve it. After I'd played fetch with him for a few minutes, a smile appeared on my face. Snowy looked content, as if he had achieved his goal and settled down at my feet, his eyes begging me to pet him.

Was it possible that Snowy was aware of my health condition? Recently diagnosed with depression, I had been experiencing bouts of sadness, lying in bed for long periods of time. I wondered if my dog was trying, in his own way, to lift my spirits. Through his actions, I learned how to help others like me who suffer from depression. Like Snowy, who never left my side when I could not get out of bed, I can support friends dealing with mental health conditions by letting them know that I'm there for them. I can offer to do things with them that bring them joy, refrain from giving unsolicited advice, and pray for them, pointing them to the Comforter and Counselor who's always with them. —Mabel Ninan

Walk of Faith: *Share an encouraging Bible verse through an email
or text with a friend who suffers from a health issue,
and let them know you're thinking of them.*

JULY 6

Bon Appétit

So I commend the enjoyment of life, because there is nothing better for a person under the sun than to eat and drink and be glad. Then joy will accompany them in their toil all the days of the life God has given them under the sun.

—ECCLESIASTES 8:15 (NIV)

THE BLACK SWALLOWTAIL caterpillars had emerged from the eggs on our fennel plants, and at first we could barely see them because they were so tiny. But David and I watched with glee as these gorgeous green-and-yellow caterpillars seemed to triple their size overnight. We loved watching as one made its way to the edge of a thin fennel branch, reared backward seemingly on its hind legs, and held on to the tip of the branch with its front legs. Next, the caterpillar proceeded to slurp the needle-thin fennel leaf until it had vanished in just seconds. Once the caterpillar decimated one branch, it moved to another. It seemed clear that the caterpillar was enjoying its feast.

We left our caterpillars for a quick trip to see our children. I excitedly prepared sugar cookies rolled in sprinkles, miniature chocolate-chip cookie bites, snickerdoodles, and a delectable three-layer strawberry cake. Unfortunately, the temperature in the car melted the frosting on the cake, and the layers slid apart. Bumping and jostling down the road formed a crevice in it the size of the Grand Canyon. I was so disappointed when I saw the cake's condition at our first rest stop.

Our family of nine converged from three states for dinner at a restaurant, and, despite my misgivings about my cake, our sons and two pregnant daughters encouraged us to bring it in, along with the other desserts. We shared cookies with our waitress, and she brought spoons for the dilapidated cake. We enjoyed our own feast as we devoured bits and pieces of cake, and everyone declared it was the most delicious strawberry cake they'd ever had.

God gives such good gifts. Whether it's a delicious, sap-filled green leaf for a caterpillar or a scrambled strawberry cake shared with family, I'm so grateful for His gifts. —Julie Lavender

Walk of Faith: *Whip up or buy a favorite treat today and share it as a gift of fellowship with someone who might need it.*

JULY 7

The Bear's Lesson

I know whom I have believed, and am persuaded that he is able to keep that which I have committed unto him against that day.

—2 TIMOTHY 1:12 (KJV)

WHILE VISITING JENNY Lake Lodge in Wyoming, I thought I saw a large black dog in the distance running straight toward the lodge. A Newfoundland, I supposed, based on its size. It was huge and running fast. But as the "dog" drew nearer, I realized it wasn't a dog at all. It was a black bear—and a big one. Both excited and a little fearful, I rose from the rocking chair, exclaiming, "It's a bear! Here comes a bear!" People milling around reacted in various ways. Some paused to see what I was pointing to. Others ignored me and went about their business. One or two even regarded me as though I was a nut case. Were they not even curious? Didn't they believe in bears?

Later, after the huge bear raced past the lodge—giving several attentive visitors a thrill and a great photo opportunity—I reflected upon the account of the blind man whom Jesus healed as recorded in the Gospel of John. Some believed the man's excited testimony. Others did not. There were those who witnessed the miracle and yet insisted the man had not been born blind at all. His parents were even brought in for questioning. There stood our Lord and Savior in their very midst—the Son of the living God. Despite what they'd seen and heard, some didn't believe. Or didn't want to. And yet others, having witnessed the miracle for themselves, believed in Jesus because of what He'd said and done.

There will always be scoffers. As Christians, we need to accept that. Just as some refused to see the galloping bear headed straight toward them, many will deny Jesus. But there will always be those of us who pay attention and believe in Him. —Shirley Raye Redmond

There are none so blind as those who will not see.
—John Heywood

ALL GOD'S CREATURES 195

JULY 8

Jumping to Conclusions

"The LORD sees not as man sees: man looks on the outward appearance, but the LORD looks on the heart."

—1 SAMUEL 16:7 (ESV)

THE RETREAT CENTER was characterized by what some call decayed elegance. Others might call it deferred maintenance. But the overgrown decorative pond was a nice place for contemplation. As I sat on a bench, deep in thought, a commotion in the pond startled me. I yelped and jumped! A splash, then concentric waves disturbed the water's surface. My adrenaline rush melted into body-shaking laughter, equal parts relief and embarrassment.

Immediately up the path came a woman I'd seen earlier in the retreat. She was stylish and elegantly dressed in a sophisticated outfit in a red hue I wouldn't be brave enough to wear even as lipstick. Here I was, in jeans and a T-shirt.

I was intimidated, and I had been avoiding her all weekend.

My squeal had brought this woman to help, but when she found me in one piece and laughing, she began to laugh too. Her eyes asked, "What's so funny?" I pointed to an ornamental green statue of a toad on a rock. "There are frogs in this pond. One just startled me." She told me a story about her son and a frog. I shared a story about chasing frogs with my dad. Soon we were sitting on rocks by the pond, getting our clothes a bit muddy, chatting like old friends.

She pointed back to the little green statue. "Who do you think put *that* here?" she asked. Just then the "statue" leaped into the pond. Splashed and wet, we laughed together again.

Unlike the spotted or colorful frogs of my childhood "hunts," this frog—which I discovered was an American bullfrog—was one consistent color. I had mistaken it for a fake, a mere garden ornament, because of its perfect-seeming appearance, monochromatic and poised on the rock. I had misjudged my new friend in a similar way. I had perceived her put-together appearance as fakery because I had been intimidated, but as we sat together now, I appreciated her friendliness, as demonstrated when she came quickly to save me from a fearsome frog. —Susie Colby

If you judge people, you have no time to love them.
—Mother Teresa

JULY 9

Just Ask!

If any of you lacks wisdom, you should ask God, who gives generously to all without finding fault, and it will be given to you.

—JAMES 1:5 (NIV)

WHILE WALKING ALONG the creek near my home, I saw a lovely bird swimming against the current. It was a warm gray color with a rust-colored head. Its slender red beak had a hook on the end of it. With its neck stretched forward, it pushed against the water and occasionally dove beneath the surface to reappear farther upstream. Moments later, I saw another bird of the same kind but with very different colors. This one had dramatic black and white plumage; the black feathers glowed a deep green when the sunlight hit them just right. I took pictures of both birds and when I got home, I went to my computer to learn their names.

I belong to a local hiking group, and we have a page on Facebook. I posted a picture of the birds and wrote, "Calling our local bird experts! Will you please help me identify these?" It didn't take long to receive an answer, and I learned the two birds were a pair of common mergansers, a type of duck. The one with the rust-colored head was the female and the gorgeous black-and-white bird was the male.

I couldn't help comparing the ease of getting answers on the "information superhighway" to the ease of getting answers from my Father in heaven. Both require only that I ask. In the case of the internet, I always double-check any info I get there. There are plenty of pictures of common mergansers to compare to my own. But in the case of answers from God, I have confidence that whatever I receive from Him needs no fact-check or corroboration. God is consistently truthful. He gives me answers generously, without stopping to say, "That's a silly question!" or "You should know this already!" He just gives. And everything He gives is good. —Marianne Campbell

> *Come, my soul, with ev'ry care.*
> *Jesus loves to answer prayer.*
> —John Newton

JULY 10

A Phantom in the Garden

Do not conform to the pattern of this world.

—ROMANS 12:2 (NIV)

THE ALMIGHTY MUST have an inordinate fondness for bugs. He certainly made enough of them—millions of different species, and ten quintillion individual bugs worldwide, give or take, according to *Smithsonian* magazine. Ten quintillion, that's a ten followed by eighteen zeroes. A billion billions. That's a lot of bugs.

One of God's most fascinating bug creations is the fellow I'm watching just now, a walking stick. One of roughly twenty-five hundred members of the *Phasmatodea* order—from the Greek word for phantom—the walking stick is about three inches long and ambles slowly through life on six spindly legs. He is a defenseless little herbivore, and you'd think he'd be easy pickings for predators, but thanks to some nifty camouflage, he is virtually invisible. Oh, look at that! An ant crawls along the length of the walking stick, from back to front, using him as a bridge from one leaf to another. The walking stick is so perfectly camouflaged that even fellow insects don't realize he is there. I watch him for a good 5 minutes, and he doesn't move a muscle. He just sits there, hiding in plain sight on my wife's Autumn Joy sedum, looking for all the world like a bumpy, wrinkled, greenish-brown twig. He blends in perfectly.

"Do not conform to the pattern of this world," says the Apostle Paul. But all too often that is exactly what I do. I conform. I go along to get along, striving to be like everyone else, keeping my Christian faith neatly folded in a drawer somewhere deep inside me. I remember how, when I was a small child, my grandmother said to me that I must always keep my faith hidden in my heart. But lately I'm thinking that my faith is a little too well hidden. It's time I open that drawer and let my faith out for the world to see. A walking stick needs to blend in, but faith needs expression. —Louis Lotz

The will of God will not take us where the grace of God cannot sustain us.
—Billy Graham

ALL GOD'S CREATURES

JULY 11

Let Me Have It

Cast all your anxiety on him because he cares for you.

—1 PETER 5:7 (NIV)

MY ADULT SON was making a decision that I didn't think was the right one. When I expressed my concerns, he said, "Mom, I love you, and I respect your opinion, but my mind is made up. I'm going to do what I think is best." Ever since that conversation, I'd been having trouble sleeping because of my worries.

As I ruminated on the problem, Piper, my Pomeranian-poodle mix, dropped a toy at my feet. She loved to play fetch. Thankful for the distraction, I threw the toy, and she dashed after it. She brought it back, but when I reached for it to throw it again, she held on tighter. I tried to wrestle the toy from her mouth. She growled playfully and dodged my hand. "Silly girl," I said. "You want me to play, but you won't let me have it." Immediately, Piper dropped the toy into my hand and wagged her tail. I wasn't sure why she'd changed her mind, but I threw the toy. Piper fetched it, but again, she didn't want to release it into my hand. Rather than attempt to wrestle it from her, I quietly said, "Let me have it." She dropped it into my hand. We played fetch for several more minutes, and every time, Piper refused to give me the toy until I said those four words.

As I rubbed Piper's silky fur, my mind drifted back to my problem. I realized that I hadn't talked to God about it at all. I'd just tried to handle it on my own. I knew that God wanted to help me with my problems, but I also knew He won't wrestle them out of my hands. Instead, He waits patiently for me to see my need for Him, and then He whispers quietly, "Let Me have it."

I bowed my head and talked to God. I laid the situation at His feet. That night, I slept well for the first time in days. —Diane Stark

Lord, help me to remember that You want to carry my burdens.
All I have to do is let You have them. Amen.

JULY 12

Follow My Lead

*"Watch me," he told them. "Follow my lead. When I
get to the edge of the camp, do exactly as I do."*

—JUDGES 7:17 (NIV)

BROTHER AND SISTER poodle mixes, Hank and Hazel, started coming to my house three times a week for daycare when they were puppies. I picked them up in the morning, then delivered them home in the evening, meaning they got into and out of the back of my station wagon twice each day. It was no big deal to lift their little bodies into the space, but getting them out at the other end of the ride was another story. A lift back and two barking, excited puppies anxious to jump out was a recipe for disaster; it could have resulted in a broken leg from the fall or an escapee dashing away.

I resolved to teach them to calmly wait for me to lift the tailgate, grab their leashes, and verbally release them so they could jump down safely. It took several months of standing and waiting for their barking and wiggling to subside, but now they sit nicely and await my OK to proceed on to adventure.

Sometime later, their "nephew," Marvin, started coming to play on occasion too. Now I had three dogs to release from the car. To my surprise and delight, it took only a few days of traveling with his older friends for Marvin to also sit calmly and wait for release. He watched Hank and Hazel and followed their lead! They showed him how to do the right thing.

I wonder who might be watching *me* and following *my* lead. What would they learn? Am I setting a good example and displaying my Christian faith by helping others and keeping to godly behavior? I will try, with God's help. —Kim Sheard

*Lord God, others may be watching me to see You. Help me to set a good
example so that if they follow my lead, they will be blessed. Amen.*

200   ALL GOD'S CREATURES

JULY 13

The Thoughts That Buzz Around

Whatever is true, whatever is honorable, whatever is just, whatever is pure, whatever is lovely, whatever is commendable, if there is any excellence, if there is anything worthy of praise, think about these things.

—**PHILIPPIANS 4:8** (ESV)

A MOSQUITO IS probably no one's favorite animal or even favorite insect. But like all animals, it has a purpose, even if it's just a place in the food chain. When I'm outside sitting on the deck and one flies up, I can admire its small, sheer wings and feathery antennae. I can appreciate its large, compound eyes. But then, it jabs its proboscis into my skin and takes a painful bite of my arm, and all of a sudden, I'm not its biggest fan! One positive thought—for such a tiny bug, the mosquito clearly catches my attention.

This makes me think of the pesky little thoughts that buzz around my head, thoughts that may seem insignificant but by their persistence become unavoidable. Thoughts like *I can't do it* and *I'm afraid* and *God doesn't care about this situation* all take painful nips at my best intentions.

To combat the mosquitoes from getting inside the house, we've placed a long mesh screen over the doorway to the deck. When we walk through it, the sides part, and then strong magnets pull the ends back together behind us. Amazingly, this rather simple contraption has proven effective and invaluable in keeping those bugs at bay.

Likewise, to combat the pesky thoughts, I need a similar barrier for my mind. Good thing that God has given us just such protection. His Word reminds me to intentionally focus my mind on all things good, honorable, and praiseworthy.

Like the mosquito, pesky thoughts can serve a purpose. They catch my attention, strengthen my resolve, and compel me to improve. But I don't need to let them penetrate and take a negative hold on me. When negative thoughts threaten, I just put up my own impermeable screen. Suddenly, I am surrounded by all that is beautiful and positive and worthy of my attention. —Peggy Frezon

A positive thinker does not refuse to recognize the negative; he refuses to dwell in it.
—Norman Vincent Peale

JULY 14

A Monsoon Miracle

*"Look at the birds of the air; they do not sow or reap or
store away in barns, and yet your heavenly Father feeds
them. Are you not much more valuable than they?"*

—MATTHEW 6:26 (NIV)

I HAD BEEN experiencing a spiritually dry season. Doubts about whether God cared about me swirled in my mind. Desperate, I asked for a sign that He still loved me and wanted to communicate with me.

Two weeks after I prayed that silent prayer, I flew to India to visit my parents. I enjoyed the cloudy skies, sudden splashing of rain, and sweet smell of wet dirt that characterized the monsoon season.

As I was on my way to my sister's house in a cab one rainy day, I thought of peacocks, because their mating season coincides with India's monsoons. The males display their emerald-green tail feathers in a fan formation as part of a mating dance to attract females. Though I had the privilege of watching the peacock shimmy quite a few times during my childhood in India, I wished I could see it one more time during this trip. Peacocks roam the wilderness in some parts of India, and they can also be found wandering on rooftops or in courtyards in villages and in some parks in urban areas. Still, the chances of me witnessing a peacock in the city of Hyderabad were slim.

When my cab turned the corner on a street that hugged a huge park, I looked through the park fence and spotted a big bird with a bright blue neck, its turquoise tail feathers fanned out. I sat up in my seat and stared at the spectacular peacock till my cab drove past the park. As I processed what had occurred, I thanked God with tears running down my cheeks. There it was—a miraculous sign that God cared about me. He never stopped listening and speaking to me. Everything about me mattered to Him, even a silly wish to see a bird dance. —Mabel Ninan

*Father, I'm in awe of Your steadfast love and goodness toward me.
You know my every need, concern, and desire, and You satisfy me
with good things. Thank You for taking care of me. Amen.*

JULY 15

Created with Purpose

*For we are God's handiwork, created in Christ Jesus to do good works,
which God prepared in advance for us to do.*

—EPHESIANS 2:10 (NIV)

BIRD ANTICS AMUSE me. Each has a little quirk, a God-given uniqueness setting it apart. The pileated woodpecker belts out his Woody Woodpecker laugh. The robin yanks a long worm from the soil, while the towhee jumps forward and back, scratching the dirt to find hidden seeds. Blue jays and doves forage on the ground, while cardinals and chickadees prefer the feeder.

Today, however, I was curious about the way a red-bellied woodpecker ate from the feeder outside my window. I'd noticed him before at the more distant feeder and thought he looked odd hanging onto its edge like a gymnast doing tricks on uneven bars. Up close, I saw he held onto the feeding tray with his feet and tucked his tail underneath. Odd as it looked, he seemed balanced as he gobbled the birdseed.

With my voracious need to learn everything about wildlife, I googled my questions. The answer filled me with awe once more of our Creator's amazing designs. A woodpecker's tail feathers bend easily because of larger muscles and vertebrae in their lower area than those of perching birds. Combined with stiffer tail feathers, their tails help anchor them. On top of that, God equipped their feet with two toes forward and two back, designed to hold onto tree trunks, instead of the normal bird feet with three toes forward and one back.

Watching my feeder, I witnessed firsthand these planned purposes at work. And I couldn't help wondering what unique things God fitted me with to do the work He put me here to do. Besides the obvious workings of my fingers to type and my eyes to see His creation, He endowed me with curiosity, a love for animals, and a family who brought me up to care for His world. How amazing I am—created in my Father's image, fit to do His work for His glory. —Cathy Mayfield

*Jesus, may I honor the uniqueness You've given me by serving
You with all I am. Amen.*

ALL GOD'S CREATURES 203

JULY 16

A Song after the Storm

Weeping may stay for the night, but rejoicing comes in the morning.

—PSALM 30:5 (NIV)

THE LAST TWO days have brought much-needed rain after a period of intense summer heat here in Florida. When we came home from church this afternoon, I immediately noticed the beautiful chorus being sung by all my backyard birds. In particular, the cardinals living just past my fence line chirped a gentle song. Their melody almost seemed to rejoice that the rain clouds had parted and the sun had reappeared after all the storms.

After listening to the cardinals for a while, I began to think about how quiet these birds become during the rain. Wondering why that may be, I did some research and learned that birds' calls may be difficult for other birds to hear over the sound of storms. Birds also tend to have a difficult time flying in bad weather, so they will stay put quietly until the storm passes. How still and strange the world becomes when the sky grows dark and the birds fall quiet!

In the same way, the storms of life sometimes leave me hunkered down. It's easy to feel as though I must take shelter and stay quiet until the storm passes. Sometimes I struggle to feel heard—or to hear the voice of God—over the sound of the wind, rain, and thunder.

But as I listen to those cardinals sing today, I'm reminded of a beautiful truth: no storm remains forever. Night always gives way to dawn. Creation will once again come alive in a song to its Creator. Though I may have to wait for some storms to pass, I can take courage knowing a song of rejoicing is coming. —Ashley Clark

The early morning hour should be dedicated to praise:
do not the birds set us the example?
—Charles H. Spurgeon

JULY 17

Everlasting Covenant

"Incline your ear, and come to Me. Hear, and your soul shall live; and I will make an everlasting covenant with you—the sure mercies of David."

—ISAIAH 55:3 (NKJV)

BIRDIE THE LOVEBIRD flew out of her cage and onto my shoulder. I'd been away traveling for several days and worried a little about her reaction. Sometimes, the normally well-behaved pet would take a peck at my earlobe when I returned from "long" absences. On this occasion, she spared me the bruise and spoiled me by whispering sweet nothings in my ear. Her tweets are music to me, letting me know she is well and happy.

Our time together began years ago, when I received a troubling call from Illinois. A friend, Andy, had been felled by a stroke and lay near death in the hospital. After packing up the car and arranging for time off work, I drove the 15-hour trip from Washington, DC, to Champaign, Illinois. After spending time with Andy at the hospital, I met his niece at my buddy's condominium. Not at all prepared for Andy's sudden illness, she asked if I would take Birdie home and care for her (I have a reputation as being a bird person). It seemed the least I could do to help take care of Andy's affairs.

Birdie nestled into a travel crate and stared at me while I headed back home. She tweeted now and then, but otherwise rode along peacefully. Birdie trusted me, though I'm not sure why.

Once home, I set Birdie up in a beautiful wooden cage—her "condo," as I called it—with a glass door. She had free range of a few rooms upstairs but went back to her condo for safety while we were out. Soon Birdie began to trust me completely, enjoying substantial time out of confinement as I wrote at the computer. I grew to love her as well. Even when she misbehaved by chewing on the wrong wooden surface, I always forgave her and cared for her with complete love. It became an important reminder of the way that God cares deeply for all of us and sees to our every need—even on our less-than-perfect days. —David L. Winters

Lord, may we always repay Your kindness with love and devotion. Teach us how much You care and just how dependable You remain.

JULY 18

A Tangled Turtle

*For it is by grace you have been saved, through faith—
and this is not from yourselves, it is the gift of God.*

—EPHESIANS 2:8 (NIV)

IDON'T KNOW what I'm after, exactly, when I go fishing. It must not be fish, because I usually don't catch any. When I do catch a fish, I take a picture with my phone camera—holding the fish close to the lens to make him appear larger—and then release him. I think I just like being outdoors. I enjoy being in my boat on a golden summer day, like today, and feeling my troubles run down the fishing line and disappear into the water.

Up ahead along the shoreline is an old willow that has tipped over, the trunk stretching out into the water. Assembled on the trunk, all in a row, are painted turtles basking in the sun. As I glide closer, they cease their sunbathing and splash into the water. All except one. He hangs on the side of the trunk at an odd angle, his fat little legs pawing frantically, but he goes nowhere. He is stuck.

Then I see it. Dangling like a cape from his carapace is a section of fish netting. The net is caught on the turtle and snagged on the willow. I cut the netting from the turtle and hold him aloft for a closer look. He is a handsome little fellow, shell dark and smooth, skin olive-green with flashy orange stripes. His little legs are still stroking, pawing the air. I slide him into the water, and he dives down into the darkness.

I wonder if he realizes, hiding down there in his weedy jungle beneath the lily pads, that he has been saved. He understands, perhaps, that he is free, but does he understand how it happened and by whose intervention?

Me, I know that I am saved, and I know who is my Savior, and I am thankful. —Louis Lotz

*Many men go fishing all their lives without knowing
that it is not fish they are after.*
—Henry David Thoreau

JULY 19

A Place to Call Home

*My people will abide in a peaceful habitation, in
secure dwellings, and in quiet resting places.*

—ISAIAH 32:18 (ESV)

EVERYONE WHO WORKS in the church bookstore with me is a cat
person. Cat rescuers, cat companions, cat lovers. There are not many
places in our downtown environment for cats to be safe, so when cats
show up, we get moving. Our goal has always been to find them a loving
home, quickly. Then Toast and Marmalade, a brother-and-sister pair of
skinny tabbies, came along.

Toast was a warm gray-brown; his sister Marmalade was bright orange,
rare for a female tabby. They had found a way into the church's basement
and made a snug little nest. They emerged to bask in the sun and eat.
Though Toast remained standoffish, Marmalade loved being petted.

The cat committee was torn about next steps: the cats were happy,
they had companionship, and they were safe. Should they be neutered?
Adopted? Or remain in the basement? Then Toast wandered off, as male
cats will do. One of the cat people said she would adopt Marmalade.
Another paid for the spay. Another helped transport her.

Despite all these good intentions, Marmalade did not adapt well to her
new life. She didn't fit in with the other cats in her new home and sat in
the window pining to be outside. Her new human had a friend who had
just lost her cat and lived on several acres. Little Marmalade moved to the
country and received a new name: Queen Esther. The queen now enjoys
room to roam, the only cat of a person who adores her.

Marmalade's experience reminds me that even when I feel like I don't
fit in, I shouldn't despair. Like everyone, I will thrive better in some environments than in others, get along with some people better than others.
Instead of wandering away, if I connect with others and allow them to
care for me, they can help me discover the places in God's kingdom where
I will find the peace, refuge, and acceptance that I seek. —Lucy Chambers

*It's a mistake to think that we have to be lovely
to be loved by human beings or by God.*
—Fred Rogers

JULY 20

Birdhouse Tree

*For our light and momentary troubles are achieving for
us an eternal glory that far outweighs them all.*

—2 CORINTHIANS 4:17 (NIV)

I WAS DOING my best to dig up a much-neglected flower bed to plant
wildflower seeds. My back hurt some, so I was going about the work
slowly. I thought I was alone, but a handful of minutes later, a pair of
small blue-gray birds began to complain and eventually swoop down
over my head.

Ah, I thought, *they're back.*

Right next to the garden bed is my birdhouse tree. I had bought a
couple of birdhouses years ago because my mom has been a birder her
whole life, and I thought I could be too. Birds bring joyful music to your
home, and they're delightful to watch. When family members saw I had
a couple of birdhouses, they kept giving them to me, and a dozen houses
of various colors and shapes are now hanging in that tree.

From my bird-watching, I have noticed that once a bird couple picks
out their home, others seemingly stay clear and find other spots to nest.
They're territorial and protective—good parent qualities. And this pair
was just doing their best to protect their eggs until they were rudely interrupted . . . by me!

After I quickly got the seed into the garden bed, I stepped back into the
shadows of our patio and waited quietly. Sure enough, what I identified
later as a blue-gray gnatcatcher flew into the largest of the birdhouses,
and her spouse flitted onto a nearby branch.

I looked over at my rather sad-looking garden bed. It wasn't picture-
perfect, that's for sure. But just as the gnatcatchers were doing their best
to be good parents, I had done what I could to make that little corner
of earth a bit prettier. And that's all God expects of us—to do our best.
—Janet Holm McHenry

Whatever you do, work at it with all your heart.
—Colossians 3:23 (NIV)

JULY 21

A Few Drops of Water

"And if anyone gives even a cup of cold water to one of these little ones who is my disciple, truly I tell you, that person will certainly not lose their reward."

—MATTHEW 10:42 (NIV)

ANOTHER BLISTERINGLY HOT Texas day. Another day among many without rain. I inspected the plants near the front door before turning on the sprinkler. There, curled up at the bottom of an empty flowerpot, was a dead skink, a small lizard with a blue tail. At least, I thought it was dead.

When I lifted the pot to remove the skink, I noticed the slightest movement of its chest. Although probably close to death, the skink was alive. I carried the pot to an area where I knew the sprinkler would reach it. Maybe a few drops of gentle water would revive the skink.

Drop by drop, the water from the sprinkler fell gently around the little guy. At first, the skink didn't move. Then his tiny tongue reached out and lapped at the water. It wasn't much to begin with, but soon his lapping increased. Before long, his chest expanded and contracted. With more water, the skink uncurled his body.

I tilted the flowerpot on its side to make it easier for the fellow to leave if he wanted and went inside. When I returned to check on him, he was gone. As I placed the empty flowerpot back where it belonged, I thought about how insignificant my small gesture seemed at first. I really wasn't sure a few refreshing drops of water would revive the dying skink. But they did.

Then I thought about people I encounter throughout my day. Some are just like that skink. Desperately in need of a few drops of compassion to revive them. A few kind words. A genuine smile. A comforting touch. It certainly did not take much on my part to help that skink. All it took was a willingness to do what I could. My encounter with this skink taught me I should have the same willingness to help all God's creatures. Especially the human ones. —Sandy Kirby Quandt

Only one life, 'twill soon be past; only what's done for Christ will last.
—Charles Thomas Studd

JULY 22

The House-Hunting Wrens

"May those who love you be secure. May there be peace within your walls and security within your citadels."

—PSALM 122:6–7 (NIV)

MESMERIZED BY THE exuberant song, I looked out the window and spotted a little bird bringing twigs to the chicken-shaped birdhouse hanging on the porch. The idea of this charming creature inhabiting my happy place brought me joy. The bird, however, seemed to look at me suspiciously and flew away, threatened by my slightest move. So I enjoyed its song from inside the house, hoping it would get used to my presence.

The song captivated me for a day, maybe two. Then it faded, becoming more distant, and the birdhouse became silent. A void took over my home and my heart. The bird was gone. Had it been hurt?

Then an old story came to mind. I had heard about a kind of bird in which the male made dummy nests for the female to choose from. Could it be the wren?

Google confirmed it was indeed the wren. The image of the bird and the audio of its song matched my missing singer. I learned that the male fills multiple cavities with twigs, and his mate will select one in which to raise their babies. It was unlikely that I had done anything to scare it away, but I was disappointed not to have this lovely bird nearby.

It occurred to me that, like the wrens that relocated away from me, the people around me make their own choices, and sometimes those choices disappoint me, leaving me feeling sad. I can advise, I can ask, I can hope, but ultimately they need to make the choice that seems best to them. My only job at that point is to let go.

As difficult as it is to let go, with God's help, I can accept the choices that others make. —Sonia Frontera

Lord, give me the wisdom to remember that others' decisions are not mine to make. When it's time to let go, please help me let go and entrust their care to Your capable hands.

JULY 23

Wash, the "Gurgle-Puss"

Be joyful in hope, patient in affliction, faithful in prayer.

—ROMANS 12:12 (NIV)

AS HE'S GOTTEN older, Wash, our 17-year-old cat, is more insistent about certain things, and his communication has gotten clearer over the years. I suppose after 17 years of living with me and my husband, Wash is delighted that we've finally learned to understand him better.

It starts out like this: there is something he wants—maybe he can see the bottom of his food dish or one of us is sitting in his favorite spot on the couch. First, he will stare at me and my husband, unblinking, for a minute or two. If this doesn't sufficiently get our attention, he'll mew using what we call the "patheti-mew" which is very plaintive, soft, and sad. We usually will commiserate by saying, "Aw, poor kitty! Such a patheti-mew!" So Wash ramps it up to a full-blown *"Meow!"* I regret to say this only inspires us to pour on the sympathy, but it gets Wash no closer to what he wants.

The last stage of Wash's communication is the rough, gurgling meow that sounds like a cross between a man forcefully clearing his throat and a howl more often heard in the wilds of Africa than our living room. "Oh no! Gurgle-Puss!" we will cry, and at that point we may check his dish or make room on the couch. Wash's persistence eventually pays off.

Thankfully, I don't have to resort to the same extreme measures as my cat. I don't need a "gurgle" cry to be heard when I make my appeals to God. In any circumstance—whether it be challenging or simple, everyday stuff—when I regularly, persistently turn to God in prayer, I can expect a result. I can trust, though He may seem slow to act, that God hears me and all things He does are for my good. —Marianne Campbell

Prayer is the Christian's vital breath, the Christian's native air.
—James Montgomery

ALL GOD'S CREATURES

JULY 24

Seal of Protection

*And you also were included in Christ when you heard the message
of truth, the gospel of your salvation. When you believed, you
were marked in him with a seal, the promised Holy Spirit.*

—EPHESIANS 1:13 (NIV)

DURING THE SPRING break, I took my son and his friend to the California Academy of Sciences, an hour's drive from our home in northern California. Out of all the exhibits we toured, the rainforest one remains etched in my mind. Spanning four floors and enclosed in a gigantic glass dome, the spectacular exhibit houses diverse trees and plants and more than fifteen hundred animals native to the rainforest. We felt as if we were transported into the Amazonian forest the moment we stepped inside the dome.

The children and I could barely contain our excitement when we found ourselves surrounded by countless butterflies on the top floor of the exhibit. My jaw dropped and my eyes widened as a blue morpho flew to a branch close to me, its iridescent blue wings capturing my attention. The brown underside of the butterfly's wings was dotted with eye-like spots. The purpose of these fake eyes, or ocelli, I discovered, was to ward off predators.

I found it fascinating that God had designed this butterfly with a protective feature. It reminded me that I too carry an inbuilt protective feature gifted to me by my Father when I accepted Jesus as my Savior. He imprinted me with the Holy Spirit to help me resist temptation and contend for my faith in Christ. No one can rob me of identity and purpose in Christ because I know I belong to the Father. The powerful seal of the Holy Spirit is not conspicuous to the naked eye like an ocelli, but in the spiritual realm, it signals that I'm a child of God, and it protects and preserves me until the day of the Lord's return. —Mabel Ninan

*Dear Father, thank You for sealing me with Your Holy Spirit.
Please help me not to be afraid of the enemy
and to remember that I'm safe and secure in You.*

JULY 25

Lady's Smile

*"When I smiled at them, they scarcely believed it;
the light of my face was precious to them."*

—JOB 29:24 (NIV)

HE WAS AS loyal a friend as a faithful dog, but our former neighbor Bob was a nuisance. While my husband recovered from a traumatic car accident, Bob called my phone multiple times a day, asking for updates on my husband's condition. I had to tell him that since the accident, my husband hadn't smiled.

Bob irritated me—he didn't call before popping in for a visit, and he had the nerve to be upset that I wasn't returning his calls. Yet there was one saving grace. Bob always brought along his lady friend—a little dog named Lady.

A mix of Australian shepherd and who knows what else, this pup seemed to display a permanent smile. Lady loved to ride shotgun in Bob's truck and went everywhere Bob went. Her black-and-white fur felt as soft as her demeanor.

Bob and Lady showed up again to visit my husband when his condition was deteriorating. He could barely sit up. I was anxious, and Bob's lack of what I thought of as good manners really got under my skin. I prayed for forgiveness for judging Bob but was still upset.

Just as my crabbiness threatened to break through, Bob pulled a dog biscuit from his pocket. Lady sat at attention, her canine smile beaming. Bob handed the biscuit to my husband, who stared at it, turning it over in his hands.

Lady whimpered and placed a freckled paw on my husband's knee. My husband held out the treat to Lady, who gently took it and then crunched it with gusto. He looked up at me. And slowly, a smile spread across his face.

My own frown turned into a grin that cured my irritation. God had reminded me that Bob cared about my husband too. —Linda S. Clare

*The gift which I am sending you is called a dog, and is, in fact,
the most precious and valuable possession of mankind.*
—Theodorus Gaza

JULY 26

The Lionfish

The wolf will live with the lamb, the leopard will lie down with the goat, the calf and the lion and the yearling together; and a little child will lead them.

—ISAIAH 11:6 (NIV)

A T ONE POINT in my life, I owned a saltwater fish tank, which I kept in my basement. Watching the exotic fish was relaxing, although maintenance of the tank was challenging. It became even more challenging when I let the pet store owner talk me into adopting a lionfish. The lionfish was magnificent to see, with its brilliant coloration and its dorsal fins capped with venomous spines. The pet store owner warned me that this fish would require a separate tank, because part of its natural diet was other fish.

So I bought a second tank, which I placed in my office. This arrangement worked smoothly until one day when I was cleaning the office tank, my lionfish went into spasms when I transferred it from its holding bucket back to the tank. I quickly put the fish back into the bucket and took it to the home tank, hoping to save its life. It dropped to the bottom of the tank and positioned itself in a corner, where it lay still. And I watched with trepidation to see if it would attack its tank mates.

The lionfish remained in the corner, eating fish food that I dropped near it, until about a week later when it began to swim around. My trepidation increased, but the anticipated attacks never happened. Somehow, perhaps through surviving its trauma and seeing its tank mates daily, the lionfish lived with them in peace.

And I thought, *How wonderful! Could I do that daily in my life?* Could I avoid the instinct to win an argument, to pick a fight, to lash out during a disagreement with hurtful words? Or maybe I could avoid those situations altogether. Surely if the lionfish could do it, so could I! —Harold Nichols

How good and pleasant it is when God's people live together in unity!
—Psalm 133:1 (NIV)

JULY 27

Laughing Loons

*"Blessed are you who hunger now, for you will be satisfied.
Blessed are you who weep now, for you will laugh."*

—LUKE 6:21 (NIV)

THE OPEN-WATER SWIMMING season had just started where my family and I live in the Land of 10,000 Lakes. With it, the local waters were accessible for people who, like me, were training to swim in competitions. I was so excited to be experiencing and rejoicing in God's creation through this sport. It's an activity I thoroughly enjoy doing outside in the purest form of nature.

In early June my coach, John Jacobson, and I visited two local lakes in Minnesota. With all our gear in place, we swam a couple of miles in lakes filled with all kinds of creatures. One of God's creations, the loon, sounded like it was laughing at us.

During a week at the cabin with my family, I saw more loons. These wonderful waterbirds are fascinating. They like to eat fish, which made me feel good about the water I swam in because one small area of the bay scared me; I wasn't sure if it had been polluted with chemicals. However, it occurred to me that if the loons were there, continuing to make their laughing sound, it must be safe.

Their laughter intrigued me so much that I finally did some research. I read that loons' "crazy laugh" is a response to a perceived threat. While I don't consider myself a threat to a loon, I do appreciate the way its distinctive call lightens my own mood and reminds me not to worry. When I feel nervous, scared, or threatened by circumstances in life, finding a way to laugh about the situation helps me relax and have fun. I pray more and more that God will provide opportunities for me to find the good humor in things.

When I feel concerned about life, I'll think of my laughing avian friends and how God used them to remind me that He is always smiling down on me. —Stacey Thureen

*Lord, You are so good to me! Show me how to laugh,
have fun, and enjoy life the way that You designed.
Remind me of how You smile down on me too. Amen.*

ALL GOD'S CREATURES 215

JULY 28

Sure-Footed

My steps have held to your paths; my feet have not slipped.

—PSALM 17:5 (NIV)

THE KALAUPAPA PENINSULA on Molokai, one of the most remote places in Hawaii, once served as a leper colony. Victims of this horrible disease were taken from their homes and transported to the colony by boat. The colony was on a relatively flat area at the foot of some of the steepest sea cliffs on Earth, so there was no way to leave except by boat or by scaling the cliffs. Today, the colony is a national historical park on a part of the island so unspoiled and beautiful that it feels like you are going back in time. The only way to visit Kalaupapa is by plane, by hiking down narrow trails in the vertical rock faces, or by mule. The 2.9-mile trail descends 1,700 feet on the edge of the tallest sea cliff in the world.

Many years ago, my husband and I were fortunate enough to visit this unique area by riding mules down to the bottom of the cliff. I must admit to feeling some trepidation as we descended straight down a narrow path on the side of the cliff. It seemed my mule plodded along without so much as looking where he was going, and it occurred to me my life depended on the sure-footedness of an animal that didn't seem all that attentive or concerned. One stumble on his part, and we both would tumble to our deaths. Full of anxiety, I monitored each of his footsteps on the way down.

When we made the return trip up the cliff, I allowed myself to relax. It was only then that I noticed the beautiful scenery. I remarked to my husband, "Did you see the gorgeous view coming up the cliff?"

"It was the same view going down," he replied. I'd missed the stunning scenery because I had been too focused on making sure my mule didn't step off the side of the cliff.

God's Word assures us if we keep our feet on His path, He will not allow us to slip. I need not worry about the steepness or the danger of the path as long as He is guiding my footsteps. —Ellen Fannon

Father, help me let go and allow You to guide my footsteps.
Let me trust that You will not allow me to stumble.

216   ALL GOD'S CREATURES

JULY 29

Beach Bunnies

The boundary lines have fallen for me in pleasant places.

—PSALM 16:6 (NIV)

I SAT ON the deck of our fourth-floor condo humming a song. Hillsong United's "Oceans" had come to mind, its lyrics stirring images of a frightened Peter walking on water.

Lord, I'm content, but help me be willing to obey if You ever call me from my comfort zone. With my *Amen,* I opened my eyes. There they were below me—two bunnies nibbling on grass. Only when a passerby startled them did they duck into the bushes along the sidewalk. Finally, the woman disappeared somewhere on the beach beyond the property's shrub-lined border. Would the duo return?

In only moments, one, then two bunnies emerged from the bushes to resume their morning nibbling. Just then, my husband joined me, coffee in hand. "Shh." I pointed to the patch of grass. "See those cuties?"

Bill looked down, then smiled. "Having breakfast, no doubt."

We watched as they hopped to a fresh spot. Then, jumping to another, they continued eating, never venturing beyond the confines of the condominium's limited property lines. The pair seemed content. With such a great big world, were they happy to simply spend their lives in so small a space?

I shook my head. "All that, just beyond them. Isn't it amazing?"

"How so?" Bill sipped his coffee.

"Those bunnies appear satisfied in that teeny patch of grass. Do you think they're ever overwhelmed by or curious about that big body of water right over there?"

"Maybe, but this is home. For now, I'm guessing they trust everything they need is right there."

He was right. For those beach bunnies, the boundary lines had fallen in pleasant places. Even with the ocean only a breath away, they were content right where they were.

And I heard Him. *You also have that kind of contentment, which is beautiful. I'll expand your faith in My time, in My ways. When My Spirit calls, you'll be able to trust without borders, walking on any water. In My presence, you'll always have everything you need too.*

Peering over the railing, I whispered, "Thank you, bunnies." —Maureen Miller

And my God will meet all your needs according to the
riches of his glory in Christ Jesus.
—Philippians 4:19 (NIV)

JULY 30

His Unseen Presence

And blessed be His glorious name forever! And let the whole earth be filled with His glory. Amen and Amen.

—PSALM 72:19 (NKJV)

OCCASIONALLY, I CATCH a glimpse of the largest representative of the woodpecker family in North America, the pileated woodpecker. They usually stick to forested areas, but luckily for me, my backyard view contains about a thousand acres of woods leading up to the Eastern Continental Divide. This affords me a better chance of seeing this crow-size bird. Both males and females have black and white feathers with a red crest on the top of their head. Though many people never get a chance to see one, there are other ways to determine their presence.

I can identify them by their long-lasting, high-pitched piping call. I also recognize their unique, rhythmic flight pattern, when their wings flap out a specific cadence. I can identify their loud drumming on hollow trees or logs as it echoes down the valley. Even the distinctive rectangular shape of the holes they hammer out show they have been here. It is rare to see them, but signs of their presence are frequent.

I have never seen God. Only a select few have. His existence may be doubted by some, but His evidence abounds. I have seen Him in the way He paints a sunset or a meadow filled with flowering blooms. I have heard Him in the testimonies of miraculous medical healings that doctors cannot explain. I have seen His handiwork in the birth of my five children. I hear it in the way He fills the early morning hour with the songs of the birds announcing the start of a new day. His presence is seen, heard, and felt throughout His wonderful creation.

I longingly look forward to that moment when I finally get to see Him face-to-face. Until then, I am content with the evidence He provides all around me. —Ben Cooper

While all that borrows life from Thee is ever in Thy care,
And everywhere that man can be, Thou, God, art present there.
—Isaac Watts

JULY 31

The Details of Grace

The grace of our Lord was poured out on me abundantly,
along with the faith and love that are in Christ Jesus.

—1 TIMOTHY 1:14 (NIV)

AS I WATCHED dark-eyed juncos hopping across our front yard and collecting birdseed, I was struck by their various colors. I was familiar with the slate-colored juncos, the males with their black backs and white bellies and the buff-brown feathers of the females. But birds of the same size and shape hopped next to them. However, these had sharply outlined solid black heads: Oregon juncos. Scanning around our feeders and in bushes, I spotted yet another color variety—the pink-sided junco, with its black eye mask and pinkish-brown sides.

There are six subspecies of dark-eyed juncos in North America. That day, I enjoyed visits from three of those subspecies in my yard. Admiring their differing color patterns, I thought of the subtle yet striking details of God's Word. The Creator who etched and painted intricate details in nature gave the same attentiveness to the words, flow, and structure of Scripture. The Bible is not merely a collection of information or a history book but also a brilliant piece of literary art reflecting God's creativity.

I think of the Greek word *charis*, often translated in the Bible as "grace." Just as I notice the breadth of the juncos' beauty as I learn their subspecies, I discover exquisite details of *charis*—God's grace—as I study His Word. Along with grace, *charis* can also be translated as goodwill, loving-kindness, favor, bounty, and delight. At first thought or read, I might view grace from only one angle. But the more I entertain God's grace in my heart and mind, the more I appreciate its details and experience God's favor and delight as He extends His goodwill in my life. —Eryn Lynum

Walk of Faith: *Challenge yourself to identify three new bird species this week.*
What can these diverse varieties tell you about the character of God?

ALL GOD'S CREATURES 219

AUGUST 1

Slow Down

"Be still, and know that I am God."

—PSALM 46:10 (NIV)

THERE IS A lean-to roof that stretches out from the south side of my barn, and on hot summer days I like to go there and sit in the shade. Sitting there just now, I notice that the dirt at my feet is pockmarked with several small conical pits, the excavation work of ant lions. Ant lions are bristly little creepy-crawlers about a quarter of an inch long, with a pair of oversized and fearsome-looking choppers. The steeply inclined pits are about 2 inches deep and 2 inches wide. The ant lion digs his little trap in the soft sand and then burrows himself into the very bottom of the pit. And there he waits.

Sooner or later an unsuspecting ant will come along and tumble down into the pit, and then—*chomp!*—the ant lion pounces. Other species have to go hunting or foraging for their daily food, but the ant lion just sits there, patiently biding his time until dinner comes to him.

For better or worse, and there is some of both, I have a type A personality. Type A folks are like ants—hardworking and industrious, always busy, always striving. Type A folks accomplish a lot in this world, but we also are prone to fall into traps of stress and depression. We tend to base our self-worth on achievement. Type A folks think we have to earn others' approval, and sometimes even God's approval, by hard work and success. So it is important for me, now and then, to stop working and go sit in the shade and relax. I need to hear the Savior whisper, *Stop trying to earn My love; you already* have *My love.* I need to slow down and savor my life, rather than always charging ahead.

I sit there watching the ground, waiting for an ant to come along. But there are no ants today. That's OK; the ant lion is in no big hurry. He can wait. —Louis Lotz

> *Lord, help me to slow down. Enable me to sense*
> *Your presence, to feel Your love. Amen.*

AUGUST 2

The Snowless Snow Leopard

I have learned in whatever situation I am to be content.

—**PHILIPPIANS 4:11** (ESV)

WITH THE HUMIDITY in the air thick enough to slice and hot sunlight beating down on me, I looked forward to reaching the snow leopard exhibit. As a volunteer at my local zoo, my job was to check on all the animals and document behavioral observations, keeping a special lookout for anything unusual.

I approached the snow leopard's home and scanned the exhibit for the big cat. I felt a special bond with him, since we both preferred winter and cold temperatures. The heat had to be making him miserable too.

There he was, a beautiful cat with gorgeous markings lying in a shaded corner on top of his elevated platform, sleeping peacefully. He looked . . . content.

But how could that be? I wiped sweat off my forehead and grimaced in discomfort. I was counting down the days until winter, grumpy and complaining about the heat, bugs, and yard work. My days were filled with discontentment, not peace.

Was that more my fault than the result of circumstances? Even though the snow leopard was designed for cold temperatures and snow, he'd found a way to calmly endure the hardship of heat without panicking or wallowing in frustration.

Could I do the same? The snow leopard's example reminded me of something I'd forgotten. I have the secret to being content in all circumstances. I have Christ in me, strengthening me to endure with patience any trial. Whether discomfort, danger, grief, or frustration, I can face all things with the peaceful forbearance of a snow leopard through Him who strengthens me. —Jerusha Agen

We can be content in Christ, regardless of our circumstances,
because in Him we have everything we need, for now and forever.
—Donald S. Whitney

AUGUST 3

Bonnie Joy's Finches

Every good and perfect gift is from above, coming down from the Father of the heavenly lights, who does not change like shifting shadows.

—JAMES 1:17 (NIV)

MY CHURCH COMMUNITY and I celebrated when our friend Bonnie Joy won a lottery for an apartment in a brand-new complex. Until then, Bonnie's income had limited her to neighborhoods that were less than ideal. In this new apartment, she would pay the same affordable rate while also feeling safe and having a home she could be proud of.

On the day a mutual friend and I helped Bonnie Joy unpack, she pulled us out to her balcony to show us a surprise she'd discovered in her new home.

"Look." She pointed to a shade tree. "I have finches. Every morning, I sit out here with my Bible and coffee, and they sing to me."

Health issues keep Bonnie Joy from driving, and her life had been difficult, but her response to the finches reflected her thankful heart. She saw her morning visitors as "a gift from my Abba Daddy."

As one who can't drive due to poor vision and has spent most of adulthood living on a low income, I related to Bonnie's gratitude for the little things that often feel like a big hug from the Father we've learned to rely on.

Over the next several weeks, Bonnie Joy texted me pictures of her finches. When the first of my yearly swallows showed up outside my bedroom window, I sent her a photo as a reply. God's care for her, demonstrated so ably in His perfect gifts—from the nice apartment to the morning finch song—reminded me how beautifully God provides for those of us who can't always provide for ourselves. Our kind Father knows exactly what we need to be safe and what will simply make us happy. —Jeanette Hanscome

Father, thank You for the little and big ways You meet my needs. I pray I will never feel so comfortable in what I have that I forget to thank You for the gifts of Your loving provision. Amen.

ALL GOD'S CREATURES   223

AUGUST 4

TV Guard Dog

Thy word have I hid in mine heart, that I might not sin against thee.

—PSALM 119:11 (KJV)

THERE SHE GOES again!" Mom picked up the penny bottle to shake while I shook my head and laughed. Becky, Mom's Scottish terrier, watches commercials and barks at any with dogs. In fact, she doesn't just watch them; she studies them, remembers the dogs, and barks ferociously when the commercials come on, even before the dogs appear.

If Becky is watching Mom cooking in the kitchen while I'm watching the television and one of the forbidden commercials comes on, in comes a black whirlwind, stamping her feet in front of the set, daring that dog to come out. On occasion, she makes a mistake, and I say, "Becky! That's not a dog. That's a miniature horse!" Or a goat, or even a cat. She turns to me with soulful eyes, as if to reply, "Sorry. I had to be sure. I must protect my humans." And off she prances to see if Mom dropped anything. But let another commercial come on that she remembers, and in she'll come—the fierce protector of the home from canine television stars.

Watching her tell off one of those dogs, I wondered how she knew from the opening chords or words that a dog would be in that particular commercial. I see her sit on my mom's recliner, watching the television most evenings. Had she truly memorized the advertisements that well?

And that led to wondering what things I know that well. Some commercial jingles pop into my head readily. But what about things that matter . . . like Scripture verses? Have I studied Scripture as Becky studies the commercials to make sure I know which ones have warnings or blessings and which have truths I should be hiding in my heart so I can warn others of coming dangers or tell them of Jesus's love? With a little black dog as my mentor, I think I'll do a bit more of that today. —Cathy Mayfield

If you are ignorant of God's Word, you will always be ignorant of God's will.
—Billy Graham

224 ALL GOD'S CREATURES

AUGUST 5

Cutouts

"I go to prepare a place for you. And if I go and prepare a place for you, I will come again and will take you to myself, that where I am you may be also."

—JOHN 14:2–3 (ESV)

I RECENTLY FINISHED a 5-hour cutout that exhausted me. What is a "cutout"? Let me explain.

Honeybees make new colonies by swarming to a new cavity opening to make a home. In nature, they use hollow trees. In urban areas, they claim an opening in a wall or floor of a house. That is when I get called to cut the bees out and remove them. Homeowners tell me, "I don't want them living here. This isn't their home." They are justified in saying it. Managed bees belong in a hive. But the bees are not fond of me doing cutouts. They react forcibly when being extracted from their home.

During the cleanup of my honey-coated equipment, I thought about the way bees find temporary homes to serve as their shelter. These homes aren't where they were created to live. Conflict arises between honeybees and humans trying to occupy shared space. Something has to be done by someone to resolve the dilemma. That is where I step in to provide a solution by doing a cutout.

As a Christian believer inhabiting this world, I am becoming more aware the world serves only as my temporary dwelling place. My eternal home is in heaven. Jesus told His followers He had to go prepare their rightful place to live with Him forever.

I use my bare hands in removing the honeycomb, and I get stung a few times. But the pain is short-lived, and I know it is part of the cost of doing a successful removal. There was also a great cost for doing my extraction from my temporary worldly home. A cost Jesus was willing to endure. It was painful but short-lived. I am truly thankful that He completed His ministry of cutting me out and preparing my natural home in heaven.
—Ben Cooper

> *This world is not my home. I'm just a-passing through.*
> *My treasures are laid up, somewhere beyond the blue.*
> —Anonymous

AUGUST 6

Learning to Identify Distractions

Let your eyes look straight ahead; fix your gaze directly before you.

—PROVERBS 4:25 (NIV)

I HEARD A familiar birdcall as my husband and I walked along the road by our house.

"Look, a killdeer," I pointed out to him. He quickly noticed a second one, and we watched the shorebirds walking together.

"Look for chicks; it's the right time of year," I said. Not a moment later, my husband exclaimed, "There they are!"

Four tiny chicks followed quickly behind their parents. They looked like little puffballs of down feathers atop tall stilt legs. We watched them for a minute before continuing on our walk.

A while later, on our way home, we walked on the opposite side of the road. I was surprised to see another killdeer in a pasture on this side of the road, across from where we'd encountered the killdeer family. Upon noticing us, this lone killdeer went into a frenzy, making all sorts of noise and flapping—then dragging—her wings along the ground.

"She's doing her broken wing display!" I told my husband.

When a killdeer feels as though its nest or family is threatened, it will divert attention by flying away from the nest and pretending to have a broken wing.

After we passed the killdeer, she regained her composure and flew back to the chicks across the road. She was the mama we'd seen with her family at the beginning of our walk, and she had successfully distracted us away from her chicks on our return.

Watching the killdeer's act, I wondered how many times I fall for distractions. Do I allow news headlines or social media posts to lure my attention or send me into a frenzy? Unlike the killdeer's clever act, such distractions rarely serve a useful purpose. As I learn to identify them, I can better train my thoughts on Christ and remain focused, no matter the noise or antics around me. —Eryn Lynum

Walk of Faith: *What regularly distracts you? Is there something that vies for your attention but is not helpful to you? Practice setting it aside and refocusing your attention on God through prayer.*

ALL GOD'S CREATURES

AUGUST 7

Live with Gusto

*Whether therefore ye eat, or drink, or whatsoever
ye do, do all to the glory of God.*

—1 CORINTHIANS 10:31 (KJV)

"THERE'S ONE, MOM!"
I stopped the car, and my son Brian hopped out. He came back carrying a robust box turtle.

Both of our sons participated in 4-H youth clubs. Every summer, our county extension office held a day of fun activities and contests. One of the highlights for our boys was the turtle race. Sometime in the weeks prior to the event, we always collected two box turtles roaming our neighborhood. My husband and sons even built a reptile-friendly domicile to keep them in until their big day.

The boys were in charge of feeding the future contestants. The turtles loved bananas, tomatoes, and other fruits and veggies, but their favorite chow was the earthworms we dug up in our yard or bought from the bait shop. The longer and juicier, the better. One day, I watched as two turtles started chomping from either end of an 8-inch night crawler and gobbled their way to the middle. Athletic champions couldn't relish their food more than those two.

To me, it didn't matter who won the turtle race. The days and weeks prior, as our sons cared for and learned from God's creatures, made the biggest impact.

And I learned something too. Watching the way the turtles approached their food reminded me to approach life with the same gusto. The Bible says that everything we do for God, no matter how mundane, brings glory to God. So, whether I start a huge ministry or change a dirty diaper, I want to show my passion for God in whatever I do.

We always released the box turtles back into the wild after the race. Now, years later, whenever I see a turtle cross the road, I wonder if it's one of my sons' contestants and remember my commitment to bring God glory in all I do. —Tracy Crump

Thou art worthy, O Lord, to receive glory and honour and power: for thou hast created all things, and for thy pleasure they are and were created.
—Revelation 4:11 (KJV)

AUGUST 8

The Confused Coyote

"Believe me when I say that I am in the Father and the Father is in me; or at least believe on the evidence of the works themselves."

—JOHN 14:11 (NIV)

A TOTAL SOLAR eclipse is such a rare event that it's worth taking a holiday to observe. The last time one was visible in the United States, I was fortunate enough to live in the zone of totality, that narrow band of territory from which the full eclipse is visible. I marveled at the sight, as did my daughter and son-in-law. The experience left me more than ever convinced of my own insignificance and of the greatness and power of God.

Moments after the sun went dark, shrouding the world in an eerie silver twilight, a coyote trotted warily out of the brush behind my daughter's house. He entered the clearing, then stopped, looking this way and that, as if unsure what to do. *What strange magic is this?* I imagined him wondering. *It isn't daylight, but it's way too soon for dark. What on earth is happening?*

A moment later he trotted back into the woods, presumably to go back to sleep until the real nightfall arrived. It seems he was confused, yes, but not all that impressed.

How often do we respond in a similar way when God makes Himself known in some grand, unexplainable way? We may feel curious or momentarily disoriented, then return to our daily routine. God's miracles are all around us. They are easy to see and impossible to explain, yet we shrug them off. Later, we ask ourselves, "Is God real? I never know for sure."

We can know. The heavens declare the glory of God. The rhythm of the tide proclaims His faithfulness. The miracles of a growing seed, a living creature, an immense universe are visible each day and far beyond our ability to understand or explain.

Don't take my word that God exists. Believe what you see. —Lawrence W. Wilson

> *For the beauty of the earth, for the glory of the skies . . .*
> *Lord of all, to Thee we raise this our hymn of grateful praise.*
> —Folliott S. Pierpoint

228   ALL GOD'S CREATURES

AUGUST 9

When Bluebirds Moved In

. . . being confident of this, that he who began a good work in you will carry it on to completion until the day of Christ Jesus.

—PHILIPPIANS 1:6 (NIV)

A T OUR OLD house, I had a favorite mockingbird who would perch on the top of my roof—directly above my living room—and sing. He came to recognize me and would even, on occasion, try to communicate with me when a predator was nearby. The bond I shared with that mockingbird was such a rare and sweet thing. Though he'd be pretty old by now, I like to think he's still alive and singing.

I visited our old house recently and noticed our neighbor had cut down the large bushes this mockingbird liked to nest in. He would often perch on the power line above these bushes. While I did see some mockingbirds on my visit, I'm not sure if "my" mockingbird was part of the group, given this change in his habitat. In his place, however, were two new visitors: bluebirds.

If you're unfamiliar with bluebirds, I'll just say they are stunning creatures that can be *very* difficult to attract. Yet as happy as I was to spot them, I still missed my mockingbird.

I sometimes struggle to hold the grief of a past season and the joy of a new season with the same two hands. But as I left our old house that day, I decided to truly notice the bluebirds. I decided to be present to what God is currently doing. Philippians 1:6 is a wonderful reminder of God's promise to "carry [His work] on" in our lives from season to season, until that work is complete. In order for His plans to continue through the seasons, we must, by necessity, go *through* these seasons. But we can trust that, in all of them, He is faithful and He is good. —Ashley Clark

Father, when I find myself looking back upon the past, remind me of the ways You are still at work in my current season, and help me to see the beauty of Your plans for me right here. Amen.

ALL GOD'S CREATURES   229

AUGUST 10

The Sacrificial Paradox of the Herd

"In this world you will have trouble. But take heart! I have overcome the world."

—JOHN 16:33 (NIV)

MY HUSBAND AND I, affectionately known as Grampy and Granny, recently drove with our two teenage grandchildren to Estes Park, Colorado. At one point we pulled over to appreciate a herd of cattle and buffalo sharing a grassy field together. Seeing American bison is always a special treat, as they are endangered.

My grandson leaned on a fence post and, in his usual astute way, asked me, "Granny, how many cows make up a herd?" Then he grinned, thinking he'd tripped me up. But this Granny has Google, and she knows how to use it, so a moment later I declared that officially three cows or more make up a herd.

My internet search brought up something called a *sacrifice paradox,* a management concept that uses the example of cattle and buffalo sharing a field to illustrate the pitfalls of making easy short-term solutions that have difficult long-term consequences. In the example, when a bad storm approaches, cattle run *away*—in the opposite direction of the approaching storm—thus the storm *follows* them, and they'll be exposed to it longer than necessary. Buffalo, on the other hand, run straight into the storm. The storm passes over them in the other direction, and they aren't exposed as long.

Yep, that's me. Like the cattle, how often have I bolted away when facing life's storm? And how many times does the storm continue to hover over me because I've gone in the wrong direction? Might it be better to act like a buffalo, put my head down, and charge straight into the storm? Through that chance stop, I realized that sometimes the best and fastest way to get through life's trials is not by ignoring the storm or trying to dodge it, but by facing it down with the Lord's Spirit in front and behind me. —Deb Kastner

Christ with me, Christ before me, Christ behind me, Christ in me, Christ beneath me, Christ above me, Christ on my right, Christ on my left, Christ when I lie down, Christ when I sit down, Christ when I arise, Christ in the heart of every man who thinks of me, Christ in the mouth of every man who speaks of me, Christ in every eye that sees me, Christ in every ear that hears me.

—Saint Patrick

AUGUST 11

Slow Down and Nibble the Flowers

Be very careful, then, how you live . . . making the most of every opportunity.

—EPHESIANS 5:15–16 (NIV)

MY FAMILY HAS taken a few backpacking trips throughout the years, and we heard that using goats could make travel easier. All we had to do was load up the goats with our gear, easing our own burdens, and blaze a trail to glorious destinations.

That's not exactly how it turned out.

Heading out to the North Cascade mountains in Washington, we rented an experienced goat and brought one of our own—Benjamin, a tall, white Lamancha with bright eyes and a mind of his own. After loading everything up, we hit the trail.

It started well. The rented goat plodded along like the expert he was, and Benjamin followed. But soon Benjamin lagged a bit behind. The gap increased as the day continued. We took turns "leading" him down the trail, but no matter what enticement we put in front of him or how we nudged him from behind, he would not go faster. He'd stop and smell the ground, nibble on flowers, or just sit and look around.

It took longer to get to camp than we'd hoped, but we got there, and while he was a source of major frustration, that stubborn goat taught me something. Those memories of Benjamin remind me that when I'm tempted to zoom through life at 60 miles an hour, I may arrive at my destination faster, but I could end up whooshing past beautiful things. Sometimes I need to slow down, nibble some flowers—I mean, smell some flowers—and enjoy the journey God has for me. The time with my kids is whizzing by. I need to slow down and make those cookies with them before they grow up and move away. I should celebrate a major accomplishment for a moment before I turn my eyes to my next goal. And above all, it is worth slowing my mind and body during my time with God to focus on what He is leading me to do today. —Kristen G. Johnson

> Walk of Faith: *Take a few moments today to slow your heart and mind to notice your surroundings. Thank God for all He's made.*

ALL GOD'S CREATURES 231

AUGUST 12

My Life Is Hard

Rejoice always, pray continually, give thanks in all circumstances;
for this is God's will for you in Christ Jesus.

—1 Thessalonians 5:16–18 (NIV)

EVERY VISIT TO my friend Susy's house in the mountains includes time with her many pets and critters. I look forward to morning greetings on the stairs by Sashi, a beautiful cat with a bushy, squirrel-like tail.

I am apparently one of the few people Sashi allows to pick her up, so I take full advantage. But first, I must validate her daily routine of whining from the depths of her soul, as if she'd lost everything dear to her during the night. As she circles her empty food dish, I can almost hear "my life is hard" through her meows.

So that's what I say to her. "I know, Sashi, your life is so difficult. You have to wait for food. The dogs get in your space. Poor baby."

The truth is, Sashi has it made at the Susy's house. She was rescued as a feral kitten. According to legend, her head and paws looked ginormous compared to the rest of her scrawny body, and Susy's family worried she wouldn't survive. But she did. She grew into her head, her legs strengthened, and now she looks like a cat featured in photos. The family keeps Sashi indoors, away from mountain predators. Contrary to her laments, she not only gets her dish filled daily but receives treats as well.

Sashi is a great example for me when I catch myself complaining about frustrations and disappointments to the point of suggesting my life is hard. Like Sashi, I don't always have what I want exactly when I think I need it, and people disrupt my plans. But God has done remarkable things in my life, filled it with good people, and allowed me to do far more than I ever imagined—writing books, traveling, learning creative skills later in life. Even when life really is hard, it's full of good. The challenge is remembering this. —Jeanette Hanscome

Walk of Faith: *What is making your life hard right now?*
How is God showing you His care and provision? Make two
side-by-side lists and pray for both today.

AUGUST 13

Call from Home

"My sheep hear My voice, and I know them, and they follow Me."

—JOHN 10:27 (NKJV)

EARLY ONE MORNING as I was sitting at my desk, I heard mooing. As in cows. Bovines. Huge creatures that chew their cud, graze in pastures, and *generally* live on farms. Seeing as how I lived in a subdivision brimming with houses—complete with a well-trafficked street—I suspected I needed more caffeine.

But when I took another swig of coffee, the mooing continued. And grew louder. When I warily glanced out my window, I came face-to-face with the soulful, long-lashed gaze of a thousand-pound cow. I reared back in shock, expecting the beast to do the same, but she just smacked her lips and continued to peruse my landscape. She and twenty or so of her besties.

Should I call wildlife services? 911? As I reached for my phone, a sudden, staccato honk returned my gaze to the window. A pickup truck drove slowly along our street, its driver tooting his horn in a precise beat while calling, "Wooowee!" from his window. The familiar sequence drew the cows' attention from the smorgasbord of shrubbery, and soon they formed a convoy behind his truck, their hooves clattering noisily along the paved road as they followed him home.

I later learned that the cows had escaped from their farmer's pasture nearly a mile away. For days afterward, social media buzzed with pictures and posts about the bovines' midnight stroll across the area, including a busy intersection not far from my home.

While the community marveled at their surprising journey, I was struck by the poise of the drifting herd. Even as they wandered—clearly lost and in danger—they remained unfazed, *certain* that their farmer would come and *call* them home. And he hadn't failed them.

Our Father won't fail us either. He's constantly correcting our paths and leading us out of trouble. Even when we can't hear Him through the roar of fear and doubt, we are His, and when the time comes, we'll recognize the sound of His hallowed voice. —Hallie Lee

Father, when I veer off in the wrong direction, please help me feel Your presence—and listen for Your holy voice.

ALL GOD'S CREATURES   233

AUGUST 14

Frog's Kiss

The blessing of the LORD be on you; we bless you in the name of the LORD.
—PSALM 129:8 (NIV)

IT WAS A hot summer afternoon, and I was outside with my kids on the back porch. I had just watered the flowers and was moving some empty terracotta pots around when I spotted a little frog inside one of them. I called my kids over to look and held the pot out to show them the little frog.

My son *oohed* and *ahhed* as he saw the little green guy in the bottom of the pot. I casually turned the pot to my daughter, and as she looked down inside, the frog jumped out and landed on her face! Splat! Right on her cheek and in her hair.

My daughter jumped back in surprise and yelled. The frog jumped right off and hopped away. "Mom, he tried to kiss me!" she said. We had been reading a lot of fairy tales. "He sure did!" I replied. "He must have thought you were a princess." We laughed together, sharing that special moment in nature.

Later that day I thought about the blessing of that frog kiss. School would be starting soon, and my daughter would be back in the fray of the social struggles of growing up. A kiss from a frog reminded my daughter that she truly is a princess in the eyes of God. She is beloved, she is of value, and God always offers her a kiss of blessing. (Even if it comes from frog lips!)

As her mother, I saw this as a moment of grace going forward. School will be hard for both of us, especially as she grows up, but God's got this. God has blessed us each in love and care. —Heather Jepsen

All things bright and beautiful, all creatures great and small,
all things wise and wonderful, the Lord God made them all.
—Cecil Frances Alexander

AUGUST 15

The Sojourn

"I am the way and the truth and the life. No one comes to the Father except through me."

—JOHN 14:6 (NIV)

THE BARN SWALLOWS arrive every spring right around lilac time. Supposedly, swallows return to the same place they nested the previous year and sometimes to the exact same rafter in the same barn. I look up into the rafters at the little feathered heads that are looking down at me from their mud-wattled nests and wonder if they are the same birds that nested here last year.

Swallows are not tidy tenants, and the floor beneath their nests is splashed with whitish droppings. Still, I like barn swallows, and I enjoy having them around. They are fun to watch, skimming low over the fields in search of insects. My bird book says that swallows can consume 60 insects an hour, gnats and mosquitos mostly. At 720 insects per day, that's roughly 22,000 fewer bugs per month that might have visited me as I sit on the deck and enjoy my morning coffee. And that's just one bird.

But now it is mid-August, and the sun's pendulum is swinging shorter each day, losing a minute with every arc. Dawn comes a little later, dusk comes a little sooner. Any day now some primordial trip wire in the swallow's pituitary gland will be triggered, and away they'll go, drawn by an overpowering urge to fly south to Brazil, even Argentina. It's a 5,000-mile flight, with many dangers along the way: headwinds, predator birds, hailstorms. And how do they know where they are going? Ornithologists think that swallows are guided by the Southern Cross, a constellation in the southern sky centered on four brilliant stars in a cross-shaped cluster.

I imagine them winging through the night sky, and I think of how I, too, am a sojourner following the cross, a pilgrim on a journey to a place I've never been, but I know the way to get there. "I am the way," said Jesus. —Louis Lotz

Through many dangers, toils, and snares, I have already come; 'tis grace hath brought me safe thus far, and grace will lead me home.
—John Newton

ALL GOD'S CREATURES 235

AUGUST 16

Nothing Better Than This

*Now may the Lord of peace Himself continually
grant you peace in every circumstance.*

—2 THESSALONIANS 3:16 (NASB)

AS MY HUSBAND drove along a busy freeway one hot August day, I
glanced over from the passenger seat at the car cruising by in the passing lane. It was a very full SUV. Rambunctious kids filled most of the back
seats. Weary parents sat in the front, looking as if they couldn't wait to
be home. It appeared to be a family returning from a camping adventure
or a trip to the beach. There wasn't an inch of space to be found between
the kids and all the gear that had aided them in their family outing. I
couldn't hear them, but I could see the energetic interaction taking place
between (what I assumed were) siblings.

Completely ignoring the chaos around him, the family dog rested its
head in the open window. He reveled in the wind that rushed past his face
and blew his ears and whiskers toward the back of the car. He was the
picture of peace, the epitome of contentment. His eyes were half shut,
partially because of the force of the breeze, partially because of his state
of rest. While only inches from where his humans were laughing and ges-
turing wildly, he was undistracted from the solitude he was experiencing.

How I wish that I could capture the posture of that dog—not the part
with his head hanging out the window, but the peace he so obviously
displayed. Chaos and distraction are all-too-familiar parts of my everyday life. I long to be able to mute the volume and shutter my eyes from
what is happening all around me. Like this family dog, I want to position
myself to let the wind of the Spirit blow over me. His peace, His assurance,
His presence is all I want and all I need, no matter what is happening in
my world. —Liz Kimmel

*Holy Spirit, come and fill me with Your presence so that I might reflect
Your peace to everyone who happens to intersect my daily life.*

AUGUST 17

Lobster Tale

Out of the depths I cry to you, LORD.

—PSALM 130:1 (NIV)

THE FIRST TIME I saw a video of squat lobsters, I laughed. With long, spindly, orangish legs, squat lobsters travel as if in slow motion, making them look like underwater spiders. These fantastic creatures are actually more closely related to hermit crabs than lobsters.

These hermit crab cousins live on the ocean's very bottom, on the empty abyssal plain, where no light and very little food comes from the world above. Yet squat lobsters have learned to make a life even in the depths. Their slow pace conserves energy so that they can get by with relatively little food.

Squat lobsters roam the Pacific Ocean coastal seabed, scavenging whatever drifts down the water column. Instead of carrying a shell on their backs, squats squeeze into crevices, leaving their claws exposed to keep other lobsters away. Their claws are formidable, sometimes growing several times longer than their bodies.

Although I'd have to submerge in a deep-sea rover to meet one, squat lobsters and their behaviors fascinate me. They showcase God's creative spirit, and they always make me laugh.

But they taught me something too. When I fall into the depths of despair, I sometimes hide between rocks too. I keep my claws sharpened for anyone who challenges my funk, and I tend to move in slow motion. Disappointment, resentment, and entitlement can drown my outlook and keep me tied to a sunken anchor of bitterness. Whenever I allow my heart to get waterlogged, I identify with squat lobsters.

These curious creatures remind me that if I wish to receive all the generous kindness that God offers, I'll need to move my claws aside, come out from behind my rock, and allow myself to be vulnerable to Him and to others who care about me and want to help. The humble squat lobster is a surprising example of a better attitude. —Linda S. Clare

Lord, when I sit at the bottom of an ocean of troubles, remind me to laugh and be open to Your love.

AUGUST 18

Flipping over Rocks

Jesus answered, "It is written: 'Man shall not live on bread alone, but on every word that comes from the mouth of God.'"
—MATTHEW 4:4 (NIV)

A BEAR!" I exclaimed as we drove along a dirt path in the foothills. My husband quickly stopped the car, ran around to open the back hatch, and pulled out our viewing scope. As he set it up, I fixed my eyes on the animal about a half mile away to avoid losing sight of it.

My husband hurriedly set up the scope and positioned it toward the black bear descending a grassy hillside.

"Here, I've got it!" my husband exclaimed as he focused the lens on the bear. With a much closer look, we could see the animal eagerly nosing its way through sagebrush and wildflowers. We watched as the young bear used its strong paws to flip over rocks, looking for insects. From where we stood, the bear was unaware of our presence, and we watched for a long while as he went about his lunchtime hunt. He left no rocks in his path unflipped, but instead took time to diligently search beneath each one.

It struck me that what to us seemed entertainment was, for him, survival. This is how the bear spends his days, flipping over rocks to find what he needs. I sometimes think of the bear when I read God's Word and wonder if I set myself on such a diligent search. Am I flipping over every rock, looking intently at the text and expectantly searching for the sustenance within? Do I leave any rock unflipped and simply skim past potential life? Like a bear eagerly searching a hillside, I want to make my way earnestly through God's Word, devoted to unearthing all its goodness. —Eryn Lynum

"Keep this Book of the Law always on your lips; meditate on it day and night, so that you may be careful to do everything written in it. Then you will be prosperous and successful."
—Joshua 1:8 (NIV)

AUGUST 19

The Very Brave Cocker Spaniel

There is no fear in love.

—1 JOHN 4:18 (NIV)

ONE OF THE great loves of my life is a black cocker spaniel named Schroeder. We adopted him 14 years ago from the animal shelter and are beyond grateful for the opportunity to care for him in his golden years. Our best estimate is that he's around 16 years old.

Schroeder and I have been through a lot together. Through every high and low life has brought along, he's never left my side—and most days, he is literally right beside me. But even after all this time together, Schroeder sometimes surprises me, just like he did last week. He actually let me clip his nails at home with little objection. Now, this may sound comical, and it is—but in years past, clipping this boy's nails has required up to three vet technicians! And as Schroeder has aged, he's also changed in other ways. I can take him for walks now without preparing for him to bolt away. Where meeting strangers once brought him panic, he now makes new friends. He has even joined us on a couple of vacations.

In the first few years after we rescued Schroeder, I watched him learn to trust us despite the difficult start he got in life before his adoption. But I didn't expect that trust to grow even deeper in his senior years. As a person who has long dealt with anxiety, I am so challenged and inspired by Schroeder's willingness to change. The neglect he suffered as a puppy was not his fault, yet he chose to overcome it.

Sometimes fears can become familiar and entrenched, and we don't remember what life was like without them. We may even feel like fear defines us. But no matter the fear or anxiety—no matter how long we've held these things—there is always hope for change. As Schroeder shows me, I can let go of my long-held fears today—and today is the perfect day to start. —Ashley Clark

Yesterday is gone. Tomorrow has not yet come.
We have only today. Let us begin.
—Mother Teresa

AUGUST 20

A Shortcut to Abundance

*They feast on the abundance of your house; you give
them drink from your river of delights.*

—PSALM 36:8 (NIV)

COATIS ARE WEIRD-LOOKING mammals. In appearance they resemble a cross between a hog (with their long, rather piglike snout) and a raccoon (in shape, size, and coloring). So their nickname, "hog-nosed raccoon," is certainly fitting. Coatis are adept at climbing trees, yet they obtain their sustenance by foraging for food on the ground.

I was first introduced to coatis while observing a bird-feeding station in Costa Rica. Coatis had assembled near the 20-foot feeder, eyes riveted on the human caretakers who were replenishing the fresh cantaloupe and melon that were impaled on protruding iron spears.

From the lodge's elevated balcony, we watched coatis circling, assessing, waiting near the feeder for the discards from last night's feeding to be tossed to the ground. All but one.

One coati climbed the nearest tree to the feeder and stealthily moved to the tip of the limb. With each movement forward, the limb bent downward more. Still the coati continued its advance. It seemed to be deliberating a jump to a structure with no safe landing space. It was evident to the horrified bystanders that this would not end well. It was a preamble to a deadly fall.

The coati hesitated yet did not turn back. We watched and grimaced from the balcony. Just as all observers braced for a reckless jump, the coati wisely decided to retreat to safety, to share in the discarded rinds and residual fruit with the rest of its kind.

How tempting it is to seek shortcuts. Like the coati, in my own way, I have sought shortcuts to God's blessings and presence through spurts of Christian activity and self-congratulating postures. What I've learned is that it is slow, steady obedience to God's Word and intimate friendship with the Lord that leads to abundant life and sustaining faith. There are no shortcuts to the fruit. —Darlene Kerr

*"Abide in me, and I in you. As the branch cannot bear fruit by itself,
unless it abides in the vine, neither can you, unless you abide in me."*
—John 15:4 (ESV)

AUGUST 21

The Harried Hummingbird

The LORD is my shepherd; I shall not want.

—PSALM 23:1 (KJV)

ZOOM, ZIP, ZOOM. It was hummingbird season, and the birds flew in a frenzy past my head. As I sat on the deck, I could feel my hair blow across my cheek as they passed by. *Zoom. Zip.* It was a race to the bird feeder.

As I quietly watched, I noticed that one particular bird seemed to be the bully of the bunch. He would sit on a branch, concealed by a few leaves, and watch the feeder as if it was his alone. As soon as a new bird came by, he would zoom down and chase it away. And he wouldn't just chase; he would also chatter. In his little hummingbird voice, he was clearly trying to be big and scary. *Peep peep peep!* "Stay away from my feeder!" he seemed to say.

At first, I wondered what his problem was. I put out fresh sugar water every day. There are plenty of sweet treats for all the hummingbirds that fly by. He was panicking over nothing. There would be more sweet water tomorrow for sure.

But then I got to thinking about how much I panic over nothing. Don't I zip and zoom throughout my day, trying to get the best of everything? I was suddenly reminded of trying to get the best parking spot, the shortest line at the grocery store, or the best deal for lunch.

I can get worried about resources too. And like the hummingbird, sometimes I feel like shoving others out of the way. I might not actually do it (I do have manners), but I can feel the inclination in my heart.

Watching the harried hummingbird showed me that I need to stop being so pushy in my life. God has got this. I am well cared for. There will be enough for me today and enough for me tomorrow. I just need to trust in Him and be willing to share. —Heather Jepsen

Dear God, help me to trust that You have things under control. If I trust in You today, there will be enough for everyone. Amen.

ALL GOD'S CREATURES 241

AUGUST 22

The Second Blue Jay

"Do not be afraid of them; the LORD your God himself will fight for you."

—DEUTERONOMY 3:22 (NIV)

FROM MY KITCHEN window, I looked into the backyard. Two blue jays rested on the edge of the birdbath. Our summer heat was unbearable. Temperatures had been in the 100s for several weeks in a row. It hadn't rained for months.

As I watched, both birds dipped their beaks into the water, took a sip, bent their heads back, swallowed, and dipped again. I must have moved, because after one bird looked in my direction, it flew off. The second bird looked at me and paused a moment, but instead of flying away, it went back to drinking.

I wondered why one bird flew away in fear, yet the other stayed and took a chance I wouldn't hurt it. Was the first bird more timid than the second? Had the first bird experienced a frightful encounter that made it wary? I continued to watch the remaining blue jay as it drank. Before long, it jumped into the water and flapped its wings, thoroughly enjoying itself. It even found a worm to eat before it flew away.

Even though I slid out of view, hoping the first bird would return, it never did. Because it flew away in fear, it lost out on the tasty snack the other bird enjoyed. Fear caused it to miss the pleasure of refreshing water on a sweltering day. The bird's fear kept it from enjoying what I provided for it.

The more I considered the blue jay that flew away, the more I realized I'm not so different. I often miss out on the good that God places in front of me because I get spooked and fly away. I need to be more like the blue jay who looked right at me, then stayed, drank the water, ate the worm, and took a bath. Like the second blue jay, I need to follow through on the opportunity God has given me, even when it gets a little scary.

—Sandy Kirby Quandt

If you want to be courageous, act as if you were—and as you act and persevere in acting, so you tend to become.
—Norman Vincent Peale

AUGUST 23

The Guardian

*But the Lord is faithful. He will establish you
and guard you against the evil one.*

—2 THESSALONIANS 3:3 (ESV)

WHEN OUR SON, Jeremy, and his family bought a house in the country, it came complete with a chicken coop and a dozen chickens. My granddaughter jumped right into caring for the hens and selling their eggs. It didn't take long, however, to learn the hard facts of country life. Other animals also like chickens—and not just for their eggs.

After losing a couple of their best layers, they began to notice that when the neighbor's Great Pyrenees, Lady, roamed their property, the chickens remained unharmed. They often heard her barking around their house at night, usually at about the same time coyotes howled nearby. Jeremy and his wife researched the protective qualities of the breed and decided to get a Great Pyrenees of their own.

I was picking up my four-year-old grandson the first time I saw Bert. The fluffy white guardian was only 7 months old but already as big as a grown golden retriever. I walked right up to him before I realized he was lying on the doorstep. He raised his head to study me but made no menacing sounds. Thank goodness he deemed me friendly, because not only are the chickens under his protection but also the other dogs, the cats, and the entire family. He has even chased off the neighbor's dog, Lady!

Bert's protectiveness reminds me of the Lord's faithfulness in protecting me. No, it doesn't mean I'll never stub my toe, but God knows me as His child. He guards me against the evil of this world as I remain established in Him. To me, that means studying His Word and praying for guidance and discernment. I can't always foresee malicious intentions, but God can.

I hope Bert will one day discern who is friend and who is foe among everyone, just as any good guardian does. Regardless, he will faithfully watch over his family—animal and human alike—just as God watches over me. —Tracy Crump

*Lord, thank You for Your faithful protection against the forces of
this world that are often too strong for us to battle.*

AUGUST 24

Caring for Dalia

*"Learn to do good. Seek justice. Help the oppressed. Defend
the cause of orphans. Fight for the rights of widows."*

—ISAIAH 1:17 (NLT)

WHEN MY SISTER Sherry's family hosted Easter, we found a surprise
at their house—a new kitten named Dalia. Sherry's house already
had its share of pets: Zoey the Australian shepherd, a funny mutt named
Red, two cats, and a rabbit. So when I heard about the most recent addition, I had to restrain myself from reacting with "Are you kidding me?
Where are you going to put her?"

Then I heard Dalia's story, and my heart turned to mush before I even
saw her.

A teenager had found her on the side of the road and taken her home
only to abandon her. So she'd been left to fend for herself twice. When
Sherry's family had rescued her, she was starved and unkempt. But when
Sherry brought Dalia out to meet the family, I saw a beautiful, healthy
tortoiseshell calico with a belly fat from good food. Her face rested on
Sherry's shoulder like a baby who knew she was safe with Mommy.

I scolded myself for ever considering this kitten as an unnecessary addition to an already full house. My sister's family had provided a home
for one of God's creatures, one who wouldn't have survived otherwise.
They'd welcomed her into their home, fed her, and given her a lovely
name. Dalia is now a scrappy kitty who can hold her own in the menagerie of pets and knows with full certainty she is loved.

By taking her in, Sherry's family demonstrated their gift for helping the oppressed. Yes, Dalia was a cat, but they have done the same for
humans in need. Though my living situation doesn't allow me to take
in abandoned animals or friends who need a place to stay, I can live out
God's Word to His people by standing up for the vulnerable in other ways.
—Jeanette Hanscome

> Walk of Faith: *Who do you admire because of their passion for
> service or care for others? Ask God for an opportunity
> to support their efforts or follow their example.*

244 ALL GOD'S CREATURES

AUGUST 25

A Name of Her Very Own

*Fear not, for I have redeemed you; I have called
you by your name; you are Mine.*

—ISAIAH 43:1 (NKJV)

ON THE ANNIVERSARY of her arrival in our home, I found myself looking back on that late August day, 2 years ago. My husband, Mike, and I were driving back from picking up our newest rescue dog, an older female golden retriever. She huddled in the back seat, her head low, her ears pinned back. I climbed in beside her and stroked her gently. "It's OK," I whispered gently, "we're going home. You're going to like it there." I had never seen a dog so frightened. I knew why. She had spent every day of her 10 years as a breeding dog in a puppy mill—an inhumane, high-volume dog-breeding facility. Now that we were preparing to give her a new home, there was one important thing left to do, and I was going to do it before we got home.

Living only in a cage, there were so many things she hadn't experienced. She'd never been inside a house. She'd never eaten nutritious food from a clean bowl. She'd never played with a toy. We would be changing all that.

There was one more thing she'd never had, something I was not willing to allow any longer. In all of her many years, she'd never had a name.

A parent knows their child's name, usually before the baby is even born. Even more remarkable, our heavenly Father knows our name. He knows each of us intimately, right down to the very hairs on our head. It is extraordinary to me that He bothers with such a detail. Because He created me and knows everything about me, I can be sure that I am important to Him.

I wanted our new dog to know she was important to us too. Important enough to call by name. So there, on a warm summer day along a quiet country road, the frightened, anonymous breeding mama from a puppy mill became known. And Sophie is her name. —Peggy Frezon

Abba God, I take great comfort in that You know my name. Because You are my loving Father, I can trust Your plans for me.

ALL GOD'S CREATURES   245

AUGUST 26

Sam's Babies

God is our refuge and strength, a very present help in trouble.

—PSALM 46:1 (ESV)

MY FRIEND PAUL did a fair amount of camping with his family when he was young. One of his favorite memories is of the time Sam came into their lives.

The family was sitting around a campfire when they noticed a dog approaching cautiously, a collie whose bedraggled appearance attested to months spent fending for herself in the wild. She stood just outside the circle of log benches, intently studying the people to determine whether they could be trusted. Satisfied with her perusal, she turned and walked away.

After a brief interval, she returned and dropped a bundle at their feet—one that looked like a . . . *skunk!* The family leaped from their seats and darted away as fast as they could. But then one crept back for a closer look and discovered that it was a black puppy with a white stripe running from its head down its back, to the tip of its tail. Intrigued, they came closer to investigate and decided that Polecat was a good name for the pup. As they examined the young one, the collie—whom they would later name Sam—returned and deposited another of her offspring next to the first. This one had tightly curled brown hair and was quickly dubbed Pussy Willow. With the delivery of her third youngster, another cutie they named Goldenrod, Sam's work for the night was done.

After bonding with the family overnight, all four dogs left the woods the next day in the family car. Sam and Polecat stayed with them, while the other two puppies found homes nearby and were able to visit often.

There are things in my life that are beyond my ability to cope with independently. I need brothers and sisters to come alongside me to provide direction, support, and fellowship. I pray that I would readily acknowledge this need and reach out to God and others with trust, just as Sam was able to do with her puppies. —Liz Kimmel

Father, Your arms are always open wide and willing to take me into Your embrace. Thank You for pointing me toward just the right help, at just the right time, no matter the circumstances of my life.

ALL GOD'S CREATURES

AUGUST 27

A Lesson from Five Deer

The LORD has done great things for us, and we are filled with joy.

—PSALM 126:3 (NIV)

OUR WEATHER WAS brutal. Triple-digit temperatures that lasted the entire summer. No rain fell for months, adding to our rain deficit from the previous summer. It was one of the hottest summers on record. The drought dried up rivers and lakes, killed plants and trees, and stressed wildlife. That's why I was surprised to see five young deer playing in a trickle of water in a roadside ditch at a local state park.

When my husband and I left the park, it was the young buck on the left side of the road that caught my attention first. He paused to make sure the road was clear before gamboling across it. The buck joined four young fawns on the other side. The fawns were frolicking in mere inches of water in a ditch. Given how dry it'd been, I had no idea where that small amount of water came from. But that didn't seem to concern the deer. They were just happy to play in it.

I felt this camping trip was a consolation prize compared to the trip we'd planned to celebrate a milestone birthday. The original vacation had to be canceled due to illness, and because of that, I was not the happiest of campers. But seeing the joy these five deer found in a shallow ditch of water caused me to rethink my attitude.

This camping trip was not just a consolation prize after all. It was an opportunity God had provided me to witness His remarkable creation. A creation that enjoyed His provision, despite the circumstances.

Those five deer in a roadside ditch reminded me of something important. Whenever my plans don't work out the way I want, I need to believe God has something else, or even better, in mind for me. —Sandy Kirby Quandt

Father, whenever I am tempted to grumble and complain when things don't go as I planned, remind me of the five deer that found joy in even the smallest thing, and to be grateful.

AUGUST 28

Inheritance

"Blessed are the meek, for they will inherit the earth."
—**MATTHEW 5:5** (NIV)

MR. WIMBERLY, A kind man from the Pineville Animal Shelter in Louisiana, told me 22 years ago that Patches was going to be a big, healthy cat. He also said she'd live a long life. I couldn't imagine how he'd know that, especially looking at the scrawny, ringworm-infected kitten clinging to the edge of the cage. She seemed uninterested in her littermates, and even her mother, but she struck a fetching Spiderman pose for me as she hooked her paws along the wire and stretched her pink button nose through the enclosure.

Patches took to her new home right away, especially delighting in our five-year-old daughter, who lined a box with blankets and fastened it with a string so she could stroll Patches around like a baby. Patches truly thrived—until the other animals came. First another cat. Then a dog. And years later, that box-strolling daughter brought her own cat home from college. Indifferent to any and every animal that entered our home, Patches isolated herself so gradually, we hardly noticed.

"She'd be happier if it was just us," my husband admitted.

As the years passed, we all grew older, and while she seemed content—if not happy—Patches didn't age as quickly as the other animals. When our gentle black cat, Geera, passed away, Patches remained aloof, but when we lost our 12-year-old papillon in 2021, everything changed.

Finally, Patches had us all to herself, and in an instant, she once more became a lap-sitting, figure-eight-weaving, loud-purring princess. At last, her patience had been rewarded and she was truly living her best life. She enjoyed 2 full years of our undivided affection, and while I miss her terribly, I'm still astounded by her endurance. And her patience.

Perhaps Patches learned to be content in every situation because she recognized the Big Picture and she knew the best was yet to come. I want to be more like Patches. —Hallie Lee

Lord, help me embrace my circumstances today, holding firm and trusting Your promise that the best is yet to come.

AUGUST 29

Life Preservers

He makes me to lie down in green pastures;
He leads me beside the still waters.

—PSALM 23:2 (NKJV)

FOR MONTHS MY walks to Wall Springs Park in Palm Harbor, Florida, meant navigating around construction trucks and workers. They rebuilt the four piers one by one and then rebuilt the boardwalk around the spring in two parts. After all the trucks had rolled away, one stray piece of wood a little over a foot long floated in the watery area of the park, Boggy Bayou.

I arrived at the park and walked across the boardwalk. Leaning against the wood railing overlooking the pond, I counted a half-dozen ducks swimming in the bayou not too far from the stray wood piece. As if waiting for my arrival, one brave hen climbed onto the floating piece of wood. She settled in and rested her webbed feet. After a few minutes' respite, she glided back into the water. Emboldened, another hen climbed upon the little raft. She stayed a minute or two and then swam away so another could have a turn.

After a while, the ducks moved to the other side of the bayou, and I continued walking until I reached one of the benches under the covered pavilion that overlooks the spring's source. Encouraged by how the ducks took a break, I sat on a bench and enjoyed a few minutes' relief from the sun's rays before I returned home.

As I overlooked the still waters, I considered Psalm 23 and how God offers me moments of respite throughout my day. Short siestas to rest in Him. But when I ignore too many of those invitations and push myself, I find myself battling an infection or the common cold. Maybe I need to be more like a duck and hop on those invitations, seeing them as life preservers. —Crystal Storms

Rest time is not waste time. It is economy to gather fresh strength. . . .
It is wisdom to take occasional furlough. In the long run,
we shall do more by sometimes doing less.
—Charles Spurgeon

ALL GOD'S CREATURES 249

AUGUST 30

My Real Live Cam

Ears to hear and eyes to see—both are gifts from the LORD.

—PROVERBS 20:12 (NLT)

OH NO! A crow just landed on the nest!" My dog lifted his head from his soft pillow to stare at me, as if to say, *And what would you like me to do about that?* I giggled as he sighed and laid his head back down. But truly, what did I want him to do? In fact, there was nothing either of us could do because the crow on the bald eagle's nest was 50 miles away—I was watching through the eagle cam on my computer.

For days, I kept my computer booted up with the eagle cam displayed. I refreshed it frequently, hoping to watch the two eggs hatch. I'd enjoyed this eagle cam for several years. Imagine getting the chance to view bald eagles, black bears, and elk living out their lives, all while sitting in my own home. Yes, I'd seen documentaries, but these were real! No, I don't understand the difference, but somehow, my heart had involved itself with these raptors.

Later that day, I sat near the computer again, doing some writing on my second computer. I kept glancing at the cam footage, anxious to see the pip widen and an eaglet burst forth. Then I noticed a flash of red. Worried about a potential threat to the eggs, I brought the computer closer, and as I did so, I realized the flash was outside my window. A bird feeder hangs inches from the window, and on it sat a brilliant male cardinal, as well as a red-bellied woodpecker. Astonished to see both on the feeder at once, I happily watched as they enjoyed their afternoon repast.

And it hit me how I'd become so focused on what was on my screen and not on what was alive and right there for me to see. What other things had I missed while spending my days focused on something happening miles away? What other things might God have for me in my own backyard? —Cathy Mayfield

Open my eyes that I may see glimpses of truth Thou hast for me.
—Clara H. Scott

AUGUST 31

I Don't Have to See It

"Night and day, whether he sleeps or gets up, the seed sprouts and grows, though he does not know how."

—MARK 4:27 (NIV)

A PILEATED WOODPECKER has taken up residence in my neighborhood. That jackhammer-like pecking is unmistakable. The sound is more like a machine gun than a birdcall, and it travels a long distance. This is no mild-mannered downy woodpecker, the quiet, gentle forager who hops from limb to limb in search of food. This is a large, long-beaked bird sporting a jaunty red crest who bores into solid oak with the relentlessness of a heavy-metal drummer. I call him Woody Woodpecker.

Here's the thing: I've never seen this particular bird. I don't have to. That distinctive sound tells me everything I need to know. Sight is useful for identifying birds, but it's not necessary in all cases. Hearing works just as well most of the time.

I know from experience that woodpeckers like Woody can be destructive, especially if they take a liking to your wood siding. But I've taken a liking to this rat-a-tat-tat sound. It reminds me that creation is alive and growing, with bees buzzing, birds chirping, dogs barking, and woodpeckers pecking, whether I can see them or not.

The Gospel is like this: the Word of God is out there, growing in the hearts of believers and taking root in the minds of unbelievers. I can hear it in words of forgiveness spoken between a wife and husband, the tears and laughter of a father's reunion with a wayward son, or the voice of a child who has learned to say, "You can go first."

Sometimes, when I feel self-important, as if God is virtually helpless to save the world without my constant work, I sit on the porch and listen to Woody rooting a carpenter ant out of a sycamore tree. And I remember that God's kingdom is doing very well despite my best efforts to help it along. —Lawrence W. Wilson

Lord, give me the faith to know that You are redeeming this world, even when I can't see it for myself.

ALL GOD'S CREATURES   251

SEPTEMBER 1

The Big Pond

*"When you pass through the waters, I will be with you; and
through the rivers, they shall not overwhelm you."*

—ISAIAH 43:2 (ESV)

I SAT ON the porch with a good friend whose daughter was preparing
to go away to college. "Is she anxious?" I asked. As the rocking chairs
creaked, I recalled a time when I was 18 and worried about leaving my
small town to make my way in a big city out of state. In my hometown,
I'd been the proverbial big fish in a small pond. How would I manage in
an immense university in a bustling city?

At that same time, I'd been looking for someone to watch over and
protect my pets while I was away. My mother had remarried, and she and
her new husband were building a log cabin in the Vermont mountains.
The family dog and cat were already there. One day I took my three goldfish from their small aquarium and tipped them into a vast pond on the
property, where they disappeared into its depths.

I had little time to wonder about those fish as I pursued my studies. But
one sunny June day, home for the summer, I visited my mother. My dog
and cat happily greeted me. "Now, come see your fish!" Mom said. We
walked to the pond and tossed in a handful of pellets. In short time, the
fish swam to the surface.

"Mom, they're huge!" I said. Those tiny goldfish had not only grown at
least 6 inches, but they'd also multiplied. Their God-given instincts had
enabled them to survive the winter, find insects and vegetation to devour,
and avoid the herons.

"And," I told my friend, leaning toward her from my rocker, "sure
enough, I thrived in my 'big pond' too." With space and opportunities,
I'd broadened my horizons and grown in ways I would have never imagined. All because I had room to grow . . . and my Father to watch over and
guide me. Together, we prayed for my friend's daughter. —Peggy Frezon

*God would not bring you through a Red Sea and turn around
and allow you to perish in a fishpond later.*
—Johnnie Dent Jr.

ALL GOD'S CREATURES   253

SEPTEMBER 2

Rush-Hour Traffic

*Even though I walk through the darkest valley, I will fear no evil,
for you are with me; your rod and your staff, they comfort me.*

—PSALM 23:4 (NIV)

TWO-WHEELERS, BOTH SCOOTERS and motorbikes, are a common mode of transport for many people in India. They are affordable and easily maneuverable on the congested roads in big cities. People use two-wheelers to transport light luggage and sometimes even small animals.

During a recent trip to India, when my car halted at a traffic stop, I observed a young man riding a motorbike with his fluffy Pomeranian. She straddled the gas tank in front of him, her tongue sticking out and ears perked up. As we dragged along in the bumper-to-bumper traffic, I noticed the dog flinch and glance at her owner whenever a vehicle got close to the bike. The man briefly looked at her and spoke a few words to calm her down. This exchange took place at least a couple of times in the rush-hour traffic.

As I noticed how the dog found comfort and safety in the words of her human friend amid a chaotic and disorderly environment, my thoughts drifted toward recent changes in my life that had left me feeling a bit lost and insecure. I brooded over all the things that could go wrong and how I could fix them.

The Pomeranian reminded me to turn to the Good Shepherd for guidance and encouragement during times of uncertainty and transitions. I can let go of my doubts and worries and count on His unchanging faithfulness, love, and wisdom to help me persevere. By fixing my eyes on Jesus and tuning my ears to listen to His assuring words, I can anchor my security and hope to Him regardless of changing circumstances.
—Mabel Ninan

*Father, please remind me to steer my thoughts toward Your steadfast love
and Your good plans for me when I feel overwhelmed by uncertainty.
May I find rest and comfort in Your presence. Amen.*

SEPTEMBER 3

Nurse Nana

He will not let your foot slip—he who watches over you will not slumber.
—PSALM 121:3 (NIV)

MS. NANA THE calico cat may be diminutive, but she has a huge heart. Even at age 18, Nana can't rest until all her humans are asleep. Her owner knew that if she didn't keep her eyes shut when Nana came by, the munchkin-size kitty would keep checking until she was satisfied. After Nana's human invited her older dad to move in, the cat simply added Dad to her list of daily duties.

Every night, Nurse Nana made her rounds. Like a dedicated nanny with a bushy tail, she visited each human family member, making sure all were fast asleep. She may be a small kitty, but she takes her job seriously.

If Nana spots anyone's eyes still open, she keeps coming back to check until she's sure they've drifted off.

One night Nana checked on Dad four times in one evening, but each time, he woke up and said, "Hi Nana." She waited across the room until he seemed asleep and then checked him again.

His daughter told him to lie still and let Nana finish checking him and leave the room before he opened his eyes. Otherwise, the concerned cat would simply keep coming back for as long as it took.

Nana's dedication makes me think of God's everlasting protection. God's love for each of us is so complete that nothing can separate us from that provision. And sleep comes a lot easier knowing a loving God is watching over all of us.

Dad learned to pretend-sleep so Nana could finish her rounds, and she watched over him for as long as he lived in the house. She was even with him when he passed away. Now a senior kitty, Nurse Nana still brings joy, a lights-out check, and a meow of approval every night. —Linda S. Clare

To sleep is an act of faith.
—Barbara G. Harrison

SEPTEMBER 4

Slow Finds Beauty

"Pay attention to this, Job. Stop and consider the wonderful miracles of God!"
—JOB 37:14 (NLT)

HAVE YOU NOTICED a sloth's face? What's not to like about an animal with a perpetual grin? It's the facial muscles around the mouth and cheeks and the downward slant to the eyes that give sloths a seemingly happy expression, regardless of their mood or situation. Sometimes the fur framing their faces closely resembles a 1960s mop-top haircut. It only adds to the hilarity of their look.

Preparing for our trip to Costa Rica, I anticipated seeing both two-toed and three-toed sloths in their natural environment. My expectations were high based upon the charming photos and animated representations I had seen. I wanted to see that cute face in real life. The reality, though, is that in spite of their relative immobility, one doesn't often get a close-up look at them in the wild. What I witnessed most often were big brown blobs high up in the tree canopy.

And when you do see sloths, they aren't terribly entertaining. They hang on an upper tree limb, most often horizontally. If you witness one moving an arm or a leg—well, you don't need to film in slo-mo to capture the action. Their movements are languid and calm and excruciatingly slow to an observer.

My encounter with sloths reminded me of a saying I once heard: "Speed normally isn't a witness to beauty." I've come to realize that speed often effectively blinds us. I can easily become blind to the moments and situations that God generously creates to restore my soul, refresh my spirit, and birth gratitude toward Him. I race through my day, mindlessly going through the motions, missing the beautiful moments that God has gifted to me.

With sloths, their slowness is not a conscious decision. It's not wisdom; it's biology. But I can choose my speed. I can slow down, really see, and offer up a string of praises to the Creator of the beautiful. —Darlene Kerr

Wisely and slow. They stumble that run fast.
—Shakespeare

SEPTEMBER 5

Always the Same

Jesus Christ is the same yesterday and today and forever.
—HEBREWS 13:8 (NIV)

AS A YOUNG wife in an animal-less apartment, I often stopped at the adoption corner at the pet store. One day, a one-eyed tabby named Captain Jack caught my attention. I talked to him and lowered my head, so it was level with his cage. Jack reached out and put a paw on my cheek. That was it! I called my husband and told him Jack had chosen me and we *had* to get him.

We brought Jack home and soon we discovered that our new five-month-old kitten was curious and playful. We'd play hide-and-seek. I'd mound up the blankets on the bed and hide behind them, then he'd smash the mound down and "find" me. As he got older, instead of playing games, he would climb onto my pillow and curl around my head as I slept. Now, as a 17-year-old senior cat, he often comes to my side, stretches his paw across my chest, and lays his head on my shoulder in a kitty hug.

Just like Jack, I've changed through the years. As I've grown from child to teen to adult, my interests and likes have changed, and my personality has changed too. I used to be incredibly shy, but now this introvert likes to meet and spend time with people. In my Christian walk, I've also changed in my understanding of God and how I relate to him. I'm grateful for the maturity and wisdom that have come as I've gotten older, and I'm excited to see what changes the coming years will bring.

While I'm thankful for the changes in me, I'm most thankful that God never changes. He'll never change His mind about what a sin is or what I need to do to be saved. He'll never call me His darling one day, then push me away the next. His Word and His solid character keep me on stable ground as I grow and change to be more like Him with every passing year. —Kristen G. Johnson

In all our efforts to find God, to please Him, to commune with Him, we should remember that all change must be on our part.
—A. W. Tozer

ALL GOD'S CREATURES   257

SEPTEMBER 6

Prayers Take Flight

And this is the confidence that we have toward him, that if we ask anything according to his will he hears us. And if we know that he hears us in whatever we ask, we know that we have the requests that we have asked of him.

—1 JOHN 5:14–15 (ESV)

IT'S LATE SUMMER and the American goldfinches find our coreopsis, eating the seeds as the plants wither. Slender flower stems bend under the weight of perched bright yellow birds. As I pull into our driveway, I witness a dozen or more goldfinches take a startled swirling flight up and out of our flower beds. It's a cheerful explosion of motion, and my spirit soars along with them.

I breathe a prayer of gratitude for birds and seeds and my eyes that can see the natural beauty of God's creation. As I watch those swirls of color rise, my thoughts turn fanciful, and I picture the multitude of prayers taking flight and making their way to the Throne of Grace.

Imagine for a moment what it would be like to see the prayers of God's people as plainly visible to the naked eye as these airborne goldfinches are to mine. The image makes me smile. Though we can't see them winging upward to Him, the Father not only receives our prayers, but He always knows exactly what we need even before we ask Him (Matthew 6:8).

Goldfinches can rise only so far before they must descend back to earth's realm, but my prayers have no such limitations, and I can be confident that they will make it all the way to heaven. Best of all, my prayers are always answered by a loving Father, and His responses are sure to be aligned with what's best for me.

My spirit soars knowing that I can confidently send the seeds of my faith on an ascending wing straight to my Father's ear. —Darlene Kerr

Lord, thank You for always hearing my prayers. I thank You that Your answers are always the right answers, because You love me.

SEPTEMBER 7

Cleanup Crew

God will supply all your needs according to His riches in glory in Christ Jesus.
—PHILIPPIANS 4:19 (NASB)

I HAD A big problem. A mild spring in our mountain valley meant that our three fruit trees—apple, plum, and apricot—were bursting with fruit in our backyard. Abundance may not seem like a problem, but since I was recovering from surgery, I didn't have the strength to harvest the fruit and then process it into sauces and jams. And while a few friends took advantage of the free fruit, a mess was growing on the ground.

But as the ripe fruit fell to the ground—first apricots, then plums, and finally apples, a whole family of helpers arrived. Half a dozen does and their young ones came nearly every day to clean things up. One mom was particularly hungry, as she had three young fawns. "Mama," as I called her, didn't skitter away as the other does did when I appeared at the kitchen door. And she was comical to watch, because one by one, she nudged her three young ones to the fruit buffet. Mama deer typically nurse for only three to four months, and it was my guess that she was tired of nursing three babies and more than ready to guide them to independence.

Like that mama deer, God nudges His children, too, through His Holy Spirit. He nudges us to seek out the people and sources that can guide us to find the bounty He has waiting for us. Sometimes that help is physical in nature. Sometimes that help is emotional—a simple desire to know we are loved. Sometimes that help is the mental guidance we need to know how to make the right decision. And sometimes it is people or resources that can help us grow in our faith. In each case, when we ask Him, He will guide us to the source in our lives that He uses to meet our needs.
—Janet Holm McHenry

Lord, thank You for the ways You nudge me toward the bounty
You have in store for me in all aspects of my life.

ALL GOD'S CREATURES 259

SEPTEMBER 8

A Real Live Dinosaur?

*"In this world you will have trouble. But take heart!
I have overcome the world."*

—JOHN 16:33 (NIV)

OH NO! AHEAD on the road lay what resembled a medium-size carcass. Days before, I'd watched deer cross there. My heart sank.

As I drew alongside, I found instead a huge snapping turtle, very much alive. Its shell measured at least 18 inches. Its beaked head raised a fraction, as though challenging me. Snapping turtles are formidable creatures. I'd been around several, and on one occasion the turtle's speed shocked us as it "snapped" a large branch in two.

Once, my brother found a tiny one by a river and raised it in an aquarium. Its slow growth was the only thing slow about it. At maturity, they look menacing, like one I saw a few years back on our property. I'd been walking our dog, Kenai, on the road bordering the yard when I spotted a huge moving rock in the grass. Astonished, I watched as it came closer. Realizing what it was and remembering how fast the one years before had moved, I hightailed it away from there!

After getting Kenai safely in the house, I went back out. If the turtle had taken up residence along our creek, we could have troubles. I didn't want to worry when we walked the dog that he would get a vicious bite. By the time I got close, the turtle had crossed the road. What I saw then astounded me! Standing on tiny tree-trunk legs, his shell about 7 inches from the ground, he looked like a miniature dinosaur tramping through the weeds. I stared while he made his way up the hill.

Recently, I've been bogged down by huge problems. They seem as ominous as that snapping turtle. They, too, had started out quite tiny and grew slowly to this point. Now, they seemed too big, too strong. That's when I have to remember I have a God who's bigger, stronger. He could snap those problems in two if I would trust Him to do so. —Cathy Mayfield

*Father, teach me to trust You to be bigger
than any trouble that comes my way. Amen.*

260 ALL GOD'S CREATURES

SEPTEMBER 9

Remain Steadfast

Therefore, my beloved brethren, be steadfast, immovable, always abounding in the work of the Lord, knowing that your labor is not in vain in the Lord.

—1 CORINTHIANS 15:58 (NKJV)

MY MOTHER OWNS two lovely Japanese coral specimens—one black and one red. The black one resembles a spindly but picturesque miniature tree. The red one appears lacy, spreading out like an old-fashioned hand fan.

For years, I thought coral was a plant. It's not. Corals are actually sea animals, small marine invertebrates. What Mom put on display upon her mantelpiece, and what jewelers transform into brooches and earrings, are the skeletons of such creatures. Sometimes coral live together in vast numbers. Their skeletons form coral reefs, many of which are hundreds of miles long, such as the Great Barrier Reef near Australia.

I also thought coral floated around near the bottom of the seafloor, carried along by the ocean currents. That's not quite true either. While baby coral larvae can swim and ride the currents, they quickly attach themselves to a safe and suitable foundation. When they do so, they remain securely anchored there for the rest of their lives. They feed on plankton and tiny plants that the ocean currents carry past them.

Occasionally when I've admired my mother's coral display, I've contemplated the beauty and steadfastness of these marine creatures. Coral is difficult to dislodge because it clings tenaciously to its foundation. I want to be like that when it comes to my faith in Jesus. I want to remain steadfast and immovable in His Truth, no matter what cultural currents may threaten to overwhelm me. Christ can and will stabilize us forever.
—Shirley Raye Redmond

Wisdom and knowledge will be the stability of your times, and the strength of salvation; the fear of the Lord is His treasure.
—Isaiah 33:6 (NKJV)

SEPTEMBER 10

Love Tops Treats

"Martha, Martha," the Lord answered, "you are worried and upset about many things, but few things are needed—or indeed only one. Mary has chosen what is better, and it will not be taken away from her."

—LUKE 10:41–42 (NIV)

MY FRIEND MARGARET'S cat, Cleo, is very affectionate and really loves treats. Whenever Margaret rattles the bag of goodies, Cleo immediately comes running.

However, more than the yummy treats, Cleo loves Margaret. Even when Margaret holds out a tempting, tasty morsel, Cleo won't take it. At least not yet. First, she rubs up against Margaret, wanting to give and receive affection. Once Margaret has loved on the kitty, she will finally accept the proffered treat.

What a smart animal to choose love over food! She knows what's most important. Margaret and Cleo's affection for each other reminds me of Mary and Martha in the Bible. It also reminds me of my relationship with God and encourages me to be more like Cleo. When I honestly reflect on my prayer life, I find I most often go to God when worried or when I need something. It's almost as if I sometimes treat God like a vending machine of treats and comfort.

Certainly, God wants to give us good things as well as comfort. But I want to be more faithful to go to Him at *all* times. To go to Him simply out of love and the desire to praise Him. I want to spend more time in prayer as if sitting at His feet, listening. I want to spend more time in Scripture getting to know Him better. I want to be like Cleo and choose the better thing. —Missy Tippens

Lord, thank You for the example Mary set by sitting at Your feet, focusing on You. Help me to be more like her, choosing the better part that can never be taken away. Amen.

SEPTEMBER 11

Choose Love

"But to you who are listening I say: Love your enemies, do good to those who hate you, bless those who curse you, pray for those who mistreat you."

—LUKE 6:27–28 (NIV)

I STOOD IN front of the 14-foot-high window and leaned against the cement wall to watch Izzy, a bottlenose dolphin at the Clearwater Marine Aquarium in Clearwater, Florida. Izzy swam in front of the window and held a pose long enough for me to take pictures of her. She appeared to smile as she swam my way. Then Izzy did somersaults in front of the window to the delight of everyone—including me.

The dolphin complex where Izzy swims holds 1.5 million gallons of water. She could easily avoid the windows with all that room. Yet Izzy chooses to interact with crowds because she loves people. That's what led her to the CMA.

Izzy lived off the shores of Texas. Her love of people meant she swam too close to boats and sustained injuries from their propellers. She ate scraps that people fed her, but that didn't give her the nutrition she needed. A few people even tried to climb on her back like one would a horse. When officials saw the posts on social media, they checked in on Izzy. Her health had declined to the point of needing intervention and medical attention. CMA became her forever home.

Still, Izzy didn't stop loving people because those she trusted turned out to be unsafe. She went to where the people were and brought smiles to those who saw her. Like Izzy, I don't want those who've hurt me to taint my love for God and those He created. I want to take a cue from this happy dolphin and bring joy to those around me. —Crystal Storms

Dear God, please give me the discernment to know when boundaries are necessary. Grant me wisdom to know how to love and pray for those from whom it's healthiest to keep some distance. Amen.

SEPTEMBER 12

The Sparrow, the Cat, and the Hawk

We don't look at the troubles we can see now; rather, we fix our gaze on things that cannot be seen. For the things we see now will soon be gone, but the things we cannot see will last forever.

—2 CORINTHIANS 4:18 (NLT)

A HOST OF little sparrows gathered inside my boxwood, making a racket with their boisterous chirping. The bush almost looked alive, the branches quivering with their activity. Once in a while a few birds popped up and perched on the top of the bush, peeking around the yard. I noticed one in particular, a plump little female with dusty-brown feathers. She seemed bright and alert as she spied the neighborhood feline out for a walk. Sensing danger, she froze. The cat walked on by, apparently well-fed or not in the mood for a chase. But the little bird was so engrossed in the cat, it didn't realize that a powerful Cooper's hawk had been watching from a nearby branch. I hadn't seen it, either, until the much larger bird was right there flapping its wings at the base of the bush. My little friend dived deep into the shrub, where the tangled branches and tight spaces protected it.

The world we live in is full of opportunities as well as hazards. Sometimes I am so focused on what I perceive as a threat that I don't see the real danger ready to pounce. Or maybe I don't see a way out of a predicament or a desirable direction. My limited vision keeps my gaze focused only on what is within my own miniscule understanding.

When I stop looking before me and behind me and instead take a heavenly focus, I get the real picture. As soon as I shift my gaze heavenward, I am trusting God to broaden my view. I am blessed, as His view is replete with infinite possibilities.

I clapped my hands and the hawk took off. The little sparrow popped up from the tangled branches and once again began singing. —Peggy Frezon

Vision is the ability to see God's presence, to perceive God's power, to focus on God's plan in spite of the obstacles.
—Charles R. Swindoll

SEPTEMBER 13

Tune In to God

My sheep listen to my voice; I know them, and they follow me.

—JOHN 10:27 (NIV)

MY GRANDMOTHER LOVED birds, and so do I. Our love of birds was one of the many things we shared. When I'd call her, she'd tell me about the array of bird varieties she could see out her window, and we'd laugh together as I described the antics of the birds in my yard.

We both especially loved blue jays—their expressive, distinctive calls ringing in the air, the unexpected indigo flashes as the birds flew from tree to tree. The ones in my yard have always been very elusive—I almost never saw them—so I always got excited when I'd hear their calls, which was only about once a week.

Sadly, three years ago, Gram lost her battle with dementia and went home to her heavenly Father. Since then, a family of blue jays has visited me on a daily basis. Hearing their voices recalls the voice of my beloved grandmother that I cherished so much in our frequent phone calls. Because I feel close to Gram when I hear them, I often find myself stopping what I am doing during the day to listen to the jays' raucous, joyous calls.

I may not always be able to find the blue jays when I look out the window, but hearing their boisterous cries throughout the day tells me they are all around me.

Though I'm still grieving Gram's loss, her love of birds led me to a deeper connection not just with her but also with God. Just as it is with the blue jays, I may not be able to see God, but when I listen for His voice, I know without a doubt He is always near. And in the same way that I've learned to tune in to the call of Gram's and my beloved blue jays, I'm also learning to stop for a moment during my busy days to tune in to the beautiful voice of my heavenly Father. —Leslie L. McKee

Walk of Faith: *Today, as you go about your day, stop to look for opportunities to listen for God's still, small voice to hear what He wants to tell you.*

SEPTEMBER 14

Horse Sense

Do not neglect to do good and to share what you have,
for such sacrifices are pleasing to God.

—HEBREWS 13:16 (ESV)

THE FARM I grew up on always had horses. That was my grandfather's doing. A local road I travel has several places with horses, and I still have the chance to see a trait I remember from my youth. Horses will partner up and stand side by side, facing opposite directions. Then they will periodically swish their tails near the other horse's face. I would think it rude to have someone come alongside me and flip their hair near my face. In horses, this behavior is beneficial. They swish the flies away from their equine partner's face.

A horse's body is too long to use its own tail. Therefore, horses rely on a willing partner to reciprocate the need for chasing pests off each other's faces. The conversation between the two might go something like this:

"Hey, buddy, are these flies getting on your nerves as much as mine? How about working together to chase them away?"

"Sure! You swish your tail every so often, and I'll swish mine."

When people saw this, they called it using "horse sense." It was interchangeable with using "common sense."

God created people with a need for others. I am not able to do everything on my own, and I need help. Today's Bible verse reads more like a command than a passing suggestion. I need to be making myself available to help and do good to others. It also tells me that God is pleased seeing me do this. If I already know I need others to get through life, it should make it easier to be willing to do the same for them.

David L. Cooper (1886–1965), the founder and president of the Biblical Research Society, is credited with this quote: "When the plain sense of Scripture makes common sense, seek no other sense." It seems the horses have taken this lesson to heart—and maybe I should as well. —Ben Cooper

Dear Lord, I am a needy person surrounded by needy people.
Give me the constant desire to share whatever resources and talents
You have given me so that I might please You. Amen.

SEPTEMBER 15

Telling the Bees

Whether we live or die, we belong to the Lord.

—ROMANS 14:8 (NIV)

MY HONEYBEES WORK at a frenzied pace in the warmer months, packing away provisions for the long Michigan winter. The bees store far more honey than they need, and I have come now, on this September morning, to take some for myself. I open the hive and cut away a chunk of honeycomb and pop it in my mouth. It is utterly delicious. Winemakers talk about the terroir of a particular wine: the way a place's geography, soil, and climate all contribute to a vintage. It is the same with honey. This year's honey is dark amber with a malty, wildflower sweetness.

Collecting honey is usually a satisfying, exultant experience. But not today. My old friend Bert, my beekeeping buddy, passed away last week, and I am sad. I'm reminded of a remarkable custom that prevailed in rural New England in the early 1800s. On the death of a family member, the honeybees were informed, and their hives were dressed in mourning, shrouded in black. The ritual was necessary, so people thought, to prevent swarms from leaving their hives and finding lodging elsewhere. John Greenleaf Whittier alludes to this odd custom in his poem, "Telling the Bees." Whittier describes how a servant girl walks slowly among the hives, announcing the sad news:

> *[T]he summer sun*
> *Had the chill of snow;*
> *For I knew she was telling the bees of one*
> *Gone on the journey we all must go!*

Chewing the honeycomb, enveloped in that gentle buzz, I tell the bees that Bert has passed away. You cannot pole-vault over the valley of the shadow of death; you have to walk it. But what sustains me in my walk is the knowledge that although death separates us from those we most love, it doesn't separate us from the God who most loves us. Whether we live or die, we belong to the Lord. —Louis Lotz

> *The grave itself is but a covered bridge, leading from light to light,*
> *through a brief darkness!*
> —Henry Wadsworth Longfellow

ALL GOD'S CREATURES 267

SEPTEMBER 16

Underwater Wonder

They glorified God and were filled with awe, saying,
"We have seen extraordinary things today."

—LUKE 5:26 (ESV)

MOST OF US can list animals, often including our pets, whose intelligence amazes us—dogs, cats, dolphins, African gray parrots, ravens, and more. Somewhat recently, scientists have begun to include a creature in that list that you might not expect: the octopus.

Scientists who study octopuses (or octopi, if you prefer—both are correct) have been surprised at the intelligence displayed by these cephalopods, a class of mollusks. Octopuses have large brains, and scientists have found that each of the octopus's eight arms also has its own brain and sensory organs! A recent discovery indicates that octopuses have some of the same DNA that determine human intelligence.

Stories abound of clever octopuses navigating mazes, using tools, working with other species to hunt for food, even using the venomous tentacle of a Portuguese man-of-war as a weapon. They have been observed unscrewing jars to retrieve the contents, as well as playing with objects in their tanks like toys. One aquarium tells the memorable story of an octopus that escaped from its tank and went down a drain in the floor to get back to the ocean. Scientists have determined that octopuses, much like crows and ravens, recognize and remember human faces—and will pick on humans they dislike. Octopuses are masters of disguise, sometimes camouflaging themselves to match their surroundings or, like the mimic octopus, actually making themselves look like animals such as sea snakes or lionfish for defensive purposes.

As amazing as the octopus is, it's mind-blowing when we to think that it is only a tiny fraction of God's magnificent creation, and the more scientists learn about the wonders of the universe, the more their discoveries add new dimensions and depth to our understanding of how wondrous His creativity truly is. When we look for God's many wonders, we can't help but be filled with praise and thanksgiving because we have seen, and continue to see, extraordinary things. —Editors of Guideposts

Lord, thank You for the new things we are learning about
Your creation—and You—every day. May I know You, love You,
and praise You more with each passing day.

268 ALL GOD'S CREATURES

SEPTEMBER 17

A Duck Dilemma

And those who know your name put their trust in you, for you, O Lord, have not forsaken those who seek you.

—PSALM 9:10 (ESV)

MALLARD DUCKS ABOUND at our three-season waterfront cottage in New York State's Adirondack Mountains. They swim past our dock every day from May to October. When our young grandchildren are visiting, the ducks stop and quack for handouts. The kids happily oblige by raiding the kitchen for cornflakes and oatmeal.

But one day last fall, a female duck showed up at our dock trailing a foot-long length of fishing line. Upon closer examination, my husband, Neil, and I discovered she had a fishhook embedded in one wing. Concerned, we tried to get her close enough to catch by luring her with food. But she always stayed just out of reach. Our younger son, Wade, did manage to snag her once, with a long-handled net. But she flew free before he could grab her.

Two weeks passed. It was time for us to close camp and for the duck to fly south for the winter. Not wanting to abandon her, Neil found our Havahart live trap, baited it with cornflakes, and set it out near our back steps. "We'll catch her now," he said. But we didn't. We caught other ducks, plenty of them. Just not her. She avoided our trap like the plague.

One by one, the mallards migrated. Only the afflicted one remained. "How can she fly a thousand miles with that hook in her wing?" I fussed.

Then one day she didn't show up. Nor did we see her the next day or the next. She'd left. Our duck had taken off despite her injury. I hoped that given time, the hook would rust and fall out by itself.

Then I made myself stop worrying. The truth is that some problems are simply too big for me to solve, despite my best efforts. When that happens, I need to let go and let God. —Aline Newman

God, give us grace to accept with serenity the things that cannot be changed, courage to change the things that should be changed, and the wisdom to distinguish the one from the other.
—Reinhold Niebuhr

SEPTEMBER 18

What Zeke Knew

"The LORD has chosen you to be a people for his treasured possession."
—DEUTERONOMY 14:2 (ESV)

ONE FALL AFTERNOON my friend Paul was hiking along a country road near Hinckley, Minnesota, when he noticed a commotion in the road up ahead. Drawing closer, he discovered that roughly forty-five cows had escaped their fence. They were ambling freely and causing immense frustration for the young woman who was desperately trying to corral them. Paul offered his assistance.

After they gathered in all the runaways, she pointed to the house at the end of the driveway and asked if he'd be interested in a black Lab puppy. He was the runt of a purebred litter. No one had yet been interested in taking a chance on him. The last thing Paul needed was another puppy, but for some reason, he said he'd take a look. As they approached her home, the tiny dog watched with excitement from the front porch.

Paul was about 4 to 5 feet away when the puppy suddenly leaped from his perch. He bounced against Paul's chest and then nestled contentedly in the arms that had come up in an automatic response to catch him. There was no way Paul could say no to that determination. In an instant, Zeke was his. He knew it then, but Zeke had known it first. The pair made their way together back to Paul's car. Zeke would not be settled in a back-seat box. Instead, he slept peacefully in Paul's lap for the entire drive back home, and the two were never separated from that point on.

Not everything in my life is a certainty. Without a season of prayer to guide me, I may not know immediately which job I should pursue or which town I should live in or how much schooling I should commit to. But because of His great love for me, I *know* that I will always belong to my heavenly Father, and He will always belong to me. —Liz Kimmel

Father, thank You for knowing and loving me from the moment I was conceived in Your heart. Thank You for helping me to choose You.

SEPTEMBER 19

Holding On for Dear Life

Because you are my help, I sing in the shadow of your wings. I cling to you; your right hand upholds me.

—PSALM 63:7–8 (NIV)

MY HUSBAND AND I headed out one beautiful fall morning to pick up a grocery order. Nothing seemed out of the ordinary—until I looked at my side mirror as we pulled out of the driveway. There, clinging to the edge of the mirror, was a small dragonfly with a long thin body, big eyes, tiny legs, and iridescent wings.

While my husband drove, I watched the little critter as our car accelerated and entered the highway. I was sure it would be blown away at any moment, losing its grip with the increased speed. Yet when I glanced at the mirror again, it was still there, gripping tightly to the mirror as the wind whipped around it.

I was amazed at how strong its thin legs were and how they clung to our fast-moving vehicle. Through it all, the dragonfly appeared unfazed by the world flying by.

As I watched it hang on for miles, I paused to consider how I handle everything that comes my way in life. I admit that on far too many occasions I get flustered and frazzled. Sometimes it feels like I'm holding on for dear life, and I forget to grab on to the One who can get me through any circumstance. I falter before I reach out to God. But like the dragonfly that hung on to our vehicle, even though it wasn't sure where we were going, I'm learning to cling to God through the ever-accelerating pace of life and trust that He has a plan. I pray for the strength to always hold on, even when I don't know where the road is headed. —Leslie L. McKee

Lord, help me to cling to You in every situation, trusting that You will hold me firm. Amen.

ALL GOD'S CREATURES   271

SEPTEMBER 20

Waiting for the Kinglets

Therefore you do not lack any spiritual gift as you eagerly wait for our Lord Jesus Christ to be revealed.

—1 CORINTHIANS 1:7 (NIV)

EVERY YEAR IN the fall, for one day only, the shrubs in my front yard play host to a flock of ruby-crowned kinglets as they migrate from north to south. Kinglets are cute, tiny olive-green birds, and I happily look forward to seeing their busy rush of motion grace my yard each year. Despite their size, they're hard to miss. When the flock lands in my garden, the twittering and scrambling among the bushes always captures my attention. I can watch them through my window and not scare them away. Still, I've had a difficult time capturing a photo of them. They simply move too fast!

Because of their size and speed, it took a couple of years of observation to gather enough unique information to identify them, but now that I know what they are called and what time of year they fly through, I can check the calendar so that I don't miss them. When the day arrives, it's a short-lived pleasure. The kinglets show up and forage frantically for only a few minutes before moving on. All that waiting for 10 minutes of delight.

Waiting for the kinglets reminds me of waiting for the King, our Lord Jesus Christ, to return. Though the waiting can be tough, boring, and even depressing, I try to cultivate an attitude of eagerness. I want to be in a state of happy expectation, not exhausted exasperation, as I wait. Though I can't mark the day on a calendar, I do look forward to the moment of His arrival. When it comes, it won't be a short-lived delight or a shallow diversion. It will be the day I go home to live with Him forever.
—Marianne Campbell

The King shall come when morning dawns, and light and beauty brings.
Hail, Christ the Lord! Your people pray: Come quickly, King of kings!
—John Brownlie

SEPTEMBER 21

A Dog to Comfort My Heart

Do not be anxious about anything, but in every situation, by prayer and petition, with thanksgiving, present your requests to God

—PHILIPPIANS 4:6 (NIV)

IT HAD BEEN a week since my dog passed away. She was a goldendoodle, part golden retriever and part poodle, and the best dog I'd ever had. She lived a wonderful 13 years.

Things were not the same in our home. It was quiet; there was no sound of the pitter-patter of dog feet on the tile and no ball dropped in my lap for an impromptu game of fetch.

My heart was missing my dog so badly that every reminder of her was a new heartbreak.

My husband and I went for a walk one morning. Our neighborhood has beautiful walking trails, and many people use the trails at all times of the day, as do many dogs. "I'm going to pet a dog," I said to my husband, reaching out to hold his hand. "I need to."

I prayed a quick prayer about it. I desperately needed to pet a furry head. About a minute after we began the walk, a beautiful golden retriever appeared on the path alongside his owner.

"Oh, my goodness," I said in a whisper. "There he is!" The dog pulled on his owner's leash as soon as he saw us, and instead of walking up to my husband who was closer to him, he beelined straight to me.

His head was in my hand before I even realized what was happening. He sniffed me, licked my hand, and let me pet his adorable furry head with the happiest of tongues hanging out of his mouth. It's remarkable how intuitive animals are and how good God is at answering our requests.

Though sad things are a part of life, indeed, God is always in the midst of it. With a little help from Him and a furry friend on the trail, my heart righted itself that day. —Heather Spiva

Lord, thank You for hearing my prayers. Even the ones that are insignificant and small are important and big to You. You are good! Amen.

SEPTEMBER 22

Dedication

Do not forsake your friend or a friend of your family.
—**PROVERBS 27:10** (NIV)

JACKIE AND SHADOW are bald eagles who have made a nest together in California's Big Bear Valley. While there are exceptions, bald eagles are generally monogamous and mate for life, and Jackie and Shadow are among them.

This pair are internet stars, with a camera attached to their nest so that scientists and the public can view their household arrangements. One year, Jackie laid three eggs, and she and Shadow dutifully tended to the eggs and each other. They took turns sitting on the eggs and gathering fish for the sitter.

Sadly, for some reason, that year the eggs did not hatch. The scientists have watched them for numerous years and have seen them raise different broods in the past, and researchers don't know why the eggs weren't viable that year. Regardless of this poor outcome, the two birds were dedicated to caring for each other. Shadow continued tending to Jackie by bringing her fish to eat.

It makes me think of times when my husband and I were disappointed—times when our plans for our future were thwarted. We didn't know why. It would've been easy for each of us to blame the other: *This wouldn't have happened if you hadn't done that!* But we chose not to blame or to be bitter with each other. Some days it was difficult to stay dedicated. It took a lot of help—God's help.

I think, too, of the dear friends who gathered around us when our plans changed. They prayed with us and cared for us with meals, rides, and listening ears. They didn't quietly disappear when times were tough for us. God provided others who were dedicated to helping us. How truly remarkable that God gives us examples of steadfast devotion and dedication, such as Jackie and Shadow, to remind us of His gift of friendship and love. We, too, can be there for each other through thick and thin, just as these majestic bald eagles are. —Virginia Ruth

Thank You, Lord, for our life partners and dear friends.
Even when life goes awry, You place those dedicated people
around us to help us on life's journey. Amen.

274 ALL GOD'S CREATURES

SEPTEMBER 23

One Curious Cat

*It is the glory of God to conceal things, but the
glory of kings is to search things out.*

—**PROVERBS 25:2** (NRSVUE)

THE KITTEN SHOWED up in my shower today—first as a shadow balancing along the tub's edge behind the curtain liner, then out popped her head, nose first, sniffing the damp vanilla-scented steam.

Later, my housemate, who has never had a feline pet, observed, "Now I know why people say curiosity killed the cat." The kitten's curiosity is why I am still finding tiny shards of my daughter's glass water bottle under the sink and around the kitchen stools. Cleo's curiosity is evidenced by pawprints on the windowsill and dust bunnies she has drawn from under the piano. The saying is meant as a warning: "Be cautious. Curiosity is dangerous." But my kitty's habits strike me more as an invitation to wonder about the world. For her, everything is endlessly interesting, a commitment of all five senses. Although she is confined to my house, lest she be prey to coyotes or a threat to birds, adventure awaits in every room. What would I discover were I to mimic my kitten's curious approach?

For most of us humans, the pause between "I wonder" and "I know" has been shortened to the time it takes to Google or ask Siri. These days I indulge in but a few speculative conversations, following trains of thought, looking for cues and connections to solve mysteries. I rarely gaze into the distance seeking when I can look down at the small screen in my hand for answers.

What do I lose by shortening the pause, by extracting wondering from the process of coming to know? If wonder is a precursor to awe and worship, might a loss of curiosity diminish and malnourish my soul? I wonder.

And there it is: I catch myself curious, pondering, following my kitten in her curious ways, exploring and seeking, and on the way to worship.
—Susie Colby

*There is a point in true worship where the mind may cease to
understand and goes over to a kind of delightful astonishment . . .
a degree of wonder without limit and beyond expression!*
—A. W. Tozer

SEPTEMBER 24

Unafraid to Ask

Let us then approach God's throne of grace with confidence, so that we may receive mercy and find grace to help us in our time of need.

—HEBREWS 4:16 (NIV)

WHEN I PICK up food donations for the farm, the animals have learned that meeting me as I arrive means treats thrown out to them. The chickens love the bread. The cats love the cheese. The horses love the apples. Goats love the bananas. All the creatures know that on donation day they get something special.

One night, after I had given food to all my waiting farm babies, to my surprise a little injured possum sat there, looking up to see what his treat would be. Old and small with a leg that dragged behind him, this possum expected his treat like all the others. He reached up and gently took the piece of bread I offered from my hand into his little possum hands and began to eat.

Seemingly unafraid, he finished his treat and then waddled off, dragging his leg behind him, but using it to keep balanced. This possum had adapted to whatever had left him hurt and changed and didn't let it deter him from confidently seeking his blessing.

As I watched him leave, I couldn't help but think of times when I deemed myself unfit for something that would undoubtedly bless me. How often have I walked away from a blessing because I didn't feel pretty enough? Smart enough? Skinny enough? Rich enough? I have said no to relationships, jobs, moves, and more just because I didn't feel worthy at the time. Looking back, I wish I had a do-over.

Do you know what makes you worthy of a blessing? The God who blesses deems you worthy. God gives us the invitation to walk right into His throne room and ask for what we need, like my little possum. He doesn't say, "Get healed and clean before you walk in," because He has done the cleaning already—just like He does the blessing. —Devon O'Day

Walk of Faith: *Approach your Father in heaven boldly in your prayers today and ask Him to let the blessing of His very presence change you for the better forever.*

SEPTEMBER 25

Change of Direction

Trust in the LORD with all your heart, and lean not on your own understanding; in all your ways acknowledge Him, and He shall direct your paths.

—PROVERBS 3:5–6 (NKJV)

LOOK OUT!" I shouted from the passenger's seat, stomping my imaginary brake pedal.

My husband slowed the car as a fat gray squirrel darted out from the side of the road and passed in front of us. And then—has this ever happened to you?—just as the squirrel reached the center of the road, the little critter changed his mind and skedaddled back in the other direction. Mike had to swerve to avoid hitting him. I let out a sigh of relief that the squirrel had made it across and hoped he'd stay put and not try to cross again until there were no cars coming in either direction.

There are times when I act like that squirrel, darting ahead with some plan, without thinking it through first. Probably, too many times to admit. I get excited about one course of action, only to change my mind and switch to a "better" way. And, if I have to be honest, sometimes I've changed my mind again and ended up back where I started.

When I behave like a hurried squirrel, lacking direction and zigzagging back and forth, I'm probably going to make a mistake or commit some sort of reckless action. I might even ignore warning signs. There is only one sure solution—to listen for God's direction. For it is God who establishes my plans. I may have the gift of free will, but God is always available to help me through clear thinking and wisdom. When I am moving in the direction God has planned for me, I can be sure that good will come out of it.

Do I think that squirrel will remember the lesson of his near miss with our vehicle? Maybe, maybe not. But I whispered a quick prayer that the next time the squirrel had to cross the street, God would direct his steps too. —Peggy Frezon

In their hearts humans plan their course, but the LORD establishes their steps.
—Proverbs 16:9 (NIV)

SEPTEMBER 26

Coyotes and Cords

*A person standing alone can be attacked and defeated, but
two can stand back-to-back and conquer. Three are even
better, for a triple-braided cord is not easily broken.*

—ECCLESIASTES 4:12 (NLT)

MY BROTHER AND sister and I often hike together. One day as we
trudged up a steep hill in North Sonoma Mountain Regional Park
in California, a large coyote trotted across the hiking trail, pausing to
take a good look at us. Sniffing in our direction, it seemed confident and
unafraid with 50 yards between us, but my sister was wary.

"What if it comes over here? We should go."

"I think, since coyotes hunt in packs and that one is alone *and*"—I
glanced around our group and nodded—"we're basically in a 'pack' of our
own, it won't bother us." My siblings agreed and we started up the hill
again. My sister was still worried, though, and glanced over her shoulder
more than once to make sure the coyote wasn't following.

The coyote kept its distance, and we did too. I remembered the verse
in Scripture that reads, "A triple-braided cord is not easily broken," and
reassured myself: my brother and sister were there, and together we were
strong enough to overcome the threat if the coyote did return. The promise from God's Word gave me confidence that we would be safe. The rest
of our hike was uneventful and refreshing. Once again, the Bible had
helped me banish my fears. What a blessing!

Each day, as I've gotten older, I see there simply isn't any circumstance
in my life that isn't covered in God's Word. Every incident and challenge,
both common and unusual, are in there, with examples given of the most
beneficial and productive responses: responses designed to draw me closer
to God. I'm so grateful to Him for providing me with this resource. With
the help of the Holy Spirit, I can develop practical knowledge that helps
me avoid dangers of all kinds—including wandering coyotes. —Marianne
Campbell

*Lead me by your truth and teach me, for you are the God
who saves me. All day long I put my hope in you.*
—Psalm 25:5 (NLT)

SEPTEMBER 27

A Source of Safety

*"He will call on me, and I will answer him; I will be
with him in trouble, I will deliver him."*

—PSALM 91:15 (NIV)

THE PING INTERRUPTED my thoughts. I checked my phone to see who'd texted. It was Beth. A friend and fellow animal lover, she'd sent a video, piquing my curiosity.

I opened it, then hit play and watched, listening to her explain: "Yesterday I rescued a baby chipmunk from my cat. Scared to death, the little guy scampered up my leg to finally nestle in my hair. I let him hang out there until he calmed down, then set him free."

Holding the phone selfie-style, Beth was able to record the top of her head, her hair twisted in a bun. As she tilted to one side, there he was. Only his fuzzy, striped noggin showed, the rest of his body completely enveloped in Beth's brown tresses.

I watched the video several more times as tears welled. I could hardly believe the timeliness of this message, as though a whisper and just for me.

It had been a difficult season. Several people we knew were struggling maritally. Others, close family and friends, had suffered losses—a miscarriage for one young couple and the passing of a loved one for another. I have to admit, occasionally I questioned God's presence in the pain and heartache. I sometimes battled fear, asking Him, *OK, Lord, what next?*

My friend's experience spoke to my heart—a reminder that our Creator cares for the tiniest of creatures when they're scared. How much more He cares for me.

The Giver of good gifts, God blesses us with friends—those with whom we can share. Who'll carry our burdens and point us to truth. Yes, those who will hide us in their embrace, speak comfort, and help us feel secure.

As I dialed her number, I brushed away tears, and before Beth answered, even before her simple hello, I knew. Like the little chipmunk, with her, I, too, was safe. —Maureen Miller

Walk of Faith: *Who is a friend with whom you feel safe?
More important, are you this sort of friend for another?
Is there a friendship you could develop to be like this?*

ALL GOD'S CREATURES

SEPTEMBER 28

Look a Little Deeper

*"I do not judge as people judge. They look at the
outward appearance, but I look at the heart."*

—1 SAMUEL 16:7 (GNT)

UGH! WHAT AN awful creature! Why would anyone want that for a pet?"

The "creature" in question was my gentle and adorable leopard gecko. I'd always wanted to own a lizard, and when I met Charlie, I was smitten. Leopard geckos are named for their chocolate-brown spots. When they're born, they actually have stripes across their lemon-and-lavender-colored skin, but as they get older, the lines scatter into playful dots. They have large, attentive eyes and are small enough to sit comfortably in the palm of your hand.

The thing that makes leopard geckos really special is their wonderful temperament. Charlie loved curling up in the crook of my elbow and seemed to lean in as I'd sing to him. My Dad took care of him when I traveled, and they formed a sweet bond. The moment Dad would walk into my house, Charlie would recognize his voice and get excited.

So imagine the knot in my stomach when strangers or, even worse, friends, would say cruel things about him!

I get that most folks will never own a lizard and that people have biases toward animals that are unusual to them, but none of that justified their comments. In those moments, all I could think was, *You're missing his beauty! You're missing his sweetness!*

Truthfully, I know I can be the same way. Not with lizards, but with people. I can get caught up in my first impressions, judging people based on their unfamiliarity and my biases. But God encourages me to look past the exterior to see what's deeper—the humanity, the grace, the heart.

He asks that because that's how He looks at each of us. And when we see others as God sees them, we see them through eyes of love. —Allison Lynn Flemming

*Lord, reveal to me times when I judge others by the way they look
or sound or act. Help me see that person the way You see them.
Help me to see their heart and love them as You love them.*

SEPTEMBER 29

Do You Remember Me?

"Remember that the Lord rescued you from the iron-smelting furnace of Egypt in order to make you his very own people and his special possession, which is what you are today."

—DEUTERONOMY 4:20 (NLT)

A FRIEND FINDS A lot of frogs in his swimming pool. Some of them struggle to get back out. So he gets his skimmer net and tries to lift them out, but many are scared and head the other direction. Some, however, don't run from the net but jump on. He believes these must be frogs that he's rescued before and who remember him. He reports that one day a young frog swam right up to him, dove under and swam around him, and then climbed on his leg like they were old friends. He's sure that this was a frog he had previously saved.

His story raised a couple of questions. First, the skeptic in me wondered, *Does a frog even have a memory?* A quick internet search revealed that there has not been much research on this issue. But there are a few studies that indicate frogs can learn and remember.

Second, I asked myself, "How frequently do I remember and recognize the One who constantly rescues me?" The Lord has rescued me more times than I can count in both my professional and my personal life. Sometimes, like the frogs running from the net, I may run from the solution. Other times, I initially attribute these rescues to good luck and tell my friends or wife, "Wow, I was sure lucky today." Until I eventually realize that just as the frogs were rescued by the efforts of my friend, my rescue was God's handiwork once again. —Harold Nichols

Walk of Faith: *This week, be aware of the times God remembers you and rescues you, in both small and large ways, and give thanks for His rescue.*

SEPTEMBER 30

Easily Distracted

Let your eyes look directly forward, and your gaze be straight before you.
—**PROVERBS 4:25** (ESV)

DURING A RECENT hike, toting my chainsaw to clear some mountain trails at the church camp I have attended for over 50 years, I was abruptly distracted when I flushed an American woodcock. She flew only a few yards away and never reached higher than 6 feet off the ground. Upon landing, she continued to hold my attention by fluttering her wings as if she were wounded. As I stepped closer to investigate the extent of her injuries, she flushed out again, drawing me further away. I now knew what she was doing. Her theatrics were worthy of an Emmy. She had successfully led me away from her nest.

This tactic is called a "distraction display." This nesting woodcock created a diversion by faking an injury to lead me, a potential predator, away from her hidden nest. Her distraction worked effectively. Once I realized what she was doing, I went on my way.

The world around me is filled with distractions. Bright lights, moving objects, and colorful images pull my eyes and attention away from important things. Checking my emails each morning can lead me down a series of rabbit holes, consuming my attention and robbing me of time.

Not all distractions are bad. Helping a person with a vehicle problem or a neighbor searching for their lost pet are things I did not schedule but are important, as I am called to help others. Godly distractions can open the door to ministering opportunities. My dilemma comes when I try to figure out the distractions worth pursuing and those to avoid.

In the moment, I need to ask myself if the distraction is pulling me away from good and godly things or is it pulling toward them. The woodcock knew exactly what she was doing when she lured me away. It was part of her protective instinct, one I'm hoping to better develop in my own life. —Ben Cooper

Gracious God, guide me when distractions come my way
and help me to discern between the healthy ones
and the bad ones. In the name of Jesus, I pray. Amen.

OCTOBER 1

Reckless Preparation

"You also must be ready, because the Son of Man will come at an hour when you do not expect him."

—LUKE 12:40 (NIV)

THE SHORTER, COOLER days of fall usher in what I call "S cubed": Silly Squirrel Season. Programmed by instinct to gather and store enough food to last the winter, the bushy-tailed rodents suddenly seem to go a little crazy, darting willy-nilly through yards populated by dogs, across busy streets, and overhead on the power lines in search of sustenance. *Reckless* is the word that most often comes to my mind when I startle and brake hard to avoid another little critter, who is just going his own way in preparing for the winter.

In my area, we see mainly eastern gray squirrels, and each one acquires between three and ten *thousand* nuts and seeds each year to eat and store, often acorns from the plentiful oaks in my region. They may bury them in hundreds of different locations and can find them later by memory and scent. And those silly squirrels can run fast: up to 20 miles per hour on the ground, not to mention those treacherous leaps from perch to perch!

They make me wonder about myself. Am I also getting ready, not for the winter, but for Christ's return? I definitely don't think about it often enough—the squirrels seem to have better instincts for preparation than I do—but when my thoughts do go there, am I reckless in my preparations like the silly squirrels, or do I play it safe? Do I take advantage of my church's opportunities to personally minister to the needy, or just throw money into the offering plate and consider my duty done? Do I strive every day to make others' lives better, or do I stroll through life merely without hurting anyone?

I hope to let those squirrels inspire me to run faster, jump farther, and be more reckless as I wait for Jesus's return. —Kim Sheard

Walk of Faith: *Write down three new things you can do in the coming months to recklessly prepare yourself and others for Christ's return.*

OCTOBER 2

The Patience of Ernest

The LORD upholds all who fall and lifts up all who are bowed down.

—PSALM 145:14 (NIV)

OUR GOLDEN RETRIEVER Ernest fell down. A lot. This was because he was very old—15—and had developed a debilitating case of arthritis, along with the types of other health issues that often accompany canines of advanced age. It broke my heart to see Ernest struggle with his mobility. We used several strategies to help—medication, rugs for traction, and a special harness with a handle to support him. But Ernest gracefully accepted the weakness in his limbs and his frequent descents. He'd just look up at me with his cataract-clouded eyes, heave a little sigh, and wait for me to assist him in rising.

He never whimpered or struggled. He knew he no longer had the power to get up again on his own. So he accepted that now, for the moment, he was on the ground. It wasn't where he was headed or where he wanted to be, but he would rest patiently in that spot until he was lifted by the loving hands that cared and provided for him. And then he would move on ahead, to the best of his ability, no matter how many more times he fell along the way.

I'm not so young anymore either, so there are times when, like Ernie, I physically take a tumble. But there are also times when I fall, metaphorically. I forget to do something. I don't perform as well as desired. I unintentionally let down a friend. During these times, I pray that I can get back up again with the same grace that Ernie displays. But I know I can't do it alone. I need to be lifted by the loving Hands that care and provide for me. So I quietly ask my Father in heaven to get me back on my feet again. And I wait, as patiently as Ernest, for the grace that is extended to me and the help that never fails. —Peggy Frezon

The world may drag you down perhaps easily a hundred times,
but God will be there to lift you up moreover than a thousand times.
—Sharon Lagueux

ALL GOD'S CREATURES

OCTOBER 3

The Power within Us

*I am sure of this, that he who began a good work in you
will bring it to completion at the day of Jesus Christ.*

—PHILIPPIANS 1:6 (ESV)

WOULDN'T IT BE cool if we could predict the future and get it right? Folklore suggests there are animals that do make predictions about the future—at least, future weather—if we humans just know what to look for.

The woolly bear caterpillar (also called a woolly worm), with its alternating bands of black and rusty brown, is thought to foretell the severity of the winter weather by the pattern of its markings, with more black indicating a harsh winter is on its way, and a broader brown band presaging a mild one.

My upbringing has trained me to take notice of these crawling critters every fall. I wish I had kept a detailed journal to confirm this foretelling over the decades of seeing the caterpillars. Here in the Northeast, any measurable edge to predict the winter weather would permit me to be more prepared for the harsher ones. The major problem, though, is the fact that woolly bear caterpillars can be all dark, all rust-colored, or mixed. That can really mess up the scientific records.

The woolly bear is blissfully unaware that it is supposed to possess this portentous power. It just does what God designed it to do, and eventually it becomes a beautiful Isabella tiger moth.

As is the case with the woolly bear caterpillar, I myself can't really predict the future. But God knows what will happen, and He's given us clues, as well as promises, about that future in His Word. By reading in the Bible about all the promises that have come true up until the present, I can be sure that those yet to come will be fulfilled just as the Bible says they will. And *that* I can predict with confidence. —Ben Cooper

I've read the last page of the Bible. It's all going to turn out all right.
—Billy Graham

286   ALL GOD'S CREATURES

OCTOBER 4

From Bugs to Beauties

You shall be called by a new name that the mouth of the Lord will give.

—ISAIAH 62:2 (ESV)

NASTY!" MY GRANDDAUGHTER'S face scrunched as she flicked the tiny insect off the toy bed in her plastic palace.

"Oh no, was that lady beetle Sleeping Beauty? Gives a whole new meaning to bedbug, huh?" I tickled Grand-Girl's tummy, attempting to make light of the situation, but I understood. I've often been annoyed with their presence in my house also.

From October until early spring, these black-spotted orange insects make their home on our walls and ceilings, and for over two decades, I've grumbled and complained. While I've always appreciated the more traditional red-and-black ladybugs, I found their orange relatives a nuisance—leaving streaks wherever they've meandered and lining every window ledge. Furthermore, their smelly "juice" (whatever *that* is) irritates the eyes.

"How do they get in?" I've inquired. My prince of a husband came to the rescue—replacing old windows with new and sealing up cracks and crevices in our old farmhouse. Still, they come!

But then I learned something. While I'd heard ladybugs are a sign of good fortune, I read that, much like a group of lions is called a pride, a group of lady beetles is a loveliness. This fact changed my attitude, replacing grumbles with grins as I use my imagination and observe more closely these little "ladies" who, once upon a time, God created.

With gratitude rather than complaint concerning what the Creator called good, I see differently—discovering this bevy is actually quite beautiful, as they wash their faces, preening themselves like tiny princesses preparing to meet Prince Charming.

Thinking about it later, it struck me how simply learning a more flattering name for these little beauties completely changed my attitude toward them. It made me wonder: are there people I've unconsciously given unflattering names in my mind? How would I feel about them if I called them by a new name? —Maureen Miller

> *A thing of beauty is a joy forever: Its loveliness increases;*
> *it will never pass into nothingness.*
> —John Keats

ALL GOD'S CREATURES

OCTOBER 5

In the Shadows

*Yea, though I walk through the valley of the shadow of death, I will fear
no evil; for You are with me; Your rod and Your staff, they comfort me.*

—PSALM 23:4 (NKJV)

MY HUSBAND, TIM, and I strolled along the trail at Homosassa Springs Wildlife State Park in Homosassa, Florida, stopping a minute or two at each exhibit. When we arrived at the enclosure of the Florida black bear, I lingered.

I asked the volunteer in front of the exhibit about the bear, whose name was Maximus. She told me Max's mother had died after being struck by a vehicle. Officials found Max nearly starved in their cave. The cub weighed barely four pounds when the Florida Fish and Wildlife Conservation Commission rescued him. The tiny baby received medical treatment, round-the-clock care, and regular feedings. Despite their best efforts, he couldn't return to the wild because he had become dependent on humans. Florida's only wildlife state park became Max's new home.

The Florida black bear is the only bear species in the state. Max serves as their mascot, educating the public about bear safety and reminding people of the importance of securing trash cans.

Max was almost five when we visited the state park. He lay in front of a large turquoise bowl and gnawed on a snack he held between his paws. His black, velvet-like fur glistened in the afternoon sun. Max wasn't quite full grown, but he would be an intimidating presence in the wild.

I've always loved bears and imagined myself stroking his fur, wondering if it was as silky soft as it looked. Max showed no outward signs of the trauma he'd experienced as a baby, but I related to his story because I'd lost my mom too. Cancer had taken her a month before our visit, and her death, while expected, left a shadow over my life.

If Max feels grief, it's not visible, and most days, my grief can't be seen. In learning to live life without my mom, I've felt the comfort of our Good Shepherd who leads me through this valley of loss—and just as people cared for Max, people will care for me during times of loss. —Crystal Storms

*As I go into a cemetery, I like to think of the time when
the dead shall rise from their graves . . . Thank God,
our friends are not buried; they are only sown!*
—Dwight L. Moody

OCTOBER 6

Starting with Rest

For thus said the Lord GOD, the Holy One of Israel, "In returning and rest you shall be saved; in quietness and in trust shall be your strength."

—ISAIAH 30:15 (ESV)

A S WE PULLED into our driveway, something in our neighbor's yard caught my attention. Neighbors on our street, including us, can regularly be found outside planting new flowers or trees or hanging bird feeders in our yards. However, it was not a new maple tree or flower bed that stole my attention but a massive six-point bull elk napping away in the front yard, only 30 feet from our driveway.

Over the next few days, our resident bull elk spent his days meandering through our yard and those of neighbors. He could be found napping in the shade of trees, occasionally waking to stand up and use his antlers to shake apples from branches for a snack. It was October, and I knew this amazing animal would soon be enduring a harsh Rocky Mountain winter, when food would be difficult to find. As I watched him resting and snacking on apples in preparation for winter, I considered how God calls me to rest before intense seasons of life.

At creation, God worked for 6 days and then rested, but Adam's first full day of life was the seventh day, a day devoted to rest. God worked, then rested, while man first rested, then set to work. Time and again, I feel God calling me to follow the pattern He established at creation. Instead of working tirelessly so I can rest, He calls me, like the elk napping beneath a shady tree, to begin with rest. Rest is not my reward for work but, instead, what equips me to faithfully carry out the work God calls me to. This regular rhythm of rest prepares me for whatever may come ahead. —Eryn Lynum

*Dear God, help me to live and work from rest rather than for rest.
Let rest be my natural starting point. Help me to thrive through
a rhythm of rest, just as You have designed nature to flourish.*

OCTOBER 7

Where He Belonged

*"By this all people will know that you are my
disciples, if you have love for one another."*

—JOHN 13:35 (ESV)

MOVEMENT BY THE green field caught my attention. A tawny dog ran toward the busy highway I drove on.

I pressed the brake pedal as the dog streaked forward. I held my breath, afraid he would dash in front of my minivan. But he swerved at the last second and darted in the opposite direction.

I frowned. *Was that the dog's idea of a game? He could have been hurt.* I'd never seen him before, though I frequently drove past that field. What if he was a stray, lost and in danger? I turned onto an intersecting road and drove to a farm that seemed the likely place the dog might live. Perhaps his owners didn't realize he was loose and running on the road.

The dog jogged alongside my van as I pulled into the driveaway. A barn door stood ajar, but I couldn't see any people. I rolled down my window and spoke to the dog. When I attempted to get out, he backed up, nervous. Not wanting to frighten the dog, I retreated to my van and watched him.

I thought he might approach the house or enter the barn, giving me some sign he belonged there and wasn't a stray in need of rescue. But he simply watched me, providing no indication either way. Thankfully, farm workers soon returned, and I could see from the dog's joyful greeting that he belonged.

As I left, a question struck me. Can people tell I belong to Christ? My life should be an obvious sign to everyone that I'm a Christian. I want to show so much love to others, especially in the Body of Christ, that people will know at first glance that I am His, and He is my home. —Jerusha Agen

*Walk of Faith: Consider how you appear to others.
Can they tell by your language and actions that you belong
to Christ? If not, ask God to change you from the inside out,
beginning today, so all will know you belong to Him.*

OCTOBER 8

Sheltered

"Remain in me, as I also remain in you."
—JOHN 15:4 (NIV)

DRIVING ALONG an interstate highway in Michigan, I noticed a Canada goose up ahead by the roadside. On second look, I realized it was not one but five geese—what appeared to be a goose, a gander, and three goslings. Traffic was light enough for me to change lanes and slow down, giving this little family a wide berth. I debated honking, no pun intended, but feared that might startle them into the roadway. *This can't end well*, I thought.

A second later, I was upon them and saw the reason for their roadside gaggle: water. There was none in the median, so they weren't trying to cross the highway. But an overnight rain had left a large puddle between the paved shoulder and the grassy area beyond. I let out a breath. *They'll be fine*, I thought—and hoped. Yes, there was danger, but as long as they stayed by the water, they would survive.

Much of my life has been an exercise in learning when to stay put. It's impossible to escape the world and its temptations, at least in this life. But too often I've tended to seek them out, leaving a place of peace and safety in search of some pleasure or satisfaction. That's always a mistake. We can exist perfectly well in proximity to some temptations, but not if we rush toward them. Even one step toward lust, rage, greed, or what may be the besetting sin of our time, envy, can bring ruin.

Yet there's no need for concern. We'll be fine as long as we remain in Christ. Sometimes the best place to go is right where we are. —Lawrence W. Wilson

Prone to wander, Lord, I feel it, prone to leave the God I love; here's my heart, Lord, take and seal it, seal it for Thy courts above.
—Robert Robinson

OCTOBER 9

When Feathers Fly

What causes fights and quarrels among you? Don't they come from
your desires that battle within you? You desire but do not have
so you kill. You covet but you cannot get what you want, so you
quarrel and fight. You do not have because you do not ask God.

—JAMES 4:1–2 (NIV)

I LOOKED OUT into my backyard on a beautiful morning. Along the firepit edges, two northern flickers hopped opposite each other, moving together like synchronized swimmers. They snapped the air with their beaks and flipped their tails at the same time, while their red feathered heads comically bobbed up and down.

Another northern flicker arrived and began bobbing in the same way. A power struggle quickly began. Two flickers started to scuffle on and off the firepit, into the dirt, and up into the air. Feathers were flying as neither one backed down. The third continued the same hop pattern while the wild pair struggled for number-one status.

A robin suddenly flew down onto the pit, scaring the others off, disputes finished or not. With no other birds around, the robin strutted completely around the firepit circle as if to say, *This is mine. And don't you ever come back.* I laughed at his boisterous spirit.

I reflected on the battles we fight for control. We want recognition for our volunteer work, create power struggles with friends over silly things, and spend more to have a better car or nicer clothes than others. There was a time in my life when the intense desire for me-centered recognition ruled my thoughts. With God's help, when I feel that familiar urge to jockey for position and power, I've begun using prayer as a lifeline that helps direct my focus off myself and away from my inner push for control, putting Him in control instead. —Twila Bennett

Lord, help me never to let my selfish desires get in the way of the life
You have for me. Guide my eyes away from power struggles
and up to You. I know Your way for me is far better.

OCTOBER 10

Old Dog, New Trick

For the Spirit God gave us does not make us timid,
but gives us power, love and self-discipline.

—2 TIMOTHY 1:7 (NIV)

I SAT AT my home computer, my fingers frozen over the keys. I'd been asked to tackle a new project at my job—something I'd never done before—and I was afraid I couldn't do it. "God, I need help," I murmured. "Can you help me overcome my fear?"

I felt a nudge on my leg. It was my terrier mix, Peyton, letting me know she needed to go outside. I followed her and our other dog, Piper, to the front door. Outside, I grabbed the tie-outs that were attached to a stake in the yard and clipped one into each dog's collar. "I'll be back in a minute," I said. "Go potty."

I headed to the kitchen to grab a drink and a snack. When I went back outside to get the dogs, Piper was sitting on the porch waiting to come back inside, but I didn't see Peyton. I looked around and saw her in the strangest place. Peyton—our nine-year-old, slightly overweight rescue dog—was making her way along the top of the retaining wall like she was a tightrope walker. I couldn't believe it. In the 5 years she'd lived with us, I'd never seen her up there. "What are you doing, Crazy Girl?" I called out to her. She wagged her tail, jumped down off the wall, and ran toward me.

I bent to pet her. "You just wanted to try something new today, huh? It was very brave of you." I stopped at my own words. If Peyton could step out of her comfort zone, I could too.

I went back to the computer. I still felt scared that I couldn't complete the task, but I took a deep breath. "Lord, please be with me," I said. I glanced down at Peyton, who immediately wagged her tail. I patted her head and thanked her for showing me that fear can be overcome. Then I got to work. —Diane Stark

Never trust your fears, they don't know your strength.
—Athena Singh

ALL GOD'S CREATURES

OCTOBER 11

Bummer the Lamb

Jesus said, "Feed my lambs."

—JOHN 21:15 (NIV)

MY FRIEND BETH Booth lived to be 100 years old and loved to tell the story of how she'd once rescued lambs. In her youth, a nearby wool farmer would bring her newborn lambs that needed extra help—often called "bummer lambs." Beth, a nurse by profession, nurtured many of these bummers.

But one bummer lamb stood out.

He was smaller than normal, and his skin hung in loose folds. He wasn't eating and was failing fast. The wool farmer thought he wasn't going to make it. But Beth stroked the lamb's head. "Let me try," she said and cradled the bummer in her arms.

The poor lamb seemed doomed, and for a time even Beth wondered if the tiny baby would live to adulthood. Yet, determined to save him, she kept the lamb in her house. Each day she sat in her rocking chair with the lamb, who she named Bummer, wrapped in a blanket on her lap. While the lamb suckled from a bottle, Beth rocked and sang to him. She prayed that the God who made the world would spare this creature.

Beth thanked God that Bummer had survived this long. She prayed that he'd grow silky wool for the farmer, even as she became more attached to the little guy. By God's grace, she knew that someday she'd have to let him go back to his flock. Slowly, Bummer started to put on weight, until he barely fit on her lap.

The lamb thrived until one day Bummer was strong enough to go back to his flock. In the field, he kicked up his heels and ran to join the other sheep.

I marvel at Beth's courage and determination to take on this lost bummer cause. It reminds me that God is always nurturing me, taking me onto His lap for love and protection. God is my Good Shepherd, constantly watching over me. —Linda S. Clare

So many of us are bummer lambs, rejected and broken. But He is the good Shepherd. He cares for our every need and holds us close to his heart. We may be broken but we are deeply loved by the Shepherd.
—Sheila Walsh

OCTOBER 12

The Master's Voice

Pay attention to what I say; turn your ear to my words.
—**Proverbs 4:20** (NIV)

MY HUSBAND AND I love watching sheepdog trials in which a border collie and its master move sheep into a pen. The dog is focused on the sheep while listening to the master. The master uses either a whistle or simple commands to guide the dog in the best way to accomplish the task of driving the three demonstration sheep into a pen. As the dog listens, it moves from one side to the next, funneling the sheep as a group in the direction the master wants them to move. If one sheep moves in a different direction, the dog herds it back so that the collective three-sheep unit enters together.

The dogs that are successful are the ones that listen to their master and heed the master's commands. There are times when they are told to lie down so that they do not "worry" the sheep by appearing too aggressive. Other times the master will direct the dog to quickly move to the left or right of the sheep to cut them off from going in a different direction.

It is only by listening to the master that the dogs can move the unruly group of sheep into the pen. The master sees the best way to move the grouping of sheep along and conveys that to the border collie.

Many times in my life I have felt that I was dealing with unruly sheep: I had several difficult situations occurring simultaneously and did not know how to proceed. It was only in listening to the Master that I knew how best to handle these situations. Sometimes God reminded me that I needed to wait and not worry the situation. Other times God nudged me to move along. Either way, God was in control. He saw the big picture and what would bring about a positive outcome. The dogs listen to the master for their direction, and when I listen to the Master, I know the way. —Virginia Ruth

And your ears shall hear a word behind you,
saying, "This is the way, walk in it."
—Isaiah 30:21 (ESV)

ALL GOD'S CREATURES 295

OCTOBER 13

My Nap with a Snake

"For I know the plans I have for you," declares the LORD, "plans to prosper you and not to harm you, plans to give you hope and a future."

—JEREMIAH 29:11 (NIV)

AFTER A LONG night caring for and worrying about my senior dog—who, as it turns out, had a simple case of conjunctivitis—I was exhausted. So tired, in fact, that I fell asleep on my patio furniture in the middle of the afternoon. When I awakened an hour later, I was surprised to find an unexpected visitor inside my screened patio—a juvenile garter snake!

This was not the first time the snake and I had crossed paths. It had been inside my screened patio once before. On that occasion, my dog practically sat on the snake before I noticed what was happening, so I already knew from experience this snake was docile. The snake seemed to be as curious about me as I was about it. After watching me for a few moments, it disappeared back into hiding. My family and I had a good laugh when I told them I'd just accidentally taken a nap with a snake.

This encounter got me thinking about the ways my mind sometimes interprets the present based on experiences from the past. If I see a snake, knowing snakes *may* be dangerous, should I automatically respond in fear? Of course not. Yet when I'm faced with a situation or a person that reminds me of a traumatic or unpleasant past event, I'm apt to bring that memory into the present and see the situation through that lens.

And when I do that, I can miss out on many good things—like the benefits this garter snake brings—because my mind has closed to it.

God has good things planned for those who trust in Him. The question is, Will we recognize them? —Ashley Clark

Walk of Faith: *As you go through your day, take inventory of the people or things in your life you've written off as "dangerous snakes." Ask yourself how God may be working in these areas, and ask Him to help you see things His way.*

OCTOBER 14

Doggy Diversity

For you created my inmost being; you knit me together in my mother's womb. I praise you because I am fearfully and wonderfully made.

—PSALM 139:13–14 (NIV)

THE AMERICAN KENNEL Club breed standard for the German short-haired pointer (GSP) describes acceptable colors and markings, size, weight, and other appearance attributes used for judging these dogs in the show ring. The AKC website also describes the typical personality traits for the breed: very affectionate with family, usually open to strangers, eager to please, usually a good watchdog, and—since this breed is a bird dog and a pointer—instinctively notice birds and point to them rather than chase.

My first GSP, Freckles, was indeed eager to please, learning many tricks and taking multiple obedience, agility, and fly-ball classes. Our current GSP, Scout, flunked Obedience 1, showing absolutely no interest in earning treats for tricks. Freckles was a good watchdog, barking at all the possible dangers outside his window. Scout silently wags at all who approach the door and would happily invite a burglar in and lead them straight to Grandma's silver. Freckles detested belly rubs and snuggling and was selective with his friends. Scout requires that a quota of belly rubs be provided each day and will jump into the laps of total strangers for love. Freckles would point birds endlessly, never chasing or harming them. Scout has zero interest in birds, but chases (and sometimes catches) chipmunks and squirrels. God clearly assigned distinct personalities to two dogs of the same breed living in the same household! I relish their differences, which often cause me to laugh in delight.

Humans are God's most special creations, and we are much more diverse than my two beloved pointers. The eight billion of us now living, plus all those who have gone before, have each been made distinct and special to God. It is difficult at times, but I try to remember to relish our differences. People who don't look or think or act like me are still God's children with special gifts to share. Thanks be to God! —Kim Sheard

We have different gifts, according to the grace given to each of us.
—Romans 12:6 (NIV)

ALL GOD'S CREATURES 297

OCTOBER 15

Who Are You Following?

So the Israelites did everything the LORD commanded Moses; that is the way they encamped under their standards, and that is the way they set out, each of them with their clan and family.

—NUMBERS 2:34 (NIV)

ONE SUNNY FRIDAY, I watched as a school bus rolled up to the gate of our local zoo carrying a load of kindergarteners. Chaperones dressed in lime-green shirts ushered the children off the bus. Their lead teacher, a cheerful soul with a booming voice, addressed her small charges.

"OK, everyone, grab your buddy and follow the flag." She raised a banner with a picture of a koala on it and marched ahead. "If you get separated," she called back, "look for the flag."

I encountered the group again later at the lemur exhibit. As we watched the funny-faced animals follow one another through the tall grass of their habitat, the teacher read from the Fun Facts about Lemurs poster in a loud voice: "Lemurs use their black-and-white bushy tails for balance and communication. When they travel together through high grass, they hold their tails high in the air, much like flags, to keep everyone together."

Watching the students march off following their flag-waving teacher, I remembered how God directed the Israelites to gather as family groups, each under the standard that represented their tribe. When He called them to pack up and travel to another location, they were to go together, led by a family leader carrying a banner that identified and unified their tribe.

Kindergarteners, lemurs, and the Israelites benefitted from following a wise leader and sticking together. We can too. When we surround ourselves with like-minded believers, we can step out in faith and follow our Sovereign's standard. God will go before us, behind us, and beside us to show us the way. —Lori Hatcher

"The LORD himself goes before you and will be with you; he will never leave you nor forsake you. Do not be afraid; do not be discouraged."
—Deuteronomy 31:8 (NIV)

298   ALL GOD'S CREATURES

OCTOBER 16

Beaver in the Stillness

He says, "Be still, and know that I am God; I will be exalted
among the nations, I will be exalted in the earth!"

—PSALM 46:10 (NIV)

WHILE ON A lakeside vacation with my in-laws in Pennsylvania, I saw something I'd never seen before: a beaver! It was dusk, and I'd been sitting quietly near the water's edge when I saw the thin wake of "something" cruising on the surface. In a moment the animal hauled itself out onto the shore, but having never seen a beaver in the wild before and because it was getting dark, I was unsure of what I was looking at. I remained still, barely breathing, and watched as the beaver groomed and smoothed its fur. I was able to watch it like this for many minutes before it hopped back in the water and swam away.

I was thankful to have been sitting at the water's edge just when it came by. *If I'd been* looking *for the beaver, I might've missed it!* I'd have been busy moving up and down the bank, seeking signs of it, and not still enough for it to make an appearance. But because I was sitting quietly, I could watch, unnoticed, and have a much better view.

This experience reminded me of the Bible verse, "Be still, and know that I am God." There are times in my life when I'm so actively looking for God that I miss Him entirely. Too often, I wear myself out with the search until I feel He's just not going to show up! But more often than not, when I am still and simply acknowledge that He's in charge, He makes an appearance immediately—often in very surprising and delightful ways.

When I am still, God can speak to me in a way I can hear. He will comfort and strengthen me when I set aside distractions and focus on Him. —Marianne Campbell

> *Be still, my soul; the Lord is on thy side. Bear patiently*
> *the cross of grief or pain. Leave to thy God to order and*
> *provide. In ev'ry change He faithful will remain.*
> —Catharina Amalia Dorothea von Schlegel

OCTOBER 17

Hop for Joy!

Rejoice in the LORD always. Again I will say, rejoice!

—PHILIPPIANS 4:4 (NKJV)

BEGINNING IN 2020 with the surge of a dormant virus from childhood, my health spiraled down while family troubles mounted daily. Days dragged by as I struggled.

In autumn of 2023, while in my happy place—Potter County, Pennsylvania—I sat on our rental cabin's porch with our dog, Kenai, trying to forget my troubles. I noticed a small animal down the lane. As I watched, I saw it jump into the air and flip its body around. A bunny! Hoping Kenai wouldn't see it, I watched as the rabbit continued to hop and leap, colorful leaves flipping into the air as it did. It reminded me of the day before when I'd kicked at fallen leaves at a park like a little kid to drive out the doldrums.

I watched until the bunny disappeared, then thought about the day ahead. My brother had moved that year to Potter County, something everyone in our family had secretly wished to do but never had, and we were going to visit him there. Excitement over seeing his new place warred with jealousy. Why was he so free to do such a thing, while I felt stuck, unable to enjoy simple pleasures? Discontentment tried to take back its hold on my heart.

Suddenly, Kenai jumped up, nose pointed toward where the bunny had slipped into the tall weeds. Though I didn't see it, I knew it must be there, and the thought of its joyful frolicking came back. It cared nothing about the dog nearby who could eat it, the hawk overhead who could swoop down and carry it off. It was simply happy in that moment with who it was, where it was. I believe God sent that tiny bunny to remind me to do the same. —Cathy Mayfield

> *When bunnies leap, my heart does too.*
> *But what if all that took was You?*
> *—C.M.*

OCTOBER 18

Chosen Citizen

*But our citizenship is in heaven. And we eagerly await
a Savior from there, the Lord Jesus Christ.*

—PHILIPPIANS 3:20 (NIV)

HOMOSASSA SPRINGS WILDLIFE State Park in Homosassa, Florida, boasts a variety of animals, including alligators, black bears, flamingos, whooping cranes, and the oldest hippopotamus in captivity. All are native Florida species except for the hippo, Lu, who's an honorary Florida resident. When the state took over the park, they were going to evict the California-born hippopotamus, but his fans successfully petitioned for him to stay.

I've always loved hippos with their small ears and tails. We visited Lu a little before his sixty-fourth birthday, and I leaned against the steel rope as the venerable beast swam back and forth in the dark waters. His big eyes seemed to take everyone in.

As I watched Lu, I thought about his honorary Florida citizenship, and it made me consider my own citizenship. Born in Colorado, I became both a Colorado and US citizen. But I've added another citizenship. When I accepted Jesus as my Savior, I became a citizen of heaven. My feet may dwell on US soil and in this world, but I'm just passing through.

When I remember that I'm a sojourner, I'm more able to view the ups and downs of this world from a heavenly perspective. Rather than worry about the unknowns of the temporary, I can choose to set my focus on my eternal home. Then the things that overwhelm me lose their weightiness. I can rest in the assurance that God will work everything for His glory and my good—just like He did for Lu, the California-born hippopotamus who retired from show biz to be with his biggest fans in Florida. —Crystal Storms

My home is in heaven. I'm just passing through this world.
—Billy Graham

OCTOBER 19

Limitless Growth

Then the angel showed me the river of the water of life, bright as crystal, flowing from the throne of God and of the Lamb

—REVELATION 22:1 (ESV)

A LOCAL STREAM gushes out hundreds of gallons of life-giving water from a deep limestone cave. I have personally seen the enormous rainbow trout that thrive there, some reaching well over 24 inches. Trout eggs hatch out in the watery haven with everything they need to grow. The frigid temperatures, neutral pH, and abundant oxygen provide a perfect habitat under a blanket of shade-providing watercress to produce impressive rainbow trout. Fishery biologists have claimed the location to be one of the best hatcheries east of the Mississippi River.

Here, trout grow quickly and are measured by counting how many individual fish it takes to hit a specific target weight. The fewer the fish, the better the site. Trout are an indicator species for water quality and respond well in a perfect environment. In this secluded location, unique circumstances all come together to check all the boxes for trout to experience limitless growth.

Oddly, though, this pristine utopia only lasts for about a quarter of a mile before the quality deteriorates. My professional career allowed me to provide options to the landowners in the watershed to install best management practices designed to improve and restore the trout habitat.

When I drive by, I often reflect on how my spiritual growth is doing, because the conditions of this world are not ideal. On the other hand, I look forward to the time yet to come when I will thrive in God's perfect habitat, heaven. As Revelation 22:1 points out, the river provides the water of life and assures me of my potential limitless growth because its source comes from both God and Jesus. There, all the requirements will be met, and all the boxes checked. An endless supply of life-giving water awaits me. What a glorious life it will be. —Ben Cooper

Father God, filter out the impurities in my surroundings here on earth until the day comes when my habitation and growth is with You. Amen.

302   ALL GOD'S CREATURES

OCTOBER 20

A Little Kindness

*"But I say unto you, Love your enemies, bless them that
curse you, do good to them that hate you, and pray for them
which despitefully use you, and persecute you."*

—MATTHEW 5:44 (KJV)

LET'S FACE IT, geese are messy. With two lakes, our subdivision attracts a variety of waterfowl. When we first moved here 40 years ago, Canada geese frequented the lakes with flocks stopping by on their migratory treks. A few years later, the Canada geese apparently decided our moderate weather was more to their liking. Now they stay year-round. Last summer, they produced record numbers of goslings, who also never leave.

Because there are now so many geese, their green droppings line the levees and cover the fishing docks and swimming platform. And no one wants to walk barefoot on the sand beach. Lakeside residents especially dislike the feathered guests who take over their yards and often get aggressive, especially during mating season. And who wants goose droppings all over their lawns? Unfortunately, many locals have been less than kind.

However, one day, I saw a homeowner ridding his yard of unwanted long-necked guests using a push broom. He gently shooed the geese across the levee to the lower lake. I don't know what kind of long-term effects resulted, but it was heartwarming to see an act of kindness.

I'll admit I've not always made kindness my first reaction if inconvenienced or when someone acts downright ugly to me. But Jesus calls me to respond in a different way. He wants me to treat others as I want to be treated (Matthew 7:12). That's not so hard if they're nice to me, but to show kindness to those who don't seem to deserve it? I sometimes have to fight myself to show Christ's love to them. But when I do, many times I see a change in the person I thought was my enemy. Kindness has a way of healing hearts.

No, it's not always easy to be kind, but it's worth it. And I may have to do it more often than I'd like because, let's face it, life is messy.
—Tracy Crump

A part of kindness consists in loving people more than they deserve.
—Joseph Joubert

OCTOBER 21

No Lacka Alpaca

The LORD is my shepherd, I lack nothing.
—PSALM 23:1 (NIV)

THOUGH MY VOICE sounded calm, anxiety stirred as I hung up the phone. I'd had to connect with my editor to let her know my project might be late. How would I accomplish all the tasks at hand? An adage about having so much to do with too little time spun in my head.

But first on the day's agenda was a planned visit with my young friend Hazel. Sitting at the dining table an hour later, we talked about her family and their farm, with its plethora of animals. "Which one's your favorite?" I inquired.

She was quiet as she considered. Finally, "I love them all, but I think it's Dia, our 18-year-old alpaca."

I laughed. "Did you say her name's Diva? That's funny."

"No, not Diva. *Dia*—spelled *D-I-A*. I looked it up online, and a name site says it means love, which is perfect, because she's my friend."

My curiosity was piqued. "How so?"

Hazel smiled. "She used to be afraid, but over time, that changed. As I've taken care of her, she's grown to trust me. Now, no matter where I lead, Dia follows." Hazel giggled. "And you know what? We play a game. I'll lean up against her, and she'll stand perfectly still, holding me up. I guess you could say I trust her too."

Her wise words pricked my conscience and served as a reminder. No matter what God entrusts to me, at home and in my work, He'll hold me up as I lean on Him, helping me accomplish what He's called me to do.

And my Good Shepherd's also my friend. No matter where He leads, I will follow. With His love, I lack nothing. —Maureen Miller

Surely your goodness and love will follow me all the days of my life.
—Psalm 23:6 (NIV)

304   ALL GOD'S CREATURES

OCTOBER 22

Don't Fence Me In

*"Have you not put a fence around him and his
house and all that he has, on every side?"*

—JOB 1:10 (NRSVUE)

OUR DOGS, FRITZ and Frannie, have a nice, fenced-in backyard to play in. But Frannie—all 5 pounds of her—can squeeze through the smallest space. We have to stack cinder blocks and bricks around the gate to keep her from escaping. Whenever the blocks are moved, like when the yard man comes, she immediately runs to the gate to see if the blocks were somehow replaced incorrectly, allowing her to sneak through. The strange thing is, however, that once she is out, she doesn't go anywhere. She usually comes around to the front porch and waits to be let into the house. I can't figure out her obsession with getting out of the yard, and it frustrates me. Doesn't she realize the fence is there for her own protection?

Yet how often do I want to wander outside the protective boundaries God has established for me? Sometimes the temptation to "see what's on the other side" is just too overwhelming. What am I missing? Does God not want me to be happy? To have fun? Why does He want to fence me in with restrictions that leave me feeling out of touch with the rest of the world? As I have grown older (and wiser) and experienced parenting rebellious children, I have come to realize that God's boundaries are there for our protection.

Satan deceives us by making us believe the boundaries God has established are confining and stifling us, when in truth, going outside God's boundaries is dangerous and always brings unpleasant consequences. I am far safer and happier remaining inside the fence, and I have also discovered the grass is not greener on the other side.

I don't think Frannie is ever going to "get it," and we will just have to try our best to keep her safe. I'm glad God gave me His Word to help me stay inside the fence. —Ellen Fannon

*Father, thank You for knowing what's best for me and
establishing boundaries to keep me safe.*

ALL GOD'S CREATURES   305

OCTOBER 23

Going with the Flow

I have learned, in whatsoever state I am, therewith to be content.

—PHILIPPIANS 4:11 (KJV)

AS A PERSON living with chronic illnesses, I found myself battling anxiety during the pandemic. Many of my friends were finding comfort and contentment in their furry friends. I have allergies, so my pet choices were limited. I remembered how much I enjoyed the aquarium when I visited. I hoped that having a fish on my desk, watching it peacefully glide around the tank, would help lower my stress and put a smile on my face.

While Giorgio, my betta, was a bit hesitant when I first put him in his new tank, it wasn't long before he made himself at home. I soon noticed I felt a bit calmer as I watched my new buddy swim around, checking out each nook and cranny. When I'd start to veer toward worrying, I'd pause what I was doing to watch Giorgio. His graceful movements and beautiful colors slowed my breathing and heart rate, and gave me a sense of peace. He seemed happy and carefree in that moment, and looking at him, I was too. And he soon recognized my voice and picked up on my daily routine—when I'd arrive for work, when I'd finish for the day, and when it was mealtime! He was doing exactly what I had hoped when I purchased him.

Over time, I realized I could learn a lot from Giorgio. When I brought him home, he was thrust into a new environment full of strange people, sights, and sounds. Even though his daily schedule changed, he adapted and settled in. Within just a week or two, he looked content and more at ease than I'd seen him in the pet store, and I started to feel more content and at ease too. Giorgio showed me that, with God's help, I, too, could be more content, at ease, and secure when I encounter stressful situations in my life. —Leslie L. McKee

Contentment is not escape from the battle, but rather
an abiding peace and confidence in the midst of the battle.
—Warren Wiersbe

OCTOBER 24

Hoot the Photobomber

*Real wisdom, God's wisdom, begins with a holy life and
is characterized by getting along with others.*

—JAMES 3:17 (MSG)

IT HAD BEEN a trying day. I'd wasted a whole morning on the phone
with technical support while working through a computer glitch that
had gobbled up several important documents. After speaking with a
series of people who were neither helpful nor sympathetic, I was left with
bruised feelings and an even bigger mess. A trip to the post office garnered
much of the same, as the clerk closed the window just as my turn neared.

When the rotten day ended, all I wanted to do was relax on the patio
with my husband. But just as I'd started to loosen up, a persistent buzzing
whirled around my chair, and a flying black insect dive-bombed my head.
"Aghh!" I screeched. "A wasp!"

"That's a dirt dauber." My husband squinted. "Look, he's carrying a
little twig."

The last thing I needed was another ornery force of nature dead set on
tormenting me. But I watched with fascination as the interloper zoomed
between us and disappeared into the iron legs of the end table.

Dirt daubers (also called mud daubers), I learned, are actually quite
docile. They feed on insects and build circular nests against buildings and
structures. While not very attractive, they are mostly harmless.

We named him Hoot.

He visited every evening, fluttering past us with his building supplies
and daily catch. One night he lingered so long I couldn't help noticing
a tiny grasshopper in his clutches. As his wings fluttered good-naturedly,
Hoot seemed to be posing, so I snapped a picture.

Hoot's visits became part of our nightly routine. And to think I'd been
suspicious of his intentions! Rather than showing up to pick a fight, Hoot
had only been going about his day . . . just like the postal worker and rude
technicians. Who knows? Maybe they'd been having a bad day as well.

Humbled, I prayed that no matter what kind of day I was having, I'd
be mindful of those around me and try to get along with everyone. Even
a photogenic dirt dauber. —Hallie Lee

Lord, help me understand that not everything is about me.

ALL GOD'S CREATURES 307

OCTOBER 25

Dog Longboarding

Carry each other's burdens, and in this way you will fulfill the law of Christ.

—GALATIANS 6:2 (NIV)

MY GRANDDAUGHTER WAS just exhausted after school and basketball practice, so when my daughter handed her the leash to walk the family's Siberian husky, Nanook, she groaned for a few moments but then got a good idea. Instead of her walking Nanook, she would let Nanook walk her—or rather *pull* her.

She went outside and grabbed her longboard—an elongated skateboard—from the garage. As soon as Nanook rounded the outside corner of the house and saw the leash in Tempe's hand, he pranced joyfully—making it a bit challenging to get the leash on. So Tempe knew today would be a good day for a test drive!

Genetically equipped to pull a dog sled, their Siberian husky found pulling my slim sixth-grade granddaughter an exciting challenge, and they did fine on the flat and a slight upward incline. But as they turned the corner and started downhill again, Nanook began sprinting for home. Tempe got a little nervous as they picked up speed, and then all of a sudden Nanook leaped over a little bump in the road, and the skateboard headed skyward too.

"I screamed," Tempe told me later, "and I'm not sure how, but I stayed on the board!" The scheme worked, though, because the husky's energy was mostly spent by the time they arrived back home.

Tempe and Nanook's longboard adventure reminds me that I, too, can ease the burden of someone who is struggling with a heavy load. Something as simple as a ride to an appointment or a warm casserole can be just the right way to lighten the burden someone else is bearing. Research shows that people who consistently help others have less depression, greater calm, fewer pains, and better health—just like a happy Siberian husky named Nanook. —Janet Holm McHenry

No one is useless in this world who lightens the burden of it for any one else.
—Charles Dickens

308 ALL GOD'S CREATURES

OCTOBER 26

A Treasure Hunt

*Come and hear, all you who fear God; let me
tell you what he has done for me.*

—PSALM 66:16 (NIV)

AS AN AVID birder, I've learned to pay attention when I see someone in
nature with a large camera and lens, as it's likely they've found something of interest. On this particular day, a photographer was not my only
clue. As my family and I walked through a grassy expanse by the river,
we noticed an A-frame sign warning visitors of owls nesting nearby. I
assumed there was a pair of great horned owls, our most common species.
But when I asked the photographer, he responded that this was a pair of
northern pygmy owls, a small species of owl I had never seen. I mustered
the courage to ask, "Would you mind showing me where they are?"

The photographer smiled as if he'd been waiting for someone to ask
and led me over to a tall pine tree. He carefully described which branch
the owl was perched on until my eyes finally landed on the small raptor,
less than half a foot tall, with wide yellow eyes, vivid striping on its chest,
and a speckled head.

I thanked the photographer as he hurried away to try to find a black
bear my husband had just spotted on a nearby hillside. I was glad that,
as the photographer had helped me locate an owl I'd never seen before,
we'd been able to direct him to another creature and photo opportunity.

Whenever I encounter another bird-watcher, I'm greeted with kindness
and generosity. It's as if we're all on a treasure hunt, looking for beauty
and eager to share it with one another. The same is true in my faith community. As we follow Jesus together, we're excited to share truths from
God's Word and encounters with His Holy Spirit. We are also on a treasure
hunt, looking for God at work and eager to share sightings of Him with
our fellow sojourners. —Eryn Lynum

*Dear God, keep me aware and attentive to see You throughout my day,
and help me to joyfully share my sightings with others.*

OCTOBER 27

The Cone of Comfort

We know and rely on the love God has for us. God is love.
Whoever lives in love lives in God, and God in them.

—1 JOHN 4:16 (NIV)

SOFIE HAS TO wear a cone after her surgery." My sister Kristy pressed her lips together to keep from bursting out laughing in front of her adolescent beagle.

I looked at Sofie, whose head tilt told me she knew we were talking about her, pictured her in a cone, and failed to stifle a snort-laugh.

It was time for fun-loving, frolicking Sofie to get spayed. I knew keeping her confined to the house and away from any favorite place that required a leap to access would be a chore for Kristy. A cone took it to the next level. Sofie would look adorably funny in her "cone of shame" when she wasn't trying to take it off.

Then Kristy started sending post-op photos of Sofie. She didn't mind the cone. Her family had sprung for a padded one like a travel neck pillow, which still got in her way but at least wasn't made of hard plastic. She seemed to know the cone kept her protected and that her family loved her enough to get her one she could rest her head on. She still looked hilarious, but the expression "cone of shame" didn't apply.

At the time, I was adjusting to a health issue that made some activities harder for me and forced changes that felt frustrating and inconvenient. I had developed lung disease despite never doing the things that often caused it. That seemed so wrong. Sofie's attitude with her temporary cone motivated me to accept my new life with a chronic health problem. When I recognized that some changes (diet, being more consistent with cardio exercise, prioritizing sleep) would make me healthier overall with or without this new challenge, I could see God's kindness in the whole thing. As His child, I could trust Him to take care of me as I made peace with my new reality. —Jeanette Hanscome

Lord, thank You for being with me always, even and perhaps especially in
times of shame, frustration, uncertainty, and change.

OCTOBER 28

Goodbye Kiss

Though he brings grief, he will show compassion,
so great is his unfailing love.

—LAMENTATIONS 3:32 (NIV)

UNFORTUNATELY, MANY OF you will relate to this. They say that having a dog will bless you with the happiest days of your life—and one of the worst. My husband, Mike, and I were blessed when God brought Ernest into our lives. And last December, for us, the worst day had come.

We sat on the floor in a dim, quiet room at the vet's, patting Ernest softly and offering him endless treats. He had never lost his appetite. Ernest had lived a wonderful and long life—unusually long for a golden retriever. He was 15 and dealing with several serious health issues. We'd known for a while that the end was nearing. I'd evaluated his quality of life every morning and night. Now, dear Ernest's quality of life was no longer acceptable. There were no more treatment or pain management options.

"You're a good boy," I said.

"We love you, and God loves you," Mike said.

Ernest crunched a dog biscuit. "Now, it's time for your goodbye kiss," I said. I peeled the silver wrapping from a Hershey's Kiss and held it on my palm. Ernest accepted it eagerly. Even though chocolate isn't good for dogs, this was the one opportunity to make an exception. "Every dog should get to experience chocolate once in their life," I said. Mike and I hugged our golden boy through our tears.

Pet loss is painful to experience, and a difficult topic to write about. But God was there to help us in our grief. I felt the warm comfort of His presence in that moment. Surely, He cares about all His creation, including Ernest. And He cares about our sorrow. "Thank You for Ernest," I said, and asked God for the peace and comfort to carry on. We said goodbye. And Ernest went to heaven with the sweet taste of chocolate on his lips.

—Peggy Frezon

"Peace I leave with you; my peace I give you. I do not give to you as the
world gives. Do not let your hearts be troubled and do not be afraid."
—John 14:27 (NIV)

ALL GOD'S CREATURES   311

OCTOBER 29

The Weaver

"Therefore everyone who hears these words of mine and puts them into practice is like a wise man who built his house on the rock. The rain came down, the streams rose, and the winds blew and beat against that house; yet it did not fall, because it had its foundation on the rock."

—MATTHEW 7:24–25 (NIV)

HEY, MOM! LOOK at that spider!"
The kids and I were coming in the front door one fall evening, and my son noticed an orb weaver spider creating a web between some beams on our deck. Orb weavers are common in Missouri, where I live, and they make large, spiral-shaped webs that look like Halloween decorations.

We stopped a moment to watch the spider work.

"It looks like she's floating in midair!" my son exclaimed.

I pointed out the foundation strands that the spider hung first, and how she then moves between those to build out her spiral.

Later that evening, as I sat and watched the spider work, I wondered about how I weave my life together. My life has so many threads; from work to church, family commitments to friends. It is a complicated pattern, for sure.

Just like the spider, I need a solid foundation to build my web. Thankfully I have an anchor line that holds my whole life together, and that is my faith in God. The orb weaver spider first builds a frame and then works on her spiral. With my trust in Him, I build a frame of faith, and then fill in the details of my life. With God as my foundation, I know I will be secure.

Talking with my son about the orb weaver's web was a good reminder to me. If I keep my foundation strong in the Lord, then the rest will follow.
—Heather Jepsen

He will be the sure foundation for your times, a rich store of salvation and wisdom and knowledge; the fear of the LORD is the key to this treasure.
—Isaiah 33:6 (NIV)

OCTOBER 30

Wisdom and the Owl

"Whoever finds me [Wisdom] finds life and obtains favor from the LORD."
—**PROVERBS 8:35** (NKJV)

A FRIEND OF mine was excited when an owl took up residence in one of the structures on his farm because he knew it would hunt pests and keep watch on the property as he slept. He's allowed me to spend some time there, watching the barn owl. Its calm and observant nature hints at the origin of the owl's reputation as a wise animal. The way it surveys the entire scene and carefully judges the right time to act and the precision with which it descends on prey suggest a well-developed brain built for accuracy.

The Bible places a high value on wisdom, as is emphasized in Proverbs 8:35. If wisdom informs our every decision, conversation, and relationship, this character trait will create new life in us and bring us favor with the Lord.

Having promised to help with a project, I went to the barn to get started. I noticed the owl in the corner—high above the hay. With its large eyes and straight posture, it scanned the barn, looking for any trace of movement. Its grayish-brown feathers and spotted beak caused it to fit in well next to the aging barnwood. Nature's camouflage is quite effective.

As my thoughts drifted into prayer, God illuminated the bird's quiet confidence and the wisdom of being slow to judgment. The latter can be a particular struggle for me. My personality, even my character strengths, can be a weakness when not mixed with God's love and patience. Why had I been so blunt in pointing out the factual error of a friend last week?

Suddenly the owl launched from its perch and dived toward a dark corner of the barn. Startled, I roused from my reflection and headed outside into the fresh new day, perhaps wiser from the encounter, and my plan for the day will include more wisdom, patience, and kindness in dealing with others. —David L. Winters

Father, You made us and unconditionally love each of Your creations.
Providentially teach us to share love as we grow in relationships.
Grant us patience and peace. Amen.

ALL GOD'S CREATURES 313

OCTOBER 31

How Do You Like Me Now?

See what great love the Father has lavished on us, that we should be called children of God! And that is what we are! The reason the world does not know us is that it did not know him.

—1 JOHN 3:1 (NIV)

WHEN I MOVED to southern Indiana, I admired the unfamiliar birds rising high over the community park. The group drifted along in circular patterns without flapping their 6-foot wings. In unison, and silently, the majestic flying squad banked, then touched down in their nests along the hillside.

Curiosity led me to ask an acquaintance about these fascinating flyers. She gave me an unpleasant look and replied, "Those are vultures and scavengers. When you see them up close and find out what they do, you will change your mind about them."

Hoping to gain insight into the species, I located two photographs of turkey vultures. In the first image they soared as black silhouettes against a blue sky and could be mistaken for eagles. I read how they glide on the warm air called thermals as a means of saving energy. The other photo zoomed in on the red, featherless turkey-like head, short whitish beak, and light-red feet. I was not expecting those features! Then I discovered that these scavengers are essential for a healthy ecosystem.

Still, I understood why public opinion was divided about this cleanup crew. You can either appreciate them or be disgusted by them.

God led me to reflect on the public perception of my actions and appearance. I may seem to be a godly woman when I volunteer at a church function, lead the ladies' prayer circle, or sing praises during worship. But what about when I attempt to hide my undesirable traits and attitudes from the public eye as I selfishly wish to be recognized for my volunteer work, pick apart someone else's prayer, or criticize the song choices?

Since God heaps love on me, even when I am not showing my best side, I can learn to love others, even at their worst. —Glenda Ferguson

Walk of Faith: *Think of an instance when God heaped His love on you, then consider how to spread that abundance of love to another.*

314   ALL GOD'S CREATURES

NOVEMBER 1

Steered in the Wrong Direction

*Am I now trying to win the approval of human beings, or of
God? Or am I trying to please people? If I were still trying
to please people, I would not be a servant of Christ.*

—GALATIANS 1:10 (NIV)

MY HUSBAND, CRAIG, raises Angus beef cattle here in California's
Sierra Valley. When he's getting animals ready to ship to auction,
he pens them up by size. This week he had five 900-pound steers in the
same pen.

The space was large enough that they had plenty of room to move
around without getting in one another's way. Nonetheless, he watched as
two steers went head-to-head in a pushing contest to see who would be
king of the pen. This typical behavior usually results in one gaining supe-
riority over the other to get a better position for feed. But while Craig was
putting the hay into the feed bunk, he watched as one steer pushed the
other one toward the opposite side of the pen—right to the water trough.
And then all of a sudden, the dominating steer gave one final push, and
the other steer lost its balance and fell right into the 4-by-8-foot trough!

It was one of my husband's *what-do-I-do-now* moments, but before he
could intervene, the doused steer righted itself, jumped back out, and
shook itself off. Then it waited until the coast was clear at the feed bunk.

Beef cattle do the craziest things, but I have to admit that sometimes
they remind me of things I do or witness. Just that day a friend had asked
if I'd take on another ministry responsibility, and I was still weighing the
yes-or-no decision. I saw the need, and I wanted to help out, but I knew
that if I took on yet another obligation, the time involved could push
me away from what I know God has called me to do. Instead of getting
steered in the wrong direction, I called her right then and told her I just
didn't have the time. And I thanked God for yet another ranch story to
remind me of His purpose for me. —Janet Holm McHenry

Walk of Faith: *When you sense that others are pushing you to take on
responsibilities, you can say, "Thank you for your confidence in me,
but God hasn't given me peace about doing that."*

NOVEMBER 2

The Wonder of Puppies

Let the morning bring me word of your unfailing love, for I have put my trust in you. Show me the way I should go, for to you I entrust my life.

—PSALM 143:8 (NIV)

MY PARENTS RECENTLY welcomed two springer spaniel puppies into their home. To say the spaniels are cute dogs is an understatement! They have adorable expressions, lanky legs, and big paws, and they give even bigger hugs. They already know they are deeply loved and look taken aback if you ever tell them no. What fun they've brought into our family. Is there anything more universally lovable than puppies?

One thing that's so special about the two of them is that the world is still brand-new. They welcome each day with a sense of wonder. Puddles and lizards and new treats are all opportunities for wonderful excitement! No new discovery is too small or insignificant. Even going outside and coming inside again is cause for tail wags and a quick round of chase. These two puppies welcome every moment with enthusiasm, excitement, and curiosity.

The older I get, the more I find myself following patterns of familiar, comfortable behavior. I so easily forget the marvels of God's creation. I pay little attention to the magnificent strength of ants, the chorus of toads after the rain, or the brilliant colors of the sunset. But I want to make an effort to maintain my sense of wonder. Wonder inspires awe, worship, and creativity. I want to be like the puppies and look forward to each new day with a heart full of anticipation—waiting for what each fresh new hour may bring. Each day is a gift, and I pray I take time to notice the creation all around me as it bears witness to God today. —Ashley Clark

Dear Lord, this is Your day, which You have given me. Help me approach it with the curiosity of a puppy and never lose sight of the joy of new discoveries. Help me see Your hand and Your love in all I see and do. Amen.

ALL GOD'S CREATURES

NOVEMBER 3

His Eye Is on the ... Pigeon

*"Look at the birds of the air; they do not sow or reap or
store away in barns, and yet your heavenly Father feeds
them. Are you not much more valuable than they?"*

—MATTHEW 6:26 (NIV)

I BELIEVE MY LOVE of animals came from my parents. They were both
animal lovers, but particularly my father. He had a soft spot when it
came to furry and feathered creatures. When I was a child, he brought
home a pigeon he had found on the road. The bird suffered from a skin
disorder that caused generalized sores on its body. My father toted the
pigeon to our veterinarian, who probably didn't know what to do with
it, but prescribed some medicine for my father to apply. When the bird
didn't get any better, he took it back to the vet again and again.

Sadly, the bird died after a couple of weeks, and my father broke down
and cried. Most people would find it strange for a grown man to cry over
a pigeon. But that's how much my father cared for God's creatures.

My heavenly Father, too, cares about our feathered friends. Jesus said,
"Are not two sparrows sold for a penny? Yet not one of them will fall to
the ground outside your Father's care" (Matthew 10:29, NIV). When I
think about how God takes notice of something that seems so insignificant as a little bird and realize that God cares even more for me, I can
hardly wrap my mind around that reality.

The Creator of the Universe, who sees every bird and knows when
each one falls to the ground, loved me enough to leave the splendor of
heaven and die an agonizing death on the cross for my sins. Because of
His sacrifice, I am free from the bondage of sin. And knowing this makes
me want to soar, just like the birds of the air. —Ellen Fannon

*In almost everything that touches our everyday life on earth,
God is pleased when we're pleased. He wills that we be as free
as birds to soar and sing our maker's praise without anxiety.*
—A. W. Tozer

318 · ALL GOD'S CREATURES

NOVEMBER 4

The Cardinal's Calling Card

*"Be careful to obey all these words that I command you, that it may
go well with you and with your children after you forever, when you
do what is good and right in the sight of the LORD your God."*

—DEUTERONOMY 12:28 (ESV)

OUR SON'S FAMILY enjoys watching a resident male cardinal that
exhibits unusual behavior. This cardinal lives near a shed at the edge
of their property. Every day he flies between the two cars parked in their
carport. He lands on the door handle of one car's passenger side, looks in
the mirror, and deposits a "reminder" of his visit. He then flies to the door
handle of the other car's driver side, looks in the mirror, and leaves another
calling card. If you are visiting, he'll greet your car in this way as well. There
is no discrimination; all cars and mirrors get the same treatment.

What does the cardinal see that makes him leave his mark? Does he
think he sees another male cardinal and feel the need to mark his territory?

I don't know the answer, but watching that cardinal made me pause to
consider the things I am leaving behind. What will be the lasting effects
of my choices in life? What will people remember about me when I am
gone from this world? Kind words or unkind? Helpful deeds or apathy?
Forgiveness or bitterness and grudges?

The things I say, the things I do, and even, to some extent, the things I
think and feel leave a mark in this world and on the lives of others. Before
I do or say something, anything, I want to remember the cardinal's quirky
behavior and consider the thing I'm about to do so that it, and what I
leave behind with that action, adds to a legacy that is "good and right
in the sight of the Lord" and to the people around me. —Harold Nichols

*For the past 33 years, I have looked in the mirror every morning
and asked myself, "If today were the last day of my life,
would I want to do what I am about to do today?"*
—Steve Jobs

NOVEMBER 5

Stopping in My Tracks

It is useless for you to work so hard from early morning until late at night, anxiously working for food to eat; for God gives rest to his loved ones.

—PSALM 127:2 (NLT)

MICHIGAN IS KNOWN for extreme temperature fluctuations that defy normal weather patterns for a particular season. My hometown of Rockford was deep into a mild fall when we experienced a November heat wave.

The staff at Camp Roger day camp, where I work, decided to take advantage of the gorgeous eighty-degree day and walk to Little Bostwick Lake. As we began the hike, I noticed a squirrel in a tree that stopped me short. The squirrel was stomach down on the bow of a substantial branch, arms draped on either side, very relaxed. Was he overheated from the unusual weather? Resting from a busy day collecting acorns? Enjoying the reds and yellows of the autumn leaves? Whatever the reason for the break in his routine, he seemed perfectly content to watch us as we stopped to observe his un-squirrel-like behavior before we continued on our hike.

Squirrels are everywhere at Camp Roger. We even have a "four o'clock squirrel" who comes down a tree each day to dumpster dive near our office and search for food on the grounds around the front of our building. I watch these creatures daily, and not once have I witnessed a squirrel at a complete stop. They are in constant motion, looking for acorns, jumping and running over leaves and up trees—busy, busy, busy. Like me.

When I stop completely to rest, it feels strange. Most days, God must look down on my constant scurrying around and wonder what I will be up to next. Sometimes I wonder that myself. When I sit down, grab a book, and force myself to slow down, I am refueled and remind myself how important it is to do this more often. —Twila Bennett

Walk of Faith: *Carve out some time today to pause. Make a cup of tea or coffee, and grab your Bible or that book you've been wanting to read. Set a timer for 30 minutes and put aside your busyness. It's worth the effort.*

NOVEMBER 6

Murphy the Eagle Dad

Who satisfies your mouth with good things,
so that your youth is renewed like the eagle's.

—PSALM 103:5 (NKJV)

I RECENTLY ENCOUNTERED a story about a bald eagle named Murphy who'd been injured and could no longer fly. Apparently, this male eagle desperately wanted to be a father. One day, the keepers at the avian sanctuary noticed Murphy building a nest and then protectively guarding it from the other birds. With no female in the picture, keepers were curious what exactly Murphy was so preciously guarding. When Murphy went to find food, they discovered the "egg" was a rock.

As it happened, the sanctuary had an abandoned eaglet on site that they'd planned to hand-raise, but with Murphy so clearly desiring to be a father, they had a better idea. They quickly removed the rock and replaced it with a baby bird. Proud daddy Murphy believed his "egg" had hatched! And not surprisingly, he was a wonderful father and has since gone on to care for a second abandoned eaglet.

I can really see myself in Murphy. How many times in my life have I built my proverbial nest only to nurture an unmoving, unchanging rock without even realizing it? I've seen this apply to my career, with jobs that went nowhere, my relationships with family and friends that were one-sided or hurtful, and even my spiritual life, pursuing different teachers or leaders who let me down. It is only when God changes that rock out with something living and breathing that I find growth. Many times I don't even recognize it's happened until much later in hindsight, when I realize my plans or desires were only rocks. Like Murphy the eagle daddy, I am grateful when God removes the rock and replaces it with an opportunity to grow. —Deb Kastner

He will cover you with his feathers, and under his wings you will
find refuge; his faithfulness will be your shield and rampart.
—Psalm 91:4 (NIV)

ALL GOD'S CREATURES   321

NOVEMBER 7

Scuppers

Where can I go from your Spirit?

—PSALM 139:7 (NIV)

BACK SO SOON?" I asked our little dog. I had opened the back door for him to relieve himself in the yard. Our deck has a motion detector sensor that only gets tripped if Scuppers goes beyond the grill on the deck. Once he hits that spot, he is at the top of the steps to go down into the yard. Generally it takes him a few minutes to do his business before he is back up the stairs and inside. The way the grill needs to be positioned, it is difficult to see him physically traversing the steps, so we relied on the light from the motion detector to know that he'd gone to the yard.

But Scuppers is smart. During inclement weather, we have watched and noticed that he waits at the top of the steps for the light to go on and then after a few moments returns inside to receive a treat. He doesn't do what he is supposed to do.

I thought about how many times I go through the motions with God but do not do what I am supposed to do. I hide out behind a facade of what I think God wants. I may appear to be kind or loving but hold back from truly helping people in need or engaging with people who "annoy" me.

God is patient with me, but He sometimes sends me back out again just like we send Scuppers back into the yard to finish his task. God returns me to the same situation or encounter with the same person so that I learn what He wants me to learn: to be loving to all people. Scuppers thinks he can hide from us, but we know what he is doing. In the same way, we think we can hide from God, but He knows what we are doing and longs for us to get it right. —Virginia Ruth

Omniscient God, where can I hide from You? You formed me. You know me. You know when I sit and when I stand. Thank You that You care so much about me and my circumstances, even if that requires me to relearn the lessons You've taught me before. Amen.

NOVEMBER 8

Oh Deer!

He makes my feet like the feet of a deer; he causes me to stand on the heights.
—2 SAMUEL 22:34 (NIV)

LOOK OUT!" I yelled as several deer crossed the busy road in front of us. My husband slammed on the brakes as one deer ran into the front of our car and then fled into the woods. Behind us, another car hit a deer that now lay on the highway. We pulled to the side.

"We need to get that deer out of the road," I said, impulsively hopping from the car and crossing the busy highway to run back to where the deer lay unmoving.

My heart fluttered to see its eyes open. How badly was it injured? I didn't want another car to hit it, possibly hurting the driver, let alone causing more trauma to the deer. With adrenaline pumping through my veins, I didn't stop to consider that I am a 68-year-old 100-pound woman. I simply grabbed the rear end of the animal and tugged it backward into the grassy median.

To my surprise, the deer sat up, its front half still in the road with its forelegs tucked underneath. I reached around and pulled its neck to try to tow the rest of its body into the median. Then, without warning, the deer jumped up and ran across the highway into the woods. Even better, no cars barreled down the street in those few seconds.

I don't suppose that deer realized I probably saved its life as it hurried to get away from me in its panic. How many times has God tried to pick me up when I lay wounded on my journey through life? Like that deer, do I try to escape from Him in my fear and pain? Or do I let Him pull me to safety? Sometimes I feel so overwhelmed that I can't find my way through the darkness, and I forget to look to the Light. Yet I know God loves me through my trials. I need not lose sight of that fact when I am lying stunned and helpless amid the world's busy traffic. —Ellen Fannon

Father, thank You for picking me up when I fall.

NOVEMBER 9

Which Is the Real Bison?

Judge not, that ye be not judged.
—MATTHEW 7:1 (KJV)

MY FIRST ENCOUNTER with bison came when we were touring Custer State Park in South Dakota. During our leisurely drive through the park, we encountered part of the park's large bison herd spread out across the road. We excitedly began taking pictures and videos from our small compact car. Our activity stimulated activity among the bison. They began moving across the road in front of and behind the car. And as the animals close to us began moving, ones further away began moving faster to keep up. I had visions of a full-fledged bison stampede, and as soon as an opening presented itself, we got our small car out of there. That encounter taught me that bison were beautiful, magnificent, dangerous animals best viewed from a distance.

My next close-up encounter came at Global Wildlife Center in Louisiana, which has added a few bison to its herd of wildlife. Imagine my surprise when this wonderful, cuddly bison stuck his head inside our tour vehicle to eat out of my hand. He let me reach around his neck and pet his furry head. The bison reminded me of a teddy bear, not at all dangerous but rather an animal to be snuggled and loved.

So which of these is the real bison? The answer, of course, is both. As I reflected on these extremely different encounters, I realized how wrong my first judgment about bison had been. And I thought about my encounters with people when I sometimes categorize or label them before I really get to know them. For me, snap judgments are rarely useful, and they can lead to bad decisions. I need to remember the bison and give people the chance to show me all the different sides of themselves.
—Harold Nichols

When you judge another, you do not define them, you define yourself.
—Wayne W. Dyer

NOVEMBER 10

Unlikely Watchdog

The Lord will fulfill his purpose for me.

—PSALM 138:8 (ESV)

I RECENTLY HAD the opportunity to meet Bella, my daughter's scoodle—a miniature poodle–Scottish terrier mix. All of a couple pounds, Bella has what's called alfalfa hair—squiggles of hair that go every which way, resembling alfalfa sprouts. Bella was the runt of a litter of perfectly wavy-haired pups with perky, playful dispositions. Instead, she kept quietly to herself—which might have been appealing for a mom with six very busy children.

As I drove up to my daughter's home with a couple of the grandchildren, Bella perked up from her cozy bed on the porch, then ran a lap around the house, in the process rousting a couple of deer from the backyard and chasing them down the street.

My granddaughter Faith laughed. Just as a teenager might quickly start picking up her bedroom when her parents pull into the driveway, Faith said Bella breaks into action when someone comes home—as if to look important and trustworthy.

"It's like she's saying, 'Look at me,'" Faith said. "'I've been taking care of business while you're away.'"

Bella clearly needs to know that she is important, that she matters, and that she has a purpose. That such a tiny dog could be a watchdog in a rural area with bears, mountain lions, and coyotes was ridiculous, of course. Instead, Bella's function is more likely to look cute in someone's handbag or backpack. In fact, her favorite and most frequent occupation is lap sitting while the family watches television.

While Bella may have been confused about her life's purpose, we can know ours. Through prayer, we can ask God to reveal His good plan for us, as well as just the right first steps to head in that direction. We don't have to run around trying to look important—God already knows we matter just the way we are. —Janet Holm McHenry

The purpose of life is a life of purpose.
—Robert Byrne

NOVEMBER 11

They Just Know

They confronted me in the day of my calamity, but the LORD was my support.
—PSALM 18:18 (ESV)

WHEN ONE OF my daughters was going through an especially tough time as a teenager, we attended a therapy group for a while. We discovered that many in the group had service dogs specifically for mental health. I don't recall emotional support animals being common at the time. It sounded like a good idea, though, so I started researching service dogs specifically trained for mental health. I found out it was way out of our league money-wise. Then my daughter bought her own dog, a Chihuahua she named Paris, and that become a less formal—but much loved—form of emotional support.

So I shelved the idea of an emotional support dog. As life went on, I forgot about it—until I experienced a particularly tough time in my own life and the idea came rushing back to me. Like most married couples, my husband and I have had many ups and downs as we've lived out our marriage vows—for better or for worse, for richer or poorer, in sickness and in health. Yeah, we've been there. We are there. My husband was just diagnosed with follicular lymphoma. The Big C. Cancer.

My emotions have been up and down (mostly down) since we started this new journey. But I've noticed one thing. My miniature schnauzer Gabby has been extra attentive, sleeping curled around my head and at my side every second of every day—except on Joe's chemo days, when Gabby stays with him. She seems to just *know*. It's amazing. Not only that, but my cat Dab, the ultimate in snooty independence, is suddenly coming to cuddle several times a day. This is not the cat I am used to, and I have no idea where this behavior came from. He just knows.

I've concluded that all pets are emotional support animals to one degree or another. They don't have to be trained. They just know. And they also understand how to help, how to offer the love and support I need to keep on trekking on this long and often tiring journey. —Deb Kastner

Lord, thank You for providing pets in our lives
who serve as emotional support animals.

326　ALL GOD'S CREATURES

NOVEMBER 12

Along Came Sofie

*You have given me greater joy than those who have
abundant harvests of grain and new wine.*

—PSALM 4:7 (NLT)

WHEN MY SISTER Kristy's family had to say goodbye to their beloved
Yorkie, Joey (aka, Joey the Highly Sensitive Dog), I didn't think it
was possible for them to find another pet with so much personality. Our
entire extended family mourned the absence of perpetually anxious Joey,
who insisted on drinking water from a mug long after a protective surgery
cone required him to. Then, in a blast of vacation photos, Kristy sent an
image of the addition to the family that they would be picking up as soon
as they unpacked: a darling beagle puppy. They named her Sofie.

From the moment I met Sofie, I knew she was exactly what Kristy's
family, as well as all of us who missed Joey, needed. I instantly fell in love.
Sofie was joy encapsulated in floppy ears, soulful eyes, awkward puppy
paws, and a white-tipped tail that spun in circles. Unlike fearful Joey, she
explored Kristy's backyard like a child at the playground and turned every
"time to go out" as a chance to frolic. When Sofie experienced snow for
the first time, she leaped through it like a gazelle. She developed a routine
of greeting me with mournful cries as if she hadn't seen me in years and
had missed me terribly.

Not only did Sofie's presence provide gladness after grief, but her spirit
resurrected my appreciation for those who spread joy. I wanted to be like
Sofie—embracing life, adventure, and every person God put in my path.
She continues to remind me that an upbeat heart is contagious, that God
created us to rejoice in all that is good, love with abandon, and praise Him
through every up and down of life. —Jeanette Hanscome

*So rejoice in the LORD and be glad, all you who obey him!
Shout for joy, all you whose hearts are pure!*
—Psalm 32:11 (NLT)

ALL GOD'S CREATURES 327

NOVEMBER 13

Stronger Than I Realized

I can do all this through him who gives me strength.

—PHILIPPIANS 4:13 (NIV)

MY COLLEGE-AGED DAUGHTER, Julia, was working at a summer internship in another state, 7 hours from home. It would be a real test for her—and for me. I'm a worrier by nature, and having my 20-year-old daughter living alone so far from home made me anxious.

Three days into her internship, Julia called me, crying. "I don't know anyone here. I'm so homesick, Mom."

I prayed—and worried—constantly. "God, help her to adjust and help me not to worry about her so much." But a week later, neither situation was improving, so I decided to visit her.

When I arrived, Julia hugged me and said, "I'm so glad you're here. I asked my coworkers for fun things we can do, and I made a whole schedule for us."

The next day, we went to the zoo. We stopped in front of the ostrich enclosure and watched several giant birds roam around. A zoo employee pointed out a nest that contained two ostrich eggs. "They're very strong," she said. "A full-grown adult could stand on an ostrich egg, and it wouldn't crack."

Over the next several days, I watched my daughter confidently navigate her new city. She introduced me to her coworkers, who had only good things to say about her. She prepared a delicious dinner for us.

On the eighth day, I packed my suitcase. "Jules, you don't need me here," I said. "You're like that ostrich egg—way stronger than either of us realized. Moving to a new city is a lot of pressure, but you're not cracking under it. You're thriving, and I'm so proud of you."

When I got home, I googled photos of ostrich eggs and printed two copies. I mailed one to Julia and kept the other for myself, as a reminder of her strength and ability to handle this change. God answered my prayer for Julia—and the one I'd prayed for myself. —Diane Stark

Remember that you are braver than you believe, stronger than you seem, smarter than you think, and loved more than you know.
—Attributed to A. A. Milne

328   ALL GOD'S CREATURES

NOVEMBER 14

Mike's Hotel Visits

No discipline seems pleasant at the time, but painful.
Later on, however, it produces a harvest of righteousness
and peace for those who have been trained by it.

—HEBREWS 12:11 (NIV)

MIKE IS THE joy of my life, a plain brown dog called a Tennessee Brown Dog or a black-mouthed cur.

He entered my life when I had just lost several of my rescue dogs to old age, all at the same time. My heart was broken, and I did not want to feel that kind of pain again. I had decided, no more dogs. And then, along came Mike and won my heart. He is afraid of his shadow and spends a great deal of his life either under the covers on the bed if I am there or under the bed if I am not. He understands even things I don't say aloud, as if he can literally read my mind.

He has healed my heart and reached places no one ever could. This worked perfectly when we were required to isolate at home. But as the world came back to life, I had to travel for work once more, and Mike had to stay at "the hotel." That is what we call the veterinarian's office, the only other place that Mike has ever been.

Because he is territorial and protective of our home space, a house sitter was not an option. But leaving him at the vet felt like such a betrayal. One look from those big, soulful eyes, tail tucked as I said goodbye, was more than either of us could take. But a young woman at the office took special care of him and changed everything for both of us.

Sometimes life requires me to "roll with it" when a situation is not what I want for myself. But as I allow myself to broaden my circle of people, experiences, and dreams, as Mike did with his "hotel" visit, I might find that new situations, new people, and new jobs can even be pleasant if given a chance. —Devon O'Day

God, give me the willingness to accept changes, even temporary ones,
so that I don't miss a gift You have prepared for me.

ALL GOD'S CREATURES   329

NOVEMBER 15

Staying Close

Draw near to God, and he will draw near to you.

—JAMES 4:8 (ESV)

"OK, BUDDY. I need my feet back now." I looked down at the 140-pound Bernese mountain dog lying on my feet under the table. No movement.

With a chuckle, I pulled my feet out from under Zander's warm, furry body and rose from the table. Then I walked up the hallway to my home office.

The thudding of large paws pursuing me as I reached the office door was no surprise. I sat at my desk, and Zander squeezed his large bulk under the wooden furniture. It wasn't enough for him to be in the same room with me. He had to be touching the people he loved. Always. So he maneuvered himself into position to make sure his shoulders made contact with my leg, and he released a deep sigh.

"Silly boy." A smile curved my mouth as I leaned down and petted Zander. His need for connection could get a little extreme. And it wasn't always the most convenient thing to be followed by a giant dog who insisted on squishing into every space I visited.

But what if Zander was setting an example for me? Maybe the Lord was using him to teach me something. Zander found peace and comfort from being close to me, his person. Could I find the peace and comfort I craved if I stuck that close to my Father?

In the busyness of life, I sometimes forget to read God's Word or spend time talking to Him in prayer. Then I become more stressed, depressed, or anxious. I need to be like Zander, to eagerly draw near to God, knowing that He promises to draw near to me too. And if I stay close, I'll experience His peace and love for all of my days. —Jerusha Agen

My Lord, I find that nothing else will do,
But follow where thou goest, sit at thy feet,
And where I have thee not, still run to meet.
—George MacDonald

NOVEMBER 16

Joy Purrs

Weeping may stay for the night, but rejoicing comes in the morning.

—PSALM 30:5 (NIV)

THE JOY I have always known is playful, rambunctious, exuberant, loud. But lately my house has been a quiet, solemn place. Gone are the days of my son's high-school basketball team taking over the kitchen with pizza and video games. The piano sits silent, and the harp and banjo are in their cases, my eldest daughter and her music-making friends having scattered to other states and provinces. My husband, the most exuberant of all, has died.

My old calico cat, Tango, and I make the best of a quiet house, sitting together on the couch with a stack of books in the early mornings.

But now my youngest daughter, who recently moved a few miles away, has determined that a new kitten is what Tango and I need to bring joy back to our home. Cleo is adorable. As playful and rambunctious as the basketball team, delightful as an ad hoc band, and almost as exuberant as my late husband, Cleo zooms around the house making a new toy of everything from lettuce to pen to toilet paper. The kitten is entertaining but mischievous; Tango is on edge. Tango has retreated from my lap to under the coffee table. As much as I love kittens, I'm a bit on edge too, and the low growl I hear from Tango doesn't help.

Working from home, I referee between the cats, playing with the little one and reassuring the older one throughout the day. In my quest for peace and equilibrium between them, to restore the quiet, I've entirely forgotten the new kitten was meant to bring joy.

By nightfall we are all exhausted. I put Cleo to bed in our guestroom, and a few moments later Tango finds her way to me and settles on my lap. The house is quiet again. And then I hear it: not the low growl, but purring. It dawns on me then: maybe joy has been here all along, contentment its own quiet version of joy. —Susie Colby

Satisfy us in the morning with your unfailing love,
that we may sing for joy and be glad all our days.
—Psalm 90:14 (NIV)

ALL GOD'S CREATURES   331

NOVEMBER 17

Salted Kitten

As a father has compassion on his children, so the
Lord has compassion on those who fear him.

—Psalm 103:13 (NIV)

WE WERE ON a quest to find unique shorebirds at the salt evaporation lagoon in Guanacaste, Costa Rica. What we found was a stray kitten.

It was a desolate location. Under a simple shelter with a concrete floor lay bags of salt awaiting transport. Lounging on the cool concrete was an adult cat and a kitten. The black-and-white kitten had heavily bandaged back legs.

Jeff and I watched the kitten hobble off, dragging its back legs, following what we assumed was its mother or perhaps surrogate mother. No one was around to ask about the kitten's apparent care. A lone worker later relayed that the kitten's paw pads had been damaged from repeated exposure to the salt. He had medicated the paws and bandaged the kitten's legs. It was apparent that the kitten was hurt, yet not unnoticed; it was awkward, but not abandoned.

This story reminds me of the beautiful way the Lord responds to you and me. During those inevitable times when I'm awkwardly dragging my hurts behind me, the Lord does not abandon me. He encircles me in His compassion. I cling to the words in 1 Peter 5:7: "Give all your worries and cares to God, for he cares about you" (NLT). Yes! He readily tends my wounds, providing hope and healing.

The little kitten found kindness in the middle of nowhere at the hands of a sympathetic worker. So, too, I find that the Lord's compassion for my hurts flows from His hand. Indeed, His compassionate care can be found in the midst of what may seem like the most desolate of places within my hurting spirit and soul. And the ointment He tenderly rubs on my wounds is His unfailing and steadfast love. —Darlene Kerr

If you would sum up the whole character of Christ in reference to ourselves, it
might be gathered into this one sentence: "He was moved with compassion."
—Charles H. Spurgeon

NOVEMBER 18

Safe Harbor

In peace I will lie down and sleep, for you alone,
LORD, make me dwell in safety.
—PSALM 4:8 (NIV)

I WAS SURPRISED to see two mallard ducks happily paddling in the pool of our Florida vacation resort. As I sunbathed, I observed them resting in the shade of the lounge chairs, and when I went in the water, I noticed the lifeguards discouraged the human swimmers from touching or feeding them. It seemed their presence had become commonplace. Over the next several days, I looked for, but never found, where the ducks bedded down, but apparently this landscaped pool area provided the ducks with everything they needed: water; bugs, worms, seeds, and plants for food; sandy soil, grasses, and shrubs for shelter; a lack of predators; and a temperate climate. It was an unusual location for wild ducks, certainly, but it provided a safe harbor that allowed the pair to thrive.

God has so far graced me with adequate food, shelter, and health care, for which I am thankful. I also am not aware of ever having been in mortal danger. In addition to my physical needs, my heavenly Father has also provided me with safe places to land, often after difficult times. A new home and fresh start following a disappointing and depressing first job experience after college. A new career as a dog walker, pet sitter, and eventual passionate owner of a pet-care business after escaping a longtime corporate job gone wrong. A welcoming new church home after being discouraged by politics in the old one.

God keeps me safe and cared for, allowing me to thrive, as He does for those mallards at the pool. I will trust in His safe harbor all my days.
—Kim Sheard

Keep me safe, my God, for in you I take refuge.
—Psalm 16:1 (NIV)

ALL GOD'S CREATURES   333

NOVEMBER 19

Moving Forward

"See, I am doing a new thing! Now it springs up; do you not perceive it?
I am making a way in the wilderness and streams in the wasteland."

—ISAIAH 43:19 (NIV)

WHEN MY HUSBAND, Neil, lost his job and found a new one in a city 90 miles away, we had to move. Rather than sell our old house, we hung onto it, planning to return home on weekends. We rented an apartment to stay in during the week.

Still, we were about to embark on a big "new normal," and I was anxious. Living in a four-room apartment in a multibuilding complex felt very different from living in our ten-room house in the country. I didn't know anyone in the city, and all my routines would have to change. I had to get used to a new grocery store, find a different doctor, a new bank, and give up my substitute teaching job.

Then there was Jitters, our middle-aged black cat. An outdoor kitty, she was used to our property and never went near the road. But city traffic? Worried, I kept her inside. That didn't work, as she paced in front of our sliding glass doors begging me to open them. Finally, I did.

And that's when I saw how adaptable she was. She avoided the busy road, never got lost, and loved exploring her new surroundings. At the same time, she immediately adjusted to riding in the car. On each trip home, she happily entered her wire crate, curled up, and fell asleep. Not only did our brave kitty not object, she embraced change. Inspired by her, I realized that I needed to change too. God was in control, and I needed to trust Him to see me through.

So, I took a chance. I signed up for daily exercise classes at the Family Y next door. Because of that, I made new friends, learned about our new community, and began enjoying our new life. —Aline Newman

Walk of Faith: *Try something new. Maybe you'd like to take*
an art class or try writing poetry but fear of failure holds you back.
Take the leap. Trust God to help you. Then give thanks when He does.

NOVEMBER 20

The Well-Connected Chrysalis

*"I give them eternal life, and they shall never perish;
no one will snatch them out of my hand."*

—JOHN 10:28 (NIV)

I DISCOVERED A chrysalis on my apple tree. Hidden beneath a small branch, it looked like just another offshoot twig. It was suspended by two slender threads and held in place by an anchor at one end. I took pictures and asked friends if they knew "who" was going to appear, and my most knowledgeable acquaintance said it would be an anise swallowtail butterfly, which is common to my area. Sometimes caterpillars that hatch late in the season "overwinter" in their chrysalis, staying dormant for many months before emerging in the spring.

But no sooner did I notice this delightful feat of nature than winter decided to unleash a ferocious storm that lasted for days. The power of the high winds and driving rain brought down trees and caused landslides elsewhere. But when the storm finally passed, the little chrysalis remained securely attached to the tree.

There are many stories and anecdotes comparing a Christian's life cycle to that of a butterfly—our life, death, and resurrection into eternal life with God—but today I find myself focused on my chrysalis stage and God's protection as I'm helplessly suspended in my life on earth.

The nascent butterfly inside the protective chrysalis can't control the powerful natural forces that swirl all around it, threatening at any moment to end its existence. It can't run away should a bird locate it and decide to have a quick snack. But it is so firmly connected to the tree, even appearing to be *part* of the tree, that wind, rain, and birds are hard pressed to harm it.

I want to be so firmly connected to God, and Him so much a part of me, that nothing this side of heaven can harm me. I'll continue to strengthen my bond with Him by reading His Word and by praying to Him, knowing I'm safe and secure in His Hand. —Marianne Campbell

I am trusting Thee, Lord Jesus; never let me fall.
I am trusting Thee forever, and for all.
—Frances R. Havergal

ALL GOD'S CREATURES   335

NOVEMBER 21

A Wren in a Bag Is Worth Two in the Bush

*After everyone was full, Jesus told his disciples, "Now
gather the leftovers, so that nothing is wasted."*

—JOHN 6:12 (NLT)

WHEN WE CLEANED out my second cousin's home in preparation for an estate sale, my siblings and I brought home a small handful of tote bags. Francis seemed to have a knack for collecting odd items she thought she might need one day. I can't for the life of me think of why an 80-something-year-old widow with no children of her own would need 20 to 30 tote bags, over 100 sticky-note pads, and quite possibly one million paper clips, but it became our task to collect a few for sentimental reasons and donate the rest to a good cause—except for one that looked destined for disposal.

"I don't want to make a special trip to Goodwill for this one bag," I told my husband. "I think I'll let you throw it in the trash." I placed it on the front porch for David to haul away. Several days went by before we noticed it again. But now, pine straw, twigs, and moss littered the porch floor under the rocking chair that held the bag. We quickly and accurately surmised that a bird had chosen to use our discarded tote bag. David peeked inside and saw the beginnings of a nest.

We watched from our dining room table as a Carolina wren made many trips inside the bag. Back and forth he flew, landing first on top of the rocking chair to survey his surroundings and then darting into the open bag. Each time, his beak carried yet another piece of building material. "He must be constructing a condominium," I commented. Before long, our old tote bag held a grand palace for four baby birds.

"I think God's trying to give me a message," I told David as we marveled at the small white eggs with brown speckles. "I think He's reminding me not to be wasteful. I plan to be more careful with my discards from now on." —Julie Lavender

*Waste does not exist in nature because ecosystems reuse everything
that grows in a never-ending cycle of efficiency and purpose.*
—Frans van Houten

NOVEMBER 22

Preparing to Care

Love is patient; love is kind. . . . It bears all things, believes all things, hopes all things, endures all things. Love never ends.

—I CORINTHIANS 13:4, 7–8 (NRSVUE)

OUR SON'S DOG, Tucker, was already a senior when my son met and married his wife, Nicole. Unfortunately, Tucker was diagnosed with cancer not long after they met. Tucker underwent surgery and chemotherapy, which was supposed to extend his life 12 to 18 months. His cancer returned, but we were blessed to have him with us for over 2 more years. Two years when he was full of life and his characteristic joy.

In his final months, to maintain his quality of life, Tucker required several medications and special care, and it was Nicole who lovingly took on that job. Because she works from home, she was able to meet his every need.

When it was time to help Tucker transition to heaven, Nicole and our son had recently learned they were expecting twins. Nicole thanked Tucker for helping prepare her for motherhood. Nurturing Tucker had blessed her with the opportunity to gain confidence in her ability to mother her future children.

I'm so thankful for the years we enjoyed with Tucker. Though our son rescued him, Tucker ended up helping our family in ways we couldn't have imagined. Our precious grand-dog had taught our children how to tenderly care for a vulnerable creature. He had helped them practice what it means to give and love selflessly in the same way God loves us. —Missy Tippens

For the joy of human love, brother, sister, parent, child, friends on earth, and friends above, for all gentle thoughts and mild, Christ, our Lord, to You we raise this, our hymn of grateful praise.
—Folliott Sandford Pierpoint

ALL GOD'S CREATURES   337

NOVEMBER 23

An Oyster Legacy

A good person leaves an inheritance for their children's children.

—PROVERBS 13:22 (NIV)

THE SUN SHONE down on us as a cool breeze made us keep our coats on. This kind of weather equaled a beautiful day in northwest Washington State, one of the rainiest spots in the US. We checked into our condo rental, and my girls squealed when the receptionist told us how to access the private beach. After unpacking, they got into their swimsuits, grabbed their towels, and headed over the bridge spanning the highway to the beach.

The moment we saw said beach, we all let out a disappointed groan. The "beach" did not have sand on which to lay our towels. It had rocks, and it was covered in oyster shells. You couldn't get to the water without crunching over hundreds of shells.

We might have wished for some bare sand, or even a smooth rock to sit on, but there was a good reason to leave the shells be. In Washington, it's against the law to take oyster shells from the beaches. The oyster larvae attach to the shells in order to grow into big oysters. They literally cling to the past as they look toward the future.

As I raise my girls and interact with other children and teenagers, I try to be like those shells, leaving behind something to which future generations will attach. What lessons will they remember, and what examples am I giving them? Many times when I mess up, I feel like I've left only crushed shells that will do my kids no good. It is then that I pray God will restore and instill in them the lessons and values that I should have taught them. Moving forward, I endeavor to leave behind "shells" that will bring them closer to Jesus and show them what it means to be women of God, how to stand for Him in a world that will often leave them scrambling for a foothold. As I live my life, I'm grateful for the example of the humble oyster, which reminds me to leave a legacy for those who will follow. —Kristen G. Johnson

Our lives speak loudly to those around us, especially the children in our home.
—Billy Graham

NOVEMBER 24

Wings of Power

Those who hope in the LORD will renew their strength. They will soar on wings like eagles; they will run and not grow weary, they will walk and not be faint.

—ISAIAH 40:31 (NIV)

A BALD EAGLE is a rare sighting at Camp Roger in western Michigan. One or two have flown over the nearby Little Bostwick Lake, but we have never seen one land in camp. That changed today when I spotted an eagle on the branch of a pine tree about 30 feet above the ground at the base of the hill I was standing on. I couldn't miss the opportunity for photos, so, with camera in hand, I slowly walked down the hill toward the tree.

Through the zoom lens, I took in every part of his impressive frame, hardly taking a breath for fear of disturbing him. His talons were sharp and created to tear his prey apart. His pointed beak, too, was made for hunting. His sharp eyes were darting around, never still. As I walked further down the hill, I angled my path to the side of a nearby building, astounded that he had not flown away. It was such a gift to have this extended time to look at this eagle so closely. I could sense that the eagle was very aware of my presence; he turned his head toward me several times. I decided to give him more space, so I walked backward up the hill and away.

In a split second, he shoved himself off the branch and with his enormous wings swooped down toward me. I gasped as he flew several yards above my head and then swung up near a building. As I watched, he darted between dozens of trees toward the lake.

I was shaking from head to toe.

Seeing an eagle soar above my head was a rare opportunity, but what was truly life-changing was witnessing its majestic strength and knowing that this is what God desires for me. It reminded me that when I am at my weakest, God gives me wings to fly! The power to dart around obstacles and to powerfully soar across the sky is the same power He wants me to have, the same power that the prophet Isaiah speaks of when he says we will soar like eagles. Let's rise up in faith. —Twila Bennett

He gives power to the weak and strength to the powerless.
—Isaiah 40:29 (NLT)

ALL GOD'S CREATURES   339

NOVEMBER 25

Assuming the Worst

You, then, why do you judge your brother or sister? Or why do you treat them with contempt? For we will all stand before God's judgment seat.

—ROMANS 14:10 (NIV)

DAISY! WHAT ARE you doing?" When the familiar gnawing sound came from the other room, I was sure I knew what was happening, and I immediately called out to our 18-month-old, mixed-breed rescue puppy to stop. We aren't sure of Daisy's parentage, but we believe there is German shepherd and terrier in the mix. Whatever her parentage, she has a greater desire than any of our other dogs to chew and destroy.

Daisy dug up and chewed every piece of rubber garden soaker hose in the backyard. She dug a 2-foot-deep hole and unearthed a 6-inch rusty roofing nail. She completely devoured one of my sandals—suede, cork, rubber, large metal buckle, and all—along with multiple pairs of house shoes. Palm tree berries and loquat fruit pits are favorites of hers. Stuffed animals and blankets are destroyed in record time. Toys that claim to be indestructible or for heavy chewers are no match for Daisy.

Which is why, when I heard her gnawing, I assumed the worst. I based my assumption of what she was doing on what she's done. Based on past experiences, my first thought was that she was chewing up her bed—again. When I finally took the time to go see what she was doing, I found she was pulling the fuzz off her tennis ball. Totally acceptable.

Daisy was innocent. She'd done nothing wrong. I assumed the worst and judged her without full knowledge of the situation. I didn't give Daisy credit for changing from her former destructive patterns.

Unfortunately, I've done the same thing with people I know. Clinging to memories of the times when they made unwise choices, I don't give them credit for being able to make positive changes.

The next time I start to judge based on past experience, I need to stop. I need to remember Daisy and her ability to make positive changes. If my puppy can change, so can the people I know. —Sandy Kirby Quandt

Father, when I start to assume the worst, remind me that, like Daisy, people can change for the better.

NOVEMBER 26

Turkey Troubles

God is not a God of confusion but of peace.

—1 CORINTHIANS 14:33 (ESV)

ON OUR WAY to church one Sunday, we drove past a familiar farm with a large horse paddock not far from the road. It's usually empty, but this day we saw a wild turkey standing forlornly in the center. We don't often see just one turkey like this. They tend to travel in groups, mostly ambling across the road as if the world is theirs and everyone else has to wait for them to get wherever they are going.

But this turkey was all alone. Where were his friends? I could imagine him thinking, *How am I going to find my friends?* He was just standing still, eyes scanning the horizon for some sight of his entourage. How long had he been caught in this predicament? How did he get inside the enclosure? I would guess that his wings played a part. But did he forget that he can fly?

As we reached the paddock on our drive home after the service, I looked to see if the turkey had resolved his situation. He had! The paddock was empty. I don't know if others came to rescue him and encourage him in the way of escape. I don't know if he figured it out for himself. Perhaps his internal muscle memory remembered that he could spread his wings and rise from the ground. In any case, he was no longer trapped. He was free, as he was meant to be.

Sometimes I get into a situation like that. Perhaps it is fear or lethargy or uncertainty that stands in my way. I should know how to remove myself from whatever has captured me, but the solution eludes me. If only I could remember that looking to God is the best—and only—way to deal with something like this. He always knows what to do. —Liz Kimmel

I'm so grateful for Your presence in my life, Father. You will never leave me stuck or trapped. You are always able to provide the way of escape, whether it is my own foolishness that has surrounded me or another outside force seeking to control.

ALL GOD'S CREATURES 341

NOVEMBER 27

Porcu-pining for a Better Me

*Let your speech always be with grace, seasoned with salt, that
you may know how you ought to answer each one.*

—COLOSSIANS 4:6 (NKJV)

THE CAR IN front of me refused to move. The light changed. Cars in
the left-turn lane next to us drove off. We sat there. To make things
worse, I could see the driver of the Prius staring down at her phone, oblivious to those behind her. I rolled down my window and bellowed, "Get
a move on, lady. We don't have all day here." My hands, as if controlled
by some otherworldly power, descended on the steering wheel, causing
the horn to punctuate my comments.

Startled, the woman looked up from her phone and drove off—just
as the light turned red again, trapping me for a penalty cycle at the
intersection.

Immediately, shame invaded. How could I behave so childishly with
my "Follow me to Living Word Church" bumper sticker posted near my
license plate? I could feel my face flush and my fingers grip the wheel a
little tighter. When would I grow up?

The gentle Holy Spirit chased the shame away with a simple object
lesson: the porcupine from a nature show I'd seen recently.

Let's see, I thought. *What do I know about porcupines?* They have quills
that they raise—and unleash—whenever they are afraid. *Bingo!* Fear is
the trigger that caused me to react badly to the other driver, releasing my
quills of impatience and irritation.

Did I fear being late? Not really. Although I had several errands to
run, nothing urgent loomed on the calendar. Perhaps I felt the woman's
actions represented disrespect.

Whatever the reason, God made me a person, not a porcupine. My
defense mechanisms need not operate without self-control. Porcupine
responses don't serve me well, making me feel immature and less
Christlike. In that moment, the Spirit gave me a gentle hug inside, as if
to remind me that my speech needs to be gracious. —David L. Winters

Grow up in all things into Him who is the head—Christ.
—Ephesians 4:15 (NJKV)

NOVEMBER 28

Picture of Surrender

*Trust in the LORD with all your heart and lean
not on your own understanding.*

—PROVERBS 3:5 (NIV)

AFTER I FINISHED an emotionally exhausting session with my counselor, I wanted to move my body and get out of my head. I leashed my Yorkie, Minnie, and made the 10-minute trek to the park up the road. She bounded back and forth as we walked, pulling me along. The crisp air refreshed my senses.

When we arrived at the park gate, I picked Minnie up as I usually do and carried her across the patches of weeds and walking paths. Something strange happened when we reached the sidewalk. She relaxed in my arms. Usually, she pedals her legs to indicate she wants me to put her down so she can walk. But that day she stayed contentedly in my arms as I walked through the park, circled the butterfly garden, and circumnavigated the natural spring that forms the centerpiece of the park.

I crossed the bridge overlooking the spring and paused to look down at Minnie lying calmly in my arms. In that moment God spoke to me. *In the same way you're carrying Minnie, I can carry you during this season.*

God's offer was an invitation to trust Him. Daily, sometimes hourly, I decide whether or not to put my faith in Him. Through Minnie, God gave me a picture of surrender. I can choose to rest in Him and allow Him to carry me, not only through this season, but through life.

Some days trusting God is easier than others. When the days are long and my energy feels spent, I can choose to trust Jesus for strength. When the bills pile higher than the checks coming in, I can choose to trust Him for provision. When decisions must be made, I can choose to trust Him for wisdom. When I trust Jesus, my heart finds rest in Him, just like Minnie found rest in my arms. —Crystal Storms

*Father, help me to release control and trust
You with every area of my life. Amen.*

NOVEMBER 29

The Reindeer at Santa Claus

I said, "Oh, that I had the wings of a dove! I would fly away and be at rest."

—PSALM 55:6 (NIV)

A MONTH BEFORE Christmas I traveled to Santa Claus, Indiana (yes, a real town), to visit with two reindeer, Gabriel and Cindy Lou (yes, real animals), who had been transported from a northern Indiana farm. I waited in line to see these magical mammals up close. The reindeer handler informed me that males and females both sprout massive antlers, which they shed at different times of the year. The pair was feeding on pellets with minerals and willow, and we learned that they are partial to oats and graham crackers. I noticed that their hooves were split in two (cloven), which makes shoveling the snow in search of food more efficient. In fact, the species' correct name is caribou, French for "snow shoveler."

Nearby I overheard a young boy ask, "Do they fly?"

The handler answered, "Only on Christmas Eve and with magic."

As I drove away, I recalled how, as a young girl, I constantly worried about my family's lack of finances during the holidays. Instead of enjoying the magic of the Christmas season, I wondered: *How will my parents pay for everything? Will we have enough money for food and still pay the bills?* I was especially drawn to the illustrations of reindeer in my childhood book *A Visit from Saint Nicholas.* The team flew through a nighttime sky lit by a full moon. To escape the worry, I prayed that I could magically fly away, like the reindeer on Christmas Eve.

I imagine psalmist David was also looking for rescue from his troubling situation by sprouting dove wings and flying away. He was confident God would rescue him. As for me, I still struggle with worry about many matters. But now at Christmas, I pray for the peace and joy that comes from the birth of Jesus, my Savior. Now *that* is the real magic of the season.

—Glenda Ferguson

Just a few more weary days and then I'll fly away,
To a land where joys shall never end. I'll fly away.
—Albert E. Brumley

NOVEMBER 30

A Kind Warning

Get rid of all bitterness, rage and anger, brawling and
slander, along with every form of malice.

—EPHESIANS 4:31 (NIV)

A MOM I knew from my children's school texted me. "I was a substitute teacher in the kindergarten class today. Nathan was being disrespectful," she wrote. When I asked for more details, she said he was acting silly during the lesson. I felt annoyed. I didn't think silliness constituted disrespect. I thanked the mom for her concern, but I didn't mean it. The next time I saw her, I still felt irritated. "God, help me not to hold a grudge," I said.

A few weeks later, I chaperoned Nathan's field trip to the zoo. The other mom was there. I waved from across the room and hoped I wouldn't have to sit with her on the bus. At the zoo, we stopped at the prairie dog exhibit and watched the little creatures poke their heads up out of their burrows and chirp at one another playfully. Then a shadow moved across the ground and the prairie dogs went into danger mode. One of them barked a warning, and the others ran to their burrows to hide. I spotted a hawk in the air. The enclosure had a net ceiling, so the hawk posed no actual danger, but the prairie dogs took no chances.

As I watched them gradually come out and return to their activities, I noticed the prairie dog who barked the warning stayed where he was, ready to sound the alarm if needed.

Although his warning was unnecessary, he had his friends' best interests in mind. I realized that the mom from school did too. She was trying to help and alert me to a potential problem with my son that I wouldn't otherwise have known. "God, thank You for helping me see the truth," I prayed.

On the bus ride back, the other mom and I had a nice conversation about how moms need to look out for one another, just as prairie dogs do. —Diane Stark

Resentment or grudges do no harm to the person against whom you hold these
feelings but every day and every night of your life, they are eating at you.
—Norman Vincent Peale

ALL GOD'S CREATURES

DECEMBER 1

A Welcome Sound

*Thou makest darkness, and it is night: wherein all
the beasts of the forest do creep forth.*

—PSALM 104:20 (KJV)

IT WAS AN unseasonably warm winter night. My husband, Neil, and I were in bed with the window open. About midnight, I heard them. A chorus of yips followed by long howls. We live in the country surrounded by farmers' fields, and occasionally I have seen coyotes sitting on the rise above our creek. Once or twice, I've seen a couple cross our yard. So at first, I assumed it was them that had woken me up.

But maybe not. It had snowed a little the day before, and Neil had pointed out several lines of fox tracks. A fox has been known to den underneath our garage, and fox tracks are quite distinctive. They leave a four-toe pawprint with a half-moon heel mark, and the tracks run in a straight line. That's because when the fox moves forward, the back paw presses into the front paw's track. A coyote's tracks look similar, but they're quite a bit larger.

Hmm, I wondered. *Were our wild noisemakers coyotes or foxes?* If I had to guess, I'd say they were a pack of coyotes, because more than one critter was carrying on. Foxes usually travel alone.

But ultimately it doesn't matter which we heard. That spine-tingling sound was a song of the wild, a call of nature. Listening to it did not frighten me. It comforted me. It reminded me of what a marvelous world God created. And I loved how He populated it with an endless variety of fascinating creatures for us to admire and enjoy. Thinking how life goes on even when we are asleep reassured me that Someone far more knowledgeable and powerful than I was in control. As the howling grew fainter, I closed my eyes and soon succumbed to nature's lullaby. —Aline Newman

*Whenever the pressure of our complex city life thins my blood
and benumbs my brain, I seek relief in the trail; and when I hear the
coyote wailing to the yellow dawn, my cares fall from me—I am happy.*
—Hamlin Garland

DECEMBER 2

The Cardinal's Visit

I know every bird in the mountains, and the insects in the fields are mine.

—PSALM 50:11 (NIV)

ISIGHED. ANOTHER dreary December morning. I looked out my window, feeling sad. As the days grow colder and shorter and the trees stand naked to the world, everything just feels harder. The clouds hide the sun, and the gray days can make me depressed.

Suddenly, a brilliant red cardinal appeared on one of the bare trees. He hopped down the length of the branch, getting closer and closer to my deck, until he finally landed on my bird feeder and looked at me.

Hey, he seemed to be saying. *Not everything out here is ugly. Take a look at me!*

With his bright red chest and his jaunty crested head, he really was a dapper fellow. And I couldn't help but smile as my spirits lifted. It felt like he was there to remind me that I was not alone. There was brightness and joy in the world; I just needed to know where to look.

Later that day as I sat down to read my mail, I opened a Christmas card from a friend. There on the front was a red cardinal. I could hardly believe the coincidence. Inside she had written about how cardinals are a reminder to her of the love of God.

"Red birds on a snowy white tree, like Christmas decorations outside. Cardinals always seem like visitors from heaven," she wrote, and she told me that I was in her prayers.

Some days when life is hard, simply looking outside my window can lift my spirits. Cardinals on a winter day remind me that I am not alone. I have a God who loves me. And I have friends who do too. —Heather Jepsen

Dear God, thank You for all the ways Your creation speaks to me of Your love. I am never alone when I am a part of Your good creation. Amen.

DECEMBER 3

Our Cow of Contentment

I have learned how to be content with whatever I have.

—PHILIPPIANS 4:11 (NLT)

SHE'S ALONE IN her pasture. At nearly a dozen years of age, it's her winter season—that is, as far as Scottish Highland cattle go.

We recently separated her from the others, mostly because the younger ones weren't being kind. She's grown quite feeble, thinner than the rest, so moving her to our lower field was for her protection, done with compassion.

Still, I sometimes wonder if she's lonely. She can safely come close to our upper pasture cows simply by sidling up to the fence. Instead, she spends much of her time in solitude, lying down among the daisies, chewing her cud.

Contentment. That's what I think of when I watch her from my window. Even on rainy days, she's a picture of peace.

I recall a time some years ago. She'd given birth to a calf. We didn't know for several days, as she kept him hidden, tucked in among the high grass of Selah Farm's meadow. When she finally gave us a peek, the wee one stood close to his mama, never wandering from her side.

Sadly, and for reasons that remain a mystery, her calf passed away. I remember her bellow, long and loud—the way she thrashed her head while down on her knees. I wept with her. And I'd have continued, except—when her bellowing stopped only moments later—her mourning ceased.

The next day, there she was, eating grass in a patch of sunshine, seemingly content once more. She never had any more calves, and her entire life has been spent on less than 50 acres, much of it not accessible due to dense rhododendron and pines.

And yet, there she is, our contented Highland cow. Despite adversity, in spite of loss, she appears to be at peace with her circumstances, in all situations.

I wonder. Does she know she's an example for me, our cow of contentment? —Maureen Miller

And blown by all the winds that pass and wet with all the showers,
she walks among the meadow grass and eats the meadow flowers.
—Robert Louis Stevenson

DECEMBER 4

Out on a Limb

Trust in the Lord with all your heart and lean not on your own understanding.

—PROVERBS 3:5 (NIV)

I HAVE CRAB apple trees on my property. They are semi-dwarf trees with a lollipop crab apple, and in the springtime they are festooned with spectacular white blossoms, like garlands of popcorn. The fragrance is divine. These particular crabbies bear what is known as persistent fruit—the small red berries do not drop to the ground; they stay attached to the branch, providing a banquet for wildlife in winter. The berries are way too high for deer to reach on this December day, but birds, of course, have no problem.

Except for turkeys. Wild turkeys look ungainly and cumbersome, but they can fly for short distances, if need be. I watch as one particular tom takes off and flies up into the crab apple tree to gobble some berries. The fruit is clustered at the far end of the branches, but the branches are slender and springy; as the turkey edges outward, he begins to lose his balance, and he falls to the ground. He fluffs his feathers, shaking off the snow, and tries again, launching himself up into the tree. Slowly now, and carefully, he walks out toward the fruit. But the willowy branch bends and wobbles under his weight, and again he loses his balance and tips over. He hangs upside down, bat-like, on the slender branch for a moment, then lets go and falls. I watch as the turkey repeatedly tries, fails, and falls. Finally, he decides, apparently, that there are easier ways to make a living, and he trundles off into the woods.

What a turkey I am, always going out onto limbs that ultimately don't deliver the stability and support I yearn for in this life. I try to find my well-being in the approval of others or in my job performance review or in my latest bank statement. But those are awfully slender branches. I need to remember that the support I long for is found only in God.
—Louis Lotz

On Christ the solid rock I stand; all other ground is sinking sand.
—Edward Mote

DECEMBER 5

Street to the Heart

*Praise be to the God and Father of our Lord Jesus Christ, the
Father of compassion and the God of all comfort, who comforts
us in all our troubles, so that we can comfort those in any
trouble with the comfort we ourselves receive from God.*

—2 CORINTHIANS 1:3–4 (NIV)

THE CHRISTMAS SEASON always brings back a sweet memory for me. It was love at first sight when the bouncy stray dog crossed my path at the entrance to El Navideno, a Christmas-themed restaurant in the mountains of Puerto Rico. She reminded me of my beloved mutt Sati, who had died on Halloween while my husband and I celebrated our tenth wedding anniversary in Hawaii. Her death had devastated me, and I was still grieving.

My friends and I exited the restaurant with the owner to see the life-size Nativity at the restaurant's event hall. The stray stood by the door, feasting on my new friend Carmen's doggie bag. I squatted to meet the dog. As I held her face, I felt Sati's love come through the dirty stray. "I want to take you home!" I said, in tears.

"Are you serious?" Carmen asked. An animal rescuer, Carmen took pictures of the dog and made phone calls to initiate the rescue.

The restaurant owner explained that this sweet dog had saved his life when she stood up to a criminal who was chasing him, allowing him to escape. He was happy that his protégé finally would be safe from animal control and have a permanent home with someone who loved her.

Two months later, the street dog boarded a flight to New Jersey to become a member of my family. I named her Natividad, which means "Nativity" in Spanish in remembrance of the place we met.

Nati quickly adapted to her new home life, feeling safe and loved. Just as quickly, she erased the pain of losing my best friend and replaced it with a feeling of unconditional love. She's my gift from Sati. —Sonia Frontera

*Lord, thank You for the beloved companion animals
You bring into our lives who embody Your compassion and comfort.*

ALL GOD'S CREATURES   351

DECEMBER 6

A Lesson from a Bull Calf

Make no friendship with a man given to anger, nor go with a wrathful man, lest you learn his ways and entangle yourself in a snare.

—PROVERBS 22:24–25 (ESV)

MY CATTLE RANCHER husband had an angry neighbor who continually was unkind to him and even yelled at him over a common fence line. Craig didn't know how to fix things with the man until he noticed the behavior of a bull calf he had bottle-fed.

Sometimes mama cows leave their babies, and my husband has to function as a surrogate mom. In those cases the calves will often be aggressively affectionate toward him, and this was the case with this particular bull calf. It's natural for a calf to headbutt its mom to get the milk flow going, and this bull calf did that to my husband—like an "I'm hungry" hint. Craig didn't think much of it at first and rubbed the calf's head affectionately while it was taking the bottle.

Eventually a dairy cow adopted the calf, but when the calf grew to about 500 pounds and continued aggressively headbutting my husband, Craig learned not to get close to that guy.

"You know," he said, "some neighbors are like that aggressive calf. At some point you learn to keep your distance."

No matter how hard you try, some relationships just can't be fixed. When we've done our best to reach out and try to restore the connection without any reciprocation, we can step away, pray for the person, and wait for God to bring about any restoration. Even Jesus taught His disciples to move on if people weren't kind. Instead, we can put the situation in God's hands and escape any future headbutting injuries. —Janet Holm McHenry

When someone shows you who they really are, believe them the first time.
—Maya Angelou

352   ALL GOD'S CREATURES

DECEMBER 7

Rejected No More

Carry each other's burdens, and in this way you will fulfill the law of Christ.
—GALATIANS 6:2 (NIV)

WHEN DUNLEY ARRIVED at his foster home, no one knew why anyone would abandon such a beautiful long-haired cat. Fighting to survive in a feral cat colony, he was battered and scrawny and his coat was matted. His foster mom figured she'd fatten him up, and then he'd be adopted.

Skittish and shy at first, Dunley slowly adjusted to his new life and became super-loving and tolerant. At first, only resident tabby Jean Grey claimed Dunley as her true love. They lounged together, groomed each other, and both seemed to understand the trauma of rejection.

Then two kittens arrived. At first, Foster Mom worried that these two short-haired panther girls might fight Jean Grey for Dunley's favor. Liberty and Independence were rambunctious youngsters as they adjusted to the new environment. The two kittens harassed Dunley and Jean Grey, and Foster Mom thought about separating them.

But when Indie injured her back legs, Dunley comforted the injured kitten, grooming her and napping next to her all day. Jean Grey tolerated the new arrangement. Liberty, not wanting to be left out, soon joined the circle and even the dog, Annie, camped out nearby.

When I'm down, I long for a friend like Dunley. The kitties love him because he loves them. God is showing me that when I need love, I can be the love to another who's suffering, until that friend shows up for me. And even if nobody steps up to assuage my grief, I can cling to the truth that God is my comforter. With Him, I'm never rejected.

When Foster Mom walked into her room, she smiled. On the bed, all four cats and the dog lay napping in a big pile. They had each other's backs, just as those of us in the family of Christ can have each other's backs. —Linda S. Clare

Lord, when I feel unwanted and rejected, please send me a friend as compassionate as Dunley.

ALL GOD'S CREATURES   353

DECEMBER 8

Surrounded by the Holy Spirit

*May the God of hope fill you with all joy and peace as you trust in him,
so that you may overflow with hope by the power of the Holy Spirit.*

—ROMANS 15:13 (NIV)

WHEN OUR KIDS were young, they were thrilled each time we got to visit the butterfly house at Callaway Gardens in Georgia, which was an hour or so from our house. The warm, humid conservatory was full of gorgeous flowering plants and hundreds of colorful butterflies flying freely. The kids would squeal with delight at the insects swirling all around them, just out of reach. Our children are adults now, but my husband and I have continued to enjoy visiting butterfly gardens in our travels.

On our last trip, we visited a garden in Tennessee. We arrived at the perfect time, right when they were releasing recently emerged, stunning blue butterflies. Children gathered around the employee who had a container and opened it to allow them to fly out. We, too, experienced the joy of watching them delicately flutter into the air. One even landed on me briefly. I felt as excited as my kids used to be!

Having all those beautiful creatures fluttering around me reminded me not only of the beauty of God's creation but also of the Holy Spirt. Whenever I pray, I feel the Spirit surrounding me and filling me. Whenever I am anxious or wondering what to do, I feel Him with me, comforting me. Whenever I need to make an important decision, I feel Him guiding me through my thoughts and through Scripture. Like those delicate butterflies that alighted on me in that garden, I feel God's Spirit alighting, and I am filled with peace and comfort. —Missy Tippens

Spirit of the Living God, fall afresh on me,
Spirit of the Living God, fall afresh on me.
Break me, melt me, mold me, fill me.
Spirit of the Living God, fall afresh on me.
—Daniel Iverson

DECEMBER 9

No Doubt about It

*But when he saw that the wind was boisterous, he was afraid;
and beginning to sink he cried out, saying, "Lord, save me!" And
immediately Jesus stretched out His hand and caught him, and
said to him, "O you of little faith, why did you doubt?"*

—MATTHEW 14:30–31 (NKJV)

MY SCHEDULED SNORKELING trip to Kauhako Crater, on the north side of Molokai near Maui, had moved up to the second day of vacation, allowing me little time to get comfortable with a very underdeveloped skill. Now, my husband and I were on a catamaran with fins, mask, and snorkel ready. As I eased myself into the chilly water, nervousness made my breathing shallow. The catamaran and I were both forcefully rocked up and down by a sudden wave. *Maybe I should just give up and get back in the boat.*

Our lifeguard excitedly pointed out an endangered Hawaiian monk seal asleep on the crater shelf, and I forced myself to look away from the waves. My brain kicked into high gear, remembering old skills, and I somehow swam over to see the chubby seal sunning without a care in the world.

Kauhako Crater is an extinct volcano, home to myriad sea creatures and fish. As I relaxed and dove beneath the waves, I could see them floating dreamily around me. I marveled that a giant geological formation that once could kill was now a peaceful haven.

That night, I was shocked to learn that the sudden larger wave that had rocked me had been caused by an earthquake on another Hawaiian island. And that seal? He is one of only 1,570 left in the world. I had been able to see one of the rarest species on earth by pushing away my fears.

That seal faces risks to his life every day—lack of food, debris entanglement, sharks, and habitat loss threaten his species' very existence. Closing his eyes and resting, confident in that nap, shows a trust that defies his odds. By keeping my eyes on Christ and not the perceived dangers around me, a boldness was built inside me during that swim, enabling me to enjoy miraculous moments gifted by an amazing Creator. —Twila Bennett

*Lord, help me remember the peace in my soul that comes from both baby
steps and giant leaps of faith.*

ALL GOD'S CREATURES   355

DECEMBER 10

A Burden Shared

*Therefore encourage one another and build each
other up, just as in fact you are doing.*

—1 Thessalonians 5:11 (NIV)

WHEN PIPPA, MY friend's beautiful tricolor Cavalier King Charles spaniel, was expecting, my friend got an emergency call from another friend whose Cavalier, Hazel, was also pregnant. She needed to leave town for several weeks to help her mother, who had been in an accident, and was distraught about leaving her pregnant dog. My friend reassured her that Hazel could come over and have her puppies in the nursery with Pippa.

Everything went as planned, and on the same night, eight little puppies were born. Pippa had three tricolor girls, and Hazel had five—two red-and-white Blenheim girls, a Ruby boy and girl, and a Blenheim boy. Everyone was ecstatic, and the moms and the babies seemed to be doing well.

Despite the best care possible, three of these little puppies failed to thrive. Within the first week, two of Pippa's girls and Hazel's Blenheim boy were gone. The vet couldn't explain it, and my friend was heartbroken. With her experience and the reading she had done about dogs grieving, she also worried that the mothers might not nurture the remaining babies. But five tiny puppies still needed round-the-clock care. For the next few weeks, she shuttled the puppies between Pippa and Hazel to ensure the most milk production possible. To her relief, both the dogs accepted all the pups as their own and cared for them devotedly. Soon, five pups had opened their eyes and were romping around.

Pippa told me that watching the two dogs care for each other's babies, accepting them as their own despite whatever grief they might have been feeling, reminded her that burdens are meant to be shared. Helping each other, Hazel and Pippa saved five darling puppies. I was inspired by their story to look for opportunities to encourage and build up others, even when I face difficult times myself. When I encourage others, I am encouraged as well. —Lucy Chambers

Here is the world. Beautiful and terrible things will happen. Don't be afraid.
—Frederick Buechner

DECEMBER 11

The Power of Puppy Love

There is no fear in love. But perfect love drives out fear.

1 JOHN 4:18 (NIV)

MY MOM COMES from a long line of women who own, adore, and spoil their canine friends. So imagine her horror when her little girl was scared of dogs!

One day, she announced, "You can't spend your life being afraid. Let's get you a dog of your own." Our neighbor's dog had just delivered a litter of puppies, so we went next door to meet them. Holding Mom's hand, I cautiously moved toward the pile of roly-poly fur balls. They seemed wild to me, but to the side sat a little white guy with black ears. Maybe he wouldn't be too scary?

I tentatively stroked his head. "Would you like him to come home with us?" Mom asked.

"All right. Can I name him Rebel?" I felt OK in the moment, but once we were back in our living room, my fear returned. After all, this creature was now in my home. He was completely unpredictable. What was this fierce beast capable of?

But Rebel knew nothing about my fear. He followed me everywhere, wanting to go wherever I was going. He brought me his toys so I could make them squeak and throw them across the room. He curled into my blanket and put his head on my lap while I read to him. We became inseparable.

Before long, I realized I wasn't afraid of Rebel at all. I was completely smitten with him, and he with me. And if I didn't need to be afraid of Rebel, maybe I didn't need to be afraid of other dogs either.

Love does that, doesn't it? It makes us feel safe. It reminds us we're not alone. It transforms our hearts. And ultimately, it gives us the courage to go into the world, loving others as we are loved. —Allison Lynn Flemming

Ever-present God, sometimes the fears and worries of life can overwhelm me. They block out the joy and wonder of Your world. Let Your love drive out all fear so that there is only room for Your peace and joy. And then, let me share that love with others. Amen.

ALL GOD'S CREATURES 357

DECEMBER 12

Seek What Nourishes

"Again, the kingdom of heaven is like a merchant looking for fine pearls."
—MATTHEW 13:45 (NIV)

WHILE I SAT on my back porch enjoying the day, the flurry of debris was hard to miss. Dried leaves and small twigs flew from the palm tree in front of me. While most visitors to the tree searched for nesting material, this determined woodpecker was searching for food. As he worked the tree, it was obvious he sought something to nourish him. This woodpecker would not settle for anything less.

I watched the bird dip its scissors-shaped beak repeatedly into the small space between the tree trunk and cut palm fronds. Side to side his beak swept until the woodpecker found what it searched for. He snatched at an insect, pecked it against the trunk, then flew away. Before long, the bird returned and performed its search all over again. Dip his beak into a space on the tree, fling debris left and right, root around, and come up with something nourishing.

At one point, the woodpecker lifted a dried palm berry from its hiding place. Was this what the bird had been searching for all along? With the berry secured in his beak, he flew off, only to return a brief time later. Had he stored the berry for later, or had he taken it to a waiting chick?

As I watched the woodpecker, I wondered if I search as diligently for the good things God provides. Do I toss worthless things aside until I reach those that nourish me spiritually? And when I find those treasures, do I willingly share them with those around me?

Anytime I begin to think studying Scripture isn't worth the extra effort, all I have to do is think about a determined woodpecker. A woodpecker that showed me it is in the extra effort that nourishment is found. God's Word is where I'll find the nourishment I truly need. Nothing else will do.
—Sandy Kirby Quandt

Singleness of purpose is one of the chief essentials for success in life, no matter what may be one's aim.
—John D. Rockefeller

DECEMBER 13

Peace without Boundaries

*"These things I have spoken to you, that in Me you may
have peace. In the world you will have tribulation; but
be of good cheer, I have overcome the world."*

—JOHN 16:33 (NKJV)

MY FAVORITE PART of Homosassa Springs Wildlife State Park in
Homosassa, Florida, is the underwater observatory. The 180-ton
floating "Fishbowl" extends across the bottom of the spring at the end of
a ramp. My husband, Tim, and I strolled hand in hand across the walkway
to the structure and then around the main section, watching manatees
swimming in the clear aqua waters.

When I made my way down the steep steps, I discovered fish that were
hidden from above. I gasped when a family of manatees swam right
beside the glass. The calf, about a third the size of its mother, stayed next
to her. Another manatee faced the window before turning and swimming
out of view.

I returned to the top for a second look. The slow, gentle movements
of the manatees, combined with the soft blue-green hues of the water,
slowed my breathing. My lips turned upward as I watched their movements. I sat down on the ground, determined to stay as long as I could,
to hold on to the peace and delight that filled my heart as I observed the
tranquil mammals.

After too short a time, Tim wanted to move on. I got up and followed
him along the trail, visiting the rest of the park.

I told Tim I wanted to see the manatees again before we got in line for
the tram to our car. He waited by a tree while I returned. The family of sea
cows clustered in the center of the crystal-clear waters. I felt a nudge in my
heart to remember that the peace and delight I experienced as I watched
the manatees wasn't exclusive to this tranquil place. Jesus promises peace
in Him and delights my heart as I seek Him—manatees not required.
—Crystal Storms

*Delight yourself also in the LORD,
and He shall give you the desires of your heart.*
—Psalm 37:4 (NKJV)

DECEMBER 14

Beautiful Squawker

*Know therefore that the Lord your God is God; he is the faithful
God, keeping his covenant of love to a thousand generations
of those who love him and keep his commandments.*

—DEUTERONOMY 7:9 (NIV)

MY FRIEND LINDI has the most beautiful blue-and-gold macaw named Chiquita. I have met her in person and can say with certainty she wasn't thrilled to meet me. She definitely likes her own people best. More often, I have heard Chiquita while talking to Lindi on the phone. The bird has quite a personality. She gets jealous when Lindi is talking to someone else and begins to squawk. Loudly. So either Lindi has to move elsewhere or we are forced to pause our conversation until Chiquita gets finished expressing her displeasure. We can't hear a word while she is demanding attention!

Lindi's family has had Chiquita since she was a baby bird, and Lindi's husband hand-fed her until she was able to eat on her own. Macaws have a very long lifespan. In human care, they can live up to 80 years or more, and she has been a part of their family for 35 years. I have always been astounded by that lifelong commitment. The family's decades of loving care for Chiquita—despite her episodes of jealous squawking—remind me of God's unconditional, forever love for me even when I complain, even when I doubt, even when I fail Him.

I am continually amazed at the depth of God's love and mercy. No matter what I do or fail to do, God remains faithful and just. He forgives me and continues loving me. I sometimes feel I don't deserve that love and goodness, yet, praise God, it is not dependent on my actions or on what I do or don't deserve. It is due to God's nature as loving and good. Just as Lindi's family is committed to a lifetime caring for Chiquita, God is even more committed to loving me—forever. —Missy Tippens

God has said, "Never will I leave you; never will I forsake you."
—Hebrews 13:5 (NIV)

360 ALL GOD'S CREATURES

DECEMBER 15

Alpacas and Christmas Bows

"And you will have joy and gladness, and many will rejoice at his birth."

—LUKE 1:14 (NKJV)

CHRISTMAS IS A happy time for me. I love every bit of it, even the busy and hectic moments. It's a time of joy to celebrate the One who came to be our Savior.

My husband, Tom, and I love to visit small towns, stopping to have lunch or coffee while enjoying the people we meet. Last Christmas, after a fresh snowfall, we ventured to Tumalo, a small town in central Oregon. My love for coffee with something sweet led us to a coffee shop on the corner—but what first caught our eyes were two beautiful alpacas at the entrance of the small cafe, each adorned with a red and silver ribbon tied in a bow around its neck.

The owner of the alpaca farm nearby greeted us with "Merry Christmas!" She held onto these exquisite, calm animals by a double leash. One was a cinnamon color, and one was blond. My love for animals led me to a conversation about alpacas, and the owner took our picture standing next to these two creatures who were gentle as lambs. Their large, dark eyes and long eyelashes, along with their ultra-soft wool, made me want to take them home.

I learned that alpaca wool is unusually fine, which makes the yarn one of the softest yarns around for those who knit. I also learned from their owner that these animals are smaller than llamas, their cousins, which have coarser wool and are used more as farm pack animals.

A simple drive the week before Christmas turned into a special memory that outweighed even the coffee and gingerbread that day. The alpacas' red and silver bows reminded me to see this encounter as a *gift* from God—the gift of an experience with God's amazing creatures. —Kathleen R. Ruckman

Dear God, help me to recognize the blessings in my life as gifts from You—some with red and silver ribbons, and some without decorations. Every gift is from above, and I thank You for the greatest Gift of all—Jesus.

DECEMBER 16

Not-So-Fun-Size Fears

"Do not fear, for I am with you; do not be dismayed, for I am your God. I will strengthen you and help you; I will uphold you with my righteous right hand."

—ISAIAH 41:10 (NIV)

MY DAUGHTER KRISTEN had described her new country as "fun-size." Now I knew why. Like a miniature candy bar compared to its full-size counterpart, much of Japan was smaller than what we were used to in the United States. As we drove to her home from the Tokyo airport, I saw miniature garbage trucks, tiny two-passenger cars, and storefront restaurants that seated eight to ten patrons.

I couldn't wait to jump into her smaller-than-normal shower and wash away the effects of my 14-hour flight from my body. I gathered a towel and my toiletries and headed to her bathroom. My scream brought her running.

"What is THAT?" I yelled, backing out of the bathroom so fast I almost knocked her over. Climbing up the side of the shower was the biggest insect I'd ever seen. About 6 inches long, it had a zillion wispy legs and two equally long antennae.

Apparently, it wasn't the first time my daughter had seen one. She grabbed a bowl, clapped it over the insect, and whisked it out the door. All my desire for a shower went with her. It was days before I gathered the nerve to step back into that shower.

Unfortunately, giant millipedes aren't the only things that frighten me. Family conflict, financial concerns, and health issues top my list of "scary." Wayward loved ones, uncertain futures, and the worries of day-to-day living often steal the sleep from my nights and the joy from my days.

Sometimes I try to battle my fear alone. Other times, I cry out to my heavenly Father and grab the weapon of God's Word. When I do, my fear shrinks and my trust in God grows. My circumstances may not change, but my perspective does. God's Word and the comfort of the Holy Spirit remind me that God is bigger than anything that threatens me—even not-so-fun-size millipedes. —Lori Hatcher

Walk of Faith: *What frightens you most right now? Talk to God about it in prayer, then trust Him to do what's best*

DECEMBER 17

Elephants Cry

"Blessed are you who hunger now, for you will be satisfied.
Blessed are you who weep now, for you will laugh."

—LUKE 6:21 (NIV)

AFRICAN AND ASIAN elephants hold a special place in my heart, and a recent documentary reminded me not only of why they are special, but also of how they reflect God's creation in beautiful ways. In spite of their massive bodies, sturdy wide feet, flapping ears, and intimidating tusks, they often seemed more human than many other animals.

Elephants are led by matriarchs, so I could relate as a mom. Calves are born only every 4 or 5 years after a gestation of 22 months. No wonder female elephants band together to care for the youngsters. Aunts, sisters, and grandmas keep the babies safe and nurtured.

Elephants care for their environment too. African elephants, the larger of the species, are known as climate heroes because of the trails they forge through forests, the seeds they distribute, and the ways their foraging thins out overgrowth. Although elephants have been victims of exploitation for their ivory and other atrocities, African and Asian countries are now partnering with these pachyderms to help save the planet.

An extraordinary thing about elephants is how they mourn and even bury their dead. Like humans, elephants grieve, looping their trunks in and around elephant bones with accompanying low vibrations that sound like a mournful cello. And elephants are actually known to cry.

One way Jesus showed His humanity while He was on earth was by weeping. Elephants remind me that our emotions are God-given—even His creatures sometimes cry. Their example, as well as Jesus's words, remind me that I need not be ashamed when I mourn and weep. —Linda S. Clare

When you are sorrowful look again in your heart, and you shall see that
in truth you are weeping for that which has been your delight.
—Kahlil Gibran

DECEMBER 18

The Curious Fox

"Nazareth! Can anything good come from there?"
Nathanael asked. "Come and see," said Philip.

—JOHN 1:46 (NIV)

TO BOARD A flight at six o'clock in the morning, I must leave my home at an unnatural hour. Stumbling toward my detached garage in the wee hours, dragging a suitcase behind me, I spied two red dots shining in the darkness. Were they taillights from a neighbor's car? No, they were far too close. Maybe a dog, wandering the alley? No, too still for that. A cat? Too high off the ground.

Intrigued, I stepped cautiously forward, then waited for my eyes to adjust to the dark. It was an animal, yes, and the creature stood still long enough for me to see its silhouette. Peering around the corner of my garage was a red fox. *That's odd,* I thought. *Right here in the middle of town.*

Remembering my drive to the airport, I proceeded to the garage, fumbling for my keys. Opening the door, I looked up. There he was again, my curious friend. He'd taken a few steps closer and stood with his head cocked to one side. Apparently, my nocturnal visitor was as confused by my presence as I was by his. We stood there, sizing each other up as if unsure about what to do next.

I've often felt that way when Christ makes Himself known to me in some unexpected way, such as in the distressing disguise of an indigent person. Or among the members of some other group, people I've been taught to fear. Or when prompting me through the Spirit to go here or there and do this or that thing.

Could that be Jesus? Is He really here, now? My first reaction is always doubt. The next is usually fear. After that comes some logical explanation for how I must be imagining things. I've found there's only one way to find out if what I'm seeing really is Christ.

Go and see for myself. —Lawrence W. Wilson

Lord, make me aware of Your presence today, and help me to believe it. Amen.

DECEMBER 19

Beyond Comprehension

But I would seek God, put my case to God, who does great things beyond comprehension, wonderful things without number.

—JOB 5:8–9 (CEB)

AFTER OWNING DOGS for most of her life, my octogenarian friend Trudy became a cat owner so she could still have furry companionship even though she wasn't as mobile as she used to be. Since I own a pet-sitting company and work daily with animals, Trudy peppers me with many questions about her girl kitties.

"Why does Mickey only vomit on the carpet, never the linoleum where it would be easy to clean up?" "Why does Pandora suddenly dash from upstairs and race through the room, scaring me to death?" "How come Mickey loves this food flavor one day and won't touch it the day after I've gone and bought a case?" "Cats are beyond my comprehension!"

Unfortunately, contrary to popular opinion, I am not a cat whisperer, and my answers are generally along the lines of, "I don't know. She's a cat. Cats are mysteries. Just enjoy them."

One day I realized the same could be said of God. We very often don't understand why He does what He does. He—and His creation—are wondrous and, in many cases, beyond our comprehension. The same winds that cool a hot day can also destroy both natural and human-made structures. Eagles soar, a beautiful sight to behold, then grab fish and small mammals in sharp talons to kill and eat. A sinless, mild-mannered Teacher dies on a cross as a criminal in place of us sinners. All God's designs—and all beyond my comprehension.

Just as Trudy need not completely understand her kitty girls to love them and enjoy their company, I don't need to completely comprehend God to love Him and enjoy His blessings. Sometimes a little mystery in life can be fulfilling. —Kim Sheard

Cats are a mysterious kind of folk. There is more passing in their minds than we are aware of.
—Sir Walter Scott

DECEMBER 20

Finding Home

Jesus replied, "Anyone who loves me will obey my teaching. My Father will love them, and we will come to them and make our home with them."

—JOHN 14:23 (NIV)

AS I PULLED into our driveway a few days before Christmas, I spotted a small dog without a collar wandering our street. Two neighbors tried to catch the stray, but it escaped. I got out of the car and joined them. The furry white dog appeared nervous and unfriendly. Using a snack, a neighbor and I lured the pooch to us and managed to put a leash on her. After some discussion, it was decided that I would keep the dog in my house while my neighbors would coordinate their efforts to find the dog's owner. My son named the poodle-terrier mix Fiona.

It took a couple of days for Fiona to become familiar with us. She did warm up to us, but did not settle in. She was restless, pawing at our backyard fence and pacing near our front door. It was as if Fiona was looking for someone or something. When our search for her owner turned up empty, we made the difficult decision to surrender her to the local shelter. Within a few days, Fiona was adopted by a wonderful family.

That Christmas, Fiona's adoption reminded me of how restless and lost I was before I found Jesus. Like a stray, I searched for belonging and rootedness. Just as my family and neighbors were instrumental in helping Fiona find a home, there were many people in my life, including my mom and Sunday school teachers, who showed me the way to Jesus. When I believed in Him and entered into a relationship with Him, my wandering stopped.

As I celebrated Christmas, my heart overflowed with gratitude toward Jesus, the Son of God who left His home in heaven and came to earth so that I could find a permanent home in Him. —Mabel Ninan

Walk of Faith: *Write down a list of blessings from being in a relationship with Jesus and spend some time worshipping and thanking Him for them.*

DECEMBER 21

Rescued!

The Lord hears his people when they call to him for help. He rescues them from all their troubles. The Lord is close to the brokenhearted; he rescues those whose spirits are crushed.

—Psalm 34:17–18 (NLT)

A SMALL STREAM cuts diagonally through our yard and meanders to a larger creek much further behind our house. Over the years, we've enjoyed toads and frogs, crayfish, an occasional snake, tadpoles, minnows, and a couple of visiting armadillos.

The stream doesn't flow year-round, only during the wetter times of the year. When we notice it drying up to become just a little muddy puddle, David and I will rescue trapped minnows or tadpoles and take them to a better location.

Just the other day, something wiggling in the small murky puddle caught our attention. At first glance, we thought it was a snake. When it surfaced, gills wiggled slightly. We couldn't bear to watch him gasping for air, his resources almost completely dried up. Possibly he wouldn't have survived another hot day in south Georgia. David ran for his net and scooped. "It's an Amphiuma," my biologist hubby declared. "Hmmmm. You know, I'm actually not sure which species this is." He leaned in and counted toes. "Four. I don't think that's an Amphiuma, after all." We hurried to get him to the larger creek behind our house.

Sometimes in my life, I feel like that little critter. Like all my resources are just about to dry up, whether that's financial resources, writing, creativity, friendships, or health options. But God always comes through. Every time, God sends a rescuer. Maybe it's someone with a really large net to rein me in from my own mistakes. Or maybe it's extra cash at Christmas from my mom or a casserole from a friend when I need it or a phone call at just the right time. God is so good like that!

Oh, and our almost-out-of-breath critter? "It's a siren," David said. With a smile, he added, "Not to be confused with the one-toed, two-toed, or three-toed Amphiuma." —Julie Lavender

Then they cried to the Lord in their trouble, and
he delivered them from their distress.
—Psalm 107:28 (ESV)

DECEMBER 22

Frog in the Flowerpot

Be still before the Lord and wait patiently for him; fret not yourself over the one who prospers in his way, over the man who carries out evil devices!

—PSALM 37:7 (ESV)

STRICKEN WITH BACK spasms, I headed to my sauna in the basement to relieve my sore muscles. For Christmas, my husband had gifted me a sauna, filling the space with plants to give my sanctuary a tropical feel.

During the pandemic, frogs started hanging out in my basement. I had no idea where they came from or how they got in. Fascinated by my guests, I learned about their species, kept track of their habits, upgraded the area with swimming facilities for them, and gave them names.

Greta was by far the largest of them. Plump and almost 4 inches long, she was a magnificent pickerel frog. I often spotted her hiding in the bushiest plant in my nursery. This time, she was facing the sauna.

As I soaked up the heat, Greta stared at me in perfect stillness, separated from me by the sauna's glass wall. She seemed to smile at me from her bed of wispy flowers and purple and green leaves.

As the heat untangled my knotted muscles, I wondered what Greta *did* as she sat there in her refuge, with no phone to doomscroll, no Netflix video to entertain her, no other frog to talk to. She's just *being*, something simple most humans can't do.

Greta didn't seem tormented about the past or worried about the future. She was not rushing to go anywhere. She enjoyed the moment, the miracle of being a frog.

I, on the other hand, found myself multitasking in this sauna that was meant to relax me, thinking about all the things I had to do and fretting about how little time I had to do them. I envied her peace.

I realized I had much to learn from my teacher in the flowerpot.
—Sonia Frontera

Walk of Faith: *What is stressing you right now? Set aside a few minutes today, and find a place to spend in silence communing with God. Turn over your worries to God and bask in His unending love.*

DECEMBER 23

A Very Rowdy Teddy Bear

The fruit of the Spirit is love, joy, peace, longsuffering, kindness, goodness, faithfulness, gentleness, self-control. Against such there is no law.

—GALATIANS 5:22–23 (NKJV)

CHALLENGING CIRCUMSTANCES CAN lead to great blessings. Never did this become more real for me than when my sister suffered a heart attack, requiring open-heart surgery. Although the procedure proved a success, the months of rehabilitation would prevent her from caring for her 75-pound goldendoodle. The 8-year-old Teddy Bear needed at least a temporary new home, and fast.

Since my sister planned to do her rehab at her daughter's home, I decided to invite Teddy to my house. She fit in well with my golden retriever and tried hard to obey the rules. Teddy enjoyed back rubs and lengthy sessions stroking her long ears.

On walks, Teddy liked to meet new friends, whether man, woman, child, or beast. She bows accordingly at first—showing her humility and good manners. What comes next hints at the other side of her personality. Once triggered by the endorphins of finding a new friend, Teddy always went crazy. She jumped on the unsuspecting recipient of her love. The dog pulled hard on her "no-pull" lead and lunged somewhat out of control in the direction of more hugs.

At home, her behavior was much the same. She would lie for hours resting or chewing contentedly on a toy. However, as soon as a car pulled in the driveway or the mail carrier walked past the front window, Teddy leaped up and went berserk: barking, rushing to the front window, and beating against the glass with her front paws. No amount of calling to her, running over and touching her, or yelling would calm her down.

During those first months, I often dreamed of returning her to my sister the minute she was healthy enough to care for Teddy. Over time, I learned to love Teddy and couldn't imagine life without her. Now she lives with me permanently. Although we've made little progress on her manners in stressful situations, I've learned an important lesson about God's love. He is patient no matter what. —David L. Winters

Father, may Your Word mature me each day. Amen.

ALL GOD'S CREATURES 369

DECEMBER 24

Watching for the Resplendent One

"Watch therefore, for you do not know what hour your Lord is coming."
—MATTHEW 24:42 (NKJV)

WE WERE TOLD to assemble at the meeting spot at 5:50 a.m. sharp. *Oh my,* I thought, *another early morning for the daybreak-averse.* Inwardly, I sighed. Our little group of ten made our way to where resplendent quetzals had been seen over the last few days, feeding on ripe avocados. "Resplendent" is not merely my description of the bird; it's part of the bird's full name.

Drawn to this place by word of mouth alone, we join a hodgepodge of bird enthusiasts. Eager eyes scour the sky to see the quetzal arrive. Scopes out, cameras poised, eyes straining to see the beautiful bird swoop down from higher elevations. A collective gasp arose as several spotted the male following the female into the avocado tree. Human eyes intently followed the "near-threatened" bird species as they flitted about the tree.

The resplendent quetzal lives in tropical forests, particularly mountain cloud forests in Central America and southern Mexico. The birds sport vibrant red, blue, and green colors. Particularly stunning is the male quetzal's approximately 30-inch-long twin tail feathers. The bird's beauty lives up to its name of resplendent, which means *shining brightly* or *characterized by a glowing splendor.*

That morning, my eyes were cast upward. My posture was expectant and anticipation coursed through my body. I had set aside my physical comfort and willingly prepared and positioned myself to await the quetzal's arrival.

Later, I recognized the spiritual analogy. I'm also awaiting the arrival of the resplendent one, my Lord and Savior Jesus Christ. He has promised to return for me, and with my every step of obedience, every act of loving service, every step of faith, I position myself in readiness to rejoice in His return. I await, faithful, eager, and full of anticipation, with my eyes always turned heavenward. —Darlene Kerr

"If I go and prepare a place for you, I will come back and take
you to be with me that you also may be where I am."
—John 14:3 (NIV)

370 ALL GOD'S CREATURES

DECEMBER 25

A Shocking Display

The light shines in the darkness, and the darkness can never extinguish it.
. . . [Jesus] said, "I am the light of the world. If you follow me, you won't
have to walk in darkness, because you will have the light that leads to life."

—JOHN 1:5; 8:12 (NLT)

IN RECENT YEARS, zoos and aquariums have become known for their often-elaborate holiday exhibits, a great way to attract visitors in what otherwise might be an off season. Did you know that electric eels have been used to make Christmas lights shine? I should hasten to clarify that in most cases the eels are not *powering* the lights, even though the eels are capable of producing 600 to 800 volts. (At one aquarium, the eels' voltage actually did power a string of lights!) Zookeepers have begun putting on displays of eel-directed Christmas lights at their zoos for a whimsical and ever-changing presentation. As the old adage says, "Don't try this at home!"

God created electric eels with unique cells that store and release energy. Using sensors as switches, the lights respond to variations in the eels' electrical shocks. In nature, their lower-voltage jolts are used as a means of communication between eels or as a sort of location system, while their strongest ones are employed to stun prey. Since the eels' shocks are strongest at mealtimes, the Christmas lights are brightest and most active around when they are being fed. Using their amazing God-given abilities, electric eels are helping people celebrate the joy of Christmas.

The eels' display can be seen as a reflection of Jesus, the Light of the World. Christmas, our celebration of His birth, arrives in the gloomiest part of the winter, its twinkling candles and bulbs bringing much-needed light to a dark world. Jesus's birth more than 2,000 years ago brought His light to a world that needed it just as much as we do today. Like the eels, we can help shine "the light that leads to life" (John 8:12, NLT) to those around us, both on Christmas Day and the rest of the year.
—Editors of Guideposts

"Arise, shine, for your light has come, and the glory of the LORD rises upon you."
—Isaiah 60:1 (NIV)

ALL GOD'S CREATURES   371

DECEMBER 26

Penny in His Pocket

You are my hiding place; You shall preserve me from trouble;
You shall surround me with songs of deliverance.

—PSALM 32:7 (NKJV)

WE HOLD THOSE we love close to our hearts, and we are naturally protective, especially of the small and vulnerable. Growing up, I was blessed with a picture of that endearing kind of love.

Uncle Bert, my father's brother, came to visit us often. I would watch him walk down the steep sidewalk in our backyard, toward our porch off the kitchen, where my mother always had a pot of coffee ready. Uncle Bert, a World War II navy veteran, knew what was important in life. He took time to visit his family and brought his little buddy along with him.

Penny, a toy Manchester terrier, poked her head out of Uncle Bert's top jacket pocket, and greeted us with the sweetest little yelp that was barely a bark. She knew she was loved and didn't fret or wiggle or try to climb out. She stayed put, content as can be, while we visited around the kitchen table. Black, shiny, and very tiny, Penny's dark brown eyes would make any heart melt. Uncle Bert was soft-spoken, and I think Penny was drawn to that gentleness.

I remember seeing Uncle Bert in the grocery store with Penny in his pocket. Tucked inside her safe shelter, Penny poked her head out to see the world. People stopped and commented on this little dog that resembled a miniscule black stallion. Children were amused to meet this amazing creature, considered a "teacup" size, as their parents stopped to say hello. I think Penny must have loved all the attention, and Uncle Bert made many new acquaintances.

This childhood memory is symbolic to me, reminding me to hold close and treasure those I love, as Uncle Bert did with Penny—and I can do this best through my loving actions and prayers for them. God holds me close and keeps me safe too, as He carries me in this big world in the "pocket" of His love. —Kathleen R. Ruckman

Thank You, dear Lord, for childhood memories that
grow more meaningful through the years.

DECEMBER 27

Natural Sabbath

There remains, then, a Sabbath-rest for the people of God.

—HEBREWS 4:9 (NIV)

A COUPLE OF MONTHS after the start of the pandemic, people began to notice that there was a change in the environment. Our natural world had a rest. With fewer internal combustion engines running both on land and sea, nature began to return to its "normal" self.

Though scientists are still debating and studying to learn what had truly changed, I was amazed that, for the duration of that difficult time, at least, things did change and that nature was resetting. Sea creatures such as sea turtles thrived during the reduction of ocean traffic. Dolphins were seen swimming in harbors that were historically too busy for them. Mammals and birds thrived without the car traffic.

I thought of God's commandment for Sabbath rest. I am often trying to squeeze in as many activities as possible and very rarely rest from my labors. The times when I have taken a Sabbath, I am amazed at how renewed and refreshed I am and how I experience a new vigor upon returning to my work.

I have also noticed that my vigor is not sustainable. By the time another week or so passes, I am in need of another Sabbath. I think that is God's design, and God's gift to us: we need to balance the energy we expend and the energy we gain from recovery. We saw that with the shift in the resetting balance of nature during our Covid shutdown, and we need to remember what we learned as we go forward. —Virginia Ruth

*Lord of the Sabbath, thank You that You know me
so well and know when I need to rest.
May I remember to balance the busyness of my life
with Your rest and renewal. Amen.*

ALL GOD'S CREATURES 373

DECEMBER 28

Barks in the Night

Do not be anxious about anything, but in everything by prayer and supplication with thanksgiving let your requests be made known to God.

—PHILIPPIANS 4:6 (ESV)

THE BARKING TUGGED me from my sleep. I blinked in the darkness of my room, listening to the familiar warning from Magnus, my Great Pyrenees. Any owner of a Great Pyrenees knows barking comes with the territory. A lot of barking.

But I wasn't too happy about his latest habit of barking overnight or in the early morning hours when I was trying to sleep. The clock read 5 a.m., which meant this alert was to tell me my neighbor had left for work and driven her car out of the driveway. Definitely a threat in his Great Pyrenees mind.

He continued to bark, though the so-called danger had long passed. I knew from experience he wouldn't stop barking until I dealt with the situation. With a sigh, I hauled myself out of bed and traipsed into the hallway, stopping where Magnus could see me from the foyer.

The moment he spotted me with his dark eyes, he stopped barking. Then he turned around, shuffled a few feet away, and plopped down to sleep. I didn't have to say a word. All Magnus needed was to see me, to know I was aware of the situation and would handle it. Then he could relax and rest.

It struck me that I should be that way too. Anytime I'm alarmed about something, I should bring my concerns to God in prayer. I try to do that regularly, but after I pray about the problem, I often continue to worry or try to fix the issue myself.

I should be like Magnus instead. When I pray, I need to look to Jesus with eyes full of faith. Once I know He's got this, I can release my burdens and rest in the peace that surpasses all understanding. —Jerusha Agen

Lord, help me to trust You so much that I can let go of worry and my desire to control because I know You hold me and all things in Your hands. Amen.

DECEMBER 29

Do You Know You Live in Paradise?

The LORD is my strength and my shield; my heart trusts in him, and he helps me. My heart leaps for joy, and with my song I praise him.

—PSALM 28:7 (NIV)

WHILE ENJOYING A picnic lunch in Glendalough, Ireland—an ancient monastic site tucked in the Wicklow Mountains—I noticed a pair of mallards waddling beside the bench where my friends and I ate. The weather was quintessentially Irish, and the lunches we'd ordered from the hotel were nothing spectacular, but I felt like I'd landed in heaven.

I looked down at the ducks. "Hello. Do you know you live in paradise?" I sensed they did. How could they not feel blessed, surrounded by lush grass, spring flowers popping up everywhere, stone ruins to shelter in, and the two lakes that gave Glendalough its name (it means *Glen of Two Lakes*).

One of my travel buddies, Edna, tossed crust from her sandwich to the duck couple. There were no signs saying we couldn't feed the birds, so tourists and hikers kept them well nourished.

Whether those ducks knew how fortunate they were to spend their lives in such beauty or not, I sensed that God used that moment as a gratitude check for me. I felt extremely fortunate to be sitting at a picnic table with eleven other writers, in one of the most glorious gaps in Ireland. Having once teetered on the poverty line, I knew full well that travel was a gift. But what about in my ordinary life at home? Did I recognize myself as blessed? Was I content? Did I know I lived in what some might consider paradise? Not always. But I wanted to.

Long after my time in Ireland had ended, I wanted to be as satisfied as those ducks. I reminded myself often to be quick to thank my Creator for each provision and recognize the loveliness of the life He crafted for me. —Jeanette Hanscome

My little sisters the birds, ye owe much to God, your Creator, and ye ought to sing his praise at all times and in all places.
—Saint Francis of Assisi

ALL GOD'S CREATURES   375

DECEMBER 30

An End-of-Year Gift

Every good and perfect gift is from above, coming down from the Father of the heavenly lights, who does not change like shifting shadows.

—JAMES 1:17 (NIV)

NEARING THE END of the year, my email inbox fills with invitations and opportunities to extend generosity to various organizations through year-end giving. Yet one year, in late December, I was the one who received a special and generous year-end gift from God.

It was two days before New Year's Day, and my husband and I, along with our four young children, took an entire day to drive through the Rocky Mountains and see what wildlife we could find. We were not disappointed.

As the sun set, I looked over our list from the day: 5 moose, over 800 elk, over 300 pronghorn, 12 white-tailed deer, 4 mule deer, 4 coyotes, 3 Wilson's snipes, 4 golden eagles, 1 bald eagle, 1 American dipper, and 6 wild turkeys. Winding our way through the foothills toward home, we were all grins as we reflected on an incredible day of watching God's creation. With darkness settling over the forest, I thought our wildlife spotting had come to a close. Yet, as we rounded a bend in the road, our headlights shone on a large animal as it darted into the woods. My husband and son saw its long, black-tipped tail and exclaimed in unison, "A mountain lion!"

My husband stopped the car and quickly grabbed his spotlight, shining it into the woods. The mountain lion sat staring at us from twenty feet away. A minute later, it ran across the road, giving us and our children a full view of its magnificence.

After the lion slipped back into the dark forest, we continued on our way, hearts racing with excitement as I added "mountain lion" to our list. Suddenly, I remembered that at the start of that year, I had told my husband that this year, our eighth year of living in Colorado, I wanted to see a mountain lion. Two days before the year's end, God gave me that gift. —Eryn Lynum

Dear God, You are the giver of every good gift. You give me everything I need, and You delight in granting me the desires of my heart.

376   ALL GOD'S CREATURES

DECEMBER 31

The Dog in the Suitcase

The Lord gave Solomon wisdom, just as he had promised him.

—1 KINGS 5:12 (NIV)

IT WAS NEW Year's Eve, some years ago. I longed to welcome the new year with my parents in Puerto Rico and looked forward to reuniting with Sati, an abused dog who had been abandoned at their house. I intended to bring her to my New Jersey home for a new beginning.

When I arrived at my parents' house, I was devastated to find Sati thin and frail. I visited the local vet to evaluate Sati and issue the certificate required for her travel to the mainland. Instead, the doctor suggested I euthanize her, asking why I would want to take in that "problem." I stormed out of his office in tears.

Seeing my distress, my friend Teresa offered to take Sati to her vet after the holidays and fly her to me when she healed.

That night, as Sati slept in my bedroom, my heart filled with angst. Was bringing Sati home with me a mistake? Unsure of what to do, I asked God for a sign before going to sleep. I woke up in the middle of the night and found Sati sleeping soundly—in my suitcase. God had spoken!

I returned home without Sati, trusting in God's promise and the certainty that Sati would heal.

Teresa's doctor diagnosed and treated Sati for heartworms, and in April, issued her travel certificate. Once in New Jersey, Sati became an affectionate companion who comforted me through illness, losing the job I loved, and my mother's death. This miracle dog encapsulated the power of love to heal.

Most importantly, Sati became my symbol for trusting God for guidance, one that I remember every New Year's Eve. Trusting in humans—like the vet who labeled Sati "a problem"—would have deprived me of her healing love. When you ask God for answers, He will deliver every time. —Sonia Frontera

Heavenly Father, grant me wisdom that can only come from You. Help me keep my eyes fixed on You and trust in You with all my heart to lead me in the right paths and to decisions that please You.

About the Authors

As a teacher and student of God's Word, **JERUSHA AGEN** is awed by the letters of love the Father writes into every moment of our lives, including through the animals we encounter. Jerusha is the daughter of two veterinarians and has always shared her life with a menagerie of pets, which she now uses as models for the animals featured in her suspense novels. You'll often find Jerusha sharing adorable photos of her two big dogs and two little cats in her e-newsletter. Get a free suspense story from Jerusha and find more of her writing at www.JerushaAgen.com.

JEAN ALFIERI is a writer, speaker, and dog fan. When her eyes locked with those of a smooshy-faced little dog who sat inside a kennel at the Humane Society, it was love at first sight. He captured her heart, and she went on to capture their many adventures in short stories starring *Zuggy the Rescue Pug*. She and her husband joke that although they pay the mortgage of their home in Colorado, it's really the dogs' house—they have three altogether. Jean finds much of her writing inspiration from her "vintage puppies" and her work at the Pikes Peak Humane Society.

TWILA BENNETT is a regular contributor to *All God's Creatures*. She is also a contributing writer to *The Cat on My Lap*, *The Dog at My Feet*, and *Guideposts One-Minute Daily Devotional*. Twila is the communications manager for Camp Roger and Camp Scottie. She is also the founder of Monarch Lane Consulting (MonarchLaneConsulting.com), helping writers create proposals and providing branding consultation. For 20 years, Twila was a branding and marketing executive for Revell Books. She loves camping, boating, and sunsets. Twila lives with her husband, Dan, in Rockford, Michigan. Connect with Twila on Facebook and Instagram.

Homemaker **MARIANNE CAMPBELL** lives in Sonoma County, California. She developed her love of animals during her childhood spent on her family's Gravenstein apple farm. Her spirit of adventure led her to visit Japan, Thailand, Nepal, Israel, and Egypt in the early 1980s. She served in the United States Navy from 1984 to 1990, where she met her husband, Scott. They have two married daughters and two grandchildren. When not writing, Marianne enjoys watching her grandchildren, reading, studying history, baking, gardening, hiking local trails, and playing *World of Warcraft*.

LUCY CHAMBERS serves Christ Church Cathedral and the downtown Houston community as the manager of the historic Cathedral Bookstore. A firm believer in the power of sharing stories to deepen connection and improve lives, she has worked with books for more than 35 years as an editor, publisher, teacher, and writer. In addition to reading and writing, she makes miniature gardens and volunteers for the altar guild and literary and green organizations. She and her husband, Sam, have two grown daughters, two very soft rabbits, a big dog, and a small dog.

LINDA S. CLARE has always loved animals, adopting dozens of cats, dogs, bunnies, and once, an anole lizard. Writing about animals can be joyful, funny, or sad, but all her stories reflect God's amazing love for creation. Linda is an author and writing coach living in the Northwest with her family. Writing her eighth book, *Thank God for Cats!*, is the most fun she's ever had in writing. Connect with Linda at lindasclare.com, at lindasclare.substack.com, or on Facebook.

ASHLEY CLARK (ashleyclarkbooks.com) writes devotions for Guideposts and southern fiction for Bethany House. With a master's degree in creative writing, Ashley teaches literature and writing courses at the University of West Florida and homeschools her son. She lives with her husband, her son, and a rescued cocker spaniel on Florida's Gulf Coast. When she's not writing, she's dreaming of Charleston and drinking all the English breakfast tea she can get her hands on.

SUSIE COLBY is proud of and entertained by her three adult kids—Caleb, Phoebe, and Lily—and one daughter-in-law, Natalie. Susie is the widow of the funniest, funnest guy ever, Steve Colby. And she is a devoted servant and referee of two cats: Tango and the Kitten. Susie has worked in student ministry for over 30 years, and if that doesn't qualify her as an animal lover, nothing would! If she hadn't been hanging out with students all these years, she might have joined Team Otter at the aquarium.

BEN COOPER is a husband, father, author, speaker, educator, and beekeeper. He grew up on a family farm in western Pennsylvania and went on to get an agricultural science degree from Penn State University. Ben retired after working as an agricultural specialist for the State of Maryland. He teaches beekeeping courses at Allegany College of Maryland and mentors new beekeepers.

Ben and his wife live in southern Pennsylvania, where they homeschooled and raised their five children. He is the author of *All Nature Sings: A Devotional Guide to Animals in the Bible* and a children's picture book series that includes *Created Critters with Wings* and *Created Critters with Fur*. Ben speaks at churches, youth groups, and camping ministries about God's wonderful creation and can be reached at cooperville@breezeline.net.

TRACY CRUMP dispenses hope in her multi-award-winning book, *Health, Healing, and Wholeness: Devotions of Hope in the Midst of Illness,* based on her experiences as an ICU nurse. Her articles and devotions have appeared in diverse publications, including *Focus on the Family, Mature Living, Ideals, The Upper Room, Woman's World,* and several Guideposts books. But she is best known for contributing twenty-three stories to Chicken Soup for the Soul books.

Tracy and her husband love observing wildlife near their country home and doting on five completely unspoiled grandchildren. Find encouragement from Tracy's blog for caregivers at tracycrump.com.

Award-winning author **ELLEN FANNON** is a retired veterinarian, former missionary, and church pianist and organist. She and her retired Air-Force-pilot-turned-pastor husband fostered more than forty children and are the adoptive parents of two sons. She has published eight novels: *Other People's Children, Save the Date, Don't Bite the Doctor, Honor Thy Father* episodes 1 and 2, and the *Love in the Wind* trilogy. Her articles and stories have appeared in *One Christian Voice,* Chicken Soup for the Soul books, *Divine Moments,* and *Guideposts.* In addition to being published in *All God's Creatures,* her devotions have been published in *Open Windows* and *The Secret Place.* She also has had stories published in *You and Me, Sasee,* and *Go* magazine. Follow Ellen's humor-at-everyday-life blog, ellenfannonauthor.com.

GLENDA FERGUSON has contributed to *All God's Creatures, Angels on Earth,* Chicken Soup for the Soul, and *Mules & More.* The Indiana Arts Commission has included her poem "The Buffalo Trace Trail: Then and Now" in the INverse Poetry Archive. Her writing encouragement comes from the Writers' Forum of Burton Kimble Farms Education Center and the ladies' prayer circle at her church. Glenda and her husband Tim live in southern Indiana, where they have an acre of land that they share with their cats, Speckles and Scrappy, plus a variety of wildlife visitors.

ALLISON LYNN FLEMMING is drawn to the power of story to grow hearts and communities. As a singer, songwriter, and worship leader, Allison and her husband, Gerald Flemming, form the award-winning duo, Infinitely More. Their ninth album, *The Sum of All Love,* explores the joys and challenges of living an authentic life of faith. Allison writes devotionals, songs, articles, and creative nonfiction to remind people how deeply they are loved by God. Publications include *All God's Creatures* (Guideposts), *The Upper Room* (devotionals), Warner Press (devotionals), and eleven stories with Chicken Soup for the Soul. Learn more about her at www.InfinitelyMore.ca.

PEGGY FREZON is a contributing editor of *Guideposts* and *Angels on Earth* magazines, and (at the time of this writing) is celebrating 20 years writing for Guideposts books and magazines! She is the author of books about the human-animal bond, especially about dogs and the people who love them. Look for her newest book coming out in the summer of 2026! Peggy and her husband, Mike, rescue senior golden retrievers at BrooksHaven, a forever retirement home for dogs. They live with their rescue goldens Pete and Sophie, and two rescue guinea pigs. Connect with Peggy at www.peggyfrezon.com and sign up for her newsletter, *Dogs of BrooksHaven,* at https://tinyurl.com/BrooksHaven.

SONIA FRONTERA is an attorney, empowerment trainer, and author from New Jersey. Her writing invites readers to discover paths to spirituality in everyday situations and personal adversity.

Though she doesn't have any creatures in her home, **JEANETTE HANSCOME** savors every opportunity to play with other people's pets and be inspired by critters she spots while traveling. She is the author of both fiction and nonfiction books, in addition to hundreds of articles and devotions. Her most recent titles are three cozies for Guideposts's Whistle Stop Café mystery series. A proud mom of two grown sons, she now has more time on her hands for her many creative pursuits and practicing ukulele. Jeanette lives in the San Francisco Bay Area.

LORI HATCHER has loved animals since she received two tiny turtles at age six. She and her husband, David, have cohabited with many fish, a pair of hermit crabs, four birds, and two amazing dogs in Lexington, South Carolina. They're currently petless due to a delightful influx of tiny humans, although they have recently acquired an amazing granddog, Halsey the Frenchie.

Lori is the author of *Refresh Your Faith, Refresh Your Prayers,* and *Refresh Your Hope.* She has also written for Guidepost's *Evenings with Jesus, Guideposts One-Minute Daily Devotional,* and *Pray a Word a Day.* She and David most recently coauthored *Moments with God for Couples* with Our Daily Bread Publishing. Connect with Lori on her blog, *Refresh,* at lorihatcher.com.

HEATHER JEPSEN is the pastor at First Presbyterian Church in Warrensburg, Missouri. She has been serving small churches for more than 18 years. She and her husband, Lars, have two kids, Olivia and Henry, as well as a wide variety of pets. When she is not pastoring or writing, Heather likes to garden, quilt, and play the harp. In addition to writing for *All God's Creatures,* Heather also writes for Guideposts's *Strength and Grace* magazine. Read more at pastorheatherjepsen.com.

KRISTEN G. JOHNSON grew up as that kid who always had her nose in a book and a pen in her hand. She enjoys many different forms of writing, including devotionals, short stories, and articles. Kristen also writes the Ophelia Starcluck middle grade series under the pen name Kristen Gwen. She is married to a pastor, and they have two adopted girls, four rabbits, and one one-eyed cat. When she pops her head up from her computer, Kristen enjoys singing, acting, hiking small mountains in search of huckleberries, and serving in her church. She and her family live in Washington State.

As a *Publishers Weekly* award-winning author of more than fifty novels and with two million books in print, **DEB KASTNER** writes contemporary inspirational and sweet western stories set in small communities, often including animals as major secondary characters.

Deb lives in beautiful Colorado with her husband, her puppers Gabby and Sadie, and two mischievous bonded brothers, black tuxedo cats Hype and Dab. She recently went through what she terms a midlife crisis and adopted her very first real live horse, whose name is Moscato.

She is blessed with three adult daughters and two grandchildren, with a third on the way. Her favorite hobby is spoiling her grandchildren, but she also enjoys reading, watching movies, listening to music (The Texas Tenors and The High Kings are her faves), singing in the church choir, and exploring the Rocky Mountains on horseback.

DARLENE KERR lives in Ohio with her naturalist husband, Jeff, on a property increasingly overflowing with native plants, flowers, and vegetables—and all the various creatures and insects that are attracted to them. She says, "Our goal is to have a living garden, where many hovering, crawling, buzzing, and burrowing critters are encouraged to thrive." Darlene is the garden tidier (with no calluses), whereas the true gardener (with calluses) is her husband. Much to her husband's chagrin, she has realized that calluses from writing are preferable, and she especially enjoys writing about God's creation, finding spiritual applications to encourage herself and others.

LIZ KIMMEL has self-published two books of Christian prose/poetry and a grammar workbook for middle-school students. She enjoys writing for Guideposts projects and for the Short and Sweet series through Grace Publishing. Married to Cary for 45 years and living in St. Paul, Minnesota, she has two children and four grandchildren. Liz provides administrative support for four nonprofits, Dare to Believe Ministries, Great Commission Media Ministries, Minnesota Christian Writers Guild, and MN House of Prayer. Her most recent book is a photo-illustrated, alliterative retelling of ten of Jesus's parables called *Putting Punch in the Parables*.

JULIE LAVENDER'S new picture book, *A Gingerbread House*, recently debuted and can be found on bookstore shelves with her other publications, including *Children's Bible Stories for Bedtime* (English and bilingual versions), *Strength for All Seasons: A Mom's Devotional of Powerful Verses and Prayers*, and *365 Ways to Love Your Child: Turning Little*

Moments into Lasting Memories. She's especially excited that her now-retired hubby, David, joins her along the writing journey. Together they've written several educational books for kids, combining his wildlife biology and entomology experiences and her education and teaching experiences. A former homeschooling military family, the Lavenders enjoyed raising and educating their kids in ten homes in six states. Julie and David are loving the retirement life, traveling often to visit their four kids, two sons-in-love, and three grandchildren.

HALLIE LEE was born and raised in Louisiana, and her writing is inspired by the southern landscape, which she says is rich with "cantankerous, salt-of-the-earth folks destined to be on the page." Her first novel, *Paint Me Fearless*, launched the bestselling Shady Gully series and was Bookfest 2022's gold-medal winner in Christian contemporary fiction. She and her family, furry kids included, currently live in Kentucky, where she aspires to write novels and devotions that gently lead us to the unfailing love of Christ. Connect with Hallie at www.HallieLee.com.

LOUIS LOTZ is an ordained minister in the Reformed Church in America and has served as president of the Reformed Church General Synod. His writings for *The Church Herald* and *RCA Today* magazines have won multiple awards from the Evangelical Press Association.

Lou and his wife, Mary Jean, live on an acreage in rural Michigan. Lou enjoys gardening, fishing, beekeeping, long walks with his bride of 51 years, and tending his grapes and fruit trees. The Lotzes have two grown children and two grandchildren.

ERYN LYNUM is a certified master naturalist, educator, and national speaker. Eryn hosts the popular podcast for kids, *Nat Theo: Nature Lessons Rooted in the Bible*. She is the author of *The Nature of Rest: What the Bible and Creation Teach Us About Sabbath Living*; *Rooted in Wonder: Nurturing Your Family's Faith Through God's Creation*; and *936 Pennies: Discovering the Joy of Intentional Parenting*. She lives in northern Colorado with her husband, Grayson, and their four children, feisty cat, German shorthaired pointer, and three pet axolotls. They spend their days hiking, camping, and adventuring through the Rocky Mountains. Eryn has been featured on broadcasts including *Focus on the Family*, *FamilyLife Today*, *Christian Parenting*, and *Raising Christian Kids*. Every opportunity she gets, she is out exploring God's creation with her family and sharing the adventures at erynlynum.com.

CATHY MAYFIELD draws much inspiration for her devotions from the animals that God has blessed her and her husband with on their partly wooded property in the mountains of central Pennsylvania. Their German shepherd mix, Kenai, adds his own crazy antics to pull from. As their youngest daughter says, "He's part kangaroo, part mountain goat!" And if there is ever a need for grandparenting devotions, Cathy is storing plenty of ideas from their five grandchildren. "They keep me feeling young—at least when I'm with them!" Cathy delights in being part of the Guideposts family of writers.

JANET HOLM McHENRY is the author of twenty-seven books. She often prayer-walks her town in California's Sierra Valley, where she encounters all kinds of God's creatures. Janet and her husband, Craig, have raised four children and a variety of pets. A journalism graduate of UC Berkeley, Janet worked as a reporter and English teacher and is the creator of an online course called *Prayer School* and host of the Sierra Valley Writers Retreat. Through her business, Looking Up!, she encourages others to pursue a praying life. She loves traveling, kayaking, and spending time with their grandchildren. Connect with her at janetmchenry.com.

LESLIE L. McKEE is an award-winning author, editor, and reviewer. She is a member of American Christian Fiction Writers and The Christian PEN. Her debut book, a devotional journal (*HOPE Amid the Pain: Hanging on to Positive Expectations When Battling Chronic Pain and Illness*), was published on October 26, 2021, with Ambassador International. In 2023, it won the Ames Award and The BookFest Award. Some of her devotions were published in compilations by Ellie Claire in 2017 and 2020. Her flash fiction stories have been published on websites and in magazines and anthologies. She enjoys reading, playing piano, crocheting, spending time with family and friends (and her turtle Speedy and fish Giorgio!), and rooting for the NY Giants. Visit leslielmckee.com. You can also find her on Facebook, Instagram, and X (formerly Twitter) @leslielmckee.

MAUREEN MILLER is an award-winning author and storyteller who writes for her local newspaper and is a contributing author in numerous collaboratives, as well as a featured blogger for several online devotional websites. She loves life in all its forms, enjoying it with her husband and their three "born in their hearts" children and grandchildren on

Selah Farm, their hobby homestead in western North Carolina. She blogs at penningpansies.com, sharing God's extraordinary character in the ordinary things of life, and she's finishing her first novel, *Gideon's Book*, for Redemption Press.

ALINE ALEXANDER NEWMAN started writing as a full-time home economics teacher, when she and Theresa Phillips coauthored an innovative textbook called *Choosing a Marriage Partner*. Aline later wrote grant requests and piloted a mobile classroom around the countryside, teaching disadvantaged adults. Since then, she has written hundreds of magazine articles (many for Guideposts publications) and seven *National Geographic* animal books for children. She's a wife, mother, and grandmother, who loves entertaining friends and family at their seasonal cottage in New York's Adirondack Mountains. That's also a favorite animal watching spot. Learn more at alinealexandernewman.com or friend her on Facebook.

HAROLD "NICK" NICHOLS is a retired university professor and administrator living in Lafayette, Louisiana, with his amazing wife of 30 years and best friend, Anna Marie. Nichols earned his PhD in theater history at Indiana University and taught at Kansas State University for 20 years before turning to administration. He served as a dean at the University of Nebraska at Kearney and at Georgia Southwestern State University before finishing his career as dean of the Mississippi State University Meridian Campus. Nick and Anna Marie have five children and thirteen grandchildren.

MABEL NINAN is an author, speaker, and host of the podcast, *Far from Home with Mabel Ninan*. In her award-winning book, *Far from Home: Discovering Your Identity as Foreigners on Earth*, Mabel draws from her personal experience as an immigrant and examines the lives of biblical heroes to shed light on how we can find purpose and joy as sojourners on earth. Her writings have appeared in *The Upper Room*, CBN.com, *Leading Hearts* magazine, AriseDaily.com, and *(in)courage.me*. She enjoys reading and traveling and lives in northern California with her husband and son. Connect with Mabel at mabelninan.com or through social media @mabel_ninan.

DEVON O'DAY is an award-winning career radio broadcaster with songwriting credits for George Strait, Dolly Parton, Hank Williams Jr., and others. As an author, she has written several books for Thomas Nelson and United Methodist Publishing House and has narrated more than one hundred audio books for HarperCollins, Thomas Nelson, and Zondervan. She has been a contributor to *All God's Creatures* since the inception of the franchise, when devotions from her book, *Paws to Reflect,* were included.

Currently Devon works for Main Street Media of Tennessee, where she hosts three lifestyle streaming shows. She lives on a rescue sanctuary therapy farm outside Nashville called Angel Horse Farm, where senior equines and special-needs livestock offer an infinite well from which to draw stories about animals and their gifts and lessons connecting us to God. Look for Angel Horse Farm on Instagram to see pictures of the animal family that inspire her devotions.

SANDY KIRBY QUANDT is a former elementary school educator and full-time writer with a passion for God, history, and travel, which often weave their way into her stories and articles. She has written numerous articles, devotions, and stories for adult and children's publications, including *Today's Christian Woman, Power for Living, The Lookout, Mature Years, Standard,* and *Alive!* Her devotions appear in *So God Made a Dog, Let the Earth Rejoice,* and several Guideposts devotional books. She has won multiple awards for writing in young adult, middle grade, and children's categories.

Are you looking for words of encouragement or gluten-free recipes? Check out Sandy's blog at sandykirbyquandt.com, where she posts twice a week. Sandy and her husband live in southeast Texas.

SHIRLEY RAYE REDMOND has written for many publications, including *Focus on the Family* magazine, *Home Life,* and *The Christian Standard.* Her devotions have appeared in multiple volumes of Guideposts's *All God's Creatures* and *Walking in Grace.* Her book *Courageous World Changers: 50 True Stories of Daring Women of God* (Harvest House) won the 2021 *Christianity Today* Book Award in the children's book category. Shirley Raye has been married for nearly 50 years to her college sweetheart. They live in Los Alamos, New Mexico, and are blessed with two adult children and five precious grandchildren.

KATHLEEN R. RUCKMAN enjoys several genres of writing. She is the published author of devotions, articles, short stories, poetry, and children's books and has taught women's Bible studies for several years. Kathleen is the mother of four adult children and nine young grandchildren, who are the loves of her life and her inspiration. Her desire as an author is to inspire readers to draw close to the heart of God and to His Word. Kathleen and her husband, Tom, and family live in Oregon, where the beauty of nature shines and all God's creatures are plentiful.

VIRGINIA RUTH and her husband are the proud owners of a rescued "only his mother knows his background" mutt named Scuppers. Virginia has been a lifelong lover of animals and words. She sees God's creation and handiwork as examples of His love for us.

Virginia has written for numerous Guideposts publications over the last 5 years and is currently working on a couple of books about lessons learned during her recent move and praying for her new neighborhood. Her website, wellofencouragement.com, provides encouraging words to fellow travelers on this road of life.

KIM SHEARD has owned a pet-sitting company in northern Virginia since 2010 and, as a result, has lots of good animal stories to tell. This is her second appearance in *All God's Creatures*, and her devotions have also appeared in Guideposts's *Pray a Word a Day Volume 2*, *The Upper Room*, *The Word in Season*, *The Secret Place*, and *Keys for Kids*. She participates in the music ministry of Vale United Methodist Church and enjoys writing liturgy for her congregation's special services. You can find her publications and flute choir arrangements listed at kimsheardauthor.com.

HEATHER SPIVA is an independent writer from Northern California. When she's not reading or writing, she is shopping for vintage clothing, hanging out with family, or having "just one more" cup of coffee. Learn more at heatherspiva.com.

DIANE STARK is a wife, mom of five, grandma of one, and dog mom. She is a contributing editor at *Guideposts* and *Angels on Earth*. She loves to write about the important things in life: her family and her faith.

CRYSTAL STORMS is an author, artist, and the calming voice behind *The Heart Rest Podcast*. With a heart to encourage, her passion is to help you release anxiety and find true peace in Christ's presence. Married to her sweetheart, Tim, since 1995, they call sunny Florida home with their adorable Yorkie, Minnie. When Crystal isn't busy creating, you'll find her exploring God's creation, snuggling with her hubby, or getting lost in a good book. Crystal would love to connect with you and help you find your own heart rest. Head over to CrystalStorms.me and say hello!

KATY W. SUNDARARAJAN enjoys writing about small things that give us pause and point us to great wonder, the things that make our hearts glad and remind us where our hope comes from. Katy lives in beautiful west Michigan, but life has given her a storehouse of very good hometowns. She and her family love to travel together but hate to leave their sweet goldendoodle home for the duration. Give Katy a good book, a pretty view, or a meal around the table with laughing people, and she'll say, "All is well."

Married since 2005, **STACEY THUREEN** is a mom of three children. Her stories have been in *Guideposts* magazine, the nonfiction book series God's Constant Presence, and once again in *All God's Creatures*. When Stacey is not putting words to paper, she can be found spending time with family. She also enjoys masters swimming and spends time at the local pool or rejoicing in God's creation by swimming in open water. Find out more at staceythureen.com.

MISSY TIPPENS is a pastor's wife, a mother of three, and an author from the Atlanta, Georgia, area. She loves being involved in their church by singing in the choir and playing handbells. Missy has cared for many fur children through the years. Her family now has two rescue dogs, and she also enjoys pet-sitting for the granddogs. After more than 10 years of pursuing her dream of publication, Missy sold her first novel to Love Inspired in 2007. She has been writing devotions for Guideposts since 2018. Visit Missy at missytippens.com.

LAWRENCE W. WILSON believes that God is love, life is good, and we can all be a bit better than we are now. He writes to remind people of simple truths so they will be inspired to live a better story. He got his start as a writer by penning and producing a play for his fourth-grade class. (It closed after one-half a performance.) Since then he has written five books and countless articles, lessons, scripts, sermons, podcasts, and news articles.

Lawrence lives in an Indiana small town, just like John Mellencamp—but not the same one.

DAVID L. WINTERS is an author and speaker living in Huber Heights, Ohio. David is a regular contributor to many Guideposts publications. His nonfiction books include *Exercise Your Faith, Taking God to Work,* and *The Accidental Missionary (A Gringo's Love Affair with Peru).* A 1981 graduate of Ohio State University, David also earned an MBA from Regent University in 2003.

Author Index

Jerusha Agen, 10, 17, 44, 93, 140, 182, 222, 290, 330, 374, 379

Jean Alfieri, iii-iv, 379

Twila Bennett, 4, 143, 292, 320, 339, 355, 379

Marianne Campbell, 18, 68, 103, 145, 197, 211, 272, 278, 299, 335, 380

Lucy H. Chambers, 14, 54, 73, 96, 110, 116, 130, 147, 176, 207, 356, 380

Linda S. Clare, 95, 124, 141, 213, 237, 255, 294, 353, 363, 380

Ashley Clark, 7, 69, 117, 127, 149, 204, 229, 239, 296, 317, 380

Susie Colby, 39, 101, 119, 163, 186, 196, 275, 331, 381

Ben Cooper, 109, 121, 154, 158, 218, 225, 266, 282, 286, 302, 381

Tracy Crump, 61, 88, 98, 123, 128, 150, 167, 227, 243, 303, 381

Editors of Guideposts, 268, 371

Ellen Fannon, 43 107, 160, 168, 216, 305, 318, 323, 381

Glenda Ferguson, 24, 42, 87, 91, 118, 126, 314, 344,382

Allison Lynn Flemming, 34, 137, 280, 357, 382

Peggy Frezon, 5, 41, 56, 174, 190, 201, 245, 253, 264, 277, 285, 311, 382

Sonia Frontera, 179, 210, 351, 368, 377, 382

Jeanette Hanscome, 26, 79, 81, 223, 232, 244, 310, 327, 375, 383

Lori Hatcher, 13, 46, 58, 90, 99, 133, 180, 298, 362, 383

Heather Jepsen, 57, 86, 136, 177, 234, 241, 312, 348, 383

Kristen G. Johnson, 27, 49, 231, 257, 338, 383

Deb Kastner, 53, 60, 97, 170, 175, 230, 321, 326, 384

Darlene Kerr, 38, 70, 159, 240, 256, 258, 332, 370, 384

Liz Kimmel, 55, 108, 135, 169, 236, 246, 270, 341, 384

Julie Lavender, 50, 152,165, 172, 194, 336, 367, 384

Hallie Lee, 37, 65, 189, 233, 248, 307, 385

Louis Lotz, 35, 80, 105, 155, 183, 198, 206, 221, 235, 267, 350, 385

Eryn Lynum, 25, 30, 115, 132, 153, 161, 219, 226, 238, 289, 309, 376, 385

Cathy Mayfield, 6, 85, 151, 203, 224, 250, 260, 300, 386

Janet Holm McHenry, 64, 131, 208, 259, 308, 316, 325, 352, 386

Leslie L. McKee, 75, 148, 265, 271, 306, 386

Maureen Miller, 74, 112, 144, 217, 279, 287, 304, 349, 386

Aline Newman, 20, 71, 269, 334, 347, 387

Harold Nichols, 2, 51, 76, 146, 164, 191, 214, 281, 319, 324, 387

Mabel Ninan, 31, 45, 138, 193, 202, 212, 254, 366, 387

Devon O'Day, 28, 40, 82, 89, 162, 276, 329, 388

Sandra Kirby Quandt, 111, 171, 209, 242, 247, 340, 358, 388

Shirley Raye Redmond, 11, 36, 72, 134, 166, 195, 261, 388

Kathleen R. Ruckman, 29, 78, 114, 139, 192, 361, 372, 389

Virginia Ruth, 21, 59, 63, 77, 122, 187, 274, 295, 322, 373, 389

Kim Sheard, 200, 284, 297, 333, 365, 389

Heather Spiva, 23, 52, 120, 185, 273, 389

Diane Stark, 15, 19, 47, 92, 199, 293, 328, 345, 390

Crystal Storms, 9, 249, 263, 288, 301, 343, 359, 390

Katy W. Sundararajan, 22, 83, 106, 129, 173, 184, 390

Stacey Thureen, 8, 67, 100, 104, 215, 390

Missy Tippens, 12, 156, 262, 337, 354, 360, 390

Lawrence W. Wilson, 32, 66, 84, 113, 181, 228, 251, 364, 391

David L. Winters, 3, 16, 48, 102, 142, 178, 205, 291, 313, 342, 369, 391

Bible Acknowledgments

Every attempt has been made to credit the sources of copyrighted material used in this book. If any such acknowledgment has been inadvertently omitted or miscredited, receipt of such information would be appreciated.

Scripture quotations marked (AMP) are taken from the *Amplified Bible*. Copyright © 2015 by The Lockman Foundation, La Habra, California. All rights reserved.

Scripture quotations marked (ASV) are taken from the *American Standard Version Bible* (public domain).

Scripture quotations marked (CEB) are taken from the *Common English Bible*. Copyright © 2011 by Common English Bible.

Scripture quotations marked (CEV) are taken from *Holy Bible: Contemporary English Version*. Copyright © 1995 American Bible Society.

Scripture quotations marked (CSB) are taken from *The Christian Standard Bible,* copyright © 2017 by Holman Bible Publishers. Used by permission.

Scripture quotations marked (ESV) are taken from the *Holy Bible, English Standard Version*. Copyright © 2001 by Crossway Bibles, a division of Good News Publishers. Used by permission. All rights reserved.

Scripture quotations marked (GNT) are taken from the *Good News Translation*® (Today's English Version, Second Edition) © 1992 American Bible Society.

Scripture quotations marked (KJV) are taken from the *King James Version of the Bible*.

Scripture quotations marked (MSG) are taken from *The Message*. Copyright © 1993, 1994, 1995, 1996, 2000, 2001, 2002 by Eugene H. Peterson.

Scripture quotations marked (NASB) are taken from the *New American Standard Bible*®, Copyright © 1960, 1971, 1977, 1995, 2020 by The Lockman Foundation. All rights reserved.

Scripture quotations marked (NIV) are taken from *The Holy Bible, New International Version*. Copyright © 1973, 1978, 1984, 2011 by Biblica, Inc. Used by permission of Zondervan. All rights reserved worldwide. zondervan.com

Scripture quotations marked (NKJV) are taken from *The Holy Bible, New King James Version*. Copyright © 1982 by Thomas Nelson.

Scripture quotations marked (NLT) are taken from the *Holy Bible, New Living Translation*. Copyright © 1996, 2004, 2007, 2015 by Tyndale House Foundation. Used by permission of Tyndale House Publishers Inc., Carol Stream, Illinois. All rights reserved.

Scripture quotations marked (NRSVUE) are taken from the *New Revised Standard Version, Updated Edition*. Copyright © 2021 by the National Council of Churches of Christ in the United States of America. Used by permission. All rights reserved worldwide.

Scripture quotations marked (VOICE) are taken from *The Voice Bible*, copyright © 2012 Thomas Nelson, Inc. The Voice™ translation copyright © 2012 Ecclesia Bible Society. All rights reserved.

A Note from the Editors

We hope you enjoyed *All God's Creatures 2026*, published by Guideposts. For more than 75 years, Guideposts, a nonprofit organization, has been driven by a vision of a world filled with hope. We aspire to be the voice of a trusted friend, a friend who makes you feel more hopeful and connected.

By making a purchase from Guideposts, you join our community in touching millions of lives, inspiring them to believe that all things are possible through faith, hope, and prayer. Your continued support allows us to provide uplifting resources to those in need. Whether through our communities, websites, apps, or publications, we inspire our audiences, bring them together, and comfort, uplift, entertain, and guide them. Visit us at guideposts.org to learn more.

We would love to hear from you. Write us at Guideposts, P.O. Box 5815, Harlan, Iowa 51593 or call us at (800) 932-2145. Did you love *All God's Creatures 2026*? Leave a review for this product on guideposts.org/shop. Your feedback helps others in our community find relevant products.

Find inspiration, find faith, find Guideposts.

Shop our best sellers and favorites at
guideposts.org/shop

Or scan the QR code to go directly to our Shop